To mom, always my biggest fan

George Edward 'Rube' Waddell, besides being a dominant pitcher in the first decade of the 1900s, was also one of the games most memorable 'characters'. Will Braund's novel brings him to vivid life in its pages. This is one hell of a funny read!"

Rick Blechta, author, *The Fallen One*

RUBE WADDELL
KING of the HALL of FLAKES

———

———

Contact info
Out of the Park
Post Office Box 695 · Marmora, ON K0K 2M0
Canada

Available as an *e-book*

ISBN: 978-0-9907609-9-3 - *hardcover*
ISBN: 978-0-9907609-7-9 - *paperback*

cover Image | **arslongaartcards**.com   design | **timmyroland**.com

KING *of the* HALL *of* FLAKES

RUBE

W A D D E L L

W.G. **Braund**

RUBE WADDELL
KING *of the* HALL *of* FLAKES

CHAPTER ONE

RESCUING KITTENS & TRAINING
GEESE FOR VAUDEVILLE

Rube got to Tennessee for training camp well ahead of the rest of the Millers, he wanted to get some fishing in on Reelfoot Lake. When he heard that some of his teammates had arrived in town, he headed to the hotel to meet them. They still had a couple of days before camp opened, so Rube proposed a fishing trip.

"How do you do it?" asked Yip Owens, the Millers' catcher, after they'd been out a while.

"Do what?"

"Find 'em when nobody else can."

"It's a combination a things. You gotta be methodical."

"Not devious?"

"Nope. Just methodical."

"And that would include what exactly?"

"Judgin' the wind, and the current, and the temperature, and then just studying."

"Studying? Studying what?"

"The surface of course."

"That old-timer said nobody'd caught anything down where you were in years. How many d'you get this morning?"

Rube looked in his basket and counted his haul. "Four catfish, two yellow bass, three largemouth, and six bluegill."

"And Jimmy, Hobe, Claude, Wid, and me tried four different spots and we caught all of two between us."

"Course your bait has a lot to do with it. You fellas were using minnows, weren't you?"

"Ya. So? What were you using?"

"Popeye jigs tipped with waxworms."

"Sounds like you got this down to a science. No wonder you catch so many."

1

"One more thing, Yip."

"What's that, Rube?"

"You gotta love what you're doin."

"Well you sure do love your fishing, we all know that. And we all know you love to eat, so how's about we get back and get your haul onto the grill?"

"That's another thing."

"What is?"

"You're not done when you catch 'em."

"What d'ya mean?"

"You gotta be ready to put in the time to cook 'em just right."

"What are you planning this time?"

"My batter is gonna be flour, baking powder, salt, buttermilk, and turmeric."

"Well you've always known what to do with a batter, Rube, but usually it's mincemeat you make outta them."

&c   &c   &c

On the morning of their second day on Reelfoot Lake a local man came up to the group with a dozen geese he was trying to get rid of.

"I'll take them, mister," said Rube.

"What in tarnation would you want with a dozen geese?" asked Yip Owens, bewildered.

"To cook for dinner," said Wid Conroy, who'd played with Rube for the Milwaukee Brewers in '01. "You know how Rube can eat."

"I'm not gonna cook 'em, Wid, I'm gonna train 'em."

"Train 'em?" asked Johnny Butler, the team's youngest player. "Why would you want to train geese?"

"In case I want to get up an act for vaudeville."

&c   &c   &c

Three days later the group passed a yard near the ballpark and saw Rube in his shirtsleeves wearing a big straw hat. He was leading the geese as they marched behind him military style in single file. The players stopped and stared, hardly believing what they were seeing.

Rube led the geese toward a rope that he'd stretched between two trees and without hesitation the geese hopped up and walked along it.

"Holy shit," said Wid Conroy. "Did you ever see geese do anything like that?"

Rube bent down and the geese took turns climbing up his left arm, walking across his huge shoulders, and then down his right arm. Then

Rube went over to the porch and got a skipping rope.

"No. You've gotta be kiddin' me," said Yip Owens. "He's not really ..."

Sure enough, Rube now had the geese skip rope. He noticed his teammates were staring at the one holding the rope.

"Couldn't get that one ta jump, so he holds the rope."

"Well that certainly makes sense," said Jimmy.

"About as much sense as *anything* Rube does," chuckled Yip.

"The man's part Paul Bunyan, part Pied Piper," added Wid.

Rube whistled to himself as he hung numbered cards on pegs along the wall of a shed. His teammates stared, wondering what could be next.

"One," Rube called, and one of the geese stepped out of the gaggle and waddled to the shed. He passed by numbers 6, 2, and 9, and picked off the card that read 1 in his beek. "Two," said Rube. The second shortest goose waddled over and picked off the card that read 2. The other geese followed suit when it was their turn.

"How in the hell d'you train 'em to do *that*?" asked Johnny.

Rube didn't answer. The geese had gathered around him as he fed them bits of bread and stroked their necks.

"Good luck with the act, Rube," said Yip. "After you've taught them how to play poker and drive a motorcar, show 'em how to throw a bender. Maybe we could use them against the Skyhawks."

In the middle of an exhibition game the next afternoon Rube thought he heard something. He had a 0-2 count on the hitter when he stopped and signalled for his teammates to be quiet. Faintly, then increasingly louder, the sound grew. Now everyone else heard what Rube had - the bell of a fire wagon that was passing the park. Rube dropped his glove on the mound and headed for the outfield exit, stripping down to his bright red underwear as he ran.

As he went out the gate he was nearly flattened by a chauffeur-driven Lambert Runabout. He leapt out of its way and looked up and down the street. He spotted a teenage liveryman and waved him down.

"Another fire, Rube?" he asked.

"That's right, Davey. I'm gonna need one a your horses again."

"Sure thing, Rube, I know you'll take good care of him."

Rube untethered one of the horses, leapt onto its back, and rode bareback at breakneck speed to where smoke was rising on the outskirts of town.

Minutes later he pulled up at the source of the smoke, a burning barn. He jumped off the horse, patted its head, and secured it to a tree. Flames shot from the barn's roof and smoke spewed out its doors. A man was hugging and trying to comfort his wife. Three firemen stood debating what to do.

"Sure is good to see you," said the oldest of the three. "Extra coat's in the wagon. We were just trying ..."

Rube grabbed the coat and pulled it on. "Anybody inside?"

"Our daughter Sadie's inside!" sobbed the farmer's wife. "She ran in to get her kittens."

"Don't worry. I'll get her," said Rube. With that he grabbed an axe from the fire wagon and smashed a huge hole in the side of the barn opposite the doors. He dropped the axe and ran in. The firemen looked at one another in astonishment.

Inside the barn Rube peered through the thick smoke. "Sadie!" he called out. "Where are you, girl?"

The only sound he heard was that of crackling wood. Suddenly a burning timber fell from the rafters. Rube saw it at the last second and batted it away just as it was about to land on him. It burned his hand but he seemed not to notice. "Sadie, where are you?"

A tiny, coughing voice called out, "We're over here. Please help us!"

Rube went toward the sound and spotted the girl, who looked to be six or seven years old. Her freckles and pigtails were covered in soot and she was hugging three kittens in her arms. Rube effortlessly scooped up the girl and her kittens in his powerful arms and carried them outside. He handed the girl to her mother.

"Sadie, darling, are you all right?"

"Yes, momma. This big man saved us!"

"So he did, and quite remarkably," said Sadie's father. "It's lucky he was here," he added, looking at the sheepish firemen, "it looked as though nobody was going to do anything."

His wife noticed Rube's badly charred hand. "Oh, my Lord, your hand! It looks terrible. You must let me tend to it."

Rube looked at it. "This? It's not so bad, I've had lots worse. Hope the girl and the kittens'll be okay, I have to go. Got a horse to return."

The astounded couple and the firemen stared as Rube jumped on the horse and rode away.

       🐾   🐾   🐾

Joe Cantillon, the Millers' manager, had decided to take the team to his hometown, Hickman, Kentucky for the rest of their training camp.

He'd picked a bad time. Hickman had seen plenty of rainy winters, but this past one had been especially bad. This time it had rained so heavily that the Mississippi was rising to record levels even before the spring thaw began. Much of Kentucky was in jeopardy of flooding. By the start of February, ice jams had caused the waters to swell dangerously. When warm weather arrived things got dramatically worse.

Hundreds of people worked tirelessly to stem the flooding with sandbags and, though he had only been in town for a few days, no one worked harder or longer than Rube. He worked so hard he became a local hero and was even named fire marshal and deputy sheriff. He spent hour after hour, day and night, in the icy waters and managed to catch a very bad cold, which inevitably turned into pneumonia. He was bedridden for a week.

℀   ℀   ℀

When Rube took the mound he was shaking and he looked awful. He gave up two long hits in the first inning and two more in the second. When the leadoff hitter, a small, pimple-faced kid of seventeen, came up in the third Rube looked in for the sign and then went into his windup. But before he got half way through he suffered a frightening coughing spell and doubled over in agony. When he finally managed to get his breath he threw a slow pitch which the kid smashed all the way to the right field fence. The right fielder threw the ball to Claude Rossman, the cut-off man, who relayed it to Jimmy Williams at second base.

"Christ almighty, the little fucker hit that one hard," Williams said to Rossman.

"Rube shouldn't be out here, Jimmy. He's way too sick to pitch."

Yip Owens took off his mask and went out to the mound. With effort, he put his arm around Rube's shoulders. "You all right, Rube?" he asked.

Rube wheezed, "A bit of a cough is all."

"A bit of a cough? Sounds like yer gonna cough up a lung," said Owens.

"It's my own damn fault, Yip. I shouldn'ta swallowed that whole bottle of creosote or whatever it was called. Doc said it was caustic."

"What were you thinking?"

"I wasn't."

Owens gestured toward the other team's bench.

"You gotta know these bums that are smackin' your pitches all over the yard wouldn'ta gotten so much as a loud foul offa you back in the day."

5

RUBE WADDELL

"You mean back when I pitched nineteen scoreless innings and whopped Cy Young? Seems like about a century ago now."

CHAPTER TWO

A REMARKABLE BOY

The rich fragrance of cedar and blossoms filled the air. Wispy clouds drifted lazily across the morning sky. A monarch butterfly fluttered, then landed on a bull rush near the shore. The only sounds were those of crickets and tree frogs. A deer wandered down to the shore of the lake and casually took a drink.

Suddenly the calm, dark green water parted and a huge fish erupted from it. Beads of sunlight shone across its majestic length as it emerged. A score of sparrows burst out of a clump of bushes as the trout splashed back down into the lake.

"Eddie, it's time to get up."

With a skill acquired from long practice he let his pointer finger slide along his line to give the fish more slack, enough line to run. He couldn't let it snap his line. He didn't want to lose this prize.

"Edward, get out of that bed this instant. You are not going to be late for school again. Do you hear me?"

"Huh," groaned Eddie. "What? Ya, ma... I'm awake."

"Do not make me come up there young man."

"No, ma. I'm gonna be right down. No fooling."

"You're right no fooling," his mother yelled up from the bottom of the stairs.

Slowly and reluctantly Eddie hauled himself upright and dragged himself out of bed. He most decidedly did not want to go to school, it was far too nice a day to be stuck in that schoolhouse for six hours. But his teacher, old man Weigle, had stopped by just last night to give Eddie's parents an account of their son's sporadic attendance record.

"We will do our best to get him to school, Mister Weigle, and we certainly appreciate you coming by to tell us what he's been up to," Eddie's father had told him. "He is kind of a character that boy of ours. Different, I guess you'd say. He does a lot of things amazingly well and he's friendly as all get out, always helping people, always tells the truth even if it'll get him in trouble, and he never has a bad word to say about anyone."

"Yes, the other students are very fond of him," Mr. Weigle admitted.

"Edward does like to play the odd practical joke though," Mr. Waddell added.

Mr. Weigle thought back to the time he'd gone to use his fountain pen only to discover that its ink had been removed and replaced with honey. He remembered another occasion when he'd opened his lunch box and watched in horror and disbelief as a huge toad leapt out of it. No one had seemed to know the culprit's identity.

"Edward is good at arithmetic, he can memorize things, his penmanship is excellent, and he reads fairly well, but he has a very short attention span."

"Did you ever hear the stories about him when he was little?" Eddie's father asked.

"No, I cannot say that I have. You folks did not live here then, did you?"

"No sir, we were in Titusville back then, we've only been in Prospect a year or so. Eddie was born in Bradford and grew up in Titusville. I'm in the oil business, like nearly everybody else around there. I rent farmland from time to time to supplement my income and Eddie's a big help with that. He works on his grandpa's farm too. The boy is so strong he could plow with two mules when he was thirteen years old. I know a lot of full grown men that can't do that."

"To what stories are you referring, Mister Waddell, apart from the plowing that is?"

"Well, to begin with, when Eddie was two years old he went missing."

"Went missing? At the age of two? What happened?"

"Mary and I went into his bedroom one afternoon while he was supposed to be having his nap. We hadn't heard a sound from his nursery in a while and we got suspicious."

"And?"

"When we went in, he was nowhere to be seen. His crib was empty and most of the bars on the one side had been broken and pulled out. I guess most younguns would have gone over the top. Not our Eddie. No sir, he busted clean outta jail."

"Where did he go?"

"It took us a while to find him. He was nowhere in the house or the yard. Eventually we did find him. He was playing in the creek. The water was cold as ice. Didn't bother little Eddie though," Mr. Waddell chuckled. "Then three years later he disappeared again."

"Where had he gone, back to the river?"

"No sir, a lot farther than that. We looked all over the farm and couldn't find him anywhere, so we started to panic. I was walking along the road calling his name when one of the local boys came running up to me. He stood panting for a second and I asked him if he knew where Eddie was. He said he was in town. I told him that wasn't possible, that Eddie was much too young to go so far on his own. 'Well Eddie's at the fire hall,' the boy told me. The firemen were letting him play with the gear until somebody came for him. Apparently he just wandered in."

Mr. Weigle was astonished.

"I suppose it shouldn't have been a *complete* surprise," said Mr. Waddell. "He always runs down to the road whenever he hears the fire wagon go by."

Mr. Weigle was beginning to understand his new student, the man-child who sat in the back row of his schoolhouse daydreaming most of the time. "Thank you kindly for the lemonade, Missus Waddell, but I must be on my way." He stood up and put on his hat. "If you do not mind my asking, what do you think the future holds in store for Edward?"

"That's a very good question, Mister Weigle," she said, picking up the teacher's empty glass as she spoke, "it's hard to know. Eddie's still like a small child, in spite of his size and strength. He just doesn't seem to take anything seriously. I pray for him all the time."

"Well, Missus Waddell, I can tell you one thing. People take to him like no boy I have ever seen. When new students move into a school the others invariably give them the cold shoulder and poke fun at them, but not Edward. The students in all the grades were doting on him from the start."

"The boy is likable, there's no doubt about that," said Mr. Waddell.

"He seems to be quite an athlete," Mr. Weigle added.

"The boy's a natural at anything physical. Too bad there's no money in fishing or shooting guns."

"Is there any money in playing baseball, Mister Waddell? I am no kind of expert on the sport, but I have seen Edward hit and throw a ball farther and harder than anyone, man or child."

"Well, Mister Weigle, there is money to be made playing ball, but only if you're one of the best in the country. And there's a chance our Eddie might just be that good."

RUBE WADDELL

Eddie really had no choice but to go to school. He washed, dressed, and put on the big straw hat he wore all the time, except at the dinner table and in school. Then he went outside to feed the chickens and collect their eggs. First, he made a trip to the outhouse - 'the outdoor convenience' his mother made him call it. Then he split logs for firewood, spread salt on the hay bales to keep them from catching fire when the chemicals inside heated up, and pumped water into the pails at the back door. He peeked inside to see if breakfast was ready.

"Looks like it's gonna be five more minutes," he said to himself. "I got time."

He opened the hatch at the back of the house and climbed down the ladder to the cellar. He went to the potato bin and took out a handful of spuds. Then he went out to the barn where he'd cut a hole in the side of a stall. He'd made it just a bit larger than a baseball. He went to the back of the barn, about sixty feet from the stall, transferred a potato to his left hand and threw it. It missed the hole by three inches. Just high and a tad left. Eddie threw another. It missed by half an inch. The next three flew right through the hole. He smiled to himself, realized that he could smell bacon, and hurried inside.

Though no one knew better than his mother just how much Eddie could eat, her son's gargantuan appetite still amazed Mrs. Waddell. This morning his two plates brimmed with four fried eggs, six sausages, home fried potatoes, half an onion, three pieces of French toast, and a tower of flannel cakes drenched in maple syrup. She'd packed him a lunch that most children would have trouble carrying much less eating, but Eddie would still be ravenous when he got home from school. After dinner it was nothing to see him wolf down a quart of ice cream for dessert. One of the women at church said she'd watched him eat an entire gallon at the soda fountain one afternoon.

"Don't you ever get stomach cramps eating so much?" his sister Maude asked Eddie.

"Not that I recall," he answered. "You gonna finish your potatoes? You hardly ever do."

"No," she answered, pushing her plate toward him. "It's a wonder you don't explode."

"Stop picking on your brother," said Mrs. Waddell. "He can't help how much he's growing."

"We'll soon be able to put him in the circus. They can call him the

Incredible Eating and Growing Boy," Maude teased.

"Never you mind, now get on upstairs and get your gloves and bonnet, young lady. Eddie, don't forget your lunch."

"Not much chance of that," chuckled Maude.

ɞ　　ɞ　　ɞ

Eddie thought he might just be able to abide school today. After all, it was March and he'd soon be needed on his grandfather's farm to help get the fields ready for seeding.

"In the British parliamentary system there are no checks and balances such as exist in the American system of government," Mr. Weigle droned, leaning forward in his chair atop the platform that had been built at the front of the schoolhouse to provide him with a better view of his charges. "A prime minister with the support of a majority in the House of Commons may enact whatever legislation and policies he so desires and if the House of Lords refuses to endorse his program the prime minster can instruct the monarch to appoint sufficient new members to ensure the measure's approval."

Sitting on the back bench with the other senior students, Eddie had no idea what his teacher was going on about. He hadn't been listening, his thoughts were of fishing, not Britain's parliament.

A row in front of him Myrtle Tanner turned around and gave Eddie a quick smile. Long blonde curls fell around her lovely oval face. "That gal's prettier than a glob a butter meltin' on a stack a wheat cakes," he thought to himself.

She looked awfully fetching in the new style of dresses that were popular now. His sister said that the tight bodices - he thought that was what she'd called them - showed off a girl's figure. An hourglass effect she called it. Whatever the style was, Myrtle sure had a nice shape to her. He wondered what she would look like in one of those bathing costumes they had in that new catalog the Sears Roebuck people had started sending out.

Myrtle was one of several girls who'd shown a great deal of interest in Eddie since he moved to town the year before. At a little over six feet tall, he towered over the other senior boys. He had a muscular back, huge shoulders, and long limbs. Eddie took pride in his appearance; his light brown hair was always parted neatly down the middle. He had high cheekbones, a lantern jaw, and clear blue eyes. His Roman nose had just a bit of a twist in it, a gift from his mother's side of the family. Unlike the other boys, he was a good listener, never bragging like the others did even when they had precious little to brag on.

One of the bigger senior boys, whose name was Daniel, loved to torment the younger students. He didn't anymore because now Eddie was around to protect them. The bully had made a comment Eddie's first day. Eddie's parents had a devil of a time keeping up to his growth spurts and his trousers were once again too short for his long legs. In front of a group of students Daniel asked him if he was expecting a flood. The others looked at Eddie to see how he'd react.

With a smile on his face that belied his embarrassment and anger, Eddie effortlessly lifted the large boy into the air with one arm and gently placed him onto a coat peg. All of the kids roared, especially the little ones Daniel had been pushing and bossing around.

"I beg your pardon, I'm not just sure I heard you clearly. What was that you said?"

"Nothing, nothing at all," stammered Daniel. "I didn't say anything. I mean I didn't mean anything. I was just fooling is all, it won't happen again." It didn't.

Eddie was easily the best athlete in the school, probably in all of Butler County. He won every wrestling match, outran all the boys, and skated faster backwards than most men could forwards. He was always the first chosen for baseball. The only trouble was Eddie threw so hard none of the boys would catch if he pitched. He could throw a ball faster than any of the men in town and he could hit balls clear over the schoolhouse roof. He was an amazing football player as well. The last fall a team from another town had come to play his school's team. In their previous match Eddie had scored six touchdowns and sacked their quarterback ten times. Now they said they wouldn't play if Waddell did.

At lunch time Eddie often played miggles with the younger boys, who were absolutely in awe of the lighthearted giant. None of the other seniors paid any attention to the younger boys, unless it was to kick them if they got in their way. But Eddie was not only kind to them, he played marbles or baseball with them whenever they asked. When they wanted to climb a tree that had no limbs near the ground Eddie would tell them to "hop aboard" and they'd climb up on his back.

The day before, after he'd polished off his huge lunch, Eddie passed the picnic table where Myrtle was sitting. She waved at him to join her. For some reason she always seemed to bring far more lunch than a 16-year old girl could possibly eat. To Eddie's delight she regularly offered him generous portions of roast beef, cheese, and slabs of apple or rhubarb pie. The day before that it had been a leg of chicken, three hard-boiled eggs, and a huge piece of cherry pie.

ℓℓ   ℓℓ   ℓℓ

As soon as he returned her smile Myrtle blushed and wheeled around. Eddie looked up at the clock. For some reason its hands weren't moving. He wondered how that could be. The clock was almost brand new. He stared intently at it, willing the wretched minute hand to move. Finally, after what seemed an eternity, it lunged ahead to the next minute. As it did, Eddie's head lurched ahead with it and he nearly fell off the seniors' bench.

Looking toward the back, Mr. Weigle had no idea what could have made the reluctant learner suddenly fall forward like that. He harrumphed and kept right on prattling about how Britain's parliament had finally reformed its membership in 1832 and again in 1867. Or had he said 1776? Or was it 1492? Eddie wasn't sure. Any one of those would have made the same sense to him.

The interminable history lesson finally came to a blessed end but there was no relief in sight. Now Mr. Weigle pontificated about how deplorable it was that so many people were employing contractions when they spoke. He looked right at Eddie when he said it. The only contractions Eddie'd heard of were the ones ladies suffered from when they were having babies. Then it was time for the class to learn when to use the subjunctive mood and the differences between the nominative and dative cases and between pronominal adjectives and indefinite pronouns. Eddie's eyelids flitted once, twice, and then closed tight. He had no idea how long he'd been asleep when his buddy Luke elbowed him hard in the mid-section.

"Eddie, for Heaven's sake, wake up! Old man Weigle ain't blind *and* deef. You bin' snorin' better part a five minutes."

"Huh. What? Oh, Luke, it's you."

Eddie shook himself awake and tried to focus. Mr. Weigle was still talking about pronouns. Eddie realized that he was again looking right at him.

"Mister Waddell, I would like you to give us a sentence containing an interrogative and a personal pronoun?"

"Who, me?" Eddie blurted.

It took the class a moment to realize how neatly Eddie had, completely by accident, composed the required sentence. Who was indeed an interrogative pronoun and me was a personal pronoun. They broke into riotous laughter.

"Well, well, you were as slick as a peeled onion that time," whispered Luke.

Mr. Weigle was not impressed. "Quiet class. That will be quite enough. Edward, you have answered my question correctly, even if it was purely by chance, so you will not need to stand in the corner for the rest of the day. Students, take out your slates and begin working on the questions on the blackboard. The top ones are for the juniors and the lower ones are of course for the seniors, who will help the younger students when they finish their own questions. Begin."

Eddie took out his slate and started to work away diligently - on a drawing of a large mouth bass rising out of the water.

CHAPTER THREE

PUZZLERS, WOBBLERS,
AND FADEAWAYS

After school Eddie headed to his favorite spot on Crab Run Creek, where he'd hidden his fishing rod under a large group of ferns just off the main road. His Snyder multiplying reel was his pride and joy. He'd put in a lot of hours punching slate for roofs and laying pipelines for the oil company his father worked for so he could send away for it. At first he kept it under his bed, but it was hard to sneak out of the house with it under his clothes on the days when he just pretended to go to school and actually went straight to the river.

For bait he used roe bags he'd made. They were the size of dimes and had trout eggs in them. He used worms and minnows to catch bass, but it was spring and the creek was teeming with steelhead trout - 'steelies' he called them. They liked the roe bags. He'd spread split shot weights along his line at just the right intervals to provide a natural-looking drift.

Eddie knew exactly how much line to let out and how fast, as well as how much play a big fish needed. It didn't serve to be impatient. "That dog won't hunt," Eddie used to say. Your line would simply snap if you pulled too fast. Sometimes it would take the better part of an hour to reel in a big one. He let three small fish go that afternoon and kept two big ones for the dinner table. The sun was still setting early and, suddenly realizing that he was famished, Eddie headed home for supper.

As he walked along the road he looked up at the sky and saw big, fluffy white clouds. They made him think of mashed potatoes. "Lord love a duck," he said out loud. "My backbone's rubbin' right up against my belly."

He decided to stop in at Howland's General Store. Several local men were sitting around the woodstove talking when he arrived. They all greeted him like he was their long lost son or nephew. Eddie looked up and down the shelves of confectionaries, pondering his selection.

Everything looked good.

"That lad is one huge son of a gun," said an old man with a long grey beard.

"And strong as an ox," said a younger man, whose name was Silas Fletcher.

"One thing's for sure. The boy has quite an arm on him," said a third man, who was puffing on a corncob pipe. "I seen him fishin' up on Lake Arthur last Sunday week. He was skippin' stones from the shore. He pretty near hit a boat seemed like it was a half mile out. Scared the fellers in it half ta death."

"Real good-natured boy, got a heart o' gold. Give ya the shirt off his back," said the bearded old-timer.

"Be way too big for my back," said Silas Fletcher.

Eddie decided. He got rock candy, toffee, peanuts in a bag, and some licorice. He got two sarsaparilla root beers as well.

"That'll be eighteen cents, Eddie," the shopkeeper said.

"Shucks, all I gots a dime, Mr. Howland."

"Don't worry about it, Eddie," said Silas Fletcher. "You can put those things on my tab, Jed."

"Thanks a heap, Mister Fletcher, much obliged."

"Least I can do after you pulled little Abe outta the river last summer."

"That was nuthin', Mister Fletcher."

"It was surely sumphin' to me and his momma."

"Thank you kindly. Guess I'd best skedaddle, you wouldn't have any backy would you?"

"Matter of fact I do. Here, Eddie, keep the bag."

*   *   *

Whenever Eddie worked in the fields he picked up rocks and stuffed them into his pockets. It wasn't just to clear the ground to make plowing and planting easier, it was because of the infernal crows. When you put your seeds in the ground the treacherous things were on them in seconds. Eddie could still recall the morning his mother'd told him that his cat had been run over by a wagon. He'd run out to the road hoping somehow to bring it back to life and been sickened by the sight of three crows pecking away at his kitty's remains. He did not like crows.

On his way along the road he picked up some good-sized stones and looked for targets in the trees. He didn't like killing squirrels the way a lot of other boys did, but he sure didn't mind killing those damn crows. A fat blue jay landed on the branch of a maple tree and a flock of finches flew overhead. Then Eddie saw a crow near the top of a walnut tree. He fired. The stone missed by inches and the crow flew off.

Two minutes later he spied a big crow seventy feet away. It was sitting on the wire that stretched along the poles that now ran from the general store all the way to Prospect. Sometimes the box on the wall behind Mr. Howland's counter would start to ring and he would put something to his ear and talk into the box. Apparently the wire had something to do with that box.

Eddie let go. The stone whistled through the air and hit the bird squarely in the breast. The crow fell to the ground. Eddie nailed another one a few minutes later, this time right in the head, just as a man he'd never seen before pulled up behind him. He climbed down from his buckboard.

"Mighty fine throwin', lad," said the man. He wasn't a local. He looked a few years older than Eddie's father, with graying hair and a day's growth of whiskers. He smelled of sweat and bourbon and wore a rumpled suit and a shirt that looked like it hadn't seen detergent in a month of Sundays.

"Thanks, Mister."

"You live in Prospect, son?"

"Do now," Eddie answered, wondering why the man would care, "moved there last year."

"Play any baseball there?"

"Yessir. For the Butler County team."

"That so? I'm on my way to see that team play. Game's tomorrow afternoon. Apparently they got a seventeen-year old twirler I need to take a look at. I do some scouting for the Franklin team in the new Iron and Oil League. Name's Wesley Baker."

He walked up to Eddie and reached out to shake his hand. Baker had always thought his hands were a fair size, but when he shook the big lad's hand it made his seem like a toddler's.

"Pleased to make yer acquaintance, Mister Baker. My name's Edward. Edward Waddell. People call me Eddie."

"Say, I'll bet you're the very fella I was told to come up and see. Are you pitching tomorrow?"

"I expect, I pitch pretty near every game now."

"Well it's good to meet you too, Eddie. Nice job on those crows, I can't stand the wretched things."

"G'bye Mister Baker." Eddie ran all the way home to tell his father the news. His dad loved baseball and took him to watch whenever a top team came to town. Now it was Eddie someone was going to see.

ℓ℮   ℓ℮   ℓ℮

There were about four hundred people in the stands to watch their darlings, the Butler County Nine, the next day. Admission was fifteen cents for the grandstand, such as it was, and a dime to bake on the bleacher benches. There was a meagre concession stand but most of the spectators brought their own snacks and beer. The smell of cigar smoke drifted through the crowd. Bettors were trying to set the odds for the game but they were having trouble because it wasn't yet certain whether Waddell would be pitching. If he was, the Butler side would be heavy favorites.

Wesley Baker bought a handful of 2-cent cigars and a bag of peanuts and took a seat directly behind home plate, a few rows up from the backstop. He wanted to see not just how fast the big kid could throw but whether he had any movement on his pitches. He knew that without movement good hitters could eventually time and catch up to even the fastest pitches.

"You a scout, mister?" the man sitting beside him asked when Baker took out a notepad.

"Traveling salesman, but the manager of the new ball club in Franklin asked me to keep my eyes open for talent. Somebody told me I should come up this way and have a look at a big kid name of Waddell."

"Worth more than a look I'd venture ta say. The kid's sumpin special if you ask me. Don't reckon he'll be pitchin' in Butler County much longer the way he fires bullets. Got a whole lot a trick pitches too he does."

"Well I am glad to have come then."

"Lucky you weren't here fer the last game."

"Why? What happened?"

"I probly shouldn't say anythin'. Wouldn't want you to think badly of the boy."

"No, please do, I assure you I'm only interested in how well he pitches."

"Well, I wasn't here, but a fella told me about it. I guess it was in The Butler Banner too. Seems the young Waddell boy was pitchin' a whale of a game and then round about the fourth or fifth inning a friend a his pulled up along the first base line in a buckboard."

"Right onto the field?"

"Yupp. Then he held up a fishin' pole. Waddell just drops his glove right there on the mound, runs over and jumps into the buggy. Seems young Eddie was more interested in fishin' than in finishin' the game."

Wondering if the trout stream would be a greater attraction than the ballgame again today Baker turned away from the man and looked for Waddell. Eddie wasn't warming up with his teammates. He was at the game though, and he was hard to miss. His light blue uniform was much too small for him and he still wore his straw hat. He was talking to a group of young kids, apparently showing them how to throw different kinds of pitches. Then he played catch with the kids for a while before putting on his baseball cap and taking the mound.

The crowd went crazy as he took his warm-up pitches.

"Go get 'em, Eddie!" a man yelled out.

Another yelled, "Mow 'em down, son."

Eddie tipped his cap to the crowd, grinning from ear to ear. His left ear was considerably higher than the other as a result of the giant plug of backy his left cheek contained.

Baker wasn't easily impressed. He'd been around to several towns to see their "can't miss" prospects, many of them big young hurlers, though maybe not as big as this Waddell kid. But now he could hardly believe what he was seeing. The lad's pitches came in at incredible speed. Baker wasn't sure major league twirlers threw that hard.

He could hear them whiz across the plate and then explode into the catcher's mitt. He felt sorry for the catcher. A couple of innings of those fast ones and a man's hand would be like tenderized meat - only a lot sorer. Nine innings and you wouldn't want to shake hands for a week. The kid was a bit wild, especially at first, but damn, could he pitch!

Baker wondered how much he'd been coached. He knew his father had played a bit. Eddie seemed to throw fast pitches, unbelievably fast in fact, that rose and others that dropped. He had apparently been taught or had figured out how to throw two and four-seamers.

Eddie walked two batters in the first inning and another hitter dribbled one weakly to the first baseman, who stepped on the bag to retire the side. From the second inning on, young Waddell was unhittable. The batters simply couldn't catch up to the speed of his pitches.

But it wasn't just the speed that gave the hitters fits and starts. They would swing at a fast pitch only to discover too late that the lightning quick pitch was actually a bender! Who threw curves at the same speed as a fastball? Baker guessed that because the kid was so strong he could grasp the ball tighter than other pitchers and impart more break to his curves. How could anyone possibly hit those? It was bad enough that his fast pitches could rise or drop.

A hitter would swing at a pitch at his waist and miss it by what seemed like a mile. He'd look back and be amazed to see that the catcher was digging the ball out of the dirt. "God damn thing dropped two feet!" Baker marveled after yet another hitter whiffed.

And that wasn't all. Left handers' curveballs broke in on right-handed batters and away from left-handed ones. This 17-year old kid could throw those easily enough, and they appeared to drop off a table as they reached the plate, but he could also throw pitches that curved the opposite way!

Baker knew of only a couple of pitchers, even in the major league, who could throw that kind of pitch. They called it a fadeaway. If a batter didn't know it was coming he could look like an chump and lean in - or out - when he should have done just the opposite.

One of the kid's fadeaways hit a batter. Eddie immediately yelled, "You all right?" as the man got up and dusted himself off. Luckily, that pitch wasn't quite the same speed as Waddell's fast ones. Getting hit with one of those could easily break a bone. Baker was glad he wasn't down there trying to get a hit off this kid.

Eddie's change of paces - Baker later learned that Eddie called them 'puzzlers' - were so slow compared to his shoots that it seemed as if a hitter could swing at them three times before they reached the plate.

But there was more, another kind of puzzler that the kid threw a few times. It seemed to flutter up to the plate and it completely baffled the hitters. It started out normally, though a great deal slower than his other pitches, then it seemed to flit the rest of the way to the plate. There was no knowing how high or low they would end up, they didn't drop like a curveball. A couple of batters flailed at the strange deliveries. One just stood there and said, "What in the hell was that!"

His speed and his ability to make the baseball behave strangely weren't the only unusual things about this young pitcher though. He had a lot more fun than twirlers were supposed to have. Most of them were intense and bore down on every pitch. Young Waddell was grinning and laughing most of the time, or calling out to people in the crowd.

"D'ya see that pitch," he yelled one time. "Watch this one," he yelled a minute later.

Even odder, between innings he didn't go to the bench with his teammates. Instead, he went to the stands to talk with people. Sometimes he'd take a seat until it was his turn to bat. One time he ordered a bag of peanuts and shared them with some kids, another time he got a beer and some popcorn.

After striking out the last two batters of the ninth inning and leaving a runner stranded at third he tossed his glove to the shortstop and did handsprings all the way off the field. To Baker, it was very strange behavior indeed, but the crowd absolutely loved it.

The other team managed two hits, both checked swings at pitches so fast that the ball traveled just over the infielders' outstretched arms. Four Butler errors led to their opponents' only runs and they won easily, 12-2. Waddell looked pretty impressive at the plate too, ripping a triple and two doubles to knock in four runs. Boosters swarmed the diamond after the victory and carried Eddie around it on their shoulders. Baker knew he had just seen something special.

He went to see Eddie's father after order had been restored, he hadn't wanted to sit with him in case the man talked his ear off and distracted him. He knew Mr. Waddell was a bit eccentric and extremely proud of his boy.

"Well, whad'ya think?"

"I have to say your boy can flat out pitch," said Baker. "He's a bit rough around the edges but he can sure fire 'em in there. Got mighty good control and a heck of an assortment of pitches."

"I don't imagine there's too many better than our Eddie."

Eddie appeared out of the stands, where he'd been talking to a pair of female admirers. His straw hat was already back on his head and he had a big shaggy dog with him. "So? How'd I do, Mister Baker?" he asked.

"Pretty darned well. You got a lotta talent, son."

"Thanks."

"What do you call those pitches that flutter?"

"I call 'em wobblers, cuz' that's what they seem to do."

"How do you throw them?"

"Offa the tips of my fingers."

"Oh, they're like knuckleballs then. No wonder they move like they do. You don't see very many twirlers who can throw knuckleballs, especially young fellas like yourself. Where did you learn how to throw them?"

"Nowhere. I was just clownin' around in the schoolyard one day and the fellas were saying they didn't wanna catch me on accounta I throw so hard. So I figured maybe holdin' the ball a different way would slow it down a bit. Never occurred to me they'd wobble like they do. They sure are hard to hit fer such slow pitches."

"They were giving the batters fits."

"Ya, it's kinda funny to watch."

"Your catcher too, he missed most of them."

"Ya, I guess you could hear him cussin' all the way up in the stands."

"So what happens now?" asked Eddie's father.

"I'm going back to Franklin and telling the manager what I saw today."

It was hot and dusty down on the diamond and Baker remembered that he had a fifth of bourbon back in his hotel room. He said farewell and told them they would likely be hearing from the Franklin skipper quite soon. The team needed good pitching, especially since their defensive skills were nearly non-existent. Eddie would soon learn just how awful they were.

CHAPTER FOUR

A VERY BAD BREAKFAST
AND OFF TO COLLEGE, JUST NOT TO CLASS

Less than two weeks later Eddie was contacted to come to Franklin. Officially, it was for a tryout, but the letter made it clear he would be pitching for the Braves no matter how he did. His mother packed his suitcase and his father hitched up the wagon and proudly took his son to play for his first real team.

When he got to the ballpark Eddie was given a uniform and the manager signaled for the catcher, Jack Nelson, to see how well the huge boy could throw. After fetching his glove Nelson crouched behind the plate. The manager yelled out, "All right, let's see what this rube can do."

To Eddie's delight the manager and Jack Nelson were both very impressed and he was told he was now on the Braves' pitching staff. But to his horror, not only did the manager continuously called him Rube, the Franklin *players* did too. Eddie hated the name and it would be a long, long time before he got used to it. No one who was close to him would ever think of calling him Rube - even long after he'd become famous throughout baseball by that name.

At first, Eddie pitched only in games that were already out of reach. It was always the other team that had the big lead. In his first appearance the Braves went down by an embarrassing score of 24-10. Mr. Baker had badly understated how horrible the team was in the field. The Braves had been fairly successful in 1895, the year before, but they had lost a lot of players and now they were terrible. The local paper was blunt after another Franklin loss, this time to Titusville.

"Any club that comes along these days can beat Franklin owing to their stupid playing and poor batting."

The team committed twelve errors that led to ten runs in Eddie's first start. The shortstop, whose name was Muff Henderson, booted six. Jack Nelson yelled out to the mound after one of Henderson's mess-ups. This time he'd bobbled a slow groundball, then recovered it, then thrown it ten feet high of the first baseman. "Don't worry about it, Rube, not your fault."

Eddie motioned for Nelson to come out to the mound.

"How long have I been on the team now, Jack?"

"Couple of weeks I guess. Why?"

"And how many times have I told you I hate bein' called rube?"

"A couple I guess."

"Try a couple a hundred."

"Sorry. Say, d'ya hear the news?"

"What news?"

"Seems the team might be folding."

"Not much of a surprise, we're only drawin' a few dozen people, even on a Saturday."

"A bunch of us are goin' to The Pig and Whistle for a couple after the game. You wanna join us?"

"Is Henderson going?"

"Don't think so, his gal's makin' him take her somewhere."

"Just as well."

"Why's that?" asked Nelson.

"You hand him a beer, he'd probably drop it."

"Good one, Rube... I mean Eddie. Let's get this thing over with. Try not to let anybody hit the ball. Especially to Muff."

Depressed about being away from home and about giving up so many runs, something that had never happened to him before, Eddie started joining the older players for drinks after the inevitable losses. Eddie could eat a lot and soon he was drinking a lot too. Mercifully, attendance got so bad the team simply folded, with a grand total of 1 in their win column, and Eddie was free to return to Prospect. He could go back to being a kid and enjoying his mother's cooking and - even better - he'd have lots of time to fish.

Soon after his return home he received a letter from Patsy Donovan, the player/manager of the National League's Pittsburgh Pirates, who'd once played centerfield for the Brooklyn Bridegrooms. Apparently one of the Pirates' scouts had seen Eddie play and the team's management had decided the kid was worth a look. Mr. Waddell was thrilled and put Eddie on the next train to the Steel City. He was to meet Donovan for breakfast and then have a tryout.

They met in the restaurant of the William Pitt Union Hotel, not far from Donovan's apartment. Presuming that Donovan would be paying, Eddie ordered a huge breakfast and had already wolfed half of it down by the time the Pirate manager had unfolded his napkin, buttered his toast, and taken a sip of his orange juice.

When he finished eating, Eddie smacked his lips audibly as he sucked bacon grease off his fingers. Donovan grimaced and pointed at Eddie's finger bowl. He looked at it, puzzled. Then he shrugged his shoulders, picked it up and drank it down. Donovan shook his head and groaned.

Eddie belched so loud that several diners looked over. Then he proceeded to wipe his mouth on his sleeve before jamming a huge wad of tobacco into his cheek. He looked around for a spittoon and, seeing none, whistled at one of the waiters to "kindly fetch" him one. It was obvious to Donovan that this country bumpkin had never eaten in a restaurant before.

Donovan had pretty much lost his appetite after watching Eddie shovel his huge meal down his throat as though he'd never seen food before. He set down his knife and fork and asked him if he played any positions apart from twirler.

"I used to catch for the school team. Nobody would catch for *me* cuz I threw too hard, so I wasn't allowed to pitch. I played some outfield in Prospect before I went to Franklin. Heck, I can play anywhere. I can throw a ball pretty near four hundred feet and I can likely outrun any player you got."

"I imagine you are a great hitter too," Donovan said, not impressed with this young braggart, even though Eddie was simply telling the truth without the social grace to be modest about his abilities.

"I sure can, I can hit a ball a country mile, maybe even clean outta your park."

"You didn't help the Franklin team much from what I hear, Waddell. Why is that, given your apparently outstanding talents?"

"The Franklin club was just plain awful, Mister Donaldson."

"It's Donovan, not Donaldson," snapped the manager.

"Huh? Oh, right, sorry." Eddie hadn't realized how nervous he was, he was usually very good at remembering names.

"I tell ya, those fellas kicked the ball around the field like it was a dried up turd in a cow pasture." More diners looked over. "Seemed like they threw to the wrong base every time they *did* catch the ball and they couldn't hit a lick either."

"I heard you were pretty wild. Walking batters doesn't help your team much."

"Well, I guess I did walk a few, but . . . "

"And I'm told you clowned around quite a bit on the mound as well. Is that true?"

"Well, I do like to have fun when I pitch. Baseball's sposed to be fun, isn't it?"

"We take it fairly seriously in the major league."

"Well, ya, I suppose you do." Eddie was sweating buckets. His mother had insisted he wear a clean white shirt, a freshly starched collar, and his wool suit. He pulled a flask out of his coat pocket and took a long swig. Then he offered some to Donovan. "Hair a the dog?"

"I don't like my players to drink very much in the evening, much less before ten o'clock in the morning," said Donovan, making no effort to hide his contempt.

"We headin' to the ballpark for that tryout out now, Mister Donaldson?"

"Once again, it's Donovan, not Donaldson and, while *I* am going to the ballpark, you are not. You can catch the next train back home. The Pittsburgh ball club has no need of your services."

Donovan put two quarters on the table and walked out, leaving Eddie alone to wonder what in the world he'd done wrong.

Three months after Eddie's botched breakfast with the Pittsburgh manager two men visited the Waddell home. One was a small man in his sixties who wore horn-rimmed spectacles and introduced himself as Professor Jenkins. The other was younger. He had dark hair and clear green eyes. He smiled and said his name was Thomas George. He wore a red flannel jacket with "Volant Athletic Department" printed across the back. In spite of the cold weather he wore a baseball cap. It had a big V on the front. The two men sat on the horsehair settee in the parlor and asked Mr. Waddell if they could speak to him and his son.

After being served coffee and some of Mary Waddell's delicious rhubarb pie the two strangers explained that they were from Volant College in Lawrence County. The older man was a professor and the director of the school's newly-established athletic department and the other was the coach of the baseball team.

"Volant is primarily a teachers' college," Professor Jenkins explained after setting down his plate. "We are trying to get some publicity in order to attract more students and we have decided the easiest and quickest way to do so is through athletics. Coach George has recruited a talented ball team, but . . ."

George interrupted. "Listen. It's like this. We're in desperate need of a good twirler. I heard about a kid from Prospect with amazing speed and I went up and saw Edward play with Franklin. The team was positively dreadful but your son displayed great skill. We would like him to pitch for us."

Eddie had little interest in academics. He hadn't really given any thought to going to college, but this offer was very tempting.

"Would Eddie have to take courses and go to classes?" asked his father.

"No," answered Jenkins. "He would have the run of the campus, but he would not be required to attend any classes. He would simply need to play baseball to the best of his abilities and deport himself in a manner befitting a student of Volant College."

They had already drawn up a contract. Eddie would be paid a dollar a game and would get free room and board. From the doorway, Mary Waddell looked on approvingly. Perhaps, even if he wasn't attending classes, the college life would have a positive influence on her aimless son.

"Could ya maybe throw in some chewing tobacco, Prof?" asked Eddie. "It throws off my balance if I don't have a plug in my mouth when I pitch."

The men looked at each other and smiled. "Why yes, I think that can be arranged," said the professor.

"Great then! I'm gonna be a college man," beamed Eddie.

& & &

Eddie arrived at the Volant College ball field on May 8. The team's first game was already in the seventh inning. Eddie explained that he had received the telegram informing him of the date just that morning. He pulled his glove out of his suitcase and, at Coach George's direction, took the mound without putting on a uniform.

There was one out. Eddie was allowed a few pitches to warm up and when the umpire called 'Play' Eddie struck out the remaining two batters. In the eighth he struck out another two hitters and then a fifth one in the ninth inning. Nobody reached base. In the team's next game, against West Sunbury Academy, Eddie was on the mound from the start and struck out an unheard of thirteen batters. He got two hits and Volant won 17-1.

RUBE WADDELL

He pitched two or three times a week for Volant and between games, since he had no classes, he would travel to nearby Greenville and pitch there. When there was no game there either, Eddie banged the drum in Volant's marching band. They played all the latest tunes, "Ole Hokie", "There'll Be a Hot Time in the Old Town Tonight", and of course "Hail Pennsylvania." When he wasn't playing the drum he would lead the band through the streets of Volant, waving a baton and throwing it what seemed like a mile into the air and then nonchalantly catching it without missing a stride when it finally returned to Earth.

He beat Clarksville, fanning twelve batters and allowing just three hits while getting three of his own, and he beat Hiram, scoring three of Volant's runs hitting in the cleanup spot. Coach George received word that Grove City and Westminster College had 'full schedules' and could not play Volant anymore.

Eddie was having a great time. On the rare occasions when a batter reached base Eddie would invariably pick him off if he took too healthy a lead. The runner would of course be focusing on Eddie's throwing hand. But he would suddenly drop his glove and throw the runner out with his right hand. The runner would get up off the ground, shake his head and mutter, "What the hell?"

A lot of what Eddie did was to impress girls. He could hardly believe how many pretty ones came to the games. They were hard to miss in their big feather hats, with pompadour hairstyles in imitation of the Gibson Girls in the magazines. Their colorful dresses had leg of mutton sleeves with puffed shoulders and, of more interest to Eddie, they were designed to show off a woman's shape. Though they often hid behind their parasols, some had a hard time disguising the fact that they were far more interested in the new twirler than they were in the progress of the game.

"He's so big and handsome," a girl named Suzanne told her friend Mabel, "and he throws the ball so hard. I swear I heard one of the batters gasp when one went pitch went by him. And they're so loud when they hit the catcher's mitt."

"I heard it took a while to find anyone brave enough to catch," said Mabel. "You can tell the *batters* are afraid."

"When he threw that curver I thought the hitter was going to jump right out of his skin," chuckled Suzanne. "It headed straight for his ear and then went right out over the plate."

"He must have been awfully embarrassed. He looked so silly."

"I wouldn't want to go up against him, that's for sure."

"I don't think I'd mind *rubbing* up against him," purred Mabel.

"You're awful!" declared Suzanne. "How could you think such a thing?

"As if you weren't."

ℓℓ   ℓℓ   ℓℓ

"Hell's bells," Eddie muttered to himself when a lovely brunette batted her long eyelashes at him as he left the bench to go out to pitch, "that gal's hotter than a two dollar pistol on a Saturday night."

Eddie often did somersaults or handsprings after striking out the last batter in an inning and winked at one girl or another when he returned to his feet. Coach George, who couldn't have been happier with Eddie, gave him quarters for sodas after each easy victory. Eddie could drink a lot of sodas, but he spent a lot of his quarters buying sodas for girls. Sometimes they would go for walks and some let Eddie take advances when they sat on a bench in a shaded lane. Edith was his favorite. She wasn't as pretty as some of the others but she was completely smitten with Eddie. She just stared at him as he downed one soda after another. She rarely touched hers.

"Did you see what they wrote about you in the New Castle Courant last week?" she asked one time. Eddie shrugged his shoulders and continued sucking on his straw. She took out the clipping and read, "'the Wampun boys could not hit the swift balls which came from pitcher Waddell.'"

"That's nice," Eddie said, returning to his soda and wishing it was a cold beer.

"They talk about that thing you do sometimes."

"Which thing?" asked Eddie.

"It says, 'In the final inning Waddell walked the first two batters, seemingly on purpose, and then instructed his fielders to leave the diamond. They could scarcely believe what Waddell was asking them to do but they reluctantly headed to the bench. Waddell proceeded to strike out the side on nine consecutive pitches.'"

"I like to put on a show for the bugs," said Eddie.

"And they go wild for you, especially the girls."

Eddie didn't need Edith to tell him he was popular. He knew he was. He always had been, wherever he'd lived, especially when he was pitching. He badly wanted to get Edith alone and see how far he could get with her this time.

They rode bicycles to a bridge on the edge of town and sat on the grass beside it. They hugged and kissed for a while and Eddie sensed that she wanted to do more. He moved his hand up along her side. She squirmed but didn't take his hand away. He squeezed her breast and she gasped a little. He began to move his hand down toward her waist and then below.

"No Eddie, you can't, I mean we can't."

"I sure would like to. I'm real sweet on you, Edith."

"I know Eddie, but I can't. If my mother ever found out..."

Her mother didn't know what Eddie and her daughter were doing, but soon enough she did learn about her daughter's bicycle rides with the gigantic ball player and she called an immediate halt to them as soon as she did. Eddie didn't see Edith again.

By now he was desperate to lie with a woman. When his Franklin teammates had bragged about what they had done with women Eddie had let on that he'd had some experience too. He hadn't. At least the college girls let him take some small liberties, the girls in Prospect hadn't been willing to do more than hold hands. Their mothers had told them they shouldn't kiss a man until they were engaged. Eddie wouldn't have to wait much longer though.

CHAPTER FIVE

BEDDED, KIDNAPPED, AND LESS
THAN A MODEL PRISONER

He'd seen her at every home game Volant had played. She always sat right behind their bench. She was in her early forties and attractive, though not stunning, mostly because her nose was a bit too big for her face. But she wore beautiful clothes and a merry widow hat, and she had one very attractive feature, two in fact. Her breasts, to which she made every effort to draw attention, were very firm and very large.

Toward the end of a game she motioned to Eddie to come over to her when he came off the mound. She handed him a note. He unfolded it and read it.

It said, "I would very much like you to come to my home at nine this evening, if you are free. I live at 22 Wilson Avenue. I would love to feel your wonderful pitching arm and see if you have other ... hidden assets."

Eddie gulped and turned as red as a beet. The note's meaning could hardly have been clearer. This woman was clearly interested in more than Eddie's shoots and puzzlers. He nodded, tipped his cap, and stuffed the invitation into his pocket.

℮℮ ℮℮ ℮℮

At 8:58 that evening Eddie nervously rang the doorbell of 22 Wilson Avenue. The woman opened the door and asked him inside. She smelled wonderful, like fresh lilacs. Eddie went into the parlor and sat down on the sofa. The room, lit only by a small Tiffany lamp in the corner, was lavishly decorated.

"I am so glad that you decided to come, Edward, if I can call you that."

"Edward's just fine, ma'am."

"Gertrude. My name is Gertrude. Gertrude Parsons. But you can call me Gertie. What can I get you to drink? Something stronger than root beer or sarsaparilla?"

"Do you have any Kentucky bourbon, Gertie?"

"I do. Relax while I get it. Take off your jacket and make yourself comfortable."

"Would you like some ice?"

"Just the way it comes, if you please."

She returned minutes later with the whiskey in a crystal glass. He got another delicious whiff of her perfume as she bent over with the glass to reveal her ample cleavage.

He took a drink and sighed, "Umm. This'd bring a tear to a glass eye."

"I'm glad you like it. You are an amazing pitcher, Edward. Before you arrived it was scarcely worth attending a Volant game. No matter how many hits they made they were sure to give up more runs than they scored. Now it's just the opposite. I've been reading about you in the newspapers. You're becoming quite the local hero."

Eddie had another sip, he normally drank a lot faster but this bourbon needed to be savoured. He tried not to stare at Gertie's chest, though she clearly welcomed it. After a few minutes in which she talked about the town, but mostly about how much she enjoyed watching Eddie play, she excused herself and left the room. When she returned she was wearing a negligee that left little to the imagination.

"I hope you don't mind my appearance or my forwardness," she purred.

"I don't much mind either," Eddie told her.

She gestured for him to follow her into the bedroom.

After he had sat down on the edge of her bed, Gertie went over to him and removed his shoes and then helped him off with his shirt and collar. Slowly and teasingly she unbuttoned his fly. Eddie wasn't wearing underwear and Gertie's eyes widened when his enormous erection popped out.

"Oh my," she gulped.

Eddie effortlessly picked Gertie up and gently tossed her onto the bed. She loved it and pulled him down on top of her. He had his way with her four times that night. "Or did she have her way with me?" he thought when he left. He wasn't sure and he didn't much care.

Gertie certainly knew what made a man happy, and not just in the boudoir. She handed him an expensive cigar when he arrived for his second visit, and another kind of whiskey, Irish this time. He worked up quite a thirst over the next two hours.

After their third time Gertie lay back on the silk sheets, sipped wine, and stared at Eddie's body. "Such a handsome and well-developed physique. How did you develop such strong arms?"

"Roofing, laying pipelines, and plowin' mostly."

"I love the way you carry me around when we're .... we're ... well, you know."

"You have the most beautiful bosoms I have ever seen, Gertie. Not that I've seen that many. They get me really ... excited."

"I noticed."

"Can I come back some other night this week?"

Gertie thought about Eddie's member and giggled, "I might just be able to squeeze you in."

Eddie planned to go back on Wednesday night. He didn't make it.

℮ ℮ ℮

He'd been out riding in a buckboard he'd borrowed from a teammate. He was supposed to pitch against Mercer that afternoon. Now he was, as usual, looking for fishing holes. It was just after 8 a.m. Sunbeams sliced through the trees as he drove along the river and he thought about how great his life was turning out. He was doing the things he loved best, fishing and playing baseball, and he was going to make love, probably several times, with a buxom and amorous woman that night.

Suddenly another buckboard pulled up alongside his. He thought he must really have been distracted not to have heard it approaching.

"That you, Waddell?" one of the men in the rig called out.

There were five of them. They were a little older than Eddie. He thought he'd seen them before. Were they players from the Mercer team? He thought so.

"You fellas from Mercer?" he yelled back.

"As a matter of fact we are," the one who was driving yelled. "Pull up for a minute. We need to talk."

"We do?" Eddie asked as he steered the buggy to the side of the road. "What about? I'm gonna pitch against you boys this afternoon, can't we talk before the game?"

"We need to talk now."

The man sitting beside the driver pulled a long-barreled revolver out of his coat and pointed it at Eddie. The driver pulled the buckboard in front of Eddie's, leaving no chance for a getaway.

"Turns out you will *not* be pitching against us this afternoon," said the driver. "You're going to spend the afternoon with this fellow," he said, motioning to the man sitting behind him. "You don't need to know his name, he has a sore arm and can't play. And neither can you."

"What the hell! You can't be serious," stammered Eddie.

33

"Oh, but we are serious. You see the odds are four to one against Mercer with you on the mound this afternoon and we've bet fifty dollars on Mercer. We believe we have a very good chance of collecting two hundred dollars if any of Volant's other pitchers toes the rubber at one o'clock."

Outnumbered five to one and facing a revolver, Eddie had no choice but to allow the man with the sore arm and the one with the gun to get into his buckboard and take him away. They drove him to a barn a couple of miles outside Mercer where Eddie watched the two play pea knuckle all afternoon.

Finally the other Mercer kidnappers arrived. They were in a rare mood. They threw a pile of bills on the table and set three bottles of liquor down beside it.

"Help yourself, we won, twelve to six," said the man who had been driving the Mercer players' buckboard. "And it was all thanks to you. You not being there that is."

"Let's play some poker, boys, you too Eddie. Lloyd, pour us some drinks," he said, motioning to the fellow in the corner.

"I got no money," said Eddie.

"You do now," said the ringleader, tossing him three dollars.

Eddie's eyes lit up. Lloyd handed him a drink. "These fellas aren't so bad after all," he thought to himself.

"You can have that money on one condition," said the ringleader.

"What's that?" asked Eddie, taking a swig of the corn liquor. It was nowhere near as good as Gertie's whiskey but tasted fine just the same.

"You pitch for Mercer tomorrow afternoon against Wampun."

"For Mercer?" Eddie asked.

"That's right," said the ringleader, placing his hand over the money he'd given to Eddie.

"Be glad to," said Eddie, pulling the money into his lap. "Got any more of that hooch, Lloyd?"

*   *   *

Eddie pitched for Mercer and won easily the next afternoon in spite of a terrible hangover. He'd lost the three dollars playing poker so he was glad when the Mercer coach gave him another dollar after the game. Eddie pocketed the bill and headed back to Volant to try to explain to the coach why he had missed the game against Mercer and to tell his teammate where his buckboard had been.

"You'd better be ready to pitch against Clarksville on Saturday, Eddie,"

Coach George said. "They'll be looking for revenge after the shellacking you gave them last time."

"I'll be even better," promised Eddie. He wasn't thinking about Clarksville, or Saturday's game though. He was thinking about a pair of delicious trout sizzling in a pan and about Gertie's amazing breasts.

&   &   &

In the third week of June the Volant baseball season came to an end and Eddie said his goodbyes to his coach and his teammates. He paid one last visit to Gertie's house and let her seduce him a few more times. The next day he packed his valise, headed back to Prospect, and rejoined the Butler County team.

The local farmers rarely left their fields to attend ball games, but when word got around that young Waddell was back they hitched up their wagons and headed in to town. He wore red underwear under his uniform in case there was a fire. In spite of Eddie's life-saving prowess the Butler manager didn't approve of his star twirler wearing bright red underwear. "You can see it right through your uniform," he insisted. Eddie finally relented. In protest, he wore no underwear at all, which led to more than a few gasps when he stripped down on his way out of the ballpark to chase another fire wagon.

&   &   &

Eddie loved military uniforms and he was particularly fond of the ones worn by the Butler County National Guardsmen that featured big shiny brass buttons. One day, on a whim, he went to the outfit's headquarters and joined up. Wearing the uniform was great, he got a lot of admiring looks from females when he walked down the street. Unfortunately he hadn't given any thought to how many rules he'd be expected to obey.

And the drills! The guardsmen marched and did maneuvers in the hot sun every morning. Even worse, the commander told them they were not allowed to have a drink, not even one, the night before a parade or an inspection. After a couple of weeks the novelty of wearing the fancy uniform wore off and Eddie stopped going. He neglected, however, to inform his commanding officer of his decision.

In the middle of a game a few days later, to the amazement of the rooters and the two teams, a detachment of guardsmen ceremoniously marched onto the field and hauled Eddie off the mound. They took him back to their barracks and threw him into the stockade. He was charged with being AWOL from his duties.

An hour later Eddie sat on the floor of his cell, whistling and tossing pebbles at the wall across from him. The commander passed by outside and gave him a withering look. When he was out of sight Eddie reached through a hole in the wall and picked up a handful of cartridges he'd noticed. He slowly took aim and threw them eighty feet across the yard into an open stove. There was a huge explosion. The cartridges had been live!

The commander ran out of a building. He looked around but saw no one. He eyed the distance between the stockade and the stove and quickly decided who had thrown the shells. He stormed over to Eddie's cell and looked in. Eddie was singing "There'll be a Hot Time in the Old Town Tonight."

"Were you responsible for that, Waddell?" he demanded.

Eddie looked at the commander with all the innocence he could muster. "For what?"

"The explosion, you hooligan."

"I *thought* I heard something. What do you suppose coulda caused it?"

The commander's face turned crimson. He called out to an officer outside the cell.

"Fitzgibbons, I've had enough of this man. Get him out of here before I organize a firing squad."

Eddie was released that night. Keeping him in line was going to be far more trouble than it was worth.

Eddie received offers from several semi-pro teams while playing for Butler. One off day he went with a group of friends to see the Evans City team play against the Mars Athletic Club. Halfway through the game Evans City ran out of pitchers.

Eddie's friends began to yell, "Hey, there's a twirler up here in the stands."

Desperate, the manager, who was also the team's shortstop, agreed to give Eddie a try. "How much worse can he do?" he asked the second baseman.

Eddie took off his straw hat, borrowed a glove, and went in to pitch. The Martians didn't manage a hit the rest of the game and the Evans City manager immediately invited Eddie to join the team. Their attendance had not been very good, in large part due to their lack of pitching. They knew Eddie could be a big draw for them, but they wanted him to go by the name he'd acquired in Franklin.

The manager, who was almost a foot shorter than his new six-foot-two starter, said, "We can promote you a lot easier as Rube Waddell. You'll draw bigger crowds and we can pay you a few more dollars."

"I'm no hayseed," Eddie told him. But, lured by the prospect of more money in his pocket, he reluctantly agreed and tried his best to get used to the name.

Before the games when Eddie, now once again Rube, was scheduled to pitch, Evans City staged a parade. He marched in his uniform behind the band and a group of boys carried a huge banner that read "Come and see Big Rube fan 'em out." It worked, rooters flocked to see him.

RUBE WADDELL
KING *of the* HALL *of* FLAKES

CHAPTER SIX

A RUBE AWAKENING

Eddie hadn't pitched in Evans City for very long when he received an offer from the Louisville Colonels of the National League to play for them for the remainder of the season for the staggering sum of five hundred dollars. They sent him a contract, a train ticket, and instructions to go to the hotel in Washington where the Colonels were staying.

He arrived in Washington at two a.m. and went directly to the hotel. He told the hotel clerk that he was Eddie Waddell, that he was joining the Louisville Colonels, and that he needed to see the manager Fred Clarke.

"It is two o'clock in the morning, Mister Waddell," the clerk pointed out.

"I know that, but I have to see Mister Clarke, immediately."

"I have instructions not to disturb Mr. Clarke."

"You don't understand, it's very important that I see him, right away."

"But you can't see him. He is not to be disturbed."

"Listen, Mister Clarke will be as mad as a March hare if he finds out that his new pitcher arrived and you wouldn't let him see him."

"I doubt that very much, Mister Waddell."

"You don't seem to understand how ball clubs work."

"I assume they do not work at *all* at two o'clock in the morning," the clerk replied sardonically.

"What's his room number?"

"I can't give you that information until eight a.m., the time at which Mister Clarke can be contacted."

"What floor is he on?"

"I can't tell you that either."

"Fine, you win, I'll just knock on every door until I find him."

"What? You can't do that!"

"How else am I gonna find him if you won't give me the damn room number?" Eddie asked, heading toward the staircase.

"All right, all right, Mister Clarke is in room three twelve, but he will not like being woken at this hour."

"He'll be fine when he finds out his new pitcher's arrived."

"His new trouble maker you mean," muttered the clerk as Eddie grabbed his valise and bounded up the stairs.

℃   ℃   ℃

"Who's there?" a voice finally answered after Eddie had been knocking on the door of room 312 for five minutes.

"It's Eddie Waddell, Mister Clarke, your new pitcher."

"Eddie who?"

"Eddie Waddell, I mean *Rube* Waddell."

"Oh, right, well what in the blazes are you doing waking me at this hour?"

"I just want to talk to you is all."

"Go away."

"I am not going anywhere until I talk to you."

"Go away and let me sleep," Clarke demanded.

"I must see you now or I will leave town," said Eddie.

"You'll what?"

"I'll leave town."

"Oh, all right then. Come in, if you absolutely must."

Rubbing his eyes, Fred Clarke opened the door. He wore blue pajamas under a brown housecoat. He had a high forehead, big ears, and beady eyes. He was twenty-five years old, five foot nine, and a hundred and sixty pounds. Eddie thought he looked to be in pretty good shape for a manager. He didn't know that Clarke was also one of the speediest and grittiest outfielders in baseball.

Clarke gestured toward a chair, but Eddie just set down his valise and started talking. He told the manager about all the games he'd won and how many batters he'd struck out. Then he told him how many different kinds of pitches he could throw and how he threw them. Then he asked about the team and about Louisville, and where he would be staying there, and how much meal money the players got.

Wondering if he would ever get rid of the kid and mercifully get back to sleep, Clarke finally interrupted. "I just had a great idea, Rube. Why don't you go around and introduce yourself to your new teammates. I'm sure they'll be delighted to meet you. What time is it now, about three a.m.?"

"I guess so. Say, that's a great idea. You got their room numbers?"

Clarke went to his night table and got a piece of paper. "Here they are. Nice meeting you, Rube. Good *night.*" Eddie said thanks and headed out. Clarke didn't notice that he'd left his valise behind.

      *   *   *

"Hans, Hans Wagner, they call me Honus," yawned the first player Eddie called on. "Vat time is eet anyway?" he grumbled in a thick German accent.

Eddie reached out and shook his hand. It was the first time he'd met anyone with hands as big as his. "Eddie Waddell's the name, folks call me Rube now though. I'm the new pitcher."

Wagner was clearly not in much of a mood for small talk and after a couple of minutes he told Eddie he had to leave. It took him an hour to wake up the other players. Some took a long time coming to the door. One or two seemed to have already been awake and he thought he could smell perfume when they opened their doors. No one seemed very pleased to meet him.

"I'm done, Mister Clarke," Eddie said through the door of room 312.

"What? You're back?" Clarke said throwing his housecoat back on and opening his door.

"I met everybody 'cept one fella. He never answered the door even though I knocked for a good ten minutes. I think I woke some people up. They seemed kinda upset."

"What room was it?" Clarke asked tiredly.

"Room one twenty-eight."

"Room one twenty-eight? That Dummy Hoy's room. The man's deaf."

"I guess that's why he didn't answer the door."

"I expect so," grunted Clarke, handing Eddie his bag.

      *   *   *

When they got off the train in Baltimore where they would play their next series against the Orioles the Colonels looked tired, all except Dummy Hoy that is. Eddie passed by a couple of his new teammates.

"The new kid sure marches to a different drummer," Topsy Hartsell told Doc Powers, one of the Colonels' two catchers. Hartsell was trying to win a spot in the Louisville outfield.

"They broke the mold when they made him," said Powers.

The Orioles had been the National League champions the last three years. Now they were in a struggle with the Boston Beaneaters for first place. The morning had been cloudy, but as game time approached the sun peeked out. It was going to be a muggy September afternoon. Just over two thousand rooters had paid an average of fifty cents for admission to Union Field. Five thousand seats were empty, the Colonels weren't much of a draw.

Sportswriters across America knew the Baltimore lineup by heart. Catching was Wilbert Robinson, Uncle Robby as he was known. The top notch infield featured Jack Doyle, Heinie Reitz, Hughie Jennings, and third baseman John McGraw, who was even more aggressive and feisty than Fred Clarke. In the outfield were Jake Stenzel, Joe Kelley, and Wee Willie Keeler, who'd hit safely in forty-four games at the beginning of the season. Half of the Orioles' lineup would wind up in the Hall of Fame.

The Baltimore press had a lot more trouble sorting out the identities of the Colonels. Several were in their first year. Heinie Smith, the second baseman, had just joined the team the week before.

When a reporter asked Fred Clarke who was pitching he grimaced and pointed at Eddie. "That man." It would be a while before he got over being wakened at two a.m.

"What's his name?" the reporter asked impatiently.

"Waddell."

"How do you spell it?"

"W E D D L E, I think," answered Clarke. "At least that's what I wrote on the lineup card."

"Who's going to catch?"

"That fellow over there," Clarke answered, pointing to a tall young man who was unpacking his gear. "And before you even ask, I have no idea how to spell *his* name. It sounds like 'shrieking ghost' to me. It's his first game, same as the pitcher."

Ossee Schreckongost was from Bethlehem, Pennsylvania which was a four hour buggy ride from Philadelphia. He had long, black wavy hair and, at five foot ten, he was one of the taller players on the team. He'd been playing for the Sunbury Nine in the New England League and had arrived that morning by train. When asked if he knew anything about the pitcher he'd be catching Schreckongost said, "Not a thing, I never laid eyes on him until a few minutes ago."

Eddie strode to the mound trying to look unfazed. He hadn't pitched an inning in the minor leagues and now he was facing the famous Orioles. "Damn, I'm as nervous as a long-tailed cat in a room fulla rocking chairs," he thought to himself.

Wee Willie "hit 'em where they ain't" Keeler led off and Eddie's first three pitches were deemed high by the umpire. He was overthrowing and getting his pitches up - at least on Keeler they were. "This fella's so short he'd have to stand up twice to cast a shadow," Eddie yelled out to the first baseman.

On the next pitch Keeler lofted a lazy fly ball to Clarke in left field for the first out. But then Jennings and Kelley hit singles and Wagner mishandled the cutoff throw, which allowed each man to advance an extra base. Now there were runners on second and third and just one out. Rooters in the bleachers started yelling at Eddie. "Hey Waddles, you walk like a duck. You throw like one too."

But Eddie fired a four seam, then a two-seam shoot past Jake Stenzel and then crossed him up with a side-armed curve to set him down on strikes. It was Eddie's first major league strikeout. He started to feel a bit better. He worked carefully to Jack Doyle, too carefully. His fourth pitch caught too much of the strike zone and Doyle ripped a single that drove in both runners. Then Reitz singled, bringing up Jack Quinn. He smashed Eddie's first pitch toward center field. Out of pure instinct Eddie reached up and knocked the ball down. He picked it up and threw to first for the third out.

In the top of the second the Colonels had one hit but failed to score. It didn't help that whenever they got a runner as far as third John McGraw would either bump him off the baseline with a well-placed hip or grab his belt when the lone umpire was watching another runner.

Eddie asked Fred Clarke how McGraw got away with it

"I don't know, but he's been doing it for years. You'd think the umpire would know enough to keep an eye on him," said Clarke.

"He's a sly one," Eddie replied, "the man could peel an orange in his pocket."

He got the first two Orioles to ground out in the home half of the second inning but Keeler lined a single between first and second and then Jennings hit a routine grounder that took a bizarre hop right over Honus Wagner's head.

"Schei spiel!" he yelled as he watched the ball roll to the outfield fence. Keeler scored all the way from first.

Anxious to get out of the inning Eddie threw one right down the middle to Kelley and he smashed it into left center. Luckily Fred Clarke made a running catch. Only one run came in this time. Baltimore got two more runs in the fourth on a double by Hugh Jennings that knocked in Keeler and Kelley. When Eddie finally settled down the Orioles began employing an assortment of tricks from their well-established playbook. They bunted and used the hit-and-run against the inexperienced Louisville fielders and stole second after almost every walk or hit. Schreckongost kept throwing them out but Heinie Smith kept dropping his hard throws.

After the fourth inning one of the only Orioles to reach base was Jennings. He got decked by one of Eddie's fadeaways.

"Sorry 'bout that," Eddie called to him after Jennings dusted himself off and trotted to first base.

"Ya, right," Jennings called back. He shook his head and muttered, "That kid really is a rube."

For some reason this rookie didn't know that pitchers were expected to throw at batters after they'd gotten big hits off them. It was part of the game and Jennings, who'd once nearly been killed by a high and tight pitch, understood. Since the Colonels could manage only one run Eddie was saddled with a loss in his major league debut, but at least he'd proven he could overcome his nerves and fare well against a top-notch lineup.

*   *   *

He and Schreckongost went to breakfast together the next morning. Schreck was in a lousy mood, not because Heinie Smith had dropped so many of his throws, but because he'd gone hitless in four at bats. They saw some of the Colonels in the lobby but none of the veterans seemed interested in eating with rookies who might not be around for long. Eddie went outside to a newsstand to get the Baltimore morning papers. He wanted to see if they'd mentioned him.

Schreck thought he had a pretty large appetite but when the mammoth breakfast Eddie had ordered arrived - on three separate plates - he couldn't believe his eyes. "This fellow never shies away from the trough," he thought to himself. It was gone in a matter of minutes and Eddie picked up one of the newspapers.

He read out loud what *The Baltimore Sun* said, "Louisville newcomer Edward Waddell, whom everyone seems to call Rube, made an admirable showing in both nerve and skill in holding the champions to five runs."

The Baltimore News reported that, "Young Waddell displayed an impressive overhand fast pitch that kept the Orioles down after the fourth inning."

Schreck wasn't listening. He was too busy admiring a blonde girl who was removing dishes from a nearby table.

"That's impressive," said Schreck, meaning the girl, not what the papers had to say about Eddie.

Just then a skinny teenager who was obviously a messenger boy hurried up to their table. "Excuse me, but is either of you Ossee Schreck

. . . Ossee Schreckon . . . Ossee . . . "

"It's Schreckongost, kid."

"Oh, good, I've been to four diners looking for you."

"What's the message?" Ossee asked.

The boy handed Schreck a piece of paper.

"What's it say?" asked Eddie.

"That I need more seasoning. They're shipping me back to New England."

"That's rotten luck, Ossee. I hope you're back up again soon."

He *would* be back in the big league before long and he and Eddie would have some very interesting and unusual times together.

RUBE WADDELL
KING *of the* HALL *of* FLAKES

CHAPTER SEVEN

A HIT WITH THE BOOSTERS
. . . BUT NOT THE BOSSES

Fred Clarke was still mad at Eddie for waking him up in the middle of the night when the team got back to Louisville and Eclipse Park II at 28th and Broadway. Now he had another reason to be annoyed with the kid. He was an absolute pain in the neck on the bench when he wasn't pitching.

Eddie got bored easily. Clarke expected his players to focus on the game at all times. When they weren't on the mound, twirlers were supposed to observe how opposition batters handled different kinds of pitches, which ones liked to work the count, and which ones tended to pull the ball or go the opposite way. They were also supposed to watch what kinds of leads enemy runners took on the bases and make note of which fielders had the best arms.

Eddie had much too short of an attention span for all that. After only a few minutes he would stop watching the action on the field and start creating some of his own. First he would start whistling, then he'd sing his favorite songs, then he would point out pretty girls in the stands. Then he'd ask about good places to fish or to have dinner or get a drink. Then he'd challenge the other players to wrestle.

Finally, just to get him off the bench, Clarke would send him out to coach first base when the Colonels were at bat. That created a whole new problem. Eddie pulled more stunts in the coaching box than he had on the bench.

"Hey pitcher," he'd yell at the mound, "you couldn't hit water if you fell out of a boat" or "bet you couldn't break a pane a glass" or "my baby sister throws harder than that."

Then he would do a comically exaggerated impersonation of the pitcher's windup and delivery, adding loud asides like, "I sure hope this one makes it to the plate" or "please don't hit this one, coach'll skin me alive iffin ya do." The boosters roared in delight.

RUBE WADDELL

But that wasn't all. Eddie would walk over to the stands and hobnob with the rooters, tell them jokes - usually quite ribald ones - or comment on their clothes, or ask them if they thought they could get a hit off this pitcher.

He talked endlessly to his teammates when they reached base, and never about baseball. A first base coach was supposed to remind the base runners how many outs there were, point out how deep the outfielders were playing, check with them to see if they'd seen the signs from the third base coach, and tell them what the pitcher did just before he threw over to pick runners off.

"D'ya ever catch a musky?" he asked one runner when he got to first. "What's the biggest steak you ever ate?" he asked another. "You ever seen that girl in the purple dress before?" he needed to know from Heinie Smith who, having just joined the team, was unlikely to know who attended their games, and more importantly was focusing on his job, to get around the bases and score a run.

Eddie caught bugs, made patterns in the dirt with his spikes, and asked boosters if they would get him a soda pop. When runners were circling the bases Eddie made cow and pig noises or pretended he was stampeding a herd of cattle. Clarke tried to remove him from the coaching box, but the crowd howled in protest and he was forced to leave him there.

Eddie knew he was a big hit. He'd put on a great show in the afternoon and carry it right into the bars until the wee hours of the morning. Word of his late night escapades soon reached the manager. Clarke was not impressed when he sent Eddie in to pitch in an exhibition game against the Indianapolis Indians, a team in the weaker Western League. The Colonels won the game but Eddie, who saw no reason to bear down in an exhibition game, gave up eleven hits. Everybody - reporters, rooters, and other players - commented on the speed of his pitches and on how much his sweeping curves broke, but clearly he was just taking it easy.

His next appearance was in a game against the Pirates. He came in with the Colonels trailing. They lost the game but a *Courier* reporter wrote about the impression that Rube Waddell made on the small number of bugs who'd gone to the game.

"It was necessary to be at the park yesterday afternoon to properly enjoy what transpired there. Rube went in to finish the contest and for more than an hour he kept the spectators splitting

their sides with laughter at his ludicrous antics. As a coacher he has no equal. He 'shoos' the runners off first and curves his body into all sorts of fantastic contortions. He made a hit - a decided hit - with the crowd. They yelled for him, roared for him, and would have no other coacher on the lines. He furnished an afternoon of genuine enjoyment. The Pittsburgh players enjoyed it too. They tried their best to get on his nerves but he parried every remark with some homespun witticism that carried a flavor of the soil."

While in his windup Eddie contorted his body so that it was hard to believe he could get the ball over the plate. He would stop right in the middle of his delivery to confuse the batters and he made noises at the top of his windup. He was overjoyed when he struck out Patsy Donovan, who'd refused to even give him a tryout after their breakfast meeting.

When the Colonels squared off against the Chicagos, who were now called the Orphans because they had lost their leader, "Pop" Anson, in '97, they faced their ace Clarke "the Old Fox" Griffith. He'd had the best E.R.A. in the league back in '88. The only Louisville pitcher with a winning record was Deacon Phillippe and he had a sore arm, so Fred Clarke reluctantly started Eddie. The Old Fox was no match for the young whippersnapper. Griffith allowed twelve hits. When the game was called due to darkness after eight innings the Colonels had a 6-1 victory and Eddie had a National League record for most strikeouts in a game, with fourteen.

"The prick can pitch, I'll give him that," Clarke muttered to himself.

℮ ℮ ℮

The Colonels lost badly to the Detroit Tigers, another team in the Western League, a few days later. It was just an exhibition game but Louisville should not have lost. Eddie beat the Tigers the next day though. He did cartwheels and handsprings off the mound and wisecracked with everyone including the umpire, who told him to get back on the mound and stop acting the fool. The bugs booed the ump, they were loving every minute of it - the Colonels had never been this entertaining.

Even though he'd given up five runs he decided to go out and paint the town red again anyway. After all, the season was almost over. Fred Clarke was not at all amused with his eccentric young fireballer. He fined Eddie a whopping fifty dollars.

Barney Dreyfuss, the Colonels' general manager, called Fred Clarke into his office. Dreyfuss had big ears and a large nose that almost obscured his tiny moustache. Papers were strewn across his desk. His familiar derby sat on top of one of the piles.

"Listen Fred," said Dreyfuss in his high-pitched voice, "I know Waddell gets on your nerves, but there's no denying the yahoo has talent."

"Oh, he has loads of it, but he's an absolute screwball," said Clarke. "He's going to drive us all around the bend."

"Well if you don't want him on the roster let's at least put him on our reserve list so no other National League team can claim him."

"I really don't want anything to do with him, Barney. I'm shipping him off to the Tigers. If he had such a good time beating them maybe he'll enjoy playing for them."

As it turned out, Eddie would. He enjoyed pretty much everything.

In late March Eddie reported to the Tigers' training camp in Nashville, Tennessee. He wore a light blue cotton suit with a bright red tie. At least his pants fit now, he'd finally stopped growing. He no longer wore his straw hat but he still had a wad of 'backy' in his mouth most of the time.

The Tigers played a series of exhibition matches on their way to Detroit to start the season. One of the stops was in Louisville. Frank Graves, the Tiger manager, wouldn't let Eddie start against the Colonels but when three other Tiger pitchers had given up a total of fifteen runs he sent him in.

"See if you can stop 'em, Rube," he said as he handed him the battered baseball.

Eddie needed no encouragement. He mowed down the Colonels inning after inning. The only run they scored was on a solo home run by Honus Wagner.

"Good one, Hans," Eddie yelled at him as the big German rounded third.

Honus grinned and yelled, "You should still be pitching for us."

"I would be if Clarke wasn't as ornery as a pit bull shittin' railway spikes."

The best thing for Eddie was that Fred Clarke batted twice and struck out both times. After the second one he threw his bat almost all the way to the grandstand before muttering and fuming his way back to the bench. Eddie snickered behind his glove.

Eddie celebrated hard and didn't make it back to the team's hotel that night, or the next night either. When he was scheduled to make his next start he was nowhere to be found. He showed up a day later, took the mound hung over to beat the band, and gave up twelve hits.

But when the team reached Detroit, where the papers had been talking about little else than the 'young giant', he was back in form. He entered a game in the sixth inning, struck out the side, and gave up just one hit the rest of the way. *The Detroit Free Press* said he was "chock full of ginger" and predicted a great future if he didn't fall by the wayside.

Eddie had his control back but he started to think he was back in Franklin whenever he allowed a hitter to make contact, the Tigers fielded as though they had paws, not gloves. In his next start he gave up just three clean hits but the Indianapolis Indians scored six unearned runs. The Tiger third baseman booted each of the first three balls hit to him.

Depressed about the tough loss, Eddie decided to take in a vaudeville show. After eating three plates of ribs and downing a few beers at The Stagger Inn he headed to the Temple Theatre. He was delighted by the animal acts, which included a cute monkey, a goat, a donkey, and a baby elephant. He thought the juggler was pretty good and the opera singer, whose face was caked in theatrical makeup, had an excellent voice,

Then a ventriloquist came out and sat on a stool. He had a dummy dressed as a cowboy on his lap. The ventriloquist asked the dummy to tell him again about the dream he'd had last night.

"I dreamt I ate a giant marshmallow," answered the dummy.

"A marshmallow?" asked the ventriloquist. "What happened?"

"When I woke up, my pillow was gone."

The audience roared.

"What did you say was the matter with your uncle?" asked the ventriloquist.

"He thinks he's a chicken," said the dummy.

"A chicken! The man is clearly insane. You should get his head examined."

"We can't. We need the eggs."

After a few more jokes the ventriloquist departed to generous applause. When girl dancers came out Eddie heard a man a few rows ahead making comments. The music was fairly loud and Eddie wasn't sure whether the man was praising and encouraging the girls or insulting them.

The master of ceremonies introduced the next act as Mr. and Mrs. Harry and Beatrice Houdini. A short man with dark hair parted in the middle and a tiny woman wearing a Louis the Fourteenth costume came onto the stage.

Stage hands brought a steamer trunk and a screen onto the stage. Harry Houdini had an audience member inspect the trunk and then he was covered with a sheet and bound tightly with ropes before being locked inside the trunk. A rope was tied around it and the screen was pulled in front. Mrs. Houdini, said, "Behold a miracle, ladies and gentlemen, a metamorphosis" and stepped behind the screen. Minutes later Harry Houdini emerged from behind the screen, pulled it aside, and pulled the rope off the steamer trunk. He opened it and Beatrice Houdini stepped out.

"Well I never," Eddie said to himself. "How in the blazes did they do that?"

Harry Houdini removed his coat to reveal a finely-muscled physique. He was wearing red tights. He did a series of flips and double somersaults and then boomeranged a playing card into the audience and did a back somersault, landing just in time to catch the incoming card.

Houdini waved a hand and two police officers came on stage. They put him in handcuffs and put irons on his legs. Then they pulled the screen in front of him. Seconds later Houdini came out and handed the officers the cuffs and irons.

"That fella is awful good," murmured Eddie.

Another policeman came out and put the magician in a strait jacket. Eddie had never seen one before. One of the policemen explained that mental asylums had started using them to control violent patients. When Houdini asked if someone could come and examine it, Rube jumped out of his seat and ran up on stage. He pulled hard at the bindings and told the audience nobody could get out of that thing. Mrs. Houdini pulled the screen in front of her husband and a minute later he came out carrying the strait jacket. The audience applauded madly.

Following a troop of acrobats the show's last act featured an extremely pretty girl with a terrific figure. She was blonde and looked to be about eighteen years old. She sang beautifully, but that wasn't enough for the man who'd yelled at the dancers.

"Nice gams, sweetie," he bellowed.

She paid no attention and kept on singing.

"Pretty swell shape you got there, honey," he yelled a minute later. She paused, but only for a second, and then kept on with the song.

Eddie reached the man just as he called out, "Why don't you take off some of those pretty duds and show us what you got."

Eddie grabbed the man and yanked him out of his seat.

"What the hell ..." he blurted.

"You are not allowed to make foul remarks while the lady is singing," Eddie growled.

"Says who?"

"Says me, you swine."

The man took a swing at Eddie. It was a mistake. Eddie punched him hard in the stomach, knocking the wind and the bravado right out of him. The theatre manager ran up with an usher. "Thank you so much for taking care of this hoodlum, sir. We'll take it from here."

Eddie let the man drop back into his seat. The singer hurried down off the stage and thanked Eddie for sticking up for her.

"That was so gallant. I'm very much obliged to you," she said.

Eddie straightened his tie and pushed his hair back into place.

"I don't know how you could ignore him for so long."

"I wish I could say he was the first masher I've had to endure," said the girl. "No one's ever come to my rescue so valiantly. I'm Lorelie."

"I'm Eddie. Say, would you like to meet me tomorrow for ice cream."

"I'd like that very much," said Lorelie without hesitation.

"How about twelve o'clock, by the clock in the park? I'll get us one of those bicycles built for two and we can go for a spin."

"That sounds divine, Eddie. I'll be there."

⁂

The next day Eddie and Lorelie went cycling and then to the amusement park.

"That was the easiest bicycle ride I've ever been on," Lorelie told Eddie as they sat at a table in a soda fountain. "I barely had to peddle. You're so strong. At the park you won the ring toss, the shooting gallery, the balloon darts, the ring the bell with the hammer, and the rope ladder climb. Is there any game you can't win?"

"Well, I'm no good at guessing which shell the fella has the pea under," said Eddie. "You sure are pretty, Lorelie."

"Why were all those boys making a fuss over you at the park?"

"I guess I shoulda mentioned, I play baseball, for the Tigers."

"Now there are more of them, staring and pointing at you through the window. I don't follow baseball very much but I've never heard of a famous player named Eddie."

"The boosters and newspaper writers call me Rube."

"Rube? As in Rube Waddell?"

"That's right."

"Why didn't you say so? I've heard people talk about you. They say you're a pitching sensation. Oh, but you must hate that name."

℀ ℀ ℀

The next morning the Detroit papers were full of accounts from people who'd seen the show at the Temple Theatre and the one-sided boxing match near the end of it. Eddie was already getting famous for how hard he threw baseballs, now he was known for throwing hard punches too.

Lorelie and Eddie saw each other only once more, for a moonlit walk and a night of passion. Then her vaudeville troupe left for parts unknown. He often looked for her on playbills and programs but he never found her.

CHAPTER EIGHT

YOU JUST HAVE TO STAND UP
TO THESE RICH FELLAS

It was a big surprise when a few days later Eddie and the Tigers won their first game, against the Columbus Senators. It ended 4-1. The Senators scored their only run in the ninth when, with the contest seemingly out of reach, Eddie started clowning around and gave up three hits. He clowned around for the next few days and nights too and when it was his turn to pitch he was in rough shape. He walked six batters, unleashed an uncharacteristic wild pitch, and lost the game.

Over the next three days the team's record fell to 1-10. Eddie started against the Milwaukee Brewers, whose manager was a tall, thin man, a former catcher named Cornelius McGillicuddy. Everyone called him Connie Mack. He was one of the most gentlemanly and well-mannered men Eddie had ever seen on a baseball diamond. For one thing he wore a suit throughout each game, even on the hottest afternoons.

Eddie walked seven batters, scattered nine hits, and struck out just two. But for a change the other side committed more errors than the Tigers, seven in all. Eddie fielded several bunts and adeptly threw out nine men at first. He also got three hits including a triple. Detroit had its second win. Days later they got their third, compliments of Eddie once again. It was clear that he was the team's biggest asset and its biggest draw as well.

The day after Eddie's third win the team was traveling to Columbus to play the Senators. Eddie got to Union Station just as a train was pulling out. He ran to the ticket window and asked if that was the train to Columbus.

"Among other destinations, yes," said the ticket agent.

"When's the next one?"

"Tomorrow morning."

"Dang," Eddie sighed. He picked up his battered suitcase and trudged out into the street. After walking a ways he passed a ball field where the Delray Athletic Club's Cigar team was playing a game. Recognizing Eddie immediately, the team's captain called out to him, "Rube, zat you? What are you doing here, I thought the Tigers were goin' to Columbus."

"They are, I'm not," said Eddie.

"If you're not doin' anything, would you mind umpin' for us? Our fella never showed up."

"Sure, be glad to."

Eddie enjoyed umpiring. He clowned around, making dramatic and exaggerated calls. In the fourth inning the second batter lined a pitch right at the first baseman. There was a cracking sound when the ball hit him in the knee and the man fell to the ground in agony. With some help from his teammates he eventually got up, but he certainly couldn't stay in the game.

"I'll play first," Eddie offered.

A man sitting alone in the bleachers was convinced to take over as umpire and Eddie took first base. Two innings later the Delray pitcher's arm gave out. He could move over and play first base where he wouldn't likely need to make many throws, but he couldn't pitch anymore. Eddie took the mound. He pitched the last four innings and was a big help with his bat. After the game he asked his new friends if there was a watering hole nearby.

"There's one just down the road," said the manager, "it's called The Bent Elbow. After the way you helped us out the team's buying."

"That'd be just grand. My mouth's so dry I could spit cotton."

Somehow, Eddie's foray with the Cigar Club made it into *The Detroit Evening Tribune*. Arthur Van Der Beck, the Tigers' owner, who'd been disgusted with his team's loose play, decided he needed to impose stricter discipline. Eddie became his first victim. Claiming that playing for another team was a violation of his contract, Van Der Beck fined Eddie twenty-five dollars.

When he found out about the fine Eddie was so mad he marched straight into Van Der Beck's office. The owner was sitting on a couch puffing on a big cigar and reading *The Racing Form*.

"Mister Van Der Beck, I could understand you fining me for drinking," yelled Eddie, "but you're fining me for playin' ball? I'm a ball player for Christ sakes! I quit."

Taking into account that Eddie was really the only quality player he had, Van Der Beck said, "Hold your horses a minute, Rube, there's no need to quit over twenty-five dollars. I tell you what, you pitch well your next game and I'll consider rescinding the fine."

"You mean you'll scrap it?"

"That's right. Hop on a train to Columbus and rejoin the club. If you show up sober and pitch well, the fine might just go away."

Eddie wasn't worried, he knew he could pitch better dead drunk than anybody else on the team could cold sober. "You got yourself a deal," he said. He strode out of Van Der Beck's office thinking that you just needed to stand up to these rich fellas and they'd back right down. Eddie got to Columbus just in time for the next game. He started well and then he got better. He walked only three and won 9-5 in spite of a lot more errors behind him.

The team headed to Minnesota to play the Minneapolis Millers. Eddie beat them handily, 12-2, striking out eleven. But the next week he gave up thirteen hits and twelve runs and lost to Charles Comiskey's St. Paul Apostles. When the team returned to Detroit the club secretary handed out the pay envelopes. When Eddie got his it was $25 short.

Eddie said nothing. He took what pay he'd been given and bought himself some new shirts and collars, a new suit, and a bright orange tie. He went to the ballpark for the Tigers' game the next day, but he didn't put on his uniform. Instead he bought a bag of peanuts and sat in the stands.

"You know what cheap sons of bitches the Detroit club are?" he asked a booster sitting next to him.

"Aren't you Waddell?" the startled man asked. "Hey, fellas," he said, turning to his friends, "it's Waddell."

"What are your doing up here, Rube?" asked one of the other spectators.

"They promised they wouldn't fine me if I won the next game and I did. And do ya know what the lyin', low-down cheats did? They went right ahead and fined me anyway."

"What are you gonna do about it?" the same man asked.

"I'm gonna quit is what I am gonna do. That'll show 'em."

"I don't know if you'd be interested," the stranger said, "but I heard some fellow behind us talking about what a great pitcher you are. He was telling this other fellow he'd pay you sixty dollars a month and free room and board to pitch for his team in Chatham if you ever got tired of playing in Detroit."

RUBE WADDELL

"The *Tigers* aren't giving me room and board. Where the devil is Chatham?" Eddie asked.

"Just across the border in Canada. Only take you an hour or so to get there."

℮   ℮   ℮

After the game Eddie left town and headed to Union Station. He hopped on board the "City of Chatham", a dilapidated little steamboat, and crossed the river to Canada. "This oughta teach the Tigers a thing or two," he thought as he tossed peanuts to the gulls that landed on the railing.

Eddie was happy pitching for the Chatham semi-pro team. The townsfolk treated him like a prince and his teammates were delighted to start winning games. A reporter from Detroit made the trip to see how he was doing. "I'm the captain and the manager too and I get a new pair of pants every time I hit a homer," Eddie told him. "I get stogies for doubles and new ties whenever I strike out the side."

In his first game against Dunnville he threw a perfect game and struck out a league record seventeen batters. He induced nine other hitters to dribble the ball meekly toward the mound so there was only one time when he needed a fielder other than the catcher and first baseman. That earned him several ties, and a nice pair of cufflinks as well. The two teams played again the next day and Eddie broke his new record, twenty strikeouts this time.

Part way though the next game a rooter who may have seen him do it before encouraged Eddie to send the rest of the team off the field. Naturally, Eddie the showman obliged. He walked the first two batters on purpose. He tried to walk the third to load the bases and add to the excitement, but the batter swung at a pitch outside the strike zone and popped it into center field.

"Oh crap!" Eddie muttered as he sprinted towards where the ball would land. The two runners scored but luckily the batter was so surprised to get a hit that he just stood at the plate and Eddie ran over and touched first. He struck out the next two men and the Chatham team scored just enough runs to win the game 3-2.

Winning wasn't enough for the fun-loving captain/manager. Eddie did tricks between innings. He juggled three baseballs and he rolled one down the back of one arm, across his shoulders, and down the other arm. He was making decent money and he was allowed to make even more by pitching for other semi-pro teams on off days. This was more like it.

Eddie was such a big draw the team added two games each week to its schedule, sometimes three. Soon he was making $150 a week. Before games he put a thick board in front of the stands and bet anyone ten dollars that he could not only hit the board, but split it in no more than three throws. He won just about every time.

At night Eddie chummed around with Chatham's mayor at the Rankin House, his unofficial campaign headquarters. Eddie graciously allowed the mayor and his supporters to buy his drinks. He rarely carried money of his own - he was so popular food and drinks were usually on the house - but he carried a shillelagh just in case a group of hoodlums appeared out of an alley on his way home. Sure enough that was exactly what happened one night after he'd finally said his slurred goodnights at the Rankin House.

Four men sprang from the shadows. "Hey Waddell," one called out, "got a few greenbacks you can spare. We hear you're makin' plenty."

Eddie sobered up in an instant. "Sorry fellas, I haven't got a red cent. Spent it all inside."

"That don't sound too likely to me, Waddell," said another tough.

"I'm not kiddin' ya, boys," Eddie told them.

"Hand it over or you won't be pitchin' for a while," threatened a third man.

Eddie struck the closest one hard with the shillelagh. The man dropped to the ground unconscious. One of the others pulled out a knife and came at Eddie. He smashed the man's arm, forcing him to scream and drop the knife. Eddie picked it up and started toward the two remaining hooligans. They looked at one other and fled.

The next morning Eddie had two visitors. One was a constable who was there to lay charges against him. He changed his mind after Eddie told him what had happened. The other was Theodore Radcliffe, a.k.a. 'Teddy', a beau of his sister Maude. Radcliffe was a member of the Homestead Athletic Club. They'd lost their last three games by lop-sided scores and decided to send Teddy to try to convince Eddie to return to Prospect. In spite of all the fun he was having in Chatham Eddie went with him. He could never say no to anyone in need.

RUBE WADDELL
KING *of the* HALL *of* FLAKES

CHAPTER NINE

"I AIN'T NO HAYSEED"

In his first start for Homestead Eddie set a league record with eleven strikeouts. His father was there for his second appearance. He went in for the last four innings of a game against East Liverpool, Ohio and struck out ten of the twelve men he faced.

In his next start, at Homestead, the Butler County hitters never got the ball past the infield. Fifteen hitters never even made contact, not so much as a foul tip. But when the two teams played again in Prospect Eddie allowed thirteen runs.

"What the hell happened out there?" Teddy asked him after the game. "You had them swinging at air in Homestead last week."

"Well I couldn't have my friends look bad in front of their neighbors."

Teddy shrugged. "I guess not, but you might have told somebody, we could have had somebody else pitch."

"Oh, sorry, I never thought a that."

In his next start, against Irwin, their left fielder, whose name was Rhinehart, constantly harassed Eddie, when he was at bat and on the mound as well. "You really are a rube, Waddell. Where's your mule? Where's the turnip cart you fell offa?" He wouldn't stop.

"Shut your damn mouth, I ain't no hayseed!" Eddie yelled back.

When Eddie headed to the mound for the seventh inning Rhinehart was running off the field. He deliberately ran past Eddie and yelled, "Anybody smell horse manure?"

"You must be lookin' for a poke in the eye," Eddie threatened.

Rhinehart dropped his glove and took a swing at Eddie. He ducked out of the way. Rhinehart threw another punch that glanced off Eddie's shoulder.

"Stay still, ya big ox," Rhinehart just barely managed to say before Eddie let loose. He hit him hard, square in the jaw. Rhinehart dropped to the ground, moaning. He didn't even try to get up. Two Irwin players had to help him to his feet. He was far too dazed to stay in the game.

The Irwin manager demanded that Eddie be ejected for injuring his player. "Your man caused the fight with his foul remarks and he threw the first punches," the umpire told him. "He got exactly what he deserved."

When the manager finally relented and went back to the bench, the umpire walked by Eddie and said, "Twas a nice punch, Rube, I'da loved to deck the loud-mouthed bastard me self."

Homestead's final game was against the Duquesne County Athletic Club. Eddie allowed two runs in the first nine innings and so did the Duquesne pitcher. Eddie struck out the side in the tenth and again in the eleventh. Darkness ended the game, still tied. Eddie had struck out twenty-three batters.

The teams decided they had to play a rematch. They knew a lot of folks would come out to see Eddie one last time. The rematch ended in darkness, tied once again. Eddie struck out twenty-two this time.

The town added extra streetcars to transport all the bugs who bought advance tickets to another rematch between the two teams. Before the game, as he often did, Eddie asked the Homestead trainer for a bucket of ice water. A young player that had just joined the team walked over to Eddie, who was dunking his left arm into the freezing water.

"I'm O'Neill," the newcomer said.

"Glad to meet you, O'Neill."

"Mind if I ask you a question?"

"Not at all, go ahead."

"Aren't you pitching today?"

"I sure am."

"With a sore arm?"

"What sore arm?"

"You're soaking it. It must be sore, how you gonna pitch?"

"My arm's not sore."

"What are you soaking it for then?"

"I usually soak it in ice cold water before a game."

"Why?"

"I got to," said Eddie.

"Huh?"

"If I don't, I throw too hard and the pitches burn up the catcher's mitt."

"Really?"

"Really."

"If you say so, Rube." The kid walked away. He hadn't been in baseball

all that long but he had certainly never heard of anything like that.

Eddie blanked Duquesne with his cooled-down arm. His teammates flocked around him after he fired strike three past the last hitter. He was the hero once again. It seemed as though he was wherever he went.

The Louisville Colonels were putting their lineup together for the '99 season. Barney Dreyfuss had heard reports about Eddie's great success with the Homestead club. "Why don't we get Waddell back?" he suggested to Fred Clarke. "He may be a yokel, but we both know the kid can pitch."

"There is no godamned way I will take Waddell back," Clarke stated emphatically.

He got his way and the Colonels did without Eddie - for now. But Clarke's friend Tom Loftus, who was part-owner of the Columbus Senators, had seen Eddie overpower hitters when he'd pitched against Columbus the year before. Loftus, a small, dapper man with a moustache that curled at the ends, was a lot more laid back than Clarke. He was more than willing to put up with some tomfoolery to have a pitcher with Waddell's talent and booster appeal.

In April, Loftus invited Eddie to pitch for the Senators. With no other offers on the table, Eddie went to play for Columbus. When he arrived, he went directly to where he'd been told to stay, Mrs. Dunning's Boarding House on E Street. The next morning he up was bright and early and spent three hours chasing squirrels on the lawn of the state capitol building. "I'm lookin' for a mascot for my new team," he explained to bewildered onlookers.

He made it to the station just in time. The Senators boarded a train to Detroit for a series against the team Eddie had deserted when he'd left to play in Canada. He pitched the first game and made the Tigers look like kittens. After eight innings they had two scratch hits and no runs. The first batter in the ninth rapped a single. Eddie hit the next two batters. Then he balked, not once but twice. Two runs scored.

The catcher went out to talk to him. "What do you think you're doing out here, Rube? Quit your dang foolin' or we'll be out here all day."

"It's Eddie. I don't like Rube."

"Fine. Eddie it is then. But buckle down. Now!"

Eddie did and easily struck out the next three hitters. Then he did handsprings off the mound and then slid into the bench. Serving as his own umpire he yelled, "Safe."

Loftus shook his head. "Crazier than a barrel a monkeys, but a hell of a twirler."

In Columbus the next week Eddie shut out Buffalo. He shut out the Tigers in his next start. Then he allowed just one meaningless ninth inning run in a lop-sided win over Indianapolis. Pitching against the league's best team, the Minneapolis Millers, he again gave up just one run, but the Senators didn't score any. It was his first loss.

Eddie was pitching on one or two days' rest, sometimes on none. He wasn't touring the saloons after every win like he had before. It paid off. He beat St. Paul twice after the loss to Minneapolis. Now he'd won six of his first seven games.

When the team played host to the Milwaukee Brewers Tom Loftus sought out Connie Mack. "We've got a new southpaw throwing for us today, Connie. The kid's an absolute screwball, but damn can he pitch."

Eddie proved Loftus right. The Milwaukee hitters couldn't get a thing brewing against him. Every couple of innings, after retiring the side, he would run into the stands. By now most of the Columbus boosters knew what Eddie wanted them to do. He wanted them to keep his luck going.

He went over to an old-timer sitting near the Senators' bench and opened up his shirt. "Do it," he said to the old man.

"Another piece, Rube?" he asked.

"Another piece," Eddie told him.

"Whatever you need to keep up yer luck," the old-timer said. He grabbed ahold of what was left of Eddie's red underwear and tore off a small piece.

"Much obliged," said Eddie as he reached into the man's bag of peanuts and removed a handful, which in Eddie's case was most of the bag.

After Eddie's fourth trip into the stands Loftus yelled over to Connie Mack, "What did I tell you," the kid's an absolute screwball.

"I've never seen anything like him, Tom," Connie yelled back.

"I tell ya, it's something crazier every day with him."

"You got your hands full there."

"I don't know whether to get him a nursemaid or a straitjacket."

"Good luck to you, you're going to need it."

"I swear, Connie, he's gonna drive me to an early grave."

"Maybe the two of you can room together in the loony bin."

CHAPTER **TEN**

AN ARM OF STEEL
AND THE PHYSIQUE OF A GLADIATOR

By the middle of July, Eddie's record stood at 20-4. All four losses, like the one to Minneapolis, were by one run. Unfortunately the rest of the Columbus staff combined didn't have close to that many wins so the team was struggling. Their only bright spot apart from Eddie was the arrival of Sam Crawford, a young outfielder from Wahoo, Nebraska. He'd been touring Midwestern towns by wagon with a semi-pro team. Sam was big at six feet tall and 190 pounds. He hit the ball hard and he could fly on the base paths. Triples and inside-the-park home runs were his specialty.

"Where's that crazy Rube?" Crawford asked manager/centerfielder George "White Wings" Tebeau while warming up for a game two weeks after his arrival.

"Didn't ya hear?"

"Hear what?"

"He's sick."

Crawford found it hard to imagine the huge force of nature getting sick, but Eddie hadn't stirred from the bed in his boarding house for three days.

"When am I ever gonna be able to get outta this bed, Florence?" Eddie asked his landlady's daughter. Florence Dunning had been taking care of Eddie ever since he'd taken sick.

"Not until your fever goes down, Edward," she told him. "Now drink your broth while it's still hot."

Florence had long brown hair but she always kept it pinned back. She had green eyes and a cute, turned up nose. She didn't wear much rouge or mascara but her full lips were always colored the same shade of red. She told Eddie it was called vermillion. He'd never heard of that. Florence dressed conservatively and she was careful not to lean too close when she fluffed Eddie's pillow.

"When can I get some real food?" he asked her.

"Feed a cold and you stave a fever," Florence told him for what seemed to Eddie like the hundredth time.

"I love the way you talk, Florence. Where are you from?"

"Georgia," she said.

"A southern belle. Are we gonna step out together when I get better?"

"Perhaps."

"You've been real good to me Florence, 'cept for not lettin' me eat."

"I am just doing what is best for you," she said.

"Well?"

"Well what?"

"You gonna step out with me when I'm better?"

"Maybe. Now get some rest."

Eddie sighed and lay back down. Florence hid a smile. She'd heard stories about Eddie being wild and even a bit crazy, but she'd never seen that side of him. She'd been dying for her handsome patient to ask her to step out, but her mother had taught her not to appear eager or available.

"Maybe I already have a beau. Did you ever think of that?"

"A course. But I haven't seen anybody callin' on ya."

"Maybe I meet a fella somewhere else," she said.

"You bin spendin' every day and night here takin' care of me. And if there ain't any beau then you might just as well be *my* girl."

"We'll see about that." She pointed to the broth and left him alone.

Eddie finally did get better and he and Florence began keeping company as soon as he did.

ℓℓ   ℓℓ   ℓℓ

He lost badly in his first game back, the fever having sapped some of his speed. But in his next start, against Mansfield, he struck out nine and won 15-3. Sam Crawford, who had acquired the nickname Wahoo Sam, hit two triples to center field. Eddie stroked two singles up the middle and then belted a home run over the right field fence.

When he wasn't scheduled to pitch, Eddie often didn't bother to go to the Senators' games. Sometimes he took Florence for a picnic at Olentangy Park. He loved the roller coaster, "the Figure Eight." Florence shut her eyes and held onto her beau for dear life. Other times they went punting on the Scioto River. Eddie liked taking Florence shopping at the huge Lazurus Department Store on High Street too, though many of its 150 male associates were handsome and he was worried Florence might take a fancy to one of them. The store's famous whistle informed shoppers and passers-by of major events. It had brought the first news of the declaration of the Spanish-American War to Columbus and a daily record of the conflict's progress had been posted in the store's windows. Florence liked the fact that the Lazurus brothers had a "one-price" policy. It meant you didn't need to haggle. Eddie enjoyed buying her pretty things, especially things to wear.

When it was his turn to pitch Eddie was often late for the game because he'd been playing with kids. Just minutes before the time for the first pitch a rumble would go through the crowd. "Here he comes, here comes Rube!" He would run down through the stands, jump onto the field, and run to the clubhouse while stripping off his shirt. Three minutes later he'd pop out in full uniform and yell, "All right, boys, let's go get 'em."

Even with Eddie and Sam Crawford, the Senators drew such sparse crowds that Tom Loftus was forced to move the team to Grand Rapids. Since they wouldn't be playing in the state capital anymore it didn't make any sense for them to be called Senators and, after much debate, they were renamed the Prodigals.

The Grand Rapids Prodigals played in front of a lot more people than they had in Columbus, especially when Eddie pitched. In his first start he drew 1,600 rooters. They'd heard a lot about the lovable and fun-loving phenom. Next he drew 2,000 and then a record 2,500 for his third start. He was now "the Great Rube" and when he was scheduled to pitch a Sunday game against the first-place Indianapolis Hoosiers 3,500 bugs were on hand to see him. Eddie didn't show up late this time. He didn't show up at all.

It was ten days before Eddie finally revealed his whereabouts. He'd gone back to Columbus to be with Florence. He sent Loftus a telegram saying he needed ten dollars or a train ticket to get back to Grand Rapids. The Prodigals had gone 1-5 while Eddie was away. Loftus wired him the money, but he was starting to lose patience with his gifted but unreliable twirler.

Even so, when Eddie got to Cedar Rapids Loftus still had Tebeau send Eddie out to pitch every other game. Unpredictable and flaky or not, he was far too big a draw to consider benching. Besides, if he had more than a day off who knew where he'd go.

Eddie gave up only a first-inning run in a win over the Hoosiers and then he beat Buffalo in the first game of a doubleheader. Still pumped up from his victory, he convinced Tebeau he could pitch the second game too. He got the start but was knocked around for seven runs in the first four innings.

"I let you down bad, George," he said after the game. "I never pitched that awful my whole life. Lemme pitch tomorrow's game. I'll show those Buffalos a thing or two."

"I guess you'll have to, Eddie," Tebeau told him. "Bumpus Jones was supposed to pitch and I just found out he's contracted malaria."

So Eddie pitched again, in spite of having thrown thirteen innings the day before. He shut out the Buffalos on four hits.

But in his next start, against Minneapolis, he gave up hit after hit and walked several of the batters who didn't hit. When his third baseman made errors on two straight ground balls in the fifth inning Eddie lost his temper. He walked off the field and left the park.

Eddie wasn't the same for the rest of the season. He gave up far more walks, hits, and runs and he didn't strike many batters out. He lost five of seven starts. People figured his arm must have finally given out from all the innings he'd pitched. The truth was that he showed up seriously hung over for almost every game. One of his two wins was against last place Kansas City and even *they* scored nine runs. He somehow failed to see any connection between his all night revelries and his poor performances. Being the toast of the town wherever he went was proving to be a curse instead of a blessing.

"What's up with you?" Sam Crawford asked him. "You don't seem to give a damn if we win or lose."

"That's not it, Sam. It's just that ... well I just shouldn't be here."

"What d'ya mean?"

"Haven't you heard? There are big league clubs after me."

"I heard. So what?"

"So I'm going back to pitch for Louisville. They want me real bad."

"Our season's not over. We got one more series left."

"I won twenty-nine games already, Sam. I think I've done enough."

Eddie left town that night and went to join the Colonels. Loftus wrote to a friend that Waddell was all used up, that his arm was dead. Eddie would have to prove him wrong in the major league.

Fred Clarke hadn't wanted Eddie back, but the Colonels were mired in ninth place. They needed a drawing card and the big fellow was certainly that. Clarke knew the kid could pitch, he wasn't sure he'd ever seen anyone with stuff like his, especially anybody so young and inexperienced. But would he be able keep Waddell on the straight and narrow?

Eddie arrived at the hotel, Garvey's at River Road and Seventh Street, just after midnight. He decided he wouldn't wake up Fred Clarke this time. Clarke didn't waste any time seeing what Eddie had left, even though he knew he'd pitched a lot of games for Columbus/Grand Rapids. His first start, once again, would be against Baltimore. When he got to Eclipse Park, Eddie put on one of the new uniforms Barney Dreyfuss had ordered for the Colonels. His was an extra large, the same size Honus Wagner wore. The uniforms were all white except for a large Gothic $\mathcal{L}$ over the left breast. Their new hats were tall and had flat tops.

"They look more like *bakers* than ball players," chuckled one bug.

Eddie pitched well against the Orioles. The score was 2-0 Baltimore after eight innings, but Louisville rallied for two runs in the top of the ninth. As he often did, Clark had opted to have the Colonels bat first so they could have first crack at the baseball before it got dirty and beaten up. Eddie would need to hold off the Orioles in their half of the inning to send the game into extra innings.

He knew that Wee Willie Keeler would bat second. Keeler already had more than two hundred hits and he was batting close to .400 after hitting .424 and .385 the last two years. Of course nobody knew exactly what they'd hit until the season ended. Each of the newspapers that covered baseball kept its own unofficial set of statistics. A week after the season ended the league published the official records.

Keeler had cut his strikeouts in half. Two years before he'd struck out four times in six hundred plus at bats. Last season, in just over six hundred trips to the plate, he'd struck out only twice. Eddie really wanted to keep Heinie Reitz, the leadoff hitter, from reaching base but he got a pitch up in the strike zone without the usual zip on it and Reitz tripled to right centerfield. Things were not looking good for the Colonels.

The Baltimore boosters made plenty of noise as Keeler strode confidently to the plate. He patiently ignored two pitches that were too low and then, with his hands choked well up the bat handle as always, he tried to punch the next pitch over the first baseman's head. It was faster than he expected and he got under it, harmlessly popping out to the second baseman. He swore to himself as he walked back to the bench.

RUBE WADDELL

John McGraw was next. He wore his usual menacing expression. Overanxious to drive in the run, he popped out to the shortstop Billy Clinqman. He had the presence of mind to fire the ball to third base to nab Keister, who'd taken too big a lead. Three out.

The Orioles sent 'Iron Man' Joe McGinnity, who got his nickname from working in iron mines in the off season, to the mound for the tenth inning and he promptly gave up two runs. Eddie held off the Orioles in the bottom of the inning and had a win in his first return appearance.

The next day he wrote a letter to Tom Loftus. It said, "I enclose these clippings from the Baltimore newspapers. They describe my work in the first game I pitched for Louisville and may serve as evidence that my arm is not dead after all. Regards, Edward Waddell."

Eddie beat Philadelphia his next time out. After his next start against Washington - another win - one reporter wrote that Waddell possessed an "arm of steel and the physique of a gladiator." When he beat the St. Louis Browns and struck out his former catcher Ossee Schreckongost twice he did handsprings and cartwheels on his way off the mound.

"Good to see you're back in the big league, Ossee," Eddie yelled when he'd finished his antics.

"I won't be for long if you keep strikin' me out," called Schreck.

"Oops. Sorry. I shoulda thought about that. You wanna go get a beer?"

"Maybe one," said Schreck.

⸺ ⸺ ⸺

Then Eddie faced the Chicago Orphans for the first time. Pitching for Chicago was Clark Griffith, who had twenty-one wins against twelve losses. Eddie easily struck out the side in the first. No one hit so much as a foul ball. Knowing that he had command of all his pitches that day, he purposely walked the first three batters in the second inning.

Fred Clarke started screaming at him from left field. Eddie looked out at him, tipped his hat and smiled. "Try to relax, Fred," he shouted, "no need to worry yourself to a frazzle."

The Orphan's third base coach laughed so hard he nearly fell over. "You'd better retire the side after telling him that," he told Eddie, "else he's liable to string you up."

Eddie calmly struck out the next three hitters. Clarke glared at him as they reached the bench. He was muttering something Eddie couldn't make out, but he was fairly sure it was not kind.

In the seventh inning Tommy Leach, who was playing third base for Louisville, and had the great fortune of being Eddie's roommate on the road, went to the mound.

"Rube, I just came over to tell you something."

"What's that?

"I'm pretty sure you're close to the National League record for strikeouts."

"Thanks fer tellin' me."

After another strikeout in the eighth Eddie sent his catcher, tall, skinny Tacks Latimer, to the press box to see how close he was now. After the last out of the game, a record-breaking thirteenth strikeout, Eddie put a finger to the top of his head and danced his way to the bench.

"What in the blazes was that?" growled Clark Griffith, who now had thirteen losses thanks to the brash rookie.

"I believe it's called a Highland fling," answered someone from the other end of the bench.

"Cocky bastard," growled Griffith.

℘   ℘   ℘

Harry Pulliman, the president of the Louisville club, could hardly believe his luck in grabbing Waddell before other National League teams discovered him. "The big farmer's a wonder," Pulliman said to Barney Dreyfuss.

"No doubt about that," said Dreyfuss.

"Have you ever seen him away from the ballpark?" Pulliman asked.

"No, but I hear he's pretty well known around town."

"Well known? That's an understatement, Barney. Rube has been in Washington, Philadelphia, Baltimore, Chicago, and St. Louis and in every place he made more friends and acquaintances in three days than I have in six years going there. Every time I turn around Rube's introducing me to people I've never met. They all act like he's their best friend!"

RUBE WADDELL
KING *of the* HALL *of* FLAKES

CHAPTER ELEVEN

NO USE HAVIN' A GUN
WITH NO BULLETS

After a Thursday afternoon game Eddie returned to Garvey's just after dinner. He was trying his best to stay in at night. There were about twenty people in the lobby. A couple of them waved and called out to him as he passed by. As he leapt up the first three steps of the staircase something heavy fell out of his pocket. It was a revolver, one of the new Smith and Wesson .38 Specials with a double-action design. Its single trigger pull was an improvement on the manual resetting of the hammer before each shot in the old single-action design. That meant it could be fired more easily.

The heavy gun bounced hard on the floor and discharged a bullet that was lodged in its chamber. The bullet ricocheted off the top of the banister and hit the huge chandelier in the middle of the lobby's ceiling. Shards of glass flew everywhere. Women screamed and men dove under chairs and sofas.

After an only partially successful effort to sooth everyone's nerves, the hotel manager said to Eddie, "We must ensure that such a thing does not happen again, Mister Waddell. Why were you carrying a revolver in your pocket and for God's sake why was it loaded?"

Eddie shrugged his shoulders and told him, "Not much point havin' a gun less you got bullets in it." The manager just stood and stared as Eddie nonchalantly headed up the stairs.

Barney Dreyfuss called Eddie into his office the next morning. "You are very lucky, Rube. The hotel manager called and told me that the hotel's insurance will cover the damage you caused yesterday, otherwise you would have had to pay to replace the chandelier. It would have been in the neighborhood of three hundred dollars."

"Jumpin' Jehosaphat! Three hundred dollars!"

"Listen, Rube, Tacks Latimer, who's been your roommate ever since

Tommy Leach refused to room with you any longer, came to see me after yesterday's game. He tells me that you have a shotgun as well as a revolver. Is that true?"

"I do, but I always keep it in my trunk. I only take it out when I go hunting."

"That is somewhat reassuring. And a knife? You have one of those as well I understand?"

"It's a dirk, Mister Dreyfuss."

"Well you're scaring Tacks half to death."

Dreyfuss recalled his recent conversation with Tacks. "I don't mind if he keeps that shotgun in his trunk," Tacks had told him, "but when he puts it together, loads it and then points it at me, that's just going too far."

"Now he doesn't want to room with you either," said Dreyfuss.

"Did Tacks tell ya why I pointed the shotgun at him?"

"No, he didn't, but what reason could you possibly have for doing such a thing?"

"Half the time when I wake up in the morning Tacks is standing right over me. He's holdin' a knife to my throat saying, 'You gotta promise you'll let me catch you whenever you pitch.'"

"Is that so? Well you put away the guns and I'll get Tacks to give me the knife," said Dreyfuss.

"I like guns."

"Well you are going to have to store them in a safe place until the end of the season."

"Fine, I guess I'll just have to stick to fishing 'til I get back home."

"And playing serious baseball."

"Ya, that too, a course."

                     ⚜   ⚜   ⚜

Eddie was 7-2 when the Colonels traveled to Pittsburgh. He was focused for a change, pulling none of his usual pranks, and he struck out one Pirate after another. He was walking, not cartwheeling, off the mound after the sixth inning when something flew out of the grandstand. He glimpsed it out of the corner of his eye. He thought it looked like a baseball, but it was too small. It hit him square in the head. It turned out to be an egg.

"You all right, Rube?" the umpire asked him.

"Sure." Eddie simply wiped off his cap and kept on walking to the bench like nothing had happened.

"You fellas today are lucky," said the umpire as Eddie passed him.

"What d'ya mean?" asked Eddie.

"They cleaned things up back in Ninety-Three, finally started protecting us umpires. My first few years I got hit by so many bottles I lost count."

"Is that why you keep your mask on between innings?"

"I guess so, old habits die hard."

"Gettin' hit with all those bottles affect your vision much?"

"Very funny, Rube. No, I see just fine."

"I was just wonderin'."

"Well don't."

        ℮   *℮*   *℮*

When he came out for the seventh Eddie told his teammates to stay on the bench. Eddie knew that at this level there was a rule against it, but he tried the stunt anyway.

"Eight players must be positioned between the foul lines," the umpire told him matter-of-factly. "Everyone except the catcher."

Eddie relented, but only a little. "Stand right behind the infielders," Eddie told the outfielders, one of whom of course was manager Clarke. The center and right fielders looked at Clarke for direction. Clarke shrugged and went to stand behind Honus Wagner.

Eddie struck out the side. Clarke just shook his head and headed to the bench.

"How can anybody throw that hard?" Tommy Leach asked him as Clarke ran past him.

"He's got some arm," said Clarke.

"And he throws so many different pitches," said Leach. "I'm sure glad I don't have to hit against him."

Eddie shut out Cincinnati in his next start and then headed off to Columbus. For a change, he had permission to leave. He was going to ask Florence Dunning to marry him.

        ℮   *℮*   *℮*

"My mother says we haven't had a proper courtship," Florence told Eddie. "She says it wouldn't be seemly."

"What's seemly?" Eddie asked.

"Proper. Respectable."

"Is she saying I don't respect you, cuz I do."

"I know, Eddie, you've been a real gentleman. But where are we going to live?"

"Wherever I'm playin' during the season and then back in Prospect - if that's okay with you."

"I suppose so, but will we be able to get by?"

"We sure will, I make a ton a money playin' ball. More every year. I'm in the big league now and all the papers say I'm getting to be one of the best pitchers that ever came down the pike. We'll be livin' high on the hog."

"Well . . . "

"What's it gonna be, Florence? We getting hitched or not?"

"Well . . . "

"Well what?"

"Well, yes we are."

Florence packed her things and headed with her fiancé to Chicago, where Eddie was scheduled to pitch. He lost 3-2. His mind was on something else. He had one more start, the last game of the season. It was in Pittsburgh, not far from home and a thousand boosters made the trip from Butler County to see the game. Florence watched her fiancé proudly from the grandstand. Eddie didn't disappoint. He gave up one run in the first on two singles and that was it. To add to his pitching performance he hit a single and a double as the Colonels won by three runs. Would he be back in Louisville or in some other major league city next year? Eddie didn't know and he really didn't care.

Eddie and Florence were married in Columbus on October 19. Friends came from Prospect, Chicago, Detroit, and Louisville. Guests described it as one of the prettiest weddings of the season. Eddie wore his best suit with a lavender boutonniere and Florence wore a stunning 3-piece French silk faille gown. They spent their honeymoon at the Neil House. Eddie would have preferred the New Chittenden or the Great Southern, but they cost $2.50 a night.

Florence wore a modest nightgown to bed. Eddie could tell she was nervous. She seemed almost on the verge of tears. His own nightshirt seemed to have a tent pole in the front. When he took it off Florence gasped.

"Are all men's . . . things that big," she asked.

"I believe this one's a tad bigger than most," Eddie told her.

He got a bottle out of his valise and poured some of its contents into his palm.

"What are you doing, Eddie?" asked Florence.

"I'm puttin' olive oil on it," Eddie told her as he spread the oil on his member. "This way it won't hurt so much."

It still hurt, and Eddie could only go in a little the first time. There was a lot of blood, but Eddie had taken the precaution of laying a towel under Florence's little bottom. They waited until the next morning to try again and Eddie got most of the way in this time. The third time he got all of the way in and Florence started to like it. A lot. Doing it was her idea the fourth time.

The newlyweds moved to Prospect, where Eddie helped out with the harvest and then got a job on a crew turning burnt trees into potash which would then be made into soap. He played some football too. He liked football almost as much as baseball. He was easily the fastest man in the league and he was by far the biggest. He soon led the league in touchdowns and tackles. The average player on the Prospect team weighed less than 140 pounds. Hauling logs around had built up Eddie's appetite beyond its already enormous proportions and he had bulked up to 235.

He was a lot stronger than the average player too. When the team from New Castle arrived for a game they towered over the Prospect players who waited anxiously for Eddie to arrive. When he did, he saw that the men from New Castle were trying to intimidate the Prospect players. He looked around and spotted two full kegs of nails ready to be used to build bleachers. He picked them up and casually carried them, one on each shoulder, over to the New Castle bench, where he gently set them down.

Then he took a huge apple out of his pocket and stood staring at the New Castle players. They looked at one another, wondering what Eddie was going to do with the apple. He looked straight at the New Castle captain and crushed the apple as if it were a grape. The New Castle team huddled and then announced that they had other things to do that afternoon.

Eddie would be paid $1,200 to pitch in 1900. But not back in Louisville. Eclipse Park had burned to the ground. The National League was on the verge of eliminating the Colonels due to poor attendance anyway, so Barney Dreyfuss had shrewdly arranged to sell the best Louisville players to the Pittsburgh Pirates and to go with them as the new team president. Fred Clarke, who would again be Dreyfuss' manager, Honus Wagner, Tommy Leach, and Eddie were among the Colonels who would now be Pittsburgh Pirates.

Eddie wouldn't be paid the way other players were. Barney Dreyfuss knew he was still too immature for that. Dreyfuss stashed away most of his salary and paid him five dollars at a time. When Eddie went to him for twenty dollars to buy new hats and clothes for Florence or to take her out to dinner and a show, Dreyfuss would give it to him out of the money he was holding back. Eddie was always delighted, thinking Dreyfuss was being very generous.

Dreyfuss arranged for a special train to take the Pirates to their training camp in Thomasville, Georgia. There were a lot of new faces and the train was hardly out of the station when Honus Wagner thought of a great way to break the ice. He organized a sandwich-eating contest.

Wagner, whose appetite was legendary, consumed one ham and cheese sandwich after another. He ended up eating eighteen of them. Eventually everyone succumbed. Everyone except Eddie. He matched Wagner sandwich for sandwich, grinning the whole time. When he'd eaten twenty-one the waiter asked how many more he would like him to make.

"That'll do, gotta leave room for some beers to wash 'em all down."

Wagner was in such agony that he thought of checking into a hospital when the train made its first stop. Eddie drank four glasses of beer and then had two big slabs of apple pie.

*   *   *

When the team reached Thomasville they didn't start working out or practicing right away. Fred Clarke sat the players down for a talk.

"Listen men, we have a chance to be a really good ball club this year. We've got a whole lot of talent here in this room."

The players looked at one another. They had a feeling something was coming.

"Men," Clarke continued, "you're professional ball players. Major league ball players. And because you are, you have certain obligations. For one, you have to get into condition and stay in condition. For another, you have to come to the park every day ready to play to the best of your ability."

"What are you getting at Fred?" asked innocent-looking Tommy Leach. "Are we supposed to stay away from loose women? Cuz my momma already warned me about *them*."

After the laughter died down Clarke said, "No I am not talking about loose women, Tommy. I am talking about laying off the booze."

"We can't have a drink all season?" groaned Tacks Latimer.

"I didn't say that. You can have a drink or two, you just can't go out and get liquored up the night before a game."

"That's a relief," said Bones Ely, the long-nosed shortstop.

Ginger Beaumont, the brawny center fielder, elbowed clean-living Deacon Phillippe in the ribs and chanted, "Praise the Lord."

"I'm not fooling. And I am not pointing fingers either. Whatever any of you may have done in the past . . . " he paused and looked right at Eddie, who looked down at his shoes, "it's all forgotten. From now on, you need to call it a night after a couple of beers and get back to the hotel so you'll be ready to play the next day. If you aren't fit and sober on game days, you can find yourself another ball club."

After a short silence Tommy Leach broke the tension that had filled the room. "Okay, skip, we understand. We'll be good boys, promise." He looked around at his teammates. "But if we gotta stay sober, can we at least bring some of those loose women back to the hotel with us?"

After waiting again for the laughter to subside Clarke pointed at the door, "Enough tomfoolery you bunch of Neanderthals, run your asses out there and get to work."

Eddie stayed out of bars - for the most part - and he picked up right where he'd left off at the end of the last season. He was supposed to pitch the middle three innings against a team from Memphis but he was throwing so well that Clarke left him in and he pitched the rest of the game. After he struck out the last batter he did three cartwheels and then walked off the field on his hands. In his next game against the Eastern League champions from Rochester none of them hit a ball out of the infield.

Eddie's first regular season start was in Cincinnati. Big Honus Wagner, now over his stomach problems, smashed three doubles and Eddie pitched a three-hit shutout. *The Cincinnati Enquirer* said that Rube Waddell made the Reds look like apes.

"At no time did Waddell give the local aggregation an opportunity to get within hailing distance of a run."

The Pirates returned home to face the Reds in their home opener at Exposition Park, which was located in Allegheny City on a small, flat piece of land just across the Allegheny River. Its twin spires of four-sided, pointed roofs were easily visible from downtown Pittsburgh, just as the city's smokestacks could be seen easily from the park. The Pirates would be wearing new uniforms that consisted of caps with a tiny *P* on the front, plain pants, a simple, buttoned jersey with a dull blue collar, and dark blue stockings with bright red stripes.

Before the game the team staged a parade. The owner of a furniture store walked alongside Eddie and kindly held an umbrella over his head to keep the sun out of his eyes.

"If you and your lovely bride decide to buy a house come and see me, Rube. I'll be sure to take care of you."

"Mighty nice a ya," Eddie told him without noticing that the umbrella Fred Fields was shading him with just happened to have *Fields Fine Furniture* printed across the top.

Sitting comfortably on new blue seat cushions the team had handed out were 11,000 boosters. It was the biggest crowd ever to watch a game in Pittsburgh. The Pirates had installed a new penny slot machine. Eddie pumped 300 pennies into it. For his three dollar investment Eddie won fifteen penny cigars.

"Just like baseball," he told Jiggs Donahue, "nothin' to it. It's a lead pipe cinch."

He might as well have been hit with a pipe. He gave up eight runs and was taken out long before the game ended.

He was scheduled to pitch on May 2 against Cy Young. Eddie didn't make it to the park. He had a good reason this time though. He was home playing with his new Irish setter, which he'd named Mickey Finn. The two were inseparable. Mickey Finn went to bars and stores and sandlot ball games with Eddie. His tail never stopped wagging.

Eddie lost his next game, to St. Louis. Tacks Latimer let two of his sinking shoots scoot through his legs and he dropped six called third strikes. It didn't matter though, Eddie gave up eleven hits. After one of them Fred Clarke ran in from left field and let into Eddie.

"What the hell do you think you're doing, Waddell? You're throwing inside to hitters who love inside pitches and slow balls to men who couldn't hit one of your fastballs in a million years! If you'd been at the meeting I called before this series you'd know what their hitters look for!"

"I ain't complaining, Fred, but how come you never said a peep to Tacks when he botched all those plays?"

"Because Tacks can't do any better than he is, you *can*."

"I'm real sorry about all those errors and dropped balls," Tacks told Eddie after the game.

"Don't you fret about it, Tacks, catchers have bin missin' my pitches since I was ten years old." Eddie threw his suit into a garbage can.

"What are you doing?" asked Tacks.

"I'm throwing out this suit."

"Why are you doing that?"

"It's dirty."

"I can use it."

"You sure?" Eddie asked.

"Ya, I always liked that suit."

Tacks got the suit dry-cleaned and it looked as good as new. Three weeks later Eddie was getting off the hotel elevator and Tacks was waiting to get on. Eddie was wearing a suit he'd purchased a few days before. Because he'd played ball with some kids in it a couple of times and then thrown it in a ball on the floor of his room it looked wrinkled, dirty, and old. Tacks was wearing the suit Eddie had given him. It looked terrific.

"That's a real nice suit," he told Tacks.

"You like it?"

"I sure do."

"Ya, it's pretty nice."

"I tell you what. You gimme that suit you're wearing and you can have this one I just bought."

"Really, you don't mind?"

Eddie gave Tacks his brand new suit in exchange for his old one.

Fred Clarke decided to sit Eddie for a while as punishment for missing the meeting. He put Jack Chesbro, who'd broken into the big league the year before, into his spot in the rotation. But when Chesbro got roughed up by the Brooklyn Superbas in the fourth inning Clarke called Eddie in to take over for him. Eddie was perfect for three innings. He was glad he had all his pitches working again. But, just when he started to relax, Wee Willie Keeler, the former Oriole, ripped one of Eddie's fadeaways deep into center field. Keeler tore around the bases for a stand-up triple and then stood looking over at Eddie with a big smile on his face.

Eddie was furious with Keeler and with himself too. "You ain't gonna see a lazy pitch like that again, Keeler," he growled at him, "nothing but smoke for you from now on."

He wheeled and threw to first base. But, with no runner on base apart from Keeler there was of course no one covering first. The ball rolled along the foul line toward the right field fence and Keeler walked home, laughing all the way.

Clarke ran to the mound. He was so mad it seemed like he was about to turn into one of Pittsburgh's smokestacks. All he said was, "Give me the fucking ball, Waddell."

Eddie lost his next start to the Boston Beaneaters, though most of the runs they scored were unearned. The Pirates weren't hitting much. Barney Dreyfuss had to give Tacks Latimer his release when his average fell below .100. Eddie left the team too, but without permission. He didn't explain where he'd gone, but it wasn't home to see Florence.

He finally came back after ten days and handed out enough fish to feed a small army.

"Don't you ever pull a stunt like that again, Waddell," Clarke yelled. "Now get in there and pitch. Eddie did. The Pirates committed five errors and Eddie lost again.

   ℀ ℀ ℀

Tommy Falcone from *The Pittsburgh Dispatch* asked Barney Dreyfuss about his oddball leftie.

"The trouble with Rube is that he is like a little boy. He wants to cut up monkey shines all the time. It's easier to take care of him on the road where he doesn't have a group of admirers following him around giving him whatever he desires."

"What kind of monkey shines are you talking about, Barney?"

"Well I heard the other night he was giving strongman exhibitions. He had a board strapped on his chest and then got two men to stand on him while he was bent over. Then he raised a chair with a heavy man on it over his head with one arm."

"Not his left arm?" asked Falcone.

"Yes. His left arm."

"Have you tried to get him to stop pulling such crazy stunts?"

"Of course we have. Fred Clarke told him to quit the side shows or else."

"And, did it work?" Falcone asked.

"You might just as well try to get the sun to stop shining as try to break Rube of his lame-brained antics."

Eddie didn't show up for his next start. A while later Clarke learned where he'd been that afternoon. On his way to the park Eddie had passed a bunch of kids playing stickball and decided to join them.

ℰ   ℰ   ℰ

A few days later Eddie was walking to Exposition Park when he saw a tavern he'd never noticed before. It was called The Fresh Flask. He decided it wouldn't hurt to go in for just one drink.

The owner served him a cold beer and said, "Boy, oh boy, would I ever like to go see that Waddell fellow pitch this afternoon. He's the Pirates' best twirler. Everybody who comes in talks about how great he is and what a show he puts on."

"Why don't ya go see him then?" asked Eddie.

"Simple. I got no one to help me here. The afternoon man quit and I'm stuck tending bar 'til the night man comes in at six. The games are over by then."

"Well I'll take care of the bar for you. I've done it before."

"You would, I mean you seem like an honest fella. I can trust you, can't I?"

"Course you can. I'll let ya keep my watch for security if you want."

"Well ... I sure would like to see Waddell pitch. There's no need to give me your watch. Beers are a nickel and shots are a dime." He handed Eddie his apron and put on his hat. "I'll see you in three hours."

ℰ   ℰ   ℰ

"Waddell didn't pitch after all," the bar owner told Eddie when he returned. "Apparently he wasn't even at the stadium today."

"Well I guess I couldn'ta bin', seein' as I was here filling in for you."

"What? You're Rube Waddell!"

"None other. Business was real good. Money's in the jar there, the tips too. See ya later."

"Well I never. What a character," the bartender muttered to himself before going behind the bar and pouring himself a big shot of rye.

RUBE WADDELL
KING *of the* HALL *of* FLAKES

CHAPTER TWELVE

A PIRATE WALKS THE PLANK

Eddie was 2-3 at the end of May. Word of his eccentricity was already getting around the league and he was being razzed mercilessly during road games.

"Why don't you go back to sloppin' hogs?" he heard time and again.

"Hey Rube, must be strange pitchin' baseballs instead of hay," a fan in Cincinnati yelled.

Harry Steinfeld, the Reds' third baseman, chimed in with a stream of vile insults. The catcher, Heinie Rietz, called Eddie names that had the ladies in the first ten rows hiding their blushing faces behind their fans. Some got up and left.

In New York, umpire Tim Hurst allowed the whole Giants' team to go out onto the field to hurl barbs at Eddie. He kept his focus in spite of all the raving from the cranks, as the newspapers had taken to calling baseball rooters. He beat the Giants in a 7-6 squeaker, then filled in effectively for 'Happy Jack' Chesbro, who was usually not the least bit happy.

Eddie beat the Phillies on June 5 and faced them again on a day's rest. Billy Shettsline, the Phillies' florid, rotund manager, was all over Eddie. "No more milk in the cow? A bit off yer feed today, Hayseed?"

"Do ya need a drink, Rube? Yer lookin' mighty thirsty," big Ed Delahanty, the Phillies' hard-hitting left fielder, yelled when he threw Eddie out at home after Eddie had been hit by a pitch and gone to third on Ginger Beaumont's double in the fifth. "The Only Del" settled for two crisp singles off Eddie, an off day for the Irish star who had batted over .400 for the third time in '99.

The *Philadelphia Inquirer* lauded the young southpaw's work.

> *"This afternoon 'Rube' Waddell was in the points for the Smoky City Crew. He fooled the Quakers with his perplexing curves, making five of them fan the air, while providing free transport to first for six, and scattering seven hits.*

The next day Eddie very nearly missed another train, this one to Boston. He'd taken a cab and the driver had driven the buggy into a ditch six miles from the train station. Normally Eddie would have stayed to pull the buggy out but he decided he'd better hightail it to the station instead. He ran the six miles and then onto the train, puffing like a racehorse.

"Swell fella that cabby," he told Honus Wagner, "only charged me half price for the ride."

Eddie didn't fare well in his first appearance in Boston but *The Boston Globe* was full of praise anyway. It said he was "the most talked about pitcher of the day, a pleasing-faced chap, tall, lithe, and muscular, with a wealth of speed and curves."

His record stood at 4-5, though he had as many strikeouts as the rest of the staff combined. In addition to shoddy defense, with the exception of Honus Wagner the Pirates just weren't hitting. They lost seven in a row. Eddie lost a heartbreaker in Chicago. He pitched thirteen scoreless innings and struck out twelve batters, but Clark Griffith hadn't allowed any runs either. The Pirates lost when Eddie walked Cupid Childs with two out in the fourteenth. He came all the way around to score when Griffith hit a towering pop up and Tommy O'Brien and Jimmy Williams let it fall between them.

O'Brien tried to console Eddie. "Twas a rotten way to lose a ball game, we done ya wrong lettin' dat ball drop like dat."

"Forget about it, Tommy," Eddie told him as they slumped into the clubhouse. "Shit like that happens. Nobody's fault. Each a ya thought the other fella was takin' it is all."

Though there were still games left on the road trip he headed back to Pittsburgh on his own.

When the team reached Pittsburgh Fred Clarke went looking for him. On his way he went to see Florence.

"I have no idea where he is," she told him as she fought back tears. "I think he loves me, but he's hardly ever home at night. He usually comes home for dinner or for lunch on an off day, but then he'll say he promised someone he would meet them or do something for them and he's gone. If anyone asks him for a favor he just drops everything and goes. When a player's moving into a new house he calls Eddie since he can carry as much as three men. If they need a new roof, they call Eddie. If they want to build a hunting cabin they call Eddie. If they want help training a new dog, they call Eddie. The last time it was Duff Cooley. He was opening a pool hall and needed Eddie to help set up the tables. Sometimes he comes home the next morning sometimes he doesn't."

Clarke really didn't want to hear about their marital problems. "Missus Waddell, I hate to ask, but is there any chance that he could he be off on a bender?"

"He goes off on them quite a lot, Mister Clarke, sometimes for two days, sometimes longer. He'll ask me if I want to go out to a show and if I say I'd rather we stayed home he gets mad and leaves."

Clarke went to all of Eddie's usual haunts. There was no sign of him, but a man at The Foaming Flask told him that, though Eddie had indeed been there a couple of times he'd heard that he was now performing at a theater.

Two nights later Clarke found him. He was with Hindman and Kummers' Union Scout Theater Company. Eddie had not only been acting on stage, he'd tried on costumes, played with props, built scenery, conducted the band in the orchestra pit, mixed with the audience, and sold songbooks.

The production had apparently not been a resounding success. A theater critic reported that "Waddell is let out for only two minutes in each scene and the repair bills are pretty hefty even for that short time."

One night he fired a pistol backstage - no one knew if it was on purpose - right in the middle of a dramatic scene. It was a rather disconcerting experience for the visiting troupe from England. They'd never seen a pistol, much less heard one fired. Of course they'd never met anyone like Eddie before either.

By the time Clarke got to the theater Eddie was no longer there. "He hasn't been here in three nights," the stage manager told Clarke, sounding much relieved.

Clarke told Barney Dreyfuss where Eddie had been.

"I just talked to Jimmy Williams and Duff Cooley," said Dreyfuss. "They checked the ball park to see if Waddell had been there. He hadn't, but they told me that Pawnee Bill's Wild West Show just opened up next door to the park. What are the chances Waddell is there?"

"Pretty damn good," answered Clarke.

Clarke and Dreyfuss went to the show. They entered a large tent and were nearly knocked over by a group of Mexican cowboys who'd just finished their performance in the center ring. They passed a group of jugglers and some Indians in head feathers and then noticed a man they assumed was Pawnee Bill. He was talking to a small woman in a bright red cowboy outfit.

"Who's this man that wants to be in the show?" the woman asked.

"He's a ball player. His name is Rube Waddell," said Pawnee Bill.

"Why would we want a ball player in the show?"

"It'll be great for business, Hazel. The park's right next store and we're bound to get baseball boosters coming in, even if it's just out of curiosity. They'll get a big kick out of seeing one of the players in the show."

"Is there anything special about this fellow?"

"Apparently. From what I hear he's the biggest draw the team has. He's supposed to be a great twirler and what's better, he's a real showman."

"What do you mean, he's a showman?"

"They say he puts on a show during the games. He does unusual things, he juggles and he does handstands and cartwheels, and he goes into the crowd and clowns around with the rooters."

"Is he allowed to do that sort of thing during a baseball game?"

"I wouldn't think so, but they say he's does it all the time."

"What would he do in our show?"

"He's going to ride around the ring on a horse and lasso some things and maybe sing a little."

"He's not riding my palomino."

"No, he is not. We got him a mustang to ride. Wait. There he is now."

Eddie appeared out of the wings in a white western outfit with red trim and a ten-gallon hat. He was riding a huge black mustang and waving a rifle over his head.

"Hey, that's Waddell," a man standing near Clarke and Dreyfuss yelled.

"No mistaking him," said the man he was with.

"What the heck is Waddell doing in a Wild West Show?"

"Who knows, that man'll do anything."

Eddie reined in his horse. He took off his ten-gallon hat and put it over his heart. Then he broke into "I Ride an Old Paint." His singing was loud and clear, but way off key.

"Hey Rube," someone called out, "that's a nice song, but that's not a paint you're riding."

Eddie ignored him and kept right on singing.

After a while Hazel rode out on a beautiful palomino. She rode toward Eddie and gave him a sour look. "Time's up, Rube, or whatever your name is. I'll take it from here."

Eddie made one more quick circuit of the ring and then rode off to a generous round of applause. Not everyone was impressed though.

Someone yelled, "Better stick to throwing baseballs, Rube," which brought a big laugh.

"Hey, there's an idea, Barney," said Fred Clarke. "How about the big jerk sticks to playing baseball."

"He never has up until now, Fred."

"Well he had better soon, or else," Clarke fumed.

ℓℓ   ℓℓ   ℓℓ

Eddie found his way to the park the next day but Clarke was not pleased with the manner in which he arrived. Eddie had apparently played another role in the Pawnee Bill Wild West Show for he arrived wearing war paint and feathers.

Of course the bugs insisted that he show off his outfit, so Clarke reluctantly sent him out to coach first base. Eddie was performing a series of high-pitched war whoops when a band of braves from the show entered through the outfield gate. Eddie led them around the infield as they whooped and brandished their tomahawks. Somehow the Pirates won the game, but Clarke was ready to go on the warpath himself. Eddie was swiftly reaching the end of the considerable length of rope Clarke had given him.

ℓℓ   ℓℓ   ℓℓ

"What d'ya mean an all-girls band?" Eddie demanded two days later when he got to the ball park. He'd run into a group of kids on the way to the park the day before and had joined the game they were playing. He hadn't made it to the Pirates' game.

"Ya, an all-girls band," Tommy Leach told him. "They played out in center field before the game. Dreyfuss got 'em as an attraction to keep folks from going over to the Wild West Show. Hey, I heard you were in it."

"Ya, the folks loved me. Say Tommy, were there any pretty gals in the band?"

"There were a lot of sweet young things. You shoulda seen the trombone player!"

"That's just swell. They have to be here on a day I'm not."

"There's a *lot* of days you're not here. What the hell do you do instead of coming to the park?"

"Lotsa things. Sometimes kids ask me to play with them and I just can't say no. I hate to disappoint 'em."

"Well you better get your mind on baseball 'cuz I think Clarke is about ready to kill you."

ℓℓ   ℓℓ   ℓℓ

RUBE WADDELL

Eddie did not get his mind on baseball and he lost his next two starts. He wasn't in the clubhouse when he was next due to pitch, but he was in the park. Teammates found him under the grandstand playing marbles with some kids.

Eddie was spending more and more nights in saloons. One night he and a group of fellow revelers decided to go out and play a ballgame under the new gas streetlights the city had installed. Eddie offered to catch and he hurt his finger. Too honest for his own good, Eddie told Fred Clarke how he'd hurt it and Clarke yelled at him for a full five minutes.

The next day Eddie ran into a group of boys. He played leapfrog, marbles, and mumblety-peg with them and then they begged him to teach them how to throw a curveball. No one had a baseball but, rather than disappoint the lads, Eddie picked up a brick and threw it several times. The next day his arm was sorer than it had ever been. Once again Eddie was truthful about how he'd hurt it. Now Clarke was completely fed up. He gave his exasperating phenom one more chance, against the first place Giants. Eddie was taken out after giving up five runs in four innings. He hadn't won a game in a month.

      ℮   ℮   ℮

"Did you see what the papers are saying about Waddell?" Clarke asked Barney Dreyfuss as they were having breakfast together. "The Gazette reporter says, 'Waddell has been petted and pampered to such an extent that he has come to the conclusion that he can do as he pleases.'"

"What are you planning to do about him, Fred?"

"I'm suspending the fool for inappropriate behavior, that's what I'm doing. And I am telling the reporters that Waddell's services are no longer required."

      ℮   ℮   ℮

Eddie read about his suspension in the newspaper. He found Fred Clarke in the locker room and asked him if it was true.

"You're damned right it is, Waddell, I've had it with you and your nonsense. Now get your stuff out of here and don't come back."

"I didn't know you felt this way, Fred. You know what? The next time I see you I am gonna shoot you full of holes."

      ℮   ℮   ℮

Where would Eddie play now? He'd pushed his luck once too often and this might just be the end of the line for him - in the big league at least. That was all right with him though, he was happy to play on sandlots.

Eddie didn't go far after he left Pittsburgh. Without letting Florence know he was leaving town, he traveled just down the road to Millvale, where he joined the local nine. He traveled with them to play in Punxsutawney and pitched the first game. He won it, 1-0, striking out eleven Punxsutawney Groundhogs. In their next game there he played the outfield and made two running catches. Millvale lost 3-1, their only run coming on a homer Eddie hit. He decided he liked the friendly little town.

The team headed home to Millvale the next day but Eddie bid them farewell and stayed to play for Punxsutawney. He still never thought to inform his new wife of his whereabouts. He pitched for the Groundhogs in their next game, against Dubois. He hit another home run and shattered several of the Dubois hitters' bats with his speed balls.

"Get rid of Waddell or we will not be playing any more games here," the Dubois manager told the Punxsutawney skipper.

Eddie kept playing, but he had to stop pitching.

Cornelius McGillicuddy had been to watch a game in Pittsburgh. Having suffered a raft of injuries, his Milwaukee Brewers were in trouble. The Pittsburgh papers made a lot out of the visit, accusing Connie Mack of being there to steal Honus Wagner away from the Pirates.

After a few minutes of small talk in the hotel lobby Connie told Dreyfuss, "I'm not here after Wagner, Barney. I want the rights to Waddell."

"Why didn't you say so, Connie? We can work something out if it's Waddell you're after. As a matter of fact you can have him cheap. He nearly drove Fred Clarke to an early grave."

"Then I can have Waddell?"

"Go ahead," said Dreyfuss. "We couldn't do a damn thing with the nut. If you think you can handle him, you're welcome to him."

Eddie was sitting in his room in Punxsutawney's only hotel, the Pantall, playing solitaire one night when he heard a knock on his door. When he opened it a bellhop told him that there was a telephone call for him. Eddie bounded down the stairs and took the ear piece from the night manager and spoke into the shiny new instrument that was mounted on the wall behind the front desk.

"Hello, Rube," Mack said, momentarily forgetting that Eddie still hated that name.

"Who the hell is this?"

"Is that you, Eddie?"

"Ya, is that you, Connie?"

"It is."

"What are *you* callin' about?"

"The folks here in Milwaukee would love to see you in a Brewers' uniform, Eddie. You'd like it here."

"Sorry Connie, no dice. The people here in Punxsutawney have done everything for me. I just couldn't let them down."

"But I'd pay you good money, Eddie. You can pitch us to the pennant and I know you'd love Milwaukee. We have a lot of breweries here."

"There's not enough money in Milwaukee to make me run out on these folks."

                                  ℮℮   ℮℮   ℮℮

Mack sent Eddie a telegram every day for the next two weeks. Each one was more flattering and promised more money. Eddie was finally getting tired of the lack of excitement in Punxsutawney and he was starting to miss Florence, even if she didn't like going places with him. He sent a three-word wire to Connie Mack. It read, "Come get me."

CHAPTER THIRTEEN

ESCAPE FROM PUNXSUTAWNEY

When Connie Mack arrived in Punxsutawney at 10 o'clock on the morning of July 25 he headed straight to the Pantall. A bellhop took him up to Eddie's room. When his door opened Mack said, "I haven't had breakfast, Eddie, care to join me?"

"Be glad to, Connie, I'm famished."

They went down to the hotel's dining room where Eddie polished off four eggs, a heap of home fried potatoes, two pitchers of coffee, and three stacks of buckwheat cakes smothered in butter.

"Aren't you still full from the breakfast you had at eight o'clock, Mister Waddell?" the incredulous waiter finally asked Eddie.

"That was what we ball players call a *warmup*, Jimmy."

Connie Mack said, "You didn't tell me you'd already eaten."

"I plum forgot to mention it. Say, Connie, we got a few hours before the 3 o'clock train. Mind if we take a walk? I got a few odds and ends to take care of."

Mack wasn't thrilled at the idea. He was nervous that the townsfolk would try to stop Eddie from leaving their team, but he agreed anyway.

"Your bill comes to twelve dollars and thirty-five cents," said the owner of the dry goods store when they made their first stop.

Connie had a pretty good idea that Eddie didn't have any money. He pulled out his wallet and said, "I'll take care of that."

Their next stop was at the Addams Express Company where Eddie owed eight dollars for a puppy he'd had sent to him COD. Connie paid the bill. There were ten more stops. At each of them Eddie owed money and Connie paid. He decided he wasn't going to lose Waddell for the sake of a few dollars. They went to the cleaners, the barber shop, the sporting goods store, the hardware store, a men's clothing store, a pawn shop - where Eddie retrieved a money clip, a silver tie pin, and a harmonica - and then visited four saloons at which Eddie had run up tabs.

Then Connie hurried Eddie back to the hotel, they still had two hours before the train and Connie was anxious about running into a delegation of townsfolk anxious to keep Eddie in town. Connie had just enough money left to pay Eddie's hotel bill. At 2:45, with just enough time to get to the station, they left. The entire hotel staff came out to the front lawn to see Eddie off.

"Thanks for moving the piano yesterday, Eddie," said the manager. "I was going to have to hire a crew to do it."

"Thanks for putting out that grease fire in my kitchen," said the chef.

"And thank ya for gettin' my son's kitty down out of that tree," said a plump, dark-skinned chambermaid.

When he and Eddie reached the station, Mack's worst fears were realized. A large delegation of men was waiting for them. Connie had wasted all that money and they weren't going to let Waddell leave Punxsutawney.

A man in a pin-striped suit and black derby stepped forward out of the group. "Are you Connie Mack?" he said as he shook Connie's hand.

"I am," said Mack nervously.

"Well on behalf of the people of Punxsutawney I want to tell you that I know you're taking Eddie away from us, but we understand that he's too fine a ball player to stay here and we want you to take good care of him. We've grown awfully fond of the big fellow and he's going to be sorely missed."

"I'll take good care of him, don't you worry about that," promised Mack.

The men all gathered around Eddie, pounded him on the back and wished him well in Milwaukee.

          ℓ   ℓ   ℓ

Connie Mack was smart enough to know that, as likable as he was, Waddell took some getting used to. Before Eddie arrived at the Lloyd Street Grounds where the Brewers played he called the other players together for a talk. The ones who came from Ohio and Pennsylvania had already heard stories about their talented but oddball new pitcher.

"All right then. The first thing I need to tell you is that even though the rooters and the reporters call him Rube, he doesn't like being called that. He is much happier if you call him Eddie. The second thing is that Waddell is . . . cut from a different cloth. I'm going to let you know right from the start that he is going to get some privileges that you fellows don't get."

"Why should he get extra privileges?" asked "Sunset" Jimmy Burke, the Brewers' third baseman.

"It's the only way to keep him around, Sunset. Otherwise he'll take off on us."

"What kind of privileges are we talkin' about?" asked Wid Conroy, the shortstop.

"Like giving him a few days off after he's pitched a bunch of innings. So he can go fishing. Eddie loves to fish."

"Should he not be watching the games to see the hitters that he will be going up against?" asked Emerson "Pink" Hawley, who was expected to do exactly that when he wasn't on the mound. Hawley had a high opinion of himself. He loved telling people that he'd once turned down a gambler's offer of $20,000 to fix a game and that his great-grandfather had masterminded the Boston Tea Party. Pink had won thirty-one games for the Pirates in '95 but he'd been 14-17 in '99.

"I can understand why you'd say that, Pink. But when you watch him pitch you'll see that he doesn't really need to know the hitters' weaknesses or proclivities to make them look like they've never had a bat in their hands. Besides, as you will certainly discover, if Rube, I mean Eddie, is not pitching he is probably not sitting on the bench watching the game anyway. He's likely to be doing almost anything else."

"Like what?" asked Conroy.

"You'll see."

"So what exactly do ya want us to do, Connie?" asked Burke.

"Just follow my lead ... and give him whatever he wants. He asks for a bat or a glove or a cigarette, just give it to him."

Eddie sauntered into the locker room wearing a new suit and a bright green tie. He had a grip with all his worldly possessions in one hand and a huge box of fishing gear in the other.

"Hello boys, how you doin? I'm here to win you a pennant."

Burke and Conroy looked at one another and rolled their eyes. Pink Hawley looked disgusted and went to get his uniform off the peg. "What a buffoon," he muttered under his breath. "He'd better be as good as Mack says he is."

In his first inning of work Eddie gave up a double and threw two wild pitches. The catcher could have gotten his mitt on both of them but he was having a lot of trouble getting used to Eddie's shoots, curves, puzzlers, wobblers, and fadeaways. He'd never seen such movement on a baseball - or such speed.

Wid Conroy mishandled two grounders and two runs scored. Eddie gave up only one more run the rest of the game but the Brewers lost 3-2. A reporter from *The Milwaukee Sentinel* asked Eddie if the errors and missed pitches bothered him and if he was upset to lose his first game.

"Heck, errors are part of the game. I'd already have a heap a gray hairs if I let 'em rile me. I played on a couple of teams where the fielders couldn't catch a cold. As for losing today, don't you worry. They're won't be much of that goin' on now that I'm here."

℮ ℮ ℮

Eddie threw a five-hitter at his former mates from Detroit a few days later. Then he beat Indianapolis and hit a home run, the first one hit over the fence that season. After each win he hopped on a streetcar and headed to Whitefish Bay on the edge of town to fish. The fishing was so good that when the team left to play in Kansas City he didn't want to go with them. He barely made it to the train station in time and got a 12-inning win over the Blues that included several of his sideshow antics between pitches, including juggling, imitating the umpire, and serenading female boosters. Off-key as usual.

He pitched the first game of a double header against Chicago. It lasted seventeen innings and took almost three hours to play. While Eddie kept the White Stockings from doing any damage, the Brewers kept putting runners on base only to see them erased by double plays or bone-headed base running. Eddie went the distance, throwing close to two hundred and fifty pitches, and won. After the last out he danced merrily off the field.

"Connie was right about Waddell being a flake. The man should be in a nuthouse," Jimmy Burke said to Wid Conroy as they trotted off the field glad the game was finally over and not looking at all forward to playing again in fifteen minutes.

Connie Mack met Eddie when he reached the bench. "Nice game Eddie, but the Chicagos want another crack at you. They're pretty sore about the way you danced off the field. They say they'll get you this time."

"You want me to pitch this game too, Connie?" Eddie asked.

"If you do you can have three days off to fish."

"Three days! Gimme the ball."

Eddie shut out Chicago in the second game. Luckily, he only needed to throw eighty pitches this time. It was his tenth win in twelve starts.

Seven of them had been shutouts. In some of the games the outfielders never had to make a play.

      ℓ℮   ℓ℮   ℓ℮

Unfortunately for Eddie, the Pirates heard all about how incredibly he was pitching for Milwaukee and they wanted him back. That was bad enough, considering how upset Eddie was with Fred Clarke. Worse, no one there would be calling him Eddie anymore, he'd be saddled with Rube from now on.

Fred Clarke was far from thrilled at the prospect of Rube returning to the Pirates, but he knew that Barney Dreyfuss was right. They were in a dogfight for first place and Waddell would be a huge help. Connie Mack would love to have kept Rube, who was performing at his best under the freedom Mack was allowing him. But he belonged to the Pirates and, unlike a lot of other baseball executives, Mack was a man of his word. He forwarded Dreyfuss' telegram requiring that Rube report to Pittsburgh.

Eddie wired back. "I will quit before I play for Clarke again."

Mack sent Dreyfuss a letter with advice on how to change Eddie's mind. It said, "Waddell has a soft spot for catchers. Send Chief Zimmer to persuade him to play for you."

Zimmer was dispatched to see Eddie. A day later he wired Dreyfuss that when he'd talked to him Rube had repeated his promise to fill Clarke full of holes the next time he saw him.

"Instruct Zimmer to buy him things," Connie Mack advised in another letter, "a new suit of clothes, some shirts and collars, a few ties, maybe some new fishing gear."

So Zimmer took Rube shopping. He bought him everything he laid his eyes on including two pairs of shoes, a shirt, an 'electric' blue suit, five striped ties, and a trunk to carry it all in. When Rube arrived in Pittsburgh, Fred Clarke assigned him the room next to his so he could keep an eye on him. The next afternoon, after the Pirates' game had been rained out, Clarke knocked on Rube's door. He was a bit surprised he was in.

"Rube, would you happen to have a spare uniform button?"

"I don't know if I do Fred, but come on in and I'll take a look." He opened up his trunk and rummaged around for a while.

"Doesn't appear as though I have any in here, Fred. Just a second though." He went into the other room.

Clarke went over and peered into Rube's trunk. He was more than a little nervous when he saw that there was a revolver inside. Rube came back into the room with a large bowie knife in his hand.

"Now just a minute, Rube, there's no need for . . . "

"No need for what, Fred?" Rube asked as he held out his other hand. It held a button from his own uniform. He'd cut it off. Now he had the same problem Clarke had just had.

On Labor Day Rube easily won his first start, even though his teammates committed four errors, and was scheduled to pitch next against Boston. He didn't show up for the game. He wasn't at the ballpark the next day either. Fred Clarke was incensed when Rube finally did show up, but Chief Zimmer managed to calm him down and Clarke sent Rube in to face Iron Joe McGinnity without saying a word to him. He battled McGinnity, who had won twenty-eight games the year before and was one his way to winning another twenty-eight, to a nine-inning tie.

He was ahead of the hard-hitting Phillies 9-2 in his third start and then eased up as he often did with a big lead. He gave up one run after another, with Clarke hollering at him from left field to bear down. The Phillies had tied the score when Rube finally got them out in the ninth. Luckily the Pirates managed to score one in the ninth and Rube closed it out for an unnecessarily close 10-9 victory.

On September 24 Rube squared off against Brooklyn's Cy Young for the first time. Young, who'd earned his nickname when he was a teenager by throwing like a cyclone, shut out the Pirates for the first seven innings while Rube shut out the Superbas. In the eighth, Bobby Wallace, the Superbas' slick-fielding shortstop, hit a fly toward Bones Ely, the Pirate center fielder. Bones mishandled it and Wallace was safe at first. He took second after tagging up on a foul out and then scored on a single by Dan NcGann. The unearned run was the only one either hurler allowed. In spite of the tough loss, Pittsburgh was still just one game out of first place.

In his next start, also against Brooklyn, Rube threw shutout ball through the first four innings, but the Brooklyn players and boosters yelled one insult after another time at him in hopes of getting him off his game.

"You big mule," one fan yelled.

"When ya going back ta Hicksville?" drawled another.

"That new bride a yours a filly or a sow?" one particularly nasty bleacher bum called out.

When Rube came up to bat in the fifth he taunted the crowd by waving his arms above his head and dancing around the batter's box. When he went back out to the mound the bugs really let him have it. Rube, who had never been known to throw at a batter, hit the first man up with a curveball that didn't curve. Since Rube always had great control of his fadeaways the cranks screamed that he must have done it on purpose. Four innings later the game was called due to darkness and Rube uncharacteristically left the park without saying a word.

He was acting even stranger than usual. After a rainout the Pirates played the Superbas again. Rube stationed himself at one of the entrances to the Brooklyn stadium beside a sign that read "Public Telephone Booths on Grand Stand, rear aisle, south end. Patrons who are expecting inward calls should leave their number with the operator". In his hand he held a huge hatchet. As the Superbas' boosters came in, Rube stared at them menacingly and methodically chopped away at one of the park's huge fence posts. He kept chopping for a half hour as the frightened rooters nervously crept past. In spite of numerous complaints about Rube and what he was doing, the Superbas' security man, who was nearly seventy, was not the least bit tempted to confront Rube.

Florence hardly ever saw him. Though she didn't know it, he'd joined a circus. Admission was the usual, fifty cents for adults, two bits for children and negroes. His act consisted of chewing live snakes. He told people he'd tasted worse, including the food at some of the hotels he'd stayed in. *The Pittsburgh Dispatch* reported on the young southpaw's latest vocation, noting that in his last start his pitches had shown "a little extra wiggle."

Rube was having trouble with his hands and it was affecting the way he gripped the baseball.

"Did you burn them?" Chief Zimmer asked.

"Ya, Chief, I singed the ends a my fingers in Milwaukee pullin' a kid's toy wagon out of a fire."

"That was awful good of you, Rube. Too bad you got burned though."

"Ya, I found out the wagon cost three dollars. My hospital bill was ten times that."

Having gone into a slump as the season wound down, the Pittsburghs now had no chance of catching the league-leading Brooklyns. But as a reward for the loyal Pirate boosters Barney Dreyfuss organized a Field Day in which the players wore costumes and competed in a variety of contests. Honus Wagner dressed up as a Dutchman. Chief Zimmer wore an Indian headdress. Bones Ely wore a tutu and batted, ran, and threw like a little girl. Rube was introduced last and the bugs went wild when he came out dressed as Uncle Sam, with a top hat and a long, pointy beard. Fred Clarke even got into the act. He pretended to be a cop and used a pair of loaded pistols to keep order during the intra-squad game.

Wagner, whose arm strength was legendary, narrowly beat Rube in the long toss by throwing the ball 398 feet against Rube's best throw of 394 feet. Rube had the fastest time in a race around the bases. He adroitly managed to keep his top hat on the whole the way.

The final event was a greased pig contest. As game as they were to try, the other Pirates were more than a little uneasy when a vicious-looking black boar was led out onto the field. It looked to weigh close to three hundred pounds.

"For the love a Pete, that it is one huge fuckin' pig!" gasped Jimmy Williams.

Rube elbowed his way through the others. "Now listen boys, greased or not, ya just can't grab one a these fellas around the middle and rassle him to the ground."

"What do you have to do?" asked Bones Ely, even though he had no intention of doing whatever it was.

"What you have to do is grab him by the hind legs."

"How are you supposed to do that before he kicks the living daylights out of you?" asked Zimmer.

"Like this," said Rube. With that he grabbed the boar's huge back legs, heaved it into the air, and flung it so far that when the startled animal landed its legs were broken. That put a quick end to the contest. The other players stared at one another in disbelief.

Rube felt terrible for having hurt the animal but its handler told him that everybody back at the farm would be thrilled that the miserable beast would be out of action for a while.

        *   *   *

Rube had two more starts before the season ended. He shut out the St. Louis Browns on four hits and then shut out the Chicago Orphans, fanning a league-high twelve batters. In two of the innings he struck out the side.

He finished the season second in the league in strikeouts with 130.

Only Noodles Hahn had more with 132, but he'd pitched 100 more innings. Rube allowed fewer hits per inning than any other pitcher in the league and he had the lowest Earned Run Average as well.

After the season ended Rube stayed in Pittsburgh. He went back to the Hindman and Kummers Theatre where the drama critic of *The Commercial Gazette* reviewed his performance.

"Rube Waddell was a huge success. The great twirler proved himself an actor of rare ability. He showed great emotion and pathos and a genuine flair for spontaneous comedy. Afterwards he led the band in a street parade. He was clad in showy raiment and handled a baton with the grace of a rheumatic woman juggling a hot potato. Between acts he sold song books for ten cents, even though the price printed on the front was twenty-five cents. Inside each one was a photograph of Mr. Waddell with the caption`Myself, the Greatest Pitcher in the World`."

RUBE WADDELL
KING *of the* HALL *of* FLAKES

CHAPTER FOURTEEN

DROP HIM OFF
THE MONONGAHELA BRIDGE!

Ban Johnson, the bellicose president of the Western League, was ready. He would abandon the clubs in Buffalo, Minneapolis, Kansas City, Indianapolis, and Milwaukee, the league's five smallest cities. In their place he would put franchises in Chicago, Boston, Philadelphia, and Baltimore in direct competition with the National League franchises there. With no Brewers left to manage, Connie Mack took over as manager and part owner of the new Philadelphia Athletics.

The American League, as it would be called, immediately began an all-out raid on the established National League clubs and achieved great success. They offered huge salary increases and scooped up Cy Young, Iron Man Joe McGinnity, Napoleon Lajoie, Jimmy Collins, and a host of other lesser-known but talented players.

Rube re-signed with the Pirates for $1,200. There was a lot of speculation that teams would go after him but his reputation for being hard to handle was well known. Rube wanted to stay in Pittsburgh anyway.

In March the Pirates headed south to Hot Springs, Arkansas. The town featured a beautiful setting in the Ouachita Mountains, nature trails, first-rate hotels, lively nightclubs, and the famous water from its natural springs. In 1886 Cap Anson had brought his Chicago White Stockings to the bustling resort and before long other teams joined them, building five new ball parks, and the annual ritual of Spring Training in southern locales was begun.

During the train ride Rube entertained his teammates by singing all the new hit songs. "On the Wabash" and "Oh Dem Goo Goo Googly Eyes" were his favorites. Then he did some push-ups in the aisle.

"Can't you ever just sit 'n relax?" asked Bones Ely.

"Never could, Bones. Folks back home used to say I was like a toad eatin' lightning."

RUBE WADDELL

When the Pirates got to Whittington Park, so-named for the creek that ran beside it, Fred Clarke put them through some calisthenics and then sent them out on a three-mile run. Rube got lost. He didn't mind though, he'd brought a gun along so he could get in some hunting. He finally showed up with a bunch of ducks he'd shot. After the run, Rube, Honus Wagner, and Sam Leever put on a trap-shooting display. Though he had just arrived in town Rube had quickly become the toast of Hot Springs, receiving several Easter baskets from townspeople when the holiday arrived. When the Pirates visited the theatre to watch moving picture shows the orchestra played "When Reuben Comes to Town." Never the shy one, Rube grabbed the baton from the conductor and took his place.

The other Pirates frequented Hot Springs' many bathhouses in the afternoons and its even more numerous casinos and gaming houses at night. Fred Clarke and Honus Wagner spent their afternoons at the race track. Gambling was one vice with which Rube was not afflicted. He spent *his* free time at the new Arkansas Alligator Farm and Petting Zoo.

Rube was looking forward to his first full season in the major leagues. He knew he would strike out lots of batters because of the new rule that foul balls would now be strikes unless the hitter already had two strikes on him. His first start was against St. Louis. He gave up a run in the first inning and then settled down a bit. He managed to make it into the seventh with a 4-2 lead. Then the wheels fell off. The Pirates lost 10-4.

Rube's second start was against the last place Chicago Orphans. He may have been a little nervous, knowing that another new league rule limited the size of rosters to sixteen players or because his father was at the game. Several of his warm up pitches flew well over Chief Zimmer's head and others bounced in the dirt all around him.

"What's the matter with you today?" Zimmer asked.

"Nuthin', Chief. I'll be fine."

He wasn't fine at all. He had no zip on his fastball, no break in his curves, and no control. Rube gave up four hits and four walks in the first inning. All nine Orphans had come to the plate. Fred Clarke, who had been yelling at Rube the whole time, had seen enough. He sent in Jack Chesbro to pitch.

Fred Clarke stormed into Barney Dreyfuss' office.

Dreyfuss could see how upset he was. "What is the matter, Fred? You look like you're ready to explode. Sit down and calm yourself."

"That's the last thing I can do right now," said Clarke.

"Is it Waddell that's got your dander up again?"

"Sell him, release him, drop him off the Monongahela Bridge for all I care! Do anything, so long as you get him the hell off my ball team."

That was going to be easy for Dreyfuss to do as it turned out. Tom Loftus, Rube's manager in Columbus, was now managing the Chicago Orphans. As soon as the team had arrived in Pittsburgh, Loftus had sought out Dreyfuss to ask him if Waddell might be available at some point. He'd offered a paltry sum for Rube, but Dreyfuss called him and told him he wouldn't have to wait for Waddell, he could have him right away. When the Orphans left town Rube was one of them.

When Ban Johnson decided to put an American League franchise in Chicago they were nicknamed White Stockings and they immediately raided Tom Loftus's cross-town Orphans. Loftus had lost Clarke Griffith and Ned Garvin, two of his best pitchers. They'd lost so many players they were now being called the Remnants. Three weeks into the season they were solidly entrenched in the National League's cellar.

The Chicago Daily Inter-Ocean was excited about the new addition.

> *"Waddell will be a great drawing card for the West Side team. Not since the days of Mike Kelly has there been an odder character than Edward Waddell, or anyone more difficult to handle. Manager after manager has tried to control big "Rube" only to abandon the effort in utter despair, and Fred Clarke must have been most distracted by the giant's antics to set him free. Tom Loftus believes he can handle the white elephant, but many other managers have thought the same thing and been beautifully deceived."*

Rube had played longer and better for Loftus than for anyone, so at least there was hope. When he got to the West Side Grounds on Saturday, May 4 several players greeted him warmly. "Glad to have you with us Rube," said Topsy Hartsel. "I remember playing for the Colonels and you waking us all up in the middle of the night when you got to Washington. The folks back home in Ohio talk about you all the time."

Only 5'5", Topsy was blonde and his eyebrows were so light it almost looked as if he didn't have any. He seemed to have a permanent smile on his face.

"Good to see ya, Topsy. You know, I used to get people to call me Eddie but I've gotten called Rube for so long now, I've finally just given in to it."

RUBE WADDELL

"Welcome aboard the sinking ship," said Cupid Childs, the second baseman who was one of the few bright lights on the Orphans. Rube remembered how walking him in the fourteenth inning had cost him a game in his first stint with the Pirates.

"Hope I can help a bit, fellas. I got off to a lousy start this year, but I'll get better."

"We'll be rootin' for you, me boy," said Dirty Jack Doyle, the first baseman born in Killorglin, Ireland. "Here's a wee sumptin to give yuz a bit uv luck," he said, handing Rube a four-leaf clover.

"Thanks, Jack, mighty nice a ya, there aren't too many of these around."

"Knock 'em dead tomorrow, Rube," said Frank Chance. At 6'1", he'd been the biggest player on the team until Rube arrived. "I'll be your battery mate. The fellas call me Husk."

They couldn't find a uniform that fit him so Rube sat in the grandstand and watched the Orphans take on the Pirates. He whistled and polished his *Smith and Wesson* revolver. Fred Clarke watched him nervously from left field wondering if the comment he'd made about dropping him off the Monongahela Bridge had gotten back to him.

The next day, Sunday, May 5, fourteen thousand Chicagoans showed up to see their team's new prize.

"This is the biggest turnout we ever had," drawled Barry McCormick, the Orphans' shortstop who hailed from Kentucky. "Give 'em a show, Rube."

It was a brilliantly sunny day, without a hint of a cloud in the sky. Of course there was still a stiff breeze, it was Chicago after all. To add to the drama of Rube's debut, Tom Loftus had him warm up by firing balls at a board fifty feet away. When his pitches made contact, the sound echoed through the stadium, sounding just like rifle shots. After a lot of 'oohs' and 'ahs' Rube took the mound in his all white uniform and solid white cap.

Fred Clarke and the other Pirates rode Rube mercilessly from the bench but he never lost his composure. Then Clarke remembered Waddell's fondness for puppies. Some teams even held one up to distract Rube when he was pitching a great game.

"Rube, come here for a minute," Clarke said as they passed each other at the end of the fourth inning.

"What d'ya want, Fred? I got nuthin' to say to you."

"I feel real bad about what happened."

"I doubt that."

"I *do*. Really bad. Listen, I've got a ranch in Kansas I never told you about and you'd be welcome to come and hunt there at the end of the season. You could help me train the new dog I just got. You can keep him if he takes a shine to you."

"All dogs take a shine to me, Fred. Hunt with your friends. If you've got any."

Rube managed to maintain his concentration, but his teammates made four errors that led to three unearned runs. The score was 4-2 Pittsburgh in the bottom of the ninth when Rube stepped up to the plate with two runners on, using the black bat he'd picked out at the Hillerich plant the Pirates had visited the year before. He jumped on a curveball and drove it over Fred Clarke's head all the way to the fence 475 feet away. The jubilant crowd rose from their seats as both runners scored. Hundreds of straw hats flew into the air.

Honus Wagner, who was playing center field, picked up the ball and fired a bullet to the third baseman. Rube flew past him before he could make the tag. He slid in just ahead of the third baseman's relay for a home run. His bright white uniform wasn't so white anymore but he had a big grin on his face as he got up and dusted himself off. Fred Clarke smacked his glove against his hip, swore, and spit a stream of tobacco juice at the ground in disgust.

"Great stuff, Rube," yelled Barry McCormick. "Looks like our bugs have a new hero."

A few minutes later a reporter tapped Rube on the shoulder. "How does it feel to be in the windy city, Rube?"

"Feels pretty good. I love playin' for Mister Loftus."

"Is he nicer than Fred Clarke?"

"All Clarke ever does is harp at his players. The man has a corncob up his ass morning 'til night."

RUBE WADDELL
KING *of the* HALL *of* FLAKES

CHAPTER FIFTEEN

SOMETIMES IT PAYS
TO STICK UP FOR THE BOSS

Three days later Rube beat the Cardinals. "Only three men could land on Waddell's pitching eccentricities," said the papers. "He not only pitched a gilt-edged game for the Chicago Nationals, he fielded sensationally." After it was over four policemen, who patted him on the back and told him how great it was to have him in Chicago, escorted Rube from the field. A group of adoring boys followed behind.

Rube quickly became a darling of Chicago's night set. He made a lot of new friends, several of whom were actors, and he met some of them to celebrate his first win, which had nudged the Orphans out of last place. After visiting a few establishments, Rube and one of his pals popped into a theater. They sat near the front and passed a flask of whiskey back and forth. It was a vaudeville show and the third act featured a lion. After watching for a few minutes Rube stood up and headed toward the stage.

"Where are you going, Rube?" asked his bewildered drinking mate, whose name was Louis.

"Up there," Rube said, pointing at the stage.

"To do *what*?"

"To pet that lion. He looks pretty tame."

"It's still a lion, you could get killed!"

"It's just a big old pussycat, Louis."

Rube hopped on stage and said, "Hello, kitty."

The startled trainer looked at the theater owner, who was standing in the wings. He shrugged his shoulders, smiled, and nodded his approval. The trainer reluctantly stepped aside to let Rube play with the lion.

"Isn't that Rube Waddell from the Orphans?" a man asked his wife.

"How should I know, Horace? I never go to base ball games."

"Well, I tell you, as sure as we are sitting here, that's Rube Waddell, the new twirler."

Rube petted the lion's mane and spoke soothingly to it. After a few minutes of play and a lot of laughs and applause from the audience the big cat playfully swiped at Rube's arm. Blood poured from a deep gash. The audience gasped.

"It's all right, folks, he didn't mean it," Rube told the audience and the trainer.

Fortunately it was his right arm. After the show it took a doctor fifteen stitches to close the wound.

"You're going to be in big trouble when your manager sees that," said Louis, who had gone with Rube to the hospital. "You had better hope this doesn't make the newspapers."

If it did, Rube would certainly be fined, perhaps even suspended. That would not do, he'd only been with the team for a few days. When he read the papers the next morning he was relieved that there was no mention of his lion taming.

"How did you get that nasty wound on your arm, Rube?" asked Tom Loftus.

"It was a terrible thing, Tom. I was attacked by a gang of robbers. I held them off for as long as I could, then one of them swung a knife at me and then they ran off. Dang lucky I'm still alive."

Loftus looked suspiciously at him, trying to decide whether to believe him. Rube *did* have a reputation for telling the truth. Then he said, "Go get packed, we leave for New York in an hour."

The Giants took the first two games from the Orphans. As soon as Rube took the mound for the third game on Thursday, May 16 the New York cranks were on him. They yelled anything they could think of to rattle him.

"My brother's in Pittsburgh taking care of that new bride of yours," one bellowed.

Rube blanked New York for seven straight innings and had an 11-0 lead when the Giants pushed across three runs in the eighth. The bleachers erupted in a cacophony of horns and other dissonant noises. Rube settled down and retired the side.

In the bottom of the ninth he walked right past the mound and out toward the bleacher benches. He took off his cap and addressed the crowd in right field from which the loudest taunts had come. There wasn't a peep as Rube spoke. He bowed and said, "Ladies and gentlemen, I must apologize. I had promised you I would pitch a shutout this afternoon but circumstances beyond my control have prevented me from doing so. I will, however, strike out the side this inning to end things satisfactorily."

His speech won over quite a few of the boosters.

"Good man, Rube," someone yelled.

"Strike 'em down, Rube," called out another.

"What do you think of that?" said Gentleman Jim Corbett to the woman sitting with him. "He shows a lot of savvy out there, doesn't he?"

"He certainly does. Do ball players *usually* talk to the bleacherites like that," she asked Jim.

"No they don't, especially the other team's cranks, and certainly not when they've been letting the player have it with both barrels all afternoon."

Rube struck out the side, as promised, though it took him twelve pitches.

After the game, which had lasted an hour and fifteen minutes, Corbett visited the locker room.

"That was quite a performance - on the mound and in the speech before the last inning," he told Rube. "I believe you may receive a less hostile greeting when you pitch here again."

"Oh, they'll probly lemme have it in both ears again. What did you say your name was?"

"Jim Corbett. I'm a boxer."

"Heck, he's not just a boxer, Rube," said Frank Chance, "he's one of the best ever."

"Have you ever boxed, Rube?' Corbett asked.

"A little. I've won a few matches here and there."

"Let's get together for some libations this evening and spar a little tomorrow at my gym."

"Sounds good to me, I'll see ya outside."

Jim and Rube became and remained great boosters of one another's work, and good friends too.

The Orphans were in trouble. Though they were winning a few games now thanks to Rube, they could only draw a crowd when he was pitching and the White Stockings were on the road. In desperation they reduced their ticket prices to twenty-five cents. To cut costs, instead of transporting the team in a tally-ho from their hotel to the ballpark and back like other teams did, Loftus had them ride in a carry-all. The wagon looked just like the one Rube's grandfather used to haul his wheat to the mill. The Orphans stared in disbelief when two grey nags pulled it up to the side entrance of the hotel.

Rube turned to Loftus and chuckled, "Put blinkers on the fellas and back 'em in."

ℓc   *ℓc*   *ℓc*

The Orphans' fielding was a big part of the problem. It seemed like wherever Rube went he ended up pitching for a team that couldn't catch the ball or throw it anywhere close to their target. In one game the Orphans committed ten errors. *The Chicago Tribune* weighed in on their deficiencies.

> *"The Orphans remind one of the Blue Island Grammar School's team. Every time an Orphan fielder boots another ground ball Willie O'Grady, their loudest rooter, stands up and yells, "Well, well, folks, there's another one. Ain't that just grand?" Rube Waddell is the only one on their staff who seems able to bag a contest."*

The Orphans nestled back into last place with a loss to the Phillies on Saturday, May 18. Rube pitched against them two days later. He was ahead 4-1 after four innings when the roof caved in. The score ended up 6-4 Philadelphia. Rube lost five of his next six starts, including a humiliating 14-4 thrashing by the Phillies. "The fielding of the locals today was disgracefully poor, their errors of the rankest order," wrote the baseball reporter for the *Daily Tribune*. Rube showed up for the next game with a bandaged right hand. When he removed the bandage Tom Loftus thought it looked as though it had been hit with a sledge hammer.

"What have you done *this* time?" Loftus asked.

Rube started to explain but didn't get far. A secretary told him that Mr. Hart wanted to see him. James Aristotle Hart, the Orphans' owner, had decided it was time he got involved. Loftus was being far too soft on the crazy young flame thrower. Tom Loftus went along to see what Hart would do.

"Judging by reports that I have received as to your whereabouts last evening, it is clear that you have taken part in a drunken melee at one of the saloons you frequent on far too regular a basis," harrumphed Hart, stroking his flowing handlebar moustache.

"I admit there is some truth to that, Mister Hart," said Rube.

"As a result of your actions, which are not in the best interests of the Chicago Orphans Baseball Club, I am docking you fifty dollars."

"But Mister Hart, couldn't I explain what happened?"

"No, you cannot. We have all had quite enough of your late night carousing."

"Come on, Jim," said Loftus. "What'll it hurt to let Rube tell us what happened?"

"Very well then. Go ahead and tell us what took place last night. But you needn't think it will influence my decision."

"I understand," said Rube contritely. "This is God's honest truth. I was at Scaller's Pumphouse last night, around ten o'clock. I was sipping on a pint of root beer, minding my own affairs, and there was a group of baseball bugs at the table next to me. There was some trouble and it was all on account of you."

"On account of me!" Hart stammered incredulously. "How in Hades could the trouble have been on account of me?"

"Well ya see - and strike me dead if there is a word of a lie in this rendition - I overheard this fellow say that Jim Hart was nothing but a cheap, cowardly son of a bitch who didn't know the first thing about baseball."

"He did, did he? What happened then?"

Rube looked Hart straight in the eye. "Well of course there was no way I was gonna let anybody get away with saying things like that about you."

"What did you do?"

"I told him that I was a friend of yours and I would not abide anyone speaking about you that way."

"What did he say to that?"

"He told me that every word he'd said was the truth."

"And then?"

And then I said he should shut his damn mouth or I'd knock him clear into the middle of next week."

"Did he stop?"

"No he did not. He commenced to jawing away about you again. And that is when I hit him. I hit him real hard, maybe a couple a times. And that's how I hurt my hand."

"What happened next?"

"Somebody ran outside and then I heard a police whistle and a constable came in and took me and the other fellow to the station. We each got a twenty-five dollar fine and had to spend the night locked up."

"And that is exactly what transpired?"

"Gospel truth, Mister Hart."

"Well in that case . . . I suppose I could see my way to forgetting about that fine."

Rube could hardly believe he'd been able to talk his way out of the spot he'd been in. "That'd be mighty decent of you." He went to leave.

"One more thing, Rube. I want to thank you for standing up for me. There aren't many that would. We baseball club owners don't have the greatest reputations these days." He took out his wallet and handed Rube a twenty dollar bill and a five.

"What's this?" asked Rube.

"It's to cover your fine."

CHAPTER SIXTEEN

THE BAD BOY
TAKES ON THE CHOIR BOY

The Orphans' most anticipated and publicized game of the season was to take place on Saturday, June 16. The Orphans would be taking on the New York Giants. And this time the banners read more than just "Come see Rube fan 'em out". Like the Orphans, the Giants were beginning to win some games because of a talented young pitcher. But the ability to throw baseballs past befuddled batters was about the only thing the two twirlers had in common.

Christy Mathewson had recently graduated from Bucknell University, where - unlike Rube at Volant - he had actually attended classes. He'd even been elected student body president. Mathewson was polished, serious, and well-mannered. Six feet tall, with blond hair and blue eyes, he was already the darling of those baseball bugs who disliked the game's rough culture of drinking, gambling, brawling, and abusing umpires. They hoped Matty could elevate the game's image.

And he was good. Mathewson had terrific control and, unlike Rube, he hated to lose. New Yorkers had taken to calling him "the Christian Gentleman." His parents were staunchly religious and had hoped he would become a minister. Christy had a girlfriend, but she wasn't the kind of girl Rube would be interested in. She was a Sunday school teacher.

The newspapers madly promoted the game as a clash of finesse versus speed and of brains versus brawn. Rube was asked for a prediction. "I expect to go into tomorrow's game and do my very best to win, but I am not braggart enough to claim a victory until the game is over and done. Mathewson is a hard man to beat."

Twelve thousand boosters came to see the classic matchup between the zany speedball hurler and the competitive choir boy. Rube's hand still hurt, but he was determined to win. Somewhat nervous, he walked George Van Haltren, the Giants' leadoff hitter, on four pitches. His first pitch to the next batter bounced just in front of the plate and skidded by Frank Chance. Van Haltren went to second on the passed ball.

Rube put everything he had into his next pitch and it sailed way over Chance's head. The ball managed to lodge itself under the grandstand and, by the time Chance dug it out, Van Haltren had scored. The Orphans were down a run and only two men had come to the plate.

Chance came out to the mound. "Listen Rube, these hitters aren't that good. You don't have to throw smoke to get them out. Throw 'em some of your puzzlers and fadeaways and you'll turn these giants into midgets."

Rube calmed down and threw strikes and the Orphans played error-free ball for a change. In the bottom of the first they got three runs on three singles and a bases-clearing triple. In the second, Sammy Strang, the Giants' third baseman, led off with a single but Rube struck out the next two batters to the delight of the Orphans' rooters. The next hitter popped out weakly to Cupid Childs.

Mathewson came to bat in the third with an opportunity to see what his teammates were up against with Rube on the hill. Rube tipped his cap to him and Matty returned the favor. A puzzler, a rising shoot, and a crazy wobbler later Matty had struck out on three pitches.

Rube had the better of Mathewson the whole afternoon.

"Cut 'em down, Rube," yelled old leather lungs Willie O'Grady. "Give 'em some a yer fancy ones."

In the bottom of the ninth Rube ripped one of Matty's pitches into deep right field for a double that knocked in the Orphans' final runs in a convincing 9-2 win. Rube ended up striking out ten Giants. It turned out Mathewson wasn't unbeatable after all. He'd given up thirteen hits and walked four batters.

"Take a look at Waddell and get an idea what a real pitcher looks like, Mathewson," piped Willie O'Grady. The next day *The Chicago Daily Inter-Ocean* said "the idol had fallen off his pedestal with a guggling glunk, like a June bug diving into a picnic lemonade."

Of Rube they said,

> *"Waddell's curves and shoots proved too much for the Giant batsmen and they appeared to pout their way through the final innings. When the young man has his mind on baseball instead of trout and pickerel he is one outstanding twirler."*

Two weeks later there was a rematch with Christy Mathewson, this time in New York. Rube loved the city that never slept and he availed himself of the Big Apple's nightlife until the wee hours. He didn't remember getting home after frequenting two theaters and three or more taverns. He vaguely recalled a couple of showgirls with long legs, heady perfume, and a lot of makeup. Once again he had made a lot of new friends. But he was in no kind of shape to pitch. He gave up nine runs in four innings as the Giants pummeled the Orphans 14-1. This time the dedicated choir boy bested the capricious man-child. Matty had been awful in their first duel and Rube had been even worse in this one. Unfortunately for baseball boosters, though they should have, the two would never face each other again. Rube's embarrassing loss in his rematch with Christy Mathewson was the first occasion in which his excessive drinking and revelry had blatantly and publicly affected his performance. Unfortunately it did not awaken him to the need to mend his ways.

When the Orphans traveled to Brooklyn for a Fourth of July doubleheader they saw that the gatepost that Rube had attacked with a hatchet had not been replaced. The Superbas wanted it left that way to rile up the bugs when Rube took the mound. The ploy worked. The Brooklyn bugs did everything they could to distract him. This time, taunts were just the beginning. The cranks broke into applause in the middle of Rube's windup, threw everything at him but the kitchen sink, let off cannon crackers, and even fired revolvers to rattle him.

Rube somehow managed to weather the storm, but his shoots weren't as fast as usual and his breaking pitches had a lot less movement. He gave up two runs in the seventh inning and another two in the eighth. Luckily the Orphans' bats saved him and Chicago rallied for a 10-9 win, but it was not one of his better outings.

He was showing up for games in worse and worse condition. Tom Loftus scheduled morning practices to work in new players he'd had to bring in due to injuries. Rube missed three of the first four. When he was a no-show for yet another one, Hart suspended him.

"Are they gonna let you come back, Rube?" a reporter asked him.

"I misbehave a bit sometimes, but Jim and Tom are fine fellows and I expect to be reinstated."

"What if you aren't?"

"Well, I've received telegrams from three different clubs offering me employment."

A reporter asked Tom Loftus for a comment on the offers Rube said he'd received.

Loftus told him, "If he's getting telegrams they're probably from his wife asking why he never sends her any money."

Hart and Loftus had hoped Waddell would see the error of his ways, but when he returned from the suspension and beat the Giants 7-4 *The Chicago Record-Herald* postulated that "the eight hits Waddell gave up may have been the result of the eight cocktails he enjoyed in a West Side tavern last night."

Rube did start attending morning practices and he showed up completely sober even for games he wasn't scheduled to pitch. He contritely told reporters that Hart had been right to suspend him, that he'd deserved it.

His next start was in St. Louis. When the Orphans got there the temperature was 113 degrees. "It's hotter than two dogs screwin' in a wool sack," said Rube as the Browns walked from the train station to their hotel.

Rube pitched well in spite of the oppressive heat, though he sweated off almost ten pounds. Unfortunately, he walked two batters in the eighth inning and then failed to back up a throw to the plate that allowed the winning run to score in a tough 2-1 loss.

The next morning Rube left for Wisconsin. He knew a great place to fish there. He didn't think to send Florence word of his plans, nor any money either.

CHAPTER SEVENTEEN

NOT FOOLING ANYONE
AT THE COUNTY FAIR

A week later Rube figured he'd caught enough fish and returned to Chicago. Jim Hart fined him, but just ten dollars. The Orphans badly needed him and Hart didn't want Rube to take off again. Obviously Rube hadn't been scheduled to start, but Hart, who was willing to try anything to get people into the usually empty seats, had organized another promotion. There were 7,000 school kids at the game so Tom Loftus, who had seen Rube joking with a bunch of boys in the bleachers when he arrived, sent him in to pitch. He would be facing the Cardinals and Loftus figured Rube would enjoy getting some revenge for the tough loss in St. Louis.

When he took the mound the roar from the kids was so loud the players had to cover their ears. Rube didn't disappoint the spirited youngsters, who cheered their hero throughout the game. He rewarded them with one of his best performances of the year. His only rough inning was the fourth when he walked two batters and hit another to load the bases. The school kids yelled encouragement.

"Strike 'em down, Rube!"

Rube tipped his cap and then chuckled as he easily struck out the next two Cardinals. Bobby Wallace was up next. He slammed his bat against the plate after whiffing at Rube's first two pitches and then hitting a harmless pop fly to Barry McCormick.

Rube won his next start, in Cincinnati, and then the Orphans traveled to Pittsburgh.

When they arrived, a large, grim-faced Allegheny County sheriff met their train.

"Mister Waddell," he said, tapping Rube on the shoulder.

"What can I do for you, officer?" Rube asked innocently.

"You can come to the station with me is what you can do Mister Waddell. We have asked your wife to make good on debts you incurred before leaving her and some very angry storekeepers behind. She informed us that you have stopped sending her a portion of your pay."

"What is this all about, officer?" asked Tom Loftus.

"It's about money that this man owes a number of people sir," the sheriff answered.

Rube, who had $1.40 in his pocket, shrugged his big shoulders and went along quietly. Luckily, when Jim Hart learned that Rube had been taken into custody for the sum of $19 he paid the bill.

His cellmates patted him on the back when he was let out.

"Been good to know ya fellas," Rube said as he put on his jacket. "Come on out to the stadium and see me pitch. If they ever let you outta here."

Rube managed to make friends no matter where he was.

⚬ ⚬ ⚬

"I'm real sorry, Flo, real sorry."

"How could you forget to send money six seeks in a row, Eddie? Here I am with almost no one in town that I know. I've had to ask the Pirates' wives for help three times now. Of course the other Orphans' wives are in Chicago with their husbands."

"I thought you would be happier here. Chicago is a long way away."

"But how could you not remember to send me anything?"

"I don't know, darlin', I guess I just get thinkin' about other things."

"Other *girls* you mean, don't you?"

"No, I didn't mean that at all, I meant fishin' and huntin' and things like that."

"I hear you've been out drinking nearly every night since you went to Chicago."

"Not every night. Sometimes I stay in or I go to see a show."

"With women?"

"No, no. With fellas. You know I'm always making friends."

"Well it sounds as though your so-called friends are not a very good influence on you."

"Let's go to bed, Flo. I don't want to fight and it's been a long time since we snuggled under the covers."

"You're right, a long time indeed, and through no fault of mine. I want to be your wife Eddie, not just a port in a storm."

Rube already had his clothes half off and Florence reluctantly started to undress. She had a hard time resisting those big eyes and wide grin. She knew she had married a big charming kid who would probably never grow up. Her mother had warned her, but Florence hadn't listened.

&r &r &r

Rather than take Florence back to Chicago, Rube put her on a train to Prospect so she could stay with his parents. At least she wouldn't go hungry there. The Orphans' next stop was in St. Louis, which had thankfully cooled down to the low nineties. All his pitches were working for Rube when he took the mound in the second game of a doubleheader and his shoots, wobblers, and puzzlers baffled the Cardinals this time around. Rube hit a home run and won 9-1, with almost no need to rely on his often unreliable fielders. The only run he allowed came on a home run hit by his former teammate Wahoo Sam Crawford. Sam wondered if Rube had taken it easy on him, it was the only pitch he'd thrown down the middle all day.

&r &r &r

Four days later in Cincinnati, Rube pitched his best game of the season, a three-hit masterpiece.

"Did you see how ridiculous Waddell made the Reds look today? That is the player we hoped we were getting when we took him off Fred Clarke's hands," Jim Hart told Tom Loftus after the game.

"He has so much talent," said Loftus, "if only he could behave himself and pitch like that all the time."

"If he could, do you really think Pittsburgh would have given up on him?"

&r &r &r

When Rube had pitched for Tom Loftus before, things were different. Loftus had owned the team. He could let Rube take off in between his starts and turn a blind eye to his other misconduct. Now Rube had to follow Jim Hart's rules and, in light of all of Rube's crimes and misdemeanors, they now stipulated that he be in his room by ten, arrive on time and sober for every game, and attend every practice.

Rube responded to the new orders the way he generally did. He left. He headed back to Wisconsin, this time to check out Lake Villa and Grays Lake where he'd heard the crawfishing was just spectacular. Jim Hart sent a detective to look for Rube. When the detective wired Hart that he'd found the delinquent star at Grays Lake, Hart instructed him to tell Rube that if he joined the team in New York he would once again be forgiven. Rube sent Hart a telegram.

I regret to inform you that I am through with organized baseball for the season. Regards, Edward Waddell.

RUBE WADDELL

Rube loved the fishing in Wisconsin. Grays Lake had plenty of musky, bass and catfish, as well as Northern pike. The hunting was great too but he needed money, so he accepted an offer to pitch for the Grays Lake Cornhuskers Athletic Club for five dollars a game. To hide his identity, Rube pitched under the name of Brown. He didn't fool anyone. His handsome face, muscular physique, and extraordinary skills were too recognizable.

His first game was played at a country fair. Rube got there well before game time. He loved fairs and he was hungry. He rode the Ferris wheel and the roller coaster and then he ate three bags of popcorn, four candy apples, and five ears of corn on the cob. He hit all the targets at the rifle shooting booth and won every single prize at the ball-throwing booth. He gave all the bears and dolls to some pretty girls who were following the handsome celebrity around.

Rube hit a home run over the fence into some startled horses and pitched the Cornhuskers to a 32-0 win. He pulled a lot of stunts for the delighted crowd, doing handsprings and calling his fielders in before striking out the side.

When the Athletic Club organized a football game they invited Rube to play fullback and linebacker and immediately named him captain. In his first game he recovered a fumble and ran fifty yards for a touchdown. Four opponents bounced right off when they tried to tackle him.

At the end of the game two men came up to talk to him. He recognized one of them. It was Frank Chance. He'd never laid eyes on the other man.

"Good to see you, Frank."

"Good to see you too, Rube. This here is Joe Cantillon. He's an umpire for the American League." Cantillon was short and serious-looking, with long brown hair and thick, dark eyebrows.

"Pleasure to know ya, Joe. What brings you fellas all the way to Grays Lake? You got kin here?"

"We came to see *you*, Rube."

"What do you want to see me for? Tom Loftus send you?"

"It has nothing to do with Loftus or the Orphans."

"What's it about then?"

"How much longer do you figure you are gonna play football?"

"I don't know, Frank. It is football season after all, and it's gettin' way too cold to play baseball."

"Maybe here. Not in California."

"California? What's California got to do with anything?"

"Players we know from different teams have put together a barnstorming tour. We're going to Los Angeles and then we'll play games all along the West Coast. The money will be good and the weather will be better. We'd love to have you with us to boost the crowds. Nobody puts on a show like you do."

"Would we have to play serious all the time?"

"No, we can take it easy and have fun and we get paid the same whether we win or lose."

"Sounds like a pretty sweet deal," said Rube.

"What d'ya say?"

"Will there be a boss to tell us when to go to bed at night?"

"There'll be no boss, Rube. Just the players."

Rube set down his helmet and said, "Count me in, boys. When do we leave?"

RUBE WADDELL
KING *of the* HALL *of* FLAKES

CHAPTER EIGHTEEN

A BIG HIT ON THE COAST

The barnstormers arrived in California at the end of November. There was a team of National League stars and another team made up of American League stars. They played each other in front of large crowds and were happy to be paid $125 a week. That was what most of them made in a month during the season. While the attendance averaged around 5,000 it was more like 12,000 when Rube Waddell was announced as the pitcher. He was terrific on the west coast. Over two back-to-back games against some of the American League's best players he notched twenty-seven strikeouts.

"It's hot out here, but comfortable," Frank Chance told Rube after the second game.

"Forget the temperature. Did you get a look at those beauties in the stands? I've never seen women with tanned skin like that."

"You *are* still married, aren't you?"

"Not for long I guess. I just got a letter from Flo. She's moving out of my folks' house and going back to Columbus."

"That doesn't sound good."

"There's more to it than that. She's asking for a divorce. Claiming I failed to provide the necessities of life and that I spend my time carousing and keeping fast company."

"I suppose you can't really argue with her on that score. I guess you'll be glad to be free of her."

"I most certainly will not. Flo's a great gal. I loved her a lot."

"You had a funny way of showing it. You hardly ever saw her."

"She never wanted to go out. She just wanted to stay home and have a game of Canasta or play the harpsichord. I'm still a young man. I need to dress up and go out on the town. Flo always dresses like a school marm. I like women in fancy clothes."

"Or no clothes at all."

RUBE WADDELL

Word went around rapidly that the California clubs were interested in Rube. Quite flattered, he told both the Oakland Mud Hens and the San Francisco Ponies he would play for them. But before the deals were finalized James Morley, the owner of the Los Angeles Loo Loos, sent him a message that he would like to meet him for lunch at The Los Angeles Hunt Club. Morley had seen how well Rube pitched against the American League stars.

Rube put on his best pinstriped suit and took a hansom cab to the posh club. He somewhat gingerly tapped the huge brass knocker against the front door and then waited a long minute until a butler opened the door.

"Edward Waddell, Mister Morley invited me."

"Indeed," said the butler. "He is expecting you. Come in Mister Waddell."

Rube was ushered down a hall illuminated by tiny lamps. On the walls were paintings of old men dressed in tuxedos that Rube assumed were directors of the club. He noticed that each had thick side whiskers but no beard. He wondered if that was some kind of rule they had. A gigantic chandelier lit the dining room. A Persian rug stretched across the floor in front of an immense fireplace. Rube had never seen such expensive-looking wallpaper. It was festooned with tiny horses and hunting dogs. The thick drapes were wide open to allow in the California sunshine.

A little man in a tuxedo met Rube at the entrance to the dining room and guided him to a table near the window. He said to the elegantly dressed man sitting there, "Your guest, Mister Waddell, sir."

"Thank you, Higgins."

Morley stood up. He was dressed in a light grey suit and his collar, like Rube's, was high and starched. His eyes were dark brown and his hair was just beginning to turn grey. He shook Rube's hand, seemed to remark to himself on the extraordinary size and strength of it, and then indicated for Rube to sit down.

A colored waiter brought them whiskey sodas. Morley ordered mushroom soup, chicken cordon bleu, and baked Alaska. Rube ordered lobster bisque, filet of sole, a Prime Rib steak, rare, with roasted potatoes and vegetables, pie, and ice cream. During dinner Morley told him about the league and about the small but rapidly growing city of Los Angeles.

When Morley finished his baked Alaska he ordered them brandy and cigars and then got down to brass tacks. "Rube, I hear you've already agreed to play for two of our league's other clubs. That was not a very wise thing to do."

"I suppose it wasn't," Rube agreed sheepishly.

"I can, however, get you out of the legal jam you have gotten yourself into. Did you sign anything?"

"I might have. Yes, I believe I did."

"Never mind, I can make things right."

"That would be mighty fine of you, Mister Morley. I can't really afford a lawyer. What would I have to do in return?"

"Agree to play for *my* club of course, for the Loo Loos."

"I'd be real happy to do just that. I like it here. Of all the places we've been to, Los Angeles is my favorite. People have been treatin' me like a prince."

"It is a beautiful city . . . except for all the oil rigs of course."

"How much would I make playing for the Loo Loos?"

"You will make two hundred and seventy-five dollars a month."

"That's pretty good money, nearly ten dollars a day."

"I can assure you it's a great deal more than any other California League player has ever been paid."

"Could I have a day or two off to go fishing once in a while?"

"Let me tell you about our schedule. Each week from April through November we play single games on Thursday, Friday, and Saturday, and then a double header on Sunday."

"Do you have practices on the other days?"

"When we do, you would not need to attend. On the off days you would be free to pitch for semi-pro teams or go fishing or do whatever else you like."

Rube took a big swig of his brandy, asked for another, and said, "You have got yourself a deal Mister Morley." A few days later the other barnstormers headed back east. Rube stayed behind to become a Loo Loo.

& & &

Los Angeles was about the same size as Columbus, but it had a lot more sunshine and lush vegetation along its broad avenues. Rube was a hit right from the start. All kinds of people invited him to dinner or bought him drinks and told him how terrific he was. He bought a whole new set of clothes, three pairs of cufflinks, and a white tie. He had his shoes shined and got a shave and a haircut at a very fancy barbershop. He was feeling like a real big shot. He gave everybody who served him a big tip. There weren't many theatres in Los Angeles yet, nothing like back east, but there were some very swanky saloons and restaurants.

In the first inning of his first game at Chutes Park against the Sacramento Mosquitos Rube blazed two strikes past Irv Rawlings, the Skeeters' centerfielder. Rawlings stared in disbelief and then turned to go to the bench.

"You've got another one coming to you," the confused umpire told him.

"You can keep it," Rawlings told him. "I want no part of it."

The Los Angeles Times reported that Waddell was "the best twirler that has ever pitched in Los Angeles."

Rube celebrated his success long and hard the night before he faced the Oakland Mud Hens, the California League's best team, and gave up eleven hits. The boosters seemed not to mind. A big crowd showed up for his next start and cheered his every move.

To satisfy the bugs who were clearly there just to see the new sensation from the East, the Loo Loos had Rube play first base or the outfield when he wasn't pitching. He made several diving catches and, more importantly as far as James Morley was concerned, he put on a show no matter what position he played.

The crowd went berserk when Rube pulled a fast one on a raw rookie who was playing his first professional game for the Skeeters. Rube was playing first base. After the rookie singled, the Loo Loos' pitcher tried to pick him off. The rookie got back to the bag in plenty of time and was feeling quite proud of himself after getting a hit in his first at bat. Rube asked him to step off the bag so he could knock the dirt off it. The rookie gladly obliged the request from the famous Rube Waddell about whom he had heard so much.

But after Rube had caught the pickoff attempt he had only *pretended* to throw the ball back to the pitcher. It was still in his glove. He tagged the kid out and then held the ball in the air to the crowd's delight. When he consoled the red-faced rookie by putting an arm around his shoulder the bugs whooped even louder.

When Rube played the outfield and caught the ball for the last out of an inning he would grin, bow, and then throw the ball on a huge arc into the bleachers. James Mooney couldn't believe his eyes when he first saw Rube do it. Baseballs cost fifty cents. But when he saw how thrilled the crowd was he had a hard time getting mad at Rube. He was making him a ton of money.

Thursday was the one day when the Loo Loos had a hard time drawing a crowd, so Morley staged a Ladies Day. Every woman who attended received a full-length picture of Rube. Jimmy Tallon, the shortstop, brought one of the huge pictures of Rube into the locker room as the players were putting on their red and yellow uniforms. "What a gorgeous specimen of a man," he said, holding up the picture for the other Loo Loos to see.

"Oh, could you sign it for me, Rube? Pretty please," teased Whitey Morgan, the center fielder. "I declare, I would be ever so grateful."

"Strike one out for me, couldn't you, Rube?" said Tallon. "I think you're the bee's knees."

"I would just die for a picture of you in a nightshirt, Rube, but not a full-length nightshirt - if you know what I mean," the catcher, Ernie Wilson said, pretending to wave a fan and batting his eyelashes.

"Laugh all you like boys," said Rube. "But I'll wager any of you a silver dollar that more than a couple of those gals will stop by my hotel tonight and they're liable to want more than just my signature."

Of course Rube had to pitch the game and he put on quite an exhibition for the ladies, bowing, tipping his cap, and playing the gallant knight. The women groaned every time one of the Mud Hens got a hit, though only four of them did, and they squealed - a sound not generally heard at baseball games - whenever Rube struck out another Mud Hen.

It turned out the west wasn't that different from the east. When Rube showed up sober and bore down he was virtually unhittable. He threw a shutout in the first game of a double header and then played first base in the second game. In the bottom of the ninth he came up with a runner on second and the Loo Loos down by a run. The first pitch was high. Rube waved his bat in the air to indicate that it was far from the strike zone. The second pitch was a bit inside. Rube jumped back three feet in mock horror. He was doing a fine job of showing up the pitcher and the crowd was loving it.

"Looks as though the man can't find the plate," called one rooter.

"Help him out, Rube, show him where the zone is," yelled another.

In frustration, the pitcher grooved the next pitch right down the middle. Rube extended his powerful arms, whipped his small bat around, and drove the ball in a long, high arc over the centerfield fence 400 feet away.

The home run, the first ball hit over the center field fence since Chutes Park opened, won the game. It also won Rube a new suit, compliments of Forsyths, Purveyor of Fine Men's Wear. The next time he took the mound he gave up just three hits and struck out ten San Francisco Ponies. He was ahead by just one run though when his third baseman bobbled an easy grounder with none out in the seventh. Rube reproachfully walked him back to third, patting him on his back.

His first pitch to the next batter was a little high. The umpire called it a ball. Rube put his hand to his heart, as if stricken. His second pitch was a little low. The umpire called, "Ball two." Rube lay down on the ground and looked in to see if it could really have been that low.

When the umpire called his next pitch ball three, Rube pretended to take off a pair of eyeglasses and offered them to him. The umpire glared at him and yelled for him to get back on the rubber and pitch. Rube waved reassuringly to the crowd and then struck out the side with his next nine pitches. Playing right field two days later he made three catches of sinking line drives, threw out two runners, and knocked in the winning run with a double.

His remarkable pitching was a sensation. *The LA Times* poetically expressed the exhilaration of seeing Rube on the mound.

There were shivers on the bleacher boards
When Rube went in to pitch
In the boxes there were tremors as
He gave his pants a hitch;
For the Looloos had been losing and
The boosters had been blue,
But they put their trust in Reuben, and
Their money on him too.
From the benches rose a mighty roar
When Rube went in to pitch.
And he twirled the shiny sphere as if
It made his fingers itch.
Then it hissed off like a rocket, and
The batter couldn't tell
If 'twere two or twenty sparks passed out
By our hero Rube Waddell.
You may bet it was a glorious game
When Rube went in to pitch;
For it made the sick man healthy, and

The poor man very rich,
As the batters fanned the climate and
They struck out one - two - three,
All before that raging multitude
It was sure a sight to see!

RUBE WADDELL
KING of the HALL of FLAKES

CHAPTER NINETEEN

A SMOLDERING ROMANCE
AND A SMOLDERING MATTRESS

On May 8 the Mud Hens came to Los Angeles for a series. Rube pitched the second game. He was ahead 2-1 in the fifth when all eyes turned from the action on the field. Something was on fire and it was inside Chutes Park. A large mattress had been hauled down to field level to serve as a backstop. In order to slide it along the grandstand the grounds crew had applied grease to it. Apparently someone had tossed a cigar or cigarette onto it. No one had noticed that smoke was slowly streaming from it. Now flames were shooting out. Panicking boosters started to flee. Then the players did. Everyone knew that Chutes Park was an old stadium made of wood and feared the worst.

Suddenly Rube appeared. He was yanking at the mattress, wrenching it from the bindings that held it down. He wrenched it free and then threw it out onto the field where it burned and then smouldered harmlessly. The only damage, besides the mattress itself, was a section of singed grass. As the grounds crew towed the smoking remains away Rube went back to the mound as if he had just stepped on a spider. He picked up the baseball and his glove and said, "Let's get on with it."

The bugs that hadn't already bolted unleashed a chorus of huzzahs. Rube retired the side and held on for the win. His double in the seventh the next day helped the Loo Loos to a win that vaulted them into first place.

When the Loo Loos staged another Ladies Day Rube didn't scan the crowd for attractive women as he had the first time. Now he had eyes for only one. Her name was Miranda Thornton. She had just arrived in town with her father, who was an oilman. Miranda was nineteen, tall, with auburn hair, sparkling blue eyes, and a sensational figure.

"Hey Whitey, did you get a gander at that gal Rube's got a hankering for?" Ernie Wilson asked.

"Are you kidding? Who could miss *her*?"

"Did ya see those eyes of hers? Enough to make a man weak in the knees."

"Probably isn't her eyes Rube's interested in. I've never seen a shape like that before."

"Don't go talking like that about her around Rube, he's positively smitten with her."

"Where do you suppose he found a beauty like that?"

"Some rich fellas that took a shine to Rube invited him to a fancy restaurant the other night. She was there with her rich daddy. He's one of the tycoons building oilrigs all over the place. He and Rube got talking about how his father was in the oil business in Ohio and the fool introduced him to his daughter.

Rube didn't pitch a shutout for Miranda, but he still put on a show for her. He gave up one earned run and two unearned ones in fourteen innings. In the ninth, he stymied the Skeeters when they placed runners on first and third and then attempted a double steal. The runner at first took off for second in hopes of drawing a throw that would allow the lead runner to score. But as the catcher's hard throw sailed over the mound, instead of ducking out of the way as a pitcher was expected to do, Rube casually reached up and snagged the ball out of the air with his bare hand. He fired it back to the catcher in plenty of time to nab the startled runner, who'd expected to be able to jog home with the winning run. Most of the ladies in the crowd were unfamiliar with baseball strategy but they knew that Rube had just done something out of the ordinary and they gave him a huge round of applause. It was a rather muffled sound, as many, including Rube's new ladylove, wore white gloves.

In the top of the fourteenth the Skeeters loaded the bases. It looked as though Rube was finally worn out. The manager certainly did not want to take his star attraction out of the game. Even if Rube was exhausted he had a much better chance of putting out this fire than any other pitcher the Loo Loos had. Besides, the thousands of ladies in attendance were sure to organize a lynch mob if he took their hero out. He reluctantly started out to the mound to see if Rube wanted to continue.

Rube waved him to go back to the bench. "I'm sound as a dollar. No need to concern yourself, I've got matters well in hand."

Rube twirled the ball in his big left hand and tossed it up in the air a couple of times. He peered in at the next batter. He smiled at him and then shook his head as if to indicate that the man need not even entertain the possibility that he might get a hit.

Suddenly Rube was seized with convulsions. The crowd gasped. Rube wrung his hands above his head. Through his mighty anatomy ran a mighty shudder and then he kicked his right leg high in the air with a flash of red from the stripes on his stockings. The batter's eyes widened to saucers.

Then Rube threw three blindingly fast shoots. The first rose through the strike zone and the batter flailed at it wildly. The second, equally fast and unhittable, whizzed low across the plate and the batter just stood and stared at it. The third was right down the middle. The hitter's eyes lit up. After having been so badly embarrassed by the first two pitches, here was one that he might hit and hit hard. He put all his might into his swing.

But as the ball reached the plate something went wrong. The ball swerved madly away from the plate. The catcher jumped two feet to his left and even then was just barely able to catch it.

"Strike three," bellowed the umpire, who could scarcely believe how far the ball had moved. Rube grinned and held his arms far apart to show how far outside the pitch had ended up.

At the plate, batting third in the line-up, Rube got five hits in eight at bats. Two of them were home runs. After the second one, which cleared the centerfield fence by forty feet, Rube decided to put on a show. As he trotted around the bases he provided the commentary. When he touched first he yelled, "At the quarter Waddell leads by a head." At second he yelled, "At the half it's Waddell by a length." When he reached third he called out, "Ladies and Gentlemen, Waddell is now ahead by a furlong," and then he slid into home and announced, "This concludes the latest demonstration by the greatest hitter in the game." Then he got up and bowed. The bugs loved it.

The Los Angeles Times scribe wrote,

> "Rube Waddell had a lady love in the grand stand today. Rueben is a lover, a squire of dames if you please. It is just for a girl that Rube is fanning out the Skeeters instead of playing in one of the big eastern leagues. He couldn't tear himself away when their seasons opened."

That night Rube celebrated with teammates at a restaurant that was among his favourites because of the huge portions of food they served. Loo Loo boosters kept buying him drinks. When he got to his hotel room just after 1 a.m. the night clerk told him there was a message for him. The message was a note. It was written on fancy linen paper and the handwriting was neat and clear. The note read . . .

My dearest Edward,
It is with a great deal of sorrow and regret that I must inform you
that my father has forbidden me to see you again.
I shall miss you more than you can know. Take care of yourself
and try not to think of me, though I shall often think of you.
With the greatest affection,
Miranda

Rube got almost no sleep. He was far too upset. The next morning he went down to the lobby. Ernie Wilson was at the desk buying a newspaper. "Wanna get some breakfast, Rube?" he asked.

"Not hungry," Rube answered.

"What? You, not hungry?"

Rube walked out of the hotel. Curious, Ernie followed him. Rube seemed to be heading for the peer. Ernie, whose legs were much shorter, struggled to keep up. "Where you headed, Rube? What's the big hurry?"

Rube ignored him and kept right on walking. When he reached the peer he walked straight out to the end. As he reached the railing he showed no sign of stopping.

"Rube! What are ya doing?" Ernie yelled.

"Killing myself," Rube answered. He dove headfirst into the ocean.

Ernie ran and looked over the railing. He tried not to laugh at what he saw. Rube had expected to dive into ten feet of water and drown but the tide was out. His head and shoulders were buried deep in mud. It took three men to extricate him.

Rube stayed in that night. He told the night clerk to send a bottle of bourbon up to his room. He got undressed and sipped away at the whiskey. At eleven o'clock there was a knock on the door. It was a bellhop. He handed Rube a telegram. Rube gave him a dime.

"*Thanks*, Mister Waddell," said the boy. "Most guests tip a nickel."

The telegram read, "Dear Rube. Must have you in Philadelphia. Your salary will be $400 per month. A ticket will be waiting for you at the train station. Signed, Connie Mack."

Rube set the telegram on the dresser. He looked out his window at the lights of downtown Los Angeles and at the palm trees that lined the boulevards. He thought about Miranda and about James Morley and the Loo Loo players who had been so good to him. Mostly he thought about

Miranda. He smoked one cigarette after another.

Finally he got into bed, though he didn't know if he could sleep with all that was weighing on his mind. He tossed and turned and then finally drifted off. He dreamt about fishing in the streams back in Pennsylvania.

The next morning he packed his trunk and headed to the train station. When he got there James Morley and several of his teammates surrounded him and pleaded with him to stay in Los Angeles. Rube had no idea how they had found out he was leaving. He broke down in tears.

"I'm sorry. I won't go," he told Mr. Morley. "You've been so good to me. I don't know what I was thinking." He handed Morley his train ticket as proof that he would stay in town.

The next day Connie Mack found out that Rube hadn't boarded the train back east. He wasn't prepared to give up, his Athletics desperately needed pitching and he knew there was no one better than Rube. He sent him another telegram offering even more money along with a promise that Rube could have days off whenever he wanted. Then he placed a phone call to Ban Johnson to tell him what had happened when Rube had tried to leave Los Angeles.

"I'll take care of it," Johnson told him. "Waddell would be a terrific asset. A lot of teams are after him and we must have him in the American League."

When he got off the phone Johnson contacted the Pinkerton Detective Agency. Connie sent Rube another telegram. Rube wired him back. *"Send me $100 cash and come and get me."*

Ban Johnson figured it would be easier to get Waddell out of California if they did it from somewhere other than Los Angeles so when the Loo Loos got to San Francisco for a series two Pinkerton agents waited for Rube at the team's hotel.

Rube didn't unpack his trunk. The next morning before the rest of the Loo Loos woke up the Pinkerton men hustled Rube out of the hotel to the train station. They boarded a Sante Fe Limited express and headed to Philadelphia. No more playing against Skeeters and Ponies. Rube was going back to the major leagues where he belonged.

RUBE WADDELL
KING *of the* HALL *of* FLAKES

CHAPTER TWENTY

THE BEST START EVER

Connie Mack received an urgent message in Baltimore where the Athletics were playing. As usual Rube had made new friends. During a stopover in Kansas City he had gotten to know featherweight boxing champion William Rothwell and his trainer Jim Manning. Rube had shown such interest in the fight game and in learning how to box that he was considering staying in Kansas City.

Mack hopped on a train to Kansas City to personally escort Rube the rest of the way to Baltimore. When he got there he reminded Rube that he had agreed to play for the Athletics and managed to get him back en route. He had made such an impression on Rothwell that he and Manning got on the train with their new best friend.

In spite of the four-day trip from Los Angeles Rube was raring to get started when he and Mack reached Baltimore.

"I want to pitch today, Connie," he announced.

"There's no need to hurry things, Eddie, you just got here. Settle in and get to know your new teammates, you can pitch tomorrow or the next day."

"Ah, come on, Connie. I don't need to settle in. I'll be just fine."

Mack reluctantly agreed. The Baltimore Orioles were a mere shadow of the powerhouse they had once been, so he figured Rube should have an easy time of it. He didn't.

Doc Powers, the Athletics' catcher, had never caught Rube when they were briefly teammates in Louisville. He held a degree in dentistry but had received no training in how to handle curve balls that broke as much as Rube's. Several of his strikes ended up as passed balls. He may have been unnerved by Powers' misses, or by the ceaseless hounding from John McGraw, the irascible Baltimore manager, or perhaps even Rube's boundless energy was a little drained after a cross country train ride. Whatever the reason, he walked three batters, hit two others, committed an uncharacteristic balk, and deservedly lost his first start in

RUBE WADDELL

Philadelphia 7-3.

      ℃   *℃*   *℃*

Mack, a former catcher himself, knew he needed someone else to catch Rube. Benjamin Shibe had never played baseball, but he had made a lot of money making baseball equipment. He'd used a chunk of it to buy the Athletics. Connie Mack told Shibe that Ossee Schreckengost, Schreck, as everyone called him, had the best glove behind the plate he had ever seen and Shibe bought the rights to Schreck. Mack didn't know that the man with the name no one could pronounce had been Rube's battery mate in his first major league game with the Louisville Colonels back in '97.

      ℃   *℃*   *℃*

The Orioles followed the Athletics to Philadelphia and Rube faced them again on July 1 at Columbia Park, which was bordered by 29th Street, Oxford Street, 30th Street, and Columbia Avenue. With Schreck behind the plate Rube was back in form. He wanted revenge for what the Orioles had done to him in Baltimore. He got it.

He faced the minimum 27 batters. Only once before had a major league twirler struck out the side in nine pitches. Rube did it in the third inning and again in the sixth. A big crowd had turned up to see the new pitcher who'd come all the way from California. Though a number of cranks had seen him pitch against the cross-town Phillies when he was with the Pirates, he was playing for the home side now and they roared their approval

In the press box atop the grandstand there was the usual cloud of cigar smoke and profanity. But there was an unfamiliar new sound. Almost all of the "ink-stained wretches" pecked away at the writing machines that had recently come into use. As Rube whiffed the side in the ninth the reporter from *The Philadelphia Record* pounded away at his typewriter that "the ball came across the plate as though it was shot from a cannon."

Only two Orioles reached base the whole afternoon. In the second inning Wilbert Robinson dribbled a ground ball past third baseman Lafayette Cross for a single. Cross, the team captain who everyone called Lave, had a long nose and his ears stuck out so far from his head they looked as though he'd stolen them from an elephant. When Robinson took his lead at first Schreck threw behind the batter and nailed Robinson without even coming out of his crouch.

Baltimore's only other hit came in the seventh, another weak single, this one off the bat of Cy Seymour. Desperate to get something going or to unnerve Waddell, McGraw sent Seymour to second on the next pitch. Schreck fired a strike to Montgomery 'Monte' Cross, the shortstop who, like first baseman Harry Davis and left fielder Danny Murphy, grew up just blocks from Columbia Park. Seymour was out by a country mile.

Rube knocked in his new team's first run by rattling a double off the left field wall. Ralph "Socks" Seybold, who sported a big nose and high, arching eyebrows and at 5'11" was tall even for an outfielder, drove in another run in the sixth to put Philadelphia ahead 2-0. When he came out for the bottom of the ninth Rube waved his cap at the grandstand and yelled, "It's all over now folks. You can go on home now."

Once again he struck out the side. A small mob dashed onto the diamond and carried their new hero off the field on their shoulders.

"Appears they're kinda fond of you," said Schreck. Rube just grinned. He and his catcher went out to partake of some of their favorite potations after the game.

                lo   lo   lo

"Say, Ossee, we made quite a pair out there today," Rube roared after their third libation at Shaver's Bar & Grill. He was in such a good mood he tipped the waiter two bits.

"You sure showed them saps, Eddie," Schreck said. "Did you see the sour look on McGraw's puss when you struck out the side in the ninth?"

"Looked good on the little cuss, didn't it?"

"You must have enjoyed sticking it to him after the things he's said and done to you. Let's have another round."

A few minutes and three beers later Rube asked Schreck, "Did you see the gal that just came in?"

Schreck turned his chair around so he could see her better. "Hot damn, she's built like a brick shithouse."

"The girl could start her own creamery," said Rube.

When they went over to her table to try to persuade her to join them they were forced to amend their assessment. Before they even reached her they took a detour, pretending they had been heading to the back door on their way to the outhouse.

"That was close," said Schreck. "She coulda turned us to stone with that face."

"The last time I saw a face like that it had a hook in its mouth," said Rube.

"Ya, but those knockers."

"I suppose the face could be forgiven, Ossee. After all, you aren't looking at the mantelpiece when you're poking the fire."

"I'll drink to that," said Schreck as he threw his arm around Rube's shoulders and they headed back to the bar.

It would be the first of many such celebrations. The boisterous battery mates roomed together, drank together, hunted and fished together, and very often got in hot water together.

The Athletics hosted Washington for a Fourth of July doubleheader. The morning game drew just over 8,000 spectators and more than 12,000 came to see Rube pitch the matinee. He was not as his best, giving up five runs to the Senators in the first inning alone. The spectators letting off fireworks to celebrate the occasion rattled him a little but he managed to hold on for a 12-9 win as the Philadelphia bats came alive for him. He showed Connie Mack and the Philadelphia faithful that he could bear down, work out of jams and win, even if he didn't have his usual pinpoint control.

He next pitched in Boston and had a 2-0 lead until the sixth when Freddy Parent reached him for a two-run homer. From then on Rube and the Americans' starter Bill Dinneen both put up zeroes inning after inning.

"How much longer do you think you can keep this up?" Socks Seybold asked Rube while Dinneen was shutting down their teammates once again in the fourteenth.

Rube pointed at Dinneen. "As long as he can."

In the top of the seventeenth Monte Cross finally put the Athletics ahead with a leadoff home run. Schreck followed with a triple and Rube knocked him in with a long sacrifice fly. He shut out the Americans in the bottom of the seventeenth and closed out his third straight win.

He beat Boston again three days later. Then he beat the White Stockings twice. Then he got two wins in relief against the Cleveland Blues. In the second one, with two out in the ninth he got two strikes on Harry Bay, the Blues' centerfielder and then called for time. No one knew what could be wrong.

"Everyone can go home now," Rube yelled toward the grandstand. "Game's over."

The cranks laughed while Harry Bay fumed in the batter's box.

"Throw the fucking ball, ya big lout," he bellowed. "I'm gonna knock the next one down yer throat." He swung hard at Rube's next offering, a wicked curve, and missed it by a foot.

"Close, Harry," said Schreck. "You just missed it."

&c   &c   &c

During the first three weeks of July, Rube had put together nine straight wins and pulled the Athletics from fourth place, just a game over .500, to eight games above .500 and just a half game out of first. Connie Mack was very happy he had brought Rube back east. Pennant fever was in the air in Philadelphia on Saturday, July 26. The St. Louis Browns were in town. The Athletics had lost the first two games of the series, but now Rube Waddell would be pitching. The skies were dark and threatening, but by 9:30 in the morning Columbia Park was filled to the brim to see the man who had turned things around so dramatically for the Athletics.

When the last of the seats was taken bugs lined the base paths and encircled the outfield. Those turned away climbed trees or telephone poles to see the action. Others stood on the roofs of nearby houses. Another crowd formed downtown outside the office of *The Philadelphia Inquirer*. Clerks inside talked to reporters at the park by telephone and then relayed the game's developments to the people in the street using megaphones.

"What is all this infernal commotion?" a woman in a huge summer bonnet asked. She hugged her poodle close to her chest as she and her husband tried to elbow their way through the tightly-packed crowd.

A man in a fedora and a suit he had obviously bought at a thrift store turned to look at her and said, "Didn't ya hear, lady? The A's are playing. And Rube's pitching." She gave him a withering look.

"Waddell. Rube Waddell, only the greatest pitcher ever," he explained.

The woman harrumphed and pushed ahead without the slightest idea what the man was talking about. Inside Columbia Park, Rube was putting on another show.

"You love the big crowds, don't ya?" Schreck said as they walked off the diamond after Rube had thoroughly embarrassed another St. Louis hitter by blazing two shoots by him and then tossing a wobbler that the man waved at helplessly.

Rube allowed just five hits. Whenever he got into trouble he would wink at Schreck, nod, and then calmly strike out the next batter. He was up 3-0 in the ninth with one out when one of the Browns lined a fadeaway that had caught a little too much of the strike zone between first and second. Rube crossed up Bobby Wallace, the next batter, and he hit a lazy fly ball to the outfield. It should have been a routine catch for Socks Seybold, but not today. The ball landed in among the crowd that stood fifteen rows deep inside the outfield walls.

According to the ground rules for the day, the umpire ruled Wallace's fly ball a double and ordered the base runner home. With Wallace now on second and a run in, the tying run came to the plate. There was still just one out. The crowd grew nervous for the first time.

Downtown, in front of *The Inquirer* office a little boy turned to his father and said, "Can Rube do it, daddy? He must be getting tired."

"Don't you worry about Rube, son, he could pitch another ten innings and those Browns wouldn't touch him again."

Back at Columbia Park, Schreck went out to the mound to talk to Rube. "What do you want to give this sumbitch?"

"Nuthin' but shoots, Ossee, nuthin' but shoots."

"What about a bender or two?"

"Nuthin' but shoots."

"All right Eddie, if you say so."

Each of Rube's three next pitches seemed faster than the last. The batter offered at one of them but just stood mesmerized as strike three exploded into Ossee's mitt.

"What'll it be tonight Eddie, steak and ale?"

"No, Ossee, I believe I am in the mood for oysters and champagne."

Their conversation ended right there. Rube was surrounded once again and carried off the field.

℃ ℃ ℃

Rube and Schreck were eating fried clams, smoking, and sipping brandy in The Lazy Duck two or three stops after their oysters and champagne at The Boathouse when Schreck said, "Eddie, do you see that fella sitting alone at the bar?"

"The man in the seersucker suit?"

"Ya, him."

"What about him?"

"He was at The Purple Onion last night and I saw him at The Boathouse too."

"You did? That's peculiar."

"Do you recognize him?"

"I don't know. Wait and see if he looks this way."

A minute later the man looked over at Rube. As soon as he realized that he was watching him the man pretended to be checking out a woman at another table.

"That's Jim Manning, Ossee. Are ya sure he was at The Purple Onion and the Boathouse too?"

"Yes, I'm sure. Who's Jim Manning?"

"He trains Willie Rothwell, the featherweight champion."

"Where do you know him from?"

"We met up in Kansas City, when I was on the way back from California. He came with Connie and me to Baltimore." Rube went over and invited Manning to join him and Schreck.

After a couple of drinks Manning admitted why he was there. Connie Mack had hired him to keep an eye on Rube. "He told me it was for your own good. That you'd pitch a lot better if you weren't out carousing every night."

Rube confronted Mack the next day. "What's the big idea of you hiring somebody to watch me?"

"I'm sorry Eddie, I guess it was a rotten thing to do. But we both know you can get yourself into a lot of trouble when you are out ... celebrating."

"Maybe the odd time. But it still isn't right what you did."

"No, it wasn't. I am going to fire Manning right away."

"Now just a minute."

"What is it? I said I would fire the man."

"Ah heck, I don't want to see Jim lose his job. I guess it won't be that much of a bother to have him tailing me. I do want to keep pitchin' well. Maybe he can help keep me on the straight and narrow."

Manning kept his job and Rube behaved himself, at least better than he usually did.

       ℓ   ℓ   ℓ

Rube was still in fine form at the beginning of August when he took the mound in Chicago on August 3rd. A lot of cranks who'd rooted for him when he was with the Orphans whooped when he struck out nine White Stockings, even though he lost 3-1.

Then he lost to Cleveland in spite of a dozen strikeouts. Connie Mack had promised him a few days off if he beat Cleveland. Rube took off anyway. When he showed up in Detroit five days later Rube's teammates expected Mack to give him Hell. But all Connie said was, "Suit up, Eddie, it's your turn."

The Athletics had been hitting the cover off the ball earlier in the year but they couldn't buy a hit now. Though they were just three games back in the unbelievably tight and exciting 1902 pennant race, they'd fallen back down to fourth place. That didn't bother Rube, he'd just shut out the Tigers until his mates figured out a way to push a run across the plate.

It turned out Rube would have to take care of the run producing as well as the run preventing. The score was 0-0 after twelve innings. He went up to bat with a runner on first in the top of the thirteenth.

As he left the on-deck circle and strode toward the plate he called over to the bench, "Don't worry fellas, I'm gonna take care of this affair right here and now."

He took the first pitch for a called strike and then lined the second one all the way to the wall in right center. He slid into third with a triple and the runner in front of him scored easily. It was Rube's third hit of the game.

"That should do it," he said to the Tiger third baseman.

He blanked the Tigers in the bottom of the thirteenth and he and Schreck went off to celebrate again. A couple of times they slowed down to make sure they didn't lose Jim Manning.

CHAPTER TWENTY ONE

TEAMS HAVE TO CHEAT
TO HAVE A PRAYER

When the Tigers came to Philadelphia for a series Rube faced them again. He outhit them. Rube had three hits - now six in his last nine at bats - and the Tigers got two. Once again he shut them out and the Athletics inched into second place, just two games back now.

Rube pitched at least two innings in all four of the games with Detroit. In the last one he took the mound in the seventh and was up by a run in the bottom of the ninth with two out. He called time and waved the outfielders off the field.

"Not allowed," the umpire bellowed. "They have to stay."

"Take a rest then, boys. Have a seat behind the infielders," Rube instructed them. They sat on their gloves.

"Get used to it," Topsy Hartsel told Socks Seybold. "Rube pulls this shit all the time. It'll get worse before it gets better."

"The cranks sure love it. Think he can pull it off?" Seybold asked.

"I wouldn't bet against him. He can usually get batters out when he takes it easy. When he bears down, they don't stand a chance."

He threw three wide ones to the next batter. The crowd, which had been cheering Rube's antics, grew deadly silent.

"Quit clowin' around," Schreck yelled out.

"Just making things interestin'," Rube yelled back. He blazed three fast ones past the next batter and the Athletics took over first place.

The White Stockings came to town next. They were jockeying with the Athletics, the Browns, and the Boston Americans for the league lead. Ben Shibe had Columbia Park's bench seats narrowed so he could fit more of them in and 18,765 tickets were sold for the game on Saturday. It was a league record.

Mack had given Rube a couple of days off and he was ready and raring to go. The crowd was in seventh heaven as he struck out five of the first nine batters. After Rube nailed down a 2-1 win, cardboard programs and straw hats filled the air. The boosters in the outfield ran in to mob Rube, who sprinted to the safety of the clubhouse.

"Affection's one thing," he yelled to Schreck, "smothering's another."

— — —

When Rube lost 5-2 back in Chicago three days later Connie Mack figured he needed a bit of a break. He rested him for a series with the Browns. Philadelphia won the first two games and moved two full games ahead of St. Louis, but when Fred Mitchell, the fourth man in the Athletics' rotation, gave up three runs at the start of the third game Mack looked down the bench at Rube. "Could you put a stop to this, Eddie?"

Rube grabbed his glove. "I sure can." He strode to the mound to the delight of the crowd.

Schreck hit a home run to right in the third and Rube followed with one to left. Apart from an unearned run in the eighth, he blanked the Browns the rest of the way. The A's won 12-4 and the giddy crowd spilled into the streets yelling. "Rube, Rube, he's our man. If he can't get 'em, no one can."

— — —

Mack slated Rube to pitch in Chicago on August 28. The White Stockings believed they had a way to beat him. For a full day the grounds crew had soaked the South Side Park diamond between home and third base. The Chicago hitters would lay down one bunt after another and hope the big lefty would slip.

"What kind of foul play is this?" Mack bellowed when he saw the field. No one had ever heard Connie yell at anyone, even an umpire. "Find some tools, men, we're going to fix this mess." He and five of his players spent more than an hour and did their best to mix dirt in with the mud. Mack wasn't sure they'd done enough.

It was hard for a batter just to make contact with one of Rube's pitches let alone do what he wanted with the ball. The White Stockings did manage to lay down a couple of bunts, but Rube fielded them successfully, slipping just a little on one of them. For the most part the White Stockings couldn't get their bats on the ball for *any* kind of hit. Rube stroked a triple in the eighth that drove in the winning run.

— — —

On the first of September in St. Louis, Jimmy McAleer, the Browns' short-haired, clean-shaven manager, tried another stunt to beat Waddell.

"Find a pair of binoculars," he told Jiggs Donahue, the Browns' big-eared backup catcher.

"Where am I gonna I find binoculars?" asked Donahue.

"Get the ones you bench jockeys use to check out women in the stands."

"Oh, right. What d'ya want me to do with them?"

"I want you to put a coat over your uniform and sit out in the center field bleachers."

"And do what, Jimmy?"

"Get the signs the A's are using, that's what. Now get out there."

It took Schreck three innings to smell a rat. He noticed that the Browns were letting all of Rube's shoots go by and confidently stepping into his fadeways as if they knew when they were coming. He knew Rube didn't tip off his pitches the way some twirlers did, so there had to be something else going on. Schreck told Connie to start watching the bleachers. It didn't take long for him to spot the culprit. In spite of the afternoon heat, there was a man in the front row of the center field bleachers wearing an overcoat. He had a clear view of home plate and he had something in his hands that looked like a pair of binoculars.

Connie nudged Ed Plank who was sitting beside him to the bench. "Hey, college man."

"Yes, Mister Mack."

"Have you noticed anything funny going on?"

"Well, Rube doesn't seem to be fooling the hitters the way he normally does if that's what you mean."

"That's exactly what I mean. The Browns seem to know exactly what he's going to throw."

"How can that be?"

"Take a look at the man in the heavy coat in the front row of the bleachers."

"A coat? In this heat? He must be crazy."

"Not quite. Watch what he's doing."

Plank watched. Every time the man held his arms up straight in the air, Rube threw a shoot. And every time the man held his arms out at his sides, Rube threw a curve.

Mack called time and went out to tell the umpire what the Browns were doing. Knowing Connie's reputation for honesty and fair play the umpire immediately called McAleer off the bench.

"What kinda game are you playin', McAleer?" he demanded.

"What are ya talkin' about, ump? We're playin' square."

"You're doing no such thing," said Mack.

"What d'ya mean?"

"We spotted your man."

"Who?"

"Donahue. That's who. Is he on the bench?"

"Who, Jiggs?"

"Ya. Jiggs," said the umpire. "Where is he?"

McAleer squinted at the bench. "He should be there. Hey fellas, anybody seen Jiggs?"

"You know perfectly well where he is, Jimmy," said Connie, with a sharp edge to his voice.

"Where's that, Connie?"

"In the center field bleachers, that's where."

"What are ya talking about? Why would he be out there?"

"Because you sent him out there."

"I never did any such thing. Honest."

"Really, Jimmy, you expect us to believe that, the way your hitters have been staring out there between pitches."

The umpire told the managers to follow him and headed out towards center field. A group of Browns gathered around them.

Connie pointed at Donahue, who was doing his best to slide under his seat. "There he is," said Mack, pointing at Donahue. "How are doing, Jiggs? Or should I say, what are you doing?"

"Watchin' the game is all," Jiggs replied innocently.

"Still denying it, Jimmy?" the umpire asked.

Jesse Burkett, the Browns' talented but slow-witted left fielder mumbled, "Oh well, we got away with it for a while."

The umpire overheard him and threw McAleer and Donahue out of the game. Unfortunately, the tipped off Browns had already done enough damage and won the game, 5-1. Now Boston was just one game back of Philadelphia.

℀   ℀   ℀

At 4:00 a.m. the A's train to Detroit was travelling along the Wabash River valley near Peru, Indiana when the players were jolted from their sleep by an awful screeching sound.

"What in the hell was that noise?" Schreck asked Rube.

"I don't know, Ossee, but it can't be anything good."

Their car lurched abruptly and violently forward. Everything went black and then the car tipped on its side along with the other cars around it. All of the players were thrown from their Pullman berths.

"Lord thunderin' Jesus!" Schreck yelled.

Rube yanked Ossee to his feet. They stood on the wall of the car, which was now the floor. "Let's get outta here while we still can."

With difficulty they made their way to the door and hopped out into the cool night air. Most of the players stood around smoking and talking while they waited for the arrival of equipment that would haul the train back up onto the tracks, but Rube was in his element. He grabbed a pair of old gloves and dug right in, working with the repair crew that was wedging boards up against the wheels. After an almost seven-hour delay the train was vertical again and Rube had made more new friends.

When they arrived in Detroit the A's were exhausted. Rube should have been more tired than anyone, especially since he'd pitched three complete games in the past five days, but he told Connie he was fine and took the mound for the early afternoon start. He won 5-1.

"That was really something," Ed Plank said to Danny Murphy as Rube did handsprings to the bench after getting the last Tiger batter to pop out.

"What was?"

"The way Rube could pitch that well after being up all night."

"Hell, Ed, it wasn't anything special."

"What do you mean?"

"Haven't you heard? Rube's *usually* up all night."

🍺   🍺   🍺

Normally Connie Mack would have been more than happy to see Rube returning to the team's hotel so early when he came in just before 10 p.m. the next night. But he was being led through the lobby by a large police constable.

Connie, who had been reading a newspaper, went to ask what Rube had done this time. "I hope it was nothing serious, officer."

"Well, sir, Mister Waddell is guilty of a misdemeanor, disturbing the peace to be precise. He was shooting at cans out behind a drinking establishment a few moments ago."

"Will he be required to go to jail?"

"No, but there is a fine."

"And how much is his fine?"

"It's ten dollars."

RUBE WADDELL

Without bothering to ask Rube if he had ten dollars, Connie extracted a ten dollar bill from his wallet and handed it to the constable. The constable said, "Thank you, sir," and left. Rube shrugged his shoulders and headed up the stairs to his room.

After finishing his pipe and his newspaper Connie decided to take a stroll in the cool September air before turning in. He wanted something to take home to his wife so he was looking in storefront windows to get some ideas. After a couple of blocks he heard noise coming from a bar called The Devil's Due. He looked inside and was a bit surprised to see a police constable sitting in a booth with his back to the window. He was with someone, another man he thought, though he couldn't be sure. On the table in front of the police man was a crumpled ten dollar bill.

When the constable turned toward the bar to call for another round Connie realized that it was the same constable to whom he had given ten dollars an hour and a half ago. And he now saw the constable's drinking companion. It was Rube.

CHAPTER TWENTY TWO

A RUN AT THE PENNANT

His on-going revelry may have been catching up with Rube while the Athletics were in Cleveland to play the Blues on the last leg of their western swing. Connie had to pull him out of a game for the first time when he started giving up walks and hits even to Cleveland's weakest hitters. He started two days later against Addie Joss, the Blues' young ace, in front of a capacity crowd. Figuring that, with the exception of Napoleon Lajoie, the Blues couldn't hit the ball that hard, he decided to throw nothing but junk, especially to the batters at the bottom of the order. As a result, several reached base and there were usually runners on when the top of the order came to bat. But every time it happened Rube would just bear down and retire the side.

In the ninth, Rube was at it again, tempting the fates once more with the A's up by just one run. With two outs Schreck went out to the mound after Rube had walked the third batter and allowed the fourth to punch the ball past third for a single that put runners on the corners. "Eddie, you can't keep getting away with throwin' that shit."

"Why not? I got two outs. We gotta get the cranks on the edge of their seats before we wrap it up. Besides, it drives the reporters crazy when they can't finish writin' their stories 'til the very end."

"Very clever, Eddie. But look who's coming up now?"

Rube looked over to see the next Cleveland batter coming out of the on-deck circle. He already knew that it was Napoleon Lajoie, the best hitter in baseball and the darling of all the Cleveland rooters. "That's what makes it interesting, Ossee. Don't you know anything about puttin' on a show?"

"So you planned this whole drama?"

"Course. Why d'ya think I let those last two fellas on?"

"Well don't fuck it up, Mister Showman."

Rube cringed a little when the umpire deemed his first two pitches to be outside. Rube could hardly groove one down the middle to Lajoie, but he was being a bit too careful. He fired a shoot past him for strike one but Lajoie tied into the next pitch and sent it sailing toward the right field foul pole. The crowd rose as one and let out a roar. The ball was fair when it reached the pole but it kept slicing and ended up foul by a few feet after veering around the pole. The boosters let out a collective groan as the ball landed in the seats.

"Foul ball," yelled the umpire. "They really ought to change that rule," he muttered to himself.

"That was close," Rube whispered to himself.

He decided to mix Lajoie up with a wobbler. It bounced in the dirt and would have bounded past most catchers, but Schreck just managed to block it and the runner on third retreated to the bag. Rube put everything he had into his next pitch. Lajoie was expecting a fast one after the wobbler. He swung as hard as he could and the bugs jumped up in anticipation of another long hit. Lajoie made contact, but nothing like he had a moment before. This time he'd just missed hitting the sweet spot. The ball climbed slowly and then died. Harry Davis called for it and made the easy catch.

"You lucky sonofabitch," said Schreck as Rube strode off the mound.

"Never any doubt my good man, never any doubt."

Two days later Connie Mack handed the ball to Rube yet again. The Athletics got out to a big lead but the Blues fought back. With the bases loaded in the ninth Rube struck out the last two batters for an 8-5 victory.

The Athletics were in first place. Rube had been with them for only 75 days and he'd won twenty games with just two losses. No twirler had contributed so greatly to his team's success since the mound was moved back to sixty feet in '93 and teams had begun using more than two starters. No other pitcher in the next 115 years would ever get off to such an incredible start.

The Athletics played two games against the Orioles and Rube won them both in relief. He'd pitched nine times in two weeks and he'd won seven games. No major leaguer would ever rack up that many victories in such a short space of time.

Between the two Thursday, September 11 games an odd-looking man in a wrinkled suit lugged a huge contraption onto the field. A young assistant followed behind, carrying a tripod. The older man went to the

A's bench and spoke with Connie Mack.

"My name is Siegmund Lubin, Mister Mack," the man said in a thick accent. "I am a feelm maker."

Lubin, a Jewish immigrant from Eastern Europe, was an optical and photography expert from Philadelphia who had been intrigued with Thomas Edison's motion picture camera and saw the potential in selling similar equipment and making films of his own. He'd built a combination camera/projector, which he called a Cineograph, rented space on the roof of a building in Philadelphia's red light district for two dollars a week to use as a studio, and begun making films for commercial release.

His first films, which he used to display his new equipment at the Pan-American Exposition in Buffalo, featured his two daughters having a pillow fight and a horse eating hay. He'd gone on to make classics called "A Cake Walking Horse", "Feeding the Rhinoceros", and the provocative sounding "How Bridget Served the Salad Undressed."

Mostly, Lubin stole plots from others. He'd shot his own versions of "The Great Train Robbery" and "Uncle Tom's Cabin", movies that Edwin S. Porter, a former employee of Edison, had made. Then he'd hired two Pennsylvania railwaymen to re-enact the hugely popular film recording of the Corbett-Fitzsimmons fight. Missing from Lubin's remake was the pistol-toting former marshall who'd refereed and provided security for the fight, Wyatt Earp. Now the fledging motion-picture companies had figured out that they could attract bigger audiences if they filmed real ballplayers in action. That was why Lubin was at the game he told Mack.

"I vould like to make a feelm of your famous twirler, Rube Waddell, Mister Mack," he told Connie, wiping sweat from his brow.

"I see. I believe Rube would enjoy that," said Mack, grinning and looking around. "He must be around here somewhere."

The young assistant spotted Rube first. "There he is, Mister Lubin," he yelled.

Rube was standing next to the grandstand talking to two young kids. Lubin went over to him.

"Good afternoon, Mister Waddell. My name ees Siegmund Lubin."

Rube looked him up and down curiously. "What can I do for ya, Siegmund?" he asked.

"As I haff explained to your manager I vould like to make a feelm of you. Pitching a baseball for my moving picture camera."

"Ya mean I'm gonna be playin' in the picture show arcades?"

"Zat ees correct. I vill pay you vun hundred dollars if you agree. All zat you vould need to do ees pitch the ball a few times and smile for ze camera."

Rube told Lubin he had a deal and went and got his glove. The assistant went and got Harry Howell, one of the few Baltimore players who still had a clean uniform, to pretend to bat. Lubin gave Howell twenty dollars and he paid Schreck twenty-five dollars to play the catcher. Rube mugged for the camera and used an even more exaggerated windup than he did when he was pitching for real. Lubin had to yell "Cut!" when Rube spat out a stream of tobacco juice. "Very sorry, Mister Waddell, but you should not do zat in za feelm. It might offend members of za weaker sex."

Lubin kept looking around as if he expected trouble any minute. Edison had filed suit against him and every other film-maker in America for copyright infringement. He often sent thugs to disrupt their shoots.

"I can't wait to see my mug on the big screen," Rube beamed when Lubin thanked him and handed him his money.

When Lubin and his assistant had left and the teams were getting ready for the second game Schreck told Rube he was glad the man hadn't tried to pay them with a check. He took Rube's money and hid it with his.

After the Athletics returned to Philadelphia a steady downpour gave them and Rube's arm a couple of much needed days off. On the 15th of September they played a double header against the Americans and Ed Plank won the first game 6-4. The second game, the series finale, attracted 16,000 cranks for a rematch between Rube and Cy Young.

The game was held up for a few minutes in the third inning when a crank jumped out of the stands and ran toward the mound. He had something in his hand. Rube's teammates looked alarmed and, fearing the worst, ran to restrain the man. Rube waved them away. The man, who appeared to be in his early twenties, took off his hat and handed Rube a box.

"What's this?" asked Rube.

"It's a watch, Rube."

"For me?"

"You'll see who it's for when you read the inscription. Rube opened the box and took out a beautiful pocket watch with a fob chain. Etched into the casing were the words, "To Rube Waddell, the greatest pitcher ever. From his biggest admirer."

"Mighty nice of you, but I'd best get back to work now."

Cy Young walked five and gave up eleven hits in one of his worst outings. Rube fired darts all afternoon. Schreck put his mitt where he wanted the pitch and Rube hit it every time. He struck out ten and won easily, 9-2.

Thanks to Rube's incredible run of victories the A's won the '02 pennant. The city of Philadelphia went mad. The Phillies had come close a couple of times but never delivered. A half million delirious boosters lined Broad Street, throwing their hats and yelling at the top of their lungs. Four hundred area baseball, bowling, and cycling teams marched in the parade. The A's rode in open carriages and waved at the crowd. Banners hung from the city's newly-erected telephone poles. Several had messages in praise of Rube. His favorite read, "You're a gem not a rube, Eddie Waddell."

At the ceremony that followed the victory parade, the mayor handed Rube another watch, this one inscribed with the words "In appreciation of your amazing work on behalf of the City of Philadelphia." Rube lost the watch the next night after thirty hours of non-stop celebrating and scores of free drinks.

He went to Connie Mack's office the next day. "What am I gonna do?" Rube asked mournfully. "Folks'll be some mad if they find out I lost it."

"I'll see if can get it back for you. Leave it to me."

Connie placed ads in three of the Philadelphia papers offering a twenty dollar reward for return of the watch. He was somewhat surprised to receive a telephone call from a bartender two days later. Rube and Mack went to the bar and Connie gave the man the twenty dollars and Rube got his watch back. Rube returned to the bar an hour later to begin consuming his twenty dollars of credit. He would lose the watch several more times at various establishments and each time Connie would pay the twenty dollars. Even though he knew full well what Rube was up to he never really minded. He wasn't paying Rube much of a salary considering how many games he won and the fact that he was drawing more rooters than any player in baseball ever had.

Barney Dreyfuss, whose Pirates had clinched the National League championship, had issued a challenge to Connie Mack as soon as it became clear that the A's would win the American League pennant. He'd proposed a ten-game series with $5,000 going to the winners. But when the season ended, Dreyfuss sent Connie another message. Initially left alone by the rival league, the Pirates' owner had since seen several of his best players, including Jack Chesbro, stolen by American League teams. He was outraged and he rescinded his challenge. There would be no championship series in 1902.

Rube had really wanted get the chance to get back at his old team, but perhaps another ten games in which he likely would have pitched six or more times might have been a bit too much even for him. He'd pitched 274 innings during the last 87 games of the Athletics' season but he had also pitched a fair chunk of the Pacific Coast League season.

The day after the last game of the season Rube picked up a newspaper in which he found his totals with Los Angeles and Philadelphia combined.

G	GS	CG	W	L	INN	Hits	K's	BB's	E.R.A
53	46	45	36	15	452	352	352	101	2.05

CHAPTER TWENTY THREE

AN OSTRICH, A GATOR,
AND A MOTORCYCLE

William Chase Temple was a wealthy sportsman who had once owned shares in the Pittsburgh Pirates. He was now one of the trustees of Rollins College, a small, private Christian college in Winter Park, Florida. Rollins had a good baseball team but they had just lost a big series to their chief rivals from Stetson University in nearby Deland. Stetson's success was largely due to its penchant for "borrowing" minor leaguers and semi-professional players. Temple figured it was time to even up the odds.

He contacted his friend Connie Mack. At first Connie thought it best that Rube rest his arm, but then he decided Rube would probably get into a lot less trouble at a Christian school than he would in a big city full of admirers eager to buy him drinks. So, at Mack's urging, Rube headed back to college. He enrolled in the business school, with no intention of actually attending classes. On campus he stood out like a sore thumb, towering over everyone and eating enough for a small army in the college dining hall.

To Rube's delight, Rollins was co-ed and he took an interest in more than just the food. He strode around the campus eying the fresh-looking and enticing young women. At first he stayed in a room on campus, but the college president quickly decided it would be best if he stayed in town. He was given an apartment above a grocery store. There would be lots of food there, but no college girls to tempt him.

Rube was immediately installed as the team's starting pitcher but he wasn't able to pitch. No one could - or would - catch for him. Ralph Evernden, the team's regular catcher, was a small young man and Rube's speed balls literally knocked him on the seat of his pants. Someone else would have to catch when Rube pitched. Temple knew just the man. Connie Mack got another call and Ossee Schreckongost was put on a train to Florida.

⚙ ⚙ ⚙

"You weren't kidding, Eddie. These college girls are a sight for sore eyes," he told his battery mate on their first stroll through the campus.

"Look at that one," said Rube as a stunning redhead went by, her hips swaying from side to side.

"Hey, sugar britches, would you care to join me in a mint julep?" Schreck asked her.

The girl looked at Schreck and then at his even bigger friend and scurried away in as ladylike a manner as she could manage.

"Gonna have to be a little more subtle, Ossee," Rube warned his friend. "These girls may look like grown women - very grown judging by the way their blouses bulge - but they're about ten years younger than you are. If you use your dick as a compass it's bound ta steer you to trouble."

"I better stick to baseball and fishing or one of their daddies is gonna have me in front of a jury or a justice of the peace."

"Or a lynch mob," chuckled Rube.

"The college boys are probably a lot more charming and clever than we are, let's go see if they can hold a candle to us in our major field of study - the effects of copious quantities of alcohol on the human body."

⚙ ⚙ ⚙

With their talented new battery, the Rollins team won their next two games handily. Their next competition would be Stetson. But as soon as the arch rivals saw Waddell and Schreckongost they went straight to the train station and headed back to Deland.

Rube pitched for Rollins, but mostly he showboated, regularly calling in the fielders and then blazing three straight into the mitt of the smiling Schreck, who sat on the ground behind the plate. The two clowned around so much that they actually lost a couple of games. They spent most of their time fishing in the lakes north of Orlando.

One morning they were hiking around a swamp when they came across an unusual farm. As they got close to it they both noticed an awful smell.

"What is that revolting stench?" asked Rube.

"I have no idea, I've never smelled anything like it," said Schreck.

"What could they be raising that'd reek that bad?"

"I have no idea. Pig manure smells a thousand times better than that."

"Wait, did you see that?" Rube asked.

"What?"

"That thing. It looked like a bird, but it couldn't have been. It was way too big. Holy shit, there's another one, and another. Ossee, there's like a hundred of them!"

"They're ostriches. Haven't you ever seen one?"

"No, and I'm glad to say I've never smelled one before either."

"It's their shit that smells."

"I figured *that* much. But *damn*, they are queer-looking things."

Suddenly a young boy went by. He was riding on the back of one of the huge birds.

"What the hell? Eddie, did you see that?"

"I sure did, that was the craziest thing I've ever seen."

"I don't think birds are supposed to be ridden, even if they're that big."

"Hey, kid. Let *me* try that," Rube called out.

"What are you doing? You aren't really going to try to ride the thing, are you?" Schreck implored Rube.

"You bet your ass I am."

"I'm not the one who's gonna look like an ass."

The boy climbed off the ostrich and looked Rube up and down. "How much you weigh, mister?"

"A little over two hundred," Rube answered.

"A little?" Schreck muttered to himself. "Try a lot."

"I don't know whether I ..."

"Aw, come on kid, it'll just be for a minute. I've never ridden a bird before."

"Well, I suppose if ..."

"Thanks, kid."

It took Rube a while to climb on the ostrich and another while to stay on it - they didn't come with saddles - but he finally managed to ride it a ways. He and the ostrich seemed to travel in several different directions at once. Schreck thought he would die laughing. He wasn't sure that he'd ever seen anything so ludicrous.

The bird hadn't seemed too alarmed or indignant when it was the boy who was riding it, but it was positively apoplectic now. It began making an ungodly hissing sound and then emitted a series of low, rumbling grunts. A couple of enormous feathers flew off it as Rube tried to get some semblance of control.

"Where's your ten-gallon hat?" Screck yelled. "You can round up some cattle with that thing. Or maybe you could ride it in Buffalo Bill's Show. I don't imagine they got an ostrich rider yet."

A big man in suspenders with a shortage of front teeth burst out of the barn. He had a pitchfork in his hand and he didn't look very happy, especially when he saw what the 225-pound stranger was doing.

"Get your arse offa that bird. Now!" yelled the farmer.

Rube half jumped and half fell off of the ostrich and landed in the middle of a mud puddle.

Schreck laughed some more. "Sorry about your bird, mister, we didn't mean any harm," he assured the man. "My friend here is just the sort that has to try anything he sees and your boy here rode by on the thing, and . . . "

The farmer checked the ostrich for damage and then glared at Rube.

"What kinda man rides another man's bird?" he demanded.

Schreck had to struggle not to start laughing again when he heard that bizarre question. "Here's something for the trouble," he said, handing the farmer two dollars. "Let's go, Eddie."

After slogging around more swamps they discovered an abandoned canoe on the shore of a huge pond and decided to borrow it. They wondered what kind of fish they might see in the dark green water.

"There's something big in there," Rube said after a few minutes. "Did you see that splash near the shore?"

"No, but I heard it," said Schreck. "Let's go see what it was."

As they neared the shoreline, Rube gazed into the water. It was far too murky for him to see anything.

"I think it might be a turtle," Rube announced. "Make pretty fine soup I expect."

"Better hope it's not a snapper."

Rube reached his hand into the water. The mystery creature turned out not to be a turtle. It was an alligator, a big one, and it snapped its huge teeth around Rube's hand. He roared in pain. Schreck madly swatted away at the gator with his paddle until it released its hold. Rube's hand was bleeding badly.

Schreck tore off his shirt and wrapped it around the nasty wound. "You are damn lucky that wasn't your throwing hand," he said as he turned the canoe around and headed back.

"Damn lucky it wasn't my *head,* d'ya see the teeth on that monster?"

Connie Mack was not amused when Rube showed up at the Athletics' training camp in Jacksonville with an enormous bandage on his right hand. Apart from a few calisthenics, Rube wasn't allowed to practice lest he throw off his delivery by favoring his damaged hand. Given time off he wandered around the countryside and eventually happened upon a bunch of pigs. He chased down one and then another and played with them as though they were puppies. He started bringing one of the pigs to the training camp and when he would talk to it Schreck laughingly told the players that among his many other talents Rube spoke Hog Latin. Rube made the pig the team's mascot and named him Dick.

Rube finally persuaded Connie Mack he was well enough to pitch and Mack put him into a game against a team from the Cummer Lumber Company. For much of the game Rube had his fielders sitting on their gloves picking dandelions while he blazed pitches past the helpless locals. After winning the game 20-0 Rube yelled to the crowd that he would pitch against the Lumber Company team the next day and would not allow a single hit.

He was in rare form the next day. Whenever one of the Cummer batters got wood on the ball it invariably dribbled toward the mound. Rube would pick up the ball and fire it behind his back to first. After giving up two hits and disappointing the large crowd just a little, Rube started throwing wobblers and curves.

In the ninth he intentionally walked the first three hitters. Schreck groaned, "Here he goes again." Rube waved at his fielders. Used to the routine by now, the outfielders shuffled in and sat behind the infielders.

"Nope. Everybody off the field, he instructed, "it's an exhibition game, normal rules don't apply. All of the players, even the first base man, headed to the bench, smiling and shaking their heads.

"See ya, Rube. Have fun," they called out. He blazed nine shoots by the next three batters to end the game.

Rube was nowhere to be seen the following day. Connie Mack offered a small reward for anyone who could find him. Was he fishing, carousing, playing with pigs, or riding ostriches this time?

"Up to one of his favorite f words I expect," suggested Topsy Hartsel.

"And what might those be?" asked Socks Seybold.

"Those would of course be fastballs, food, fishing, females, fires, and firewater," Harstel explained.

It turned out to be none of them. At least not his time.

RUBE WADDELL

After having dinner at their hotel the next night a group of the players went for a walk. As a publicity stunt, the Roof Garden Theatre had hired a minstrel band to parade down Bay Street.

"Hey, look who's leading the band," said Monte Cross.

Wearing a scarlet military uniform with a three-foot tall shako, Rube marched at the head of the band, expertly twirling a baton. Every few steps he would throw it high in the air, spin around, and catch it behind his back without missing a beat.

"Rube's a one-man circus troop," said Lave Cross.

"You just never know what he's going to pull next," said Topsy.

"He sure is enjoying himself," said Connie Mack.

"Isn't he *always*?" asked Lave.

Connie Mack didn't want to upset Rube, who was obviously having a wonderful time and for a change not doing something dangerous. Mack crouched down behind a mailbox so Rube wouldn't see him. As Rube passed by he ducked down, whispered, "Hey Connie" and kept right on going.

When the Athletics headed back to Philadelphia they played an exhibition game against the Phillies. In the first inning Rube fanned all three batters. He went on to shut out the Phillies for nine innings. He looked more than ready for the real games to begin.

Given a day off Rube walked aimlessly around Philadelphia until he heard a loud noise coming from a deserted race track. The horses were long gone. They'd been replaced by colorful two-wheeled machines that were roaring around the oval spewing gigantic clouds of dust from their wheels. Rube found a man who seemed to be in charge. His name turned out to be Jack Prince. "What d'ya call those machines?" asked Rube.

"They're called motorcycles. Say, don't I know you?"

"The name's Eddie. Eddie Waddell, Mister Prince."

"You're the famous ball player. Don't they call you Rube?"

"Yepp, have been for a while. How fast do those things go?"

"Upwards of fifty miles an hour on a straightaway."

"Gee willikens, that's some fast. They hard to ride?"

"A little at first, like a bicycle only a whole lot faster."

It didn't take Rube long to get the hang of it. He told some of the Athletics about the noisy machines and when they came to check them out they saw Rube showing people how to start them up.

"Give it a try," Rube told Socks Seybold.

"I don't know," said Seybold, "I think Connie'd be awful sore if he saw us on one of those contraptions. They don't look very safe to me."

"Ya, Eddie. We got a clause in our contracts that says we're not supposed to engage in any dangerous pursuits," Lave Cross pointed out.

Knowing a good thing when he saw one, Jack Prince made Rube a track official. He sold tickets and made a big show of waving the flag to start the races. The patrons loved it and so did Rube. But when Connie Mack came and saw him speeding recklessly around the track with the orange scarf around his neck trailing straight out behind him he told him he needed to be at the ballpark.

RUBE WADDELL
KING *of the* HALL *of* FLAKES

CHAPTER TWENTY FOUR

NO MORE CRACKERS IN BED

When the Athletics arrived in Boston for their first series of the 1903 regular season Connie Mack asked Schreck to come to his hotel room. Mack was sitting at a desk by the window with a stack of papers in front of him when Ossee arrived.

"Thanks for coming up, Ossee, I have a new contract here for you. I think you are going to be quite happy with it. Even though you didn't hit all that well last year, due to your excellent work behind the plate - especially when Rube was pitching - there's a nice little raise in it for you."

Schreck looked it over. "Seems fair to me, Connie, thanks."

Mack handed Ossee his fountain pen. He didn't take it.

"What's the matter? I thought you were happy with the contract."

"Pleased as punch, but I got a problem with Rube."

"You do? I thought the two of you were as thick as the hair on a dog's back."

"We are. And I like catchin' him, even though he still hurts my hand with his speed."

"Even with that hinged glove you invented?"

"Yupp. But, at least the ball's dry when it comes in. Eddie wouldn't think of throwing spitters. Says it ain't sanitary. Last spring I asked Billy Sullivan what it's like catchin' Ed Walsh. After three or four innings he feels like he needs to wring the ball out."

"So what has Rube got to do with your contract?"

"I need a clause added to it."

"A clause that says what?"

"A clause that says Eddie can't eat animal crackers in bed anymore."

"What did you say?"

"I said I want it added to my contract that Eddie can't eat animal crackers in bed anymore. I didn't object when he brought mocking birds and a small reptile or two into our room down south, but I'm sick and tired of waking up with cowhorns and elephant tusks sticking into my ribs. Happens every morning."

Connie stifled a laugh. He thought it was by far the most unusual stipulation he'd ever been asked to consider, but he knew full well that he'd never be able to get any of the other players to room with Rube. "All right, Ossee, you've got it. Send Eddie up to see me and I'll tell him."

A few minutes later Connie had finished telling Rube that he would have to swear off eating animal crackers in bed. Rube promised he would and then went to leave.

"Just a minute, Eddie."

"What is it?"

"Sit down. I want to show you something."

Mack went and got a glass and a handkerchief from the nightstand. Inside the handkerchief were two live worms he'd pulled out of the hotel's garden.

Rube chuckled. "You fixin' ta show me a magic trick, Connie?"

"Not magic, just a bit of science."

Connie got a bottle of bourbon from his suitcase and poured three fingers of whiskey into the glass. Within a few seconds both of the worms were dead.

"Well?" asked Connie.

"Well what?"

"Do you understand what I'm trying to show you?"

"I sure do."

"And what do you suppose it is that I'm trying to show you?"

"You're trying to set my mind at ease."

"Set your *mind* at ease?"

"Yes, you're trying to show me that a drinking man doesn't ever have to worry about having worms in his stomach."

"No, that's not at all what I . . . Never mind, Eddie, get out of here. And remember, no more animal crackers."

"Right, Connie. Whiskey's okay, but no animal crackers. I got it."

"Good *night* Edward."

Connie Mack made sure Rube got in early the night before the Athletics' home opener and it paid off. The skies were dark and menacing as the mayor proudly hoisted the 1902 pennant flag over Columbia Park, but Rube brightened the atmosphere considerably by fanning ten and winning easily, 6-1.

As the season progressed, however, it became painfully obvious that, although the Athletics' line up was the same as in 1902 - with the exception of outfielder Ollie Pickering who'd come over from the Cleveland Blues - they just could not hit with any consistency. On April 24th Rube struck out ten but lost 4-0. On the 29th he finally got some runs and won a laugher. Then he disappeared.

Rube was walking along Market Street a few days after he'd left the team. He was thinking that he really should go back, but wasn't sure how he would explain his lengthy absence. Just before he reached the corner of Market Street and Franklin Avenue, Rube bent down to pet a border collie a man was walking. He heard a loud noise from directly behind him and looked around just in time to see an out of control delivery wagon bearing down on him. The wagon narrowly missed him before barrelling into a lamp post and spilling its load all over the street.

"What in the hell do you think you're doing?" Rube yelled at the two teamsters who'd climbed out to see if the horses were all right and if the wheels were still intact.

"What did you say?" one of the men replied. He had a dark beard and had a large pot belly that made his suspenders look as though they were about to burst.

"Maybe you can't hear any better than you can drive a wagon. I said what the hell do you think you're doing?"

"We didn't hit you, mister. What's your problem?" the other teamster grunted. He was tall and muscular and had huge mutton chops.

"You almost killed me and this man and his dog, you stupid fools. That's my problem."

"That's a real fine suit you're wearing. Did we get some dirt on it, dandy man?" said the first teamster. Rube noticed that both of them had nasty scars.

"How about you apologize and maybe I'll forget about how you just about ran me into the ground," Rube suggested.

"And how about you just walk away and we won't beat the livin' daylights out of you," threatened the one who'd been driving.

"I could lick the both a you with one arm tied behind my back," Rube retorted.

The driver lurched at Rube, who deftly stepped out of the way and landed a fist squarely on the man's jaw. The other one hit Rube with a glancing blow to the side of his head. Rube reeled a little but swung and hit him hard in the stomach. The man doubled over, his breath gone. Someone had obviously called the police when they saw the teamsters narrowly miss running Rube over. A constable blew his whistle and ran toward the combatants. Another policeman came out of an alley and grabbed one of the teamsters from behind.

"That'll be enough of that, ya damned hooligans," ordered the constable who'd blown the whistle.

"These galoots nearly killed me and then they wanted to fight," Rube tried to explain.

"You can tell it all to the magistrate," said the constable who'd appeared out of the alley.

Connie Mack was called to the police station that night. He and Rube were relieved when the man with the collie told the magistrate that the teamsters were the guilty parties. No charges were laid against Rube.

He started to make up a story about where he had been the past five days but Connie said, "Never mind, Eddie, just beat the Chicagos tomorrow afternoon and we'll forget all about it." Rube struck out thirteen batters the next day and beat the White Stockings 3-1.

After the game Ed Plank went over to talk to Lave Cross.

"The prick got away with it again," said Plank.

"With what?"

"Taking off on us again. The bugger gets away with murder."

"Yes, he does," Cross agreed. "But we're all real happy when he turns up and pitches like that, aren't we?"

CHAPTER TWENTY FIVE

A HOTEL ESCAPADE

The Athletics travelled to St. Louis and, as usual, Rube pitched the first game of the series. Jesse Burkett hit a home run with a man on in the first, but Rube settled down and posted goose eggs the rest of the way, striking out thirteen. Philadelphia won 4-2 and after Rube struck out the side in the ninth he did an Indian war dance off the mound.

After the game he and Schreck went for a ride on a scenic railway in Forest Park. They had only been aboard for five or ten minutes when the train jerked violently and barely managed to stay on the tracks. Rube had been leaning out the side when it happened and he was thrown several feet. He landed in the middle of a bush and was extricating himself from it when Schreck whispered, "Stay down."

"What?"

"Don't get up just yet."

"Why not?"

"Hold on to your left arm and groan."

"Why would I wanna do that, Ossee? I'm fine."

"Just do it, there's somebody coming."

Rube grabbed his arm just as the conductor and an older man in an expensive-looking suit arrived on the scene. The conductor looked at Rube and then back at the train to judge how far he'd been thrown. The other man introduced himself as the park manager. He looked worried.

"Are you hurt, sir?" he asked.

"He sure is," answered Schreck.

"I am so sorry about this, gentlemen. I really don't know how this could have happened." He gave the conductor a withering look.

"He must have been leaning out the ..."

"Silence," the manager commanded him.

"Yes, sir."

"Do you know who this is?" Schreck asked, gesturing toward Rube. He looked hard at Rube. "I'm not certain that I do."

"Have you ever heard the name Rube Waddell?" asked Schreck.

"*That's* who this is, boss, I knew he looked awful familiar," said the conductor. "I've never seen him play, but he's supposed to be about the best pitcher in baseball."

"And that, gentlemen," said Schreck, pointing at the arm Rube was holding onto, "is his throwing arm."

"Oh my," said the park manager. "Listen, I want to offer you something by way of compensation … to help you to forget about this whole unfortunate incident. Would fifty dollars suffice?"

"I think that would help to ease the pain a little," Rube told him, gently rubbing his arm and trying his best to suppress a grin.

"That was quick thinking back there," he told Ossee as they left the park.

"Are you in much pain?" asked Schreck.

"Right around fifty dollars' worth, I'd say."

"That was some pretty fair acting you did back there."

"Well then I might as well tell you."

"Tell me what?"

"I got offered a job last night while you were visitin' your aunt."

"Doing what?"

"*Acting.* I signed on with Billy Garen of the Havlin Theatre Company."

"What are you gonna be in?"

"A play called Stain of Guilt. I get forty dollars a week to play a policeman and then I do something called a tableau. It's gonna be called Reuben Striking Them Out. They're writin' it just for me."

"How are you going to do that when you got three more months of baseball left?"

"I come back here in October, soon as the season's over."

"Already a famous twirler and soon to be a world-renowned thespian," said Schreck, "your head's going to be so swollen you won't be able to fit it through doors."

"What did you call me?" Rube asked.

"A thespian."

"Watch your mouth, Ossee."

& & &

When word of his new vocation reached Philadelphia, Alf Jones, an enthusiastic cub reporter from the *Inquirer,* wondered whether Rube had any serious acting ability but suggested that "if any fruit is thrown at him he'll be able to pick it up and curve it back from whence it came with smashing effect."

Rube beat the Browns in the last game in St. Louis and then pitched a three-hit shutout to open a series in Cleveland. He beat them 3-1 in the final game there, allowing just four hits and striking out twelve. The next morning the headline at the top of the sports page of *The Cleveland Plain Dealer* read "Cleveland Wants No More Waddell."

In New York, Rube blanked the Highlanders, whom the press had labelled "the Invaders" for his fourth straight win. He struck out the side in the ninth and then danced a jig. On June 1st in Washington he shut out the Senators on two hits, facing just twenty-eight batters, one shy of a perfect game. Even the mighty Ed Delahanty could manage only two long foul balls off "the inimitable Rube."

The Athletics were in a pennant race, the closest one the young American League had seen, and Connie Mack was proving to be a genius in his lenient treatment of his outstanding new twirler. Rube wasn't at his best when he took on Bill Donovan, who had "jumped" from the Superbas to the Tigers, but he beat Detroit's new ace 4-3 for his seventh straight win to move his record to 11-3.

In his next start he beat Chicago, giving up just one run and four hits. Then he faced Cleveland and their fireballer Addie Joss. Joss could throw hard and he was in top form. For the first five innings he didn't allow a single base runner. For his part, Rube struck out five of the first six men he faced. Each team scored a run in the sixth, but that would be it for a long, long time. Rube pitched perfect ball the rest of the way. The game lasted fourteen innings. Ollie Pickering ended the thriller in the bottom of the fourteenth with a home run and was carried off the field on the shoulders of giddy cranks. *The Inquirer* gushed that it was "a game that future old-timers will talk about for years, the most sensational game of ball ever played in this city" and went so far as to propose that Rube receive laurels and have a monument erected in his honor.

Rube won his next game too, besting St. Louis 9-3 for his tenth straight victory and boosting the Athletics into first place. Though only a third of the season had been played, Rube had already struck out 138 batters. To top off the day he won an ice-cream eating contest that was held at a local drug store and then hurried to join his teammates at the train station for another western swing.

In Chicago, the White Stockings bunted on him whenever they got a chance. The ploy worked. They tired Rube out and in frustration he started throwing wild to first. He survived his errors but, with his concentration all but gone, he gave up a home run to light-hitting Nixey Callahan in the eighth, his first in five years. Little Ducky Holmes hit one in the ninth that gave the White Stockings a 2-1 win.

Rube lost his next start in St. Louis too. Then it rained for two days, a welcome relief from the heat, and Rube and Schreck used the opportunity to go fishing. When they got back they visited the bar at Sportsman's Park before getting into their uniforms. It showed in their work. Schreck made a critical error and Rube pitched as though he would rather still be fishing. Another loss. Rube and Ossee went right back to the bar after the game.

When the Athletics arrived in Detroit for their next series Connie Mack called the two together and told them they could not leave the hotel. They were not to go out - not even for a newspaper. They sat in their room for an hour playing cards, looking out the window, and feeling sorry for themselves.

"I win nine games in a row and then when I lose a couple Connie tells me to go to my room," whined Rube.

"And I make one goddam error and I'm in the doghouse," said Ossee.

"Are we really gonna sit here staring at the walls all night?"

"I don't see where we got much choice. Connie finds out we left the hotel he'll suspend us for sure."

"The hotel has liquor doesn't it?"

"Ya, so?"

"And they got room service, don't they?"

Ossee's face brightened. "Ya. They could probably send up some steaks and maybe a bottle of bourbon or two."

"Might as well. Can't dance, never could sing, and it's too wet to plough," said Rube.

The meal was hardly the best they'd had. The steaks were overcooked and the potatoes were as hard as rocks. But the bourbon tasted good enough that they soon forgot how bad the food had been. When the second bottle was almost gone Rube asked Schreck if he happened to have a baseball in his trunk.

"Why the hell would I have a baseball in my trunk?"

"Just askin', I thought we could play some catch."

"Well I ain't got no fuckin' baseball in my trunk, ya rube."

"Then find something else we can play catch with."

After rummaging around in their luggage for a few minutes they settled on a bottle of cologne. Ossee sat on the floor by the window and

Rube threw from an imaginary mound in the doorway to the bathroom. Schreck used a cushion for a mitt. Rube's first three throws were dead on target and Ossee caught them with ease.

"Strike three!" Ossee yelled at the non-existent batter. "Come on, Eddie, you can throw harder than that? You're throwin' like a little girl."

"Like a little girl, am I? How's this?"

Rube fired the bottle at Ossee, who ducked just as it was about to hit him in the head. The bottle shattered when it hit the wall. It made a large hole and its contents ran down the flowered wallpaper.

"That was a ball," announced Ossee.

"What are we gonna use now?" asked Rube.

"How 'bout this?" Ossee suggested, picking up a cigar lighter from a table.

"Good enough, Schreckie boy. Toss it over."

Rube was less accurate with the cigar lighter than he had been with the bottle of after shave. Ossee managed to corral his first pitch but the second hit the window, which shattered into even more pieces than the bottle had.

"Damn," said Ossee. "Now we're outta things to play catch with."

Rube shrugged. "If we can't play baseball, we'll have to switch over to football."

This time a pillow served as the ball. Rube scored a touchdown by reaching the end of the carpet before Ossee got to him, but the two smashed into a table, which cracked and fell apart, along with the lamp that had sat on it.

Schreck went and picked up a bottle. It was empty. He tossed it aside, smashing it. He picked up the other bottle and saw there was still some whiskey in it. "Could I interest you in another drink?" he asked Rube.

Rube stared at Ossee. "Does a duck's boner drag in the weeds?"

Somehow during the night another lamp got broken and the tub was split in two.

         *   * *   * *

Rube managed to pitch the next day and gave up only three hits, though Connie Mack could tell he was badly hung over. Schreck allowed a passed ball that led to a run. Luckily the Tigers didn't bunt very often, but the Athletics managed just five hits off Wild Bill Donovan, who edged Rube 2-1. Three days later Rube tired in the final innings and lost another close one in Cleveland, 4-3 this time. It was Rube's fourth loss in a row. In addition to looking worn out late in the games Rube wasn't striking batters out the way he usually did. Suddenly the Athletics were three games out of the lead.

      *   *   *

When they boarded the train back to Philadelphia Connie Mack told Rube he wanted to talk to him. They went to the club car together and Rube immediately ordered a whiskey. "On second thought, make it a double," he told the waiter.

"Make it a coffee," Connie told the waiter.

Rube grunted and asked Connie what he wanted to talk to him about.

"I am going to have to fine you a hundred dollars."

"A hundred dollars! For what?"

"For that deplorable hotel escapade in Detroit. When I went to pay our bill I was told about all the damage you and Ossee caused. I had to pay for the repairs."

"All right, Connie, go ahead and fine me," said Rube, getting up to leave, "but I'll tell you something."

"What's that?"

"There *ain't* no Hotel Escapade in Detroit."

CHAPTER TWENTY SIX

A BIG HITTER IN THE STANDS

The Athletics returned home for a Fourth of July double header with the Tigers. Ed Plank pitched the first game and won 4-3. Rube spent much of the game in the bleachers firing blanks from his new revolver. He pitched the second game and suffered his fifth straight loss. By the fifth inning a lot of cranks were booing him and calling for Mack to take him out. Rube knew he deserved it.

Pitching on one day of rest, Rube faced the Tigers again on July 6th and gave up five runs. Luckily Schreck homered over the right field wall in the eighth to give him a one-run lead. After he struck out the first two batters in the ninth and whizzed two fast ones by Sport McAllister, Topsy Hartsel made a terrific running catch to save the victory when McAllister drove the next pitch into deep left field.

On July 16 Rube finally returned to form against Chicago, pitching better than he had since the 14-inning marathon against Addie Joss. His shoots hit Schreck's mitt like peas shot from a canon, his drop balls baffled the batters, and his curves broke wickedly. The White Stockings didn't stand a chance. Whenever it appeared as though they were about to mount a rally, Rube snuffed it out like a candle. He struck out fourteen and the A's won 2-0.

Rube's mother arrived in Philadelphia that night for a visit. When he met her at the Broad Street station the St. Louis Browns were getting off a train along with a number of boisterous supporters who'd accompanied them. They appeared to have spent most of the trip in the bar car. Even though he'd just pitched the day before, Rube asked to work the first game against the Browns. His mom had never seen him pitch in the big leagues, she'd only read about her famous son in the newspapers.

With one out and one on in the first, Rube walked the next three batters and a run crossed the plate. The Athletics scored two of their own in the fourth, one of them on a double by Rube that brought a smile to his mother's face. "That's my *son*," she told everyone around her.

RUBE WADDELL

It was at that point that things started to get ugly. The Browns knew that some of the St. Louis bugs who were traveling with them had placed sizable wagers on them. They hadn't counted on Waddell starting again today. They figured their best chance was to distract Rube and they started to encourage their rooters to get on him.

The cranks gave it everything they had. They yelled insults, they threw potatoes, onions, tomatoes, and cantaloupes, they blew horns, and they even let off fireworks in the middle of Rube's windup. Then some of them started yelling at Rube's mother to put him off his game. Mrs. Waddell called one of them a slimy polecat, "accidentally" tripped another on his way down the aisle as he was asking her if Rube had been born in a barn, and whacked a third with her umbrella. They left her alone after that.

Rube was as mad as a wet hen. As the jeering got more intense he threw harder and harder. Maurice Blau, a well-known ticket scalper and gambler, urged the Browns' boosters to really let Rube have it.

Rube called Harry Davis over to the mound. "Jasper, where's the asshole who's getting them all riled up? I can hear him, but I can't spot him."

"He's up there," said Davis, pointing at a big man in a tweed suit wearing a derby. He was waving his arms at the rooters behind him, exhorting them to more and more outrageous behavior. He had a huge diamond ring on his left hand and had a cigar sticking out of his mouth.

"What's his name?"

"Blau. Ben Shibe says he's the worst of the gamblers, he carries out his business right out in the open like nobody can do anything to him."

Blau had often been seen moving through the stands before games arranging bets. He hung around the lobbies of hotels where the teams stayed and had tried on many occasions to get players to throw games. The St. Louis cranks hooted and howled as Rube prepared to face the next batter. "Hey farm boy, is yer pig here?" one bellowed. "Oh, wait, that's your *momma*."

That was it, Rube'd had enough. He dropped his glove, shouted "I got you, ya son of a bitch," and ran to the stands. He vaulted the railing into the box seats and ran up the aisle. When he reached Blau he knocked his hat off, pulled his cigar out of his mouth and threw it away. Then he pulled the big man out of his seat as though he were a mischievous four-year old. Alf Jones reported that Rube "shook him like a terrier. There was murder in the eyes of the famous pitcher."

Rube punched Blau once in the nose and twice in his huge gut. Then he dragged him all the way down the aisle and out onto the field, where a policeman relieved Rube of his burden. The umpire, Bert Cunningham, saw no reason to eject Rube from the game. Two plainclothes policemen took Blau, whose fancy clothes were now bloody and torn, out in handcuffs and Ben Shibe banned him from Columbia Park.

As luck would have it, Rube was the first batter up after the incident. There were a few hisses from the St. Louis cranks but they were quickly drowned out by cheers, especially from the ladies in attendance who had been disgusted by the abuse Mrs. Waddell had received. Rube waved his cap and tore into the first pitch for another double. Then he returned to work on the mound, struck out twelve and won 4-1. The Browns' rooters lost a pile of money.

Unfortunately, league president Ban Johnson had been at the game and witnessed Rube going into the stands. Johnson had made it his mission in life to return baseball to its gentlemanly origins and to eliminate rowdyism. He handed Rube a five-game suspension. Rube didn't mind, after putting his proud mother back on the train he went fishing.

When Rube returned from his fishing trip he easily beat the last-place Senators. Their biggest star, Big Ed Delahanty, the '02 American League batting champion, had fallen off a bridge a few nights before and his body had been swept over Niagara Falls. Rube hadn't seen any newspapers during his fishing trip and hadn't heard what had happened to "the Only Del." As a result, he was the only man on the field without a black armband. It took him a while to figure out why he was being booed.

&c   &c   &c

Two days later he allowed Washington just two runs but lost anyway. When the Senators followed the A's back to Philadelphia for another series Rube begged Mack to let him pitch. This time he shut out Washington on five hits. But when he took the rubber against them again two days later he tired in the sixth inning and had to be pulled.

"I hear you were up all night again, Eddie. Was it a dame or a bottle this time?" Harry Davis asked him after the game. "You can usually pitch all afternoon."

"Didn't ya hear what happened?" Rube asked him.

"No, what?"

"There was a big fire at the Hotel Vendig last night."

RUBE WADDELL

"Ya, Harry," said Topsy Hartsel, "our Rube was a hero again. This time he pulled two firemen and three kids out of the flames. Saved their lives."

Hartsel went over to the table in front of his locker and got the newspaper he'd just been looking at. He flipped through its pages until he found the story about the previous night's fire. He scanned down until he found the part about Rube and handed the paper to Davis. The story had all the details.

"Apparently Athletics' star pitcher Rube Waddell had been in the United Cigar Store adjacent to the hotel when he smelled smoke and ran out into the street to learn its source. He immediately saw flames emanating from the Vendig and ran to see what he could do. The fire had started in the hotel's kitchen and flames were engulfing the lobby when Waddell ran into the building with a complete lack of regard for his own safety. He quickly determined that the elevators were inoperative and dashed up the stairs to see if the guests were escaping the blaze.

Firefighters, many of whom the pitcher knew from his having attended other fires, assured him that the first three floors had already been evacuated and pointed up the staircase to indicate they had not checked the higher floors yet. Upon reaching the fourth floor Waddell began banging on doors. When he got no response he took out his revolver and fired a shot into the air. He heard cries for help coming from one of the rooms and rushed to their source. When he banged on the door and no one answered he used his shoulder to smash the door open and when he entered the room he saw a woman and a child huddled in the corner. Waddell picked the two up in his arms and carried them down to the lobby and then out into the street where they received assistance.

Waddell went right back in and again ran up the staircase. A man was running ahead of him trying to reach the fifth floor. He yelled at the man to go back down to safety but the man told him he had to get some important papers out of his room. When he refused to comply with the instruction to go back down the stairs the pitcher punched the man, rendering him unconscious. Waddell then threw the man over his shoulder and carried him back down to the lobby, where the firemen had managed to stop the spread of flames.

Editor's Note: Our reporter later learned that Waddell, who suffered minor burns during his rescues, helped to extinguish the flames on the upper floors and assisted several hotel patrons' desperate efforts to climb down the building's flimsy and precarious fire escapes. The hero also carried to safety two firemen who had been overcome by smoke inhalation.

"And then the boys made me go out and celebrate with them at The Mechanics Bar after we put out the fire," Rube explained. "You get a lot of soot in your mouth in that kind of work."

"And whiskey and beer wash it down better than water?" asked Connie Mack, who had been eavesdropping.

"Seems to."

Mack just smiled. Though he hadn't been able to go the distance this time, having pitched five times in seven days, Rube had almost single-handedly pulled the slumping and light-hitting Athletics back into contention.

He gave up just four hits to the New York Highlanders in his next start. Oddly, umpire-baiting, foul-mouthed pepper pot Norm "the Tabasco Kid" Elberfeld got all four of them. After the game Rube told a reporter, "If I had just walked him all four times I would've had a no-hitter."

RUBE WADDELL
KING *of the* **HALL** *of* **FLAKES**

CHAPTER TWENTY SEVEN

A BIG HITTER ON THE STAGE

Rube did well in his next start in Chicago, until the White Sox started bunting on him again. He let one roll right past him, picked up another and threw wildly past first base, and then fell trying to field another. By the time order was restored he'd given up five runs and been sent to the showers. In St. Louis Connie Mack handed Rube the ball for the first game against the Browns and Willie Sudhoff, their second best twirler. Rube pitched well, giving up just four hits, but a throwing error in the second by Danny Hoffman allowed two runners to scamper home and that was all St. Louis needed. Sudhoff held the offensively-challenged Athletics to just one run. It was Rube's fourth straight loss. After his impressive winning streak Rube had just five wins in his last sixteen decisions.

Two days later, some St. Louis rooters who'd lost bets in Philadelphia the day Rube went into the stands after Maurice Blau hooted at him throughout the game. They'd heard he would be appearing at the Havlin Theatre at the end of the season.

"You'd better *act* better than you pitch!" yelled a man sitting in the box seats.

"Hey Romeo, where's Juliet, back on the farm milkin' the cows?" yelled the man beside him.

Rube responded by doffing his cap and bowing after every strikeout. Schreck did his part as usual, doing his best to distract the hitters. The Browns were trying out a rookie catcher named Branch Rickey. He was struggling at the plate and behind it as well. He'd gone home to Flay, Ohio to visit his ailing mother and had missed the Browns' last three games.

"How's your mother?" asked Schreck.

As Rickey told him, "I think she's going to be all right," he heard a bang and realized that Schreck was throwing the ball back to the mound. He heard the umpire say, "Strike one." As Schreck said, "My ma gave me quite a scare a while back," Rickey heard another bang and Schreck was throwing the ball back to the mound again. Now the umpire said, "Strike two." Then Rickey saw a blur and heard a third bang and the umpire said, "You're out." Years later Rickey, by then a respected baseball executive would recall, "When Waddell had his control and some sleep . . . he was absolutely unhittable."

In the sixth, John Anderson, the Browns' first baseman, hit a lazy infield popup. It would have been an easy play for Rube but instead of camping underneath it he got down on his knees facing Monte Cross, who was playing short that day. On the bench between innings Rube had prepared for a play like this. Figuring that since two of his infielders were named Cross and that one of them might have an easy play at some point, he'd composed a verse for the mocking cranks.

Now, as Monte prepared to make the routine catch, Rube began to loudly and melodramatically serenade him.

"Wherefore art thou, Cross?
I shall not waver in my trust.
Use your wit or use your mitt,
But trap yon fly thou must."

Monte grinned and shook his head in amazement. He caught the ball and then bowed in imitation of Rube's theatrics. The cranks howled. They weren't in quite such a good mood after Rube had fanned a dozen Browns en route to his twentieth win of the year.

Three days later in Detroit, Rube watched Charles Bender, a big, hard-throwing 19-year old Chippewa from a reservation in Crow Wing County, Minnesota Connie Mack had signed, and Ed Plank lose both ends of a double header. The A's and Tigers would be playing another double header the next day.

"I'll pitch 'em both, Connie," Rube told Mack.

"You can have three days off if you do," Connie promised him.

Rube faced Wild Bill Donovan in the first game and he shut out the Tigers on three hits. The second didn't go as well. Rube pitched out of a jam in the second but walked in a run in the third. He muttered, "I never walk in a fucking run," and spat a stream of tobacco juice half way to the outfield grass in disgust. He settled down and shut out the Tigers until the eighth. The A's had scored a run to tie things up 1-1. Rube went out to pitch the bottom of the eighth, his seventeenth inning of the day.

Deacon McGuire hit a groundball that bounced off the glove of Lave Cross at third. On the next pitch he took off for second. The Tigers' first baseman grounded the next pitch to Danny Murphy, but he'd left his position to cover second. The ball rolled to the outfield. Socks Seybold ran in and scooped the ball up and fired home. Schreck had to go up the line a bit but caught the ball and then dove back to the plate. McGuire slid under the tag and Detroit won 2-1.

Rube ran off the diamond and straight to Connie Mack. He didn't even get a chance to open his mouth before Connie said, "Yes, Eddie, you can still go fishing."

"Thanks, boss, I tried my best."

"Yes you did. Now go and catch a couple for me."

       ℓ   ℓ   ℓ

Rube did not handle the time off well. He didn't spend much time fishing. He was supposed to be back with the team by August 24 to start against Cleveland but he didn't appear. Mack put Ed Plank in to pitch in his place even though Plank never fared well against the Blues. He lost. Rube finally showed up that night and Mack told him to stay in his room to be ready for the next day. As soon as Mack had gone up to his room Rube snuck down to the front desk and asked for ten dollars.

"Put it on the team's bill," he told the clerk. Then he went on a drinking binge.

       ℓ   ℓ   ℓ

Rube had gone too far this time. Mack called the reporters into his office.

"What are you going to do with Rube?" one asked.

"Are you fed up with him, Connie?" asked another.

"Waddell has been given his release. He is suspended the rest of the season for misconduct," Mack told them. "I have nothing further to say on the matter."

       ℓ   ℓ   ℓ

When the season ended two weeks later *The Sporting News* printed the final statistics. In the 1903 season Waddell had struck out more hitters than any pitcher in history. His total of 302 was 115 more than second place Bill Donovan's. Fireballers Addie Joss and Cy Young hadn't reached 300 strikeouts *combined*. Asked for a comment, Connie Mack shrugged, sighed, and said, "That Waddell, if he ever grows up ... goodness me."

       ℓ   ℓ   ℓ

RUBE WADDELL

After he was suspended Rube wandered around Philadelphia for a few days. He'd heard about a new kind of store that had opened on Chestnut Street called Wanamaker's Department Store. It was enormous, like five or six stores rolled into one. You could buy almost everything there - from candy to curtains, from watches to wallets, from parasols to perfume. The store was lit with electricity and it had huge circular counters in each section. Behind each counter were two or more pretty young sales girls in smart dresses.

Each of the items that Wanamaker's sold had a little piece of cardboard attached to it. Printed in small letters was the amount the item cost. It was such a clever idea that Rube wondered why no one had thought of it before. Amazingly, you could return anything that you purchased and get your money back. There didn't even have to be anything wrong with the item, you could just say you'd changed your mind. It didn't matter.

There were a lot of things in Wanamaker's that Rube dearly wanted. The problem was he had no money. One of the clerks told him that he could pay by check but Rube had never had a bank account. He tried on a suit that had caught his eye. It was grey and pinstriped. The sales manager came out and the clerk explained to him that Rube had no cash and could not pay by check. The sales manager eyed Rube up and down. With his broad shoulders and tall frame Rube looked very handsome. He made the suit look good.

"How would you like to be a mannequin?"

"A man a what?" Rube asked.

"A mannequin."

"What would I have to do?"

"You would have to stand in the store window without moving."

"Why would I wanna do that?"

"Because we would pay you."

"You'd pay me just to stand still?"

"Yes, to model our clothes, so people could see how attractive they might look in them."

"Sounds easier than firing shoots for two hours in the blazin' sun. I'll give it a whirl."

The next day Rube stood in the Wanamaker's front window. He shuffled and twitched a bit at first, but then he got the hang of it and found that he could go several minutes without blinking or moving a muscle. People passing the store would stop and stare at the large, real-as-life mannequin. Often a woman would be looking at Rube and her husband would join her. Invariably the husband would get a quizzical look on his face and finally say to his wife, "I'll be darned if that mannequin doesn't look just like Rube Waddell."

The wife usually had no idea who or what a Rube Waddell was. "I don't believe there is a line of clothing or a suit called a Rube Waddell, dear," she would say.

"No, the star twirler for the Athletics."

"It's just a mannequin," she would explain.

"Well I know that, but I tell you, it looks just like Rube Waddell."

Rube would wait a while and then he'd bow and say, "Rube Waddell, at your service," and the couple would nearly jump out of their skin.

The store paid Rube four dollars a day, which was more than Connie Mack was giving him, and he was able to buy a lot of clothes and a hair brush and some cologne and a kite and a model motorcycle he'd had his eye on. The candy department had a new confection called a Tootsie Roll that was delicious. After a couple of weeks Rube grew bored of just standing still though. He headed to the Grog Barrel in Camden to tend bar for a while and then he was off to St. Louis to pursue his career on stage.

In *The Stain of Guilt* a woman must choose between a suitor of high moral fiber and another whose motives are much less pure. Rube didn't have the lead, he played the heroine's brother, a guileless soul who could always be counted on to look out for his little sister.

During the play's climax the lecherous suitor has the heroine in a compromising situation and Rube was to rush on stage, yell "Unhand that woman, you evil cur," and punch the villain.

Rube took his work seriously but he wasn't able to learn the trick of delivering a punch without actually landing it. He often knocked the villain right off the stage, sometimes right over the footlights and into the orchestra pit.

"Just brush me and I'll fall," the actor playing the villain pleaded.

The director, whose name was Finnegan, tried again and again to teach Rube the theatre punch. He carefully demonstrated it. "You see, Rube, you don't even make contact. You hit the air behind the actor's head but the audience can't see that you have missed. We make a sound effect off stage so it sounds like you landed the blow."

Rube never did the knack of it and one actor after another quit the show after being knocked senseless in the line of duty. Finnegan finally wrote the punch out of the play. Rube would now just wrestle the villain. But the next night, when the villain put up token resistance, Rube picked him up and threw him into the third row of seats.

At least Rube couldn't hurt anyone during his recitation of *Reuben Striking Them Out* and he received a number of curtain calls. *The Stain of Guilt* was a big hit and Finnegan took it on the road for eight weeks. Rube was praised for knowing his lines and for delivering them in a clear voice with a natural style. But the production was forced to close down when no one could be found who was brave enough to play the villain.

ℓℓ   ℓℓ   ℓℓ

Rube went to stay with his parents, who had moved to St. Mary's, Pennsylvania. He joined the fire department and performed at the local opera house where he would shatter one-inch thick planks with his pitches. He enjoyed his mother's cooking and he put on a few pounds. Best of all, he trained his parents' dog Angel, a yellow Lab, to roll over, play dead, and fetch slippers and newspapers. Angel went everywhere with Rube, he hated to leave her when it was time to go.

ℓℓ   ℓℓ   ℓℓ

Connie Mack had no interest in returning to Jacksonville, there had been too many diversions. This time the Athletics would train in Spartanburg, South Carolina. Players were encouraged to engage in healthy pursuits when they weren't at the practice facility. Charles Bender, who had instantly - and quite predictably - been nicknamed Chief, was the most experienced horseback-rider on the club. Rube had no trouble keeping up with him though. He told people horses were a lot easier to ride than ostriches.

A reporter from *The Inquirer* had accompanied the team and he told the readers back home that "Waddell has become a great favorite with the residents down here due to his skill with a gun and a fishing rod. He often goes hunting or fishing after the day's workout and returns at sundown with ducks, quails, and fish. As a result of his endeavors the A's are eating very well."

Connie Mack was reading on the veranda one evening when a young boy ran up and told him he should come right away. He said two men were staging a raree a block away. Mack was a bit puzzled as to why the boy thought he would want to see it, but he did his best to keep up with the lad until they finally reached a street corner where a crowd had gathered. With some difficulty he managed to elbow his way close enough to see what had drawn so many people. There was a man in a strange costume holding a large alligator on a leash. All of a sudden another man, whom Mack quickly realized was Rube, picked up the alligator and spun it around. The gator flashed its teeth and whipped its huge tail menacingly but Rube deftly grabbed the gator and wrestled it to the ground. He had obviously done this before.

The onlookers cheered. Mack wasted no time in getting Rube out of there. In spite of his apparent expertise, Mack told Rube in no uncertain terms that he should do no more alligator wrestling while a member of the Philadelphia Athletics.

On the trip back to Philadelphia, the A's stopped in Richmond, Virginia to play a team from Montreal. After the game Rube used his actor's card to get the team front row seats at the theater.

"I guess it pays to have a famous actor in our midst," said Ed Plank, not really meaning it. Ball players didn't usually get special treatment. Often they got the opposite because of their rough reputation. This night at least they felt like big shots.

The reporter from *The Inquirer* predicted, "Rube is going to break all the records he has already set and there will be no sideline diversions. When the Rube is hooked up that way, he is practically invincible."

Rube would be even better than ever in 1904. But would the A's get him any runs?

RUBE WADDELL
KING of the HALL of FLAKES

CHAPTER TWENTY EIGHT

THE TOP TWIRLERS GO
HEAD TO HEAD

Rube pitched the home opener against the New York Highlanders. He gave up a couple of early runs but Harry Davis hit one that just cleared the right field fence, Danny Murphy swatted a triple in the eighth, and Jasper ended things when he knocked in the winning run in the twelfth. Rube ended the day with a win and sixteen strikeouts.

A reporter from *The Inquirer* caught up with him as he was hopping on a trolley car to head uptown.

"Great game, Rube," he said as he followed him on.

"Thanks, Joe," said Rube.

The reporter was pleased that Rube remembered his name. "You tied the record today, Rube."

"What record?"

"The one for strikeouts. You had sixteen today."

"I did? I guess I lost count. I knew I had a lot."

"Do you know whose record you tied?"

"I don't know, Cy Young, Kid Nichols?"

"No, a younger fellow. Goes by the name of Eddie Waddell but everyone calls him Rube."

"You don't say. Sounds like a hellluva twirler, this Waddell fellow."

"Oh he is, a bit of a character too, or so they say."

"Do they now?"

"Apparently he has been known to imbibe a potation or two after a big win."

"That sounds like a right smart thing for him to do. Let's get us a couple of cold beers, Joe. I know just the place. I will even let you buy the first round."

"I'd be happy too," he answered, thinking that he would end up paying for a lot more than one round and would have quite a nasty headache in the morning. He was right on both counts.

There was a huge buildup for the Athletics' game on April 24. They were to face the Boston Americans who'd won the first interleague championship series five months before in what had been dubbed the World Championship Series. Pitching for Boston would be Cy Young.

The Americans couldn't do a thing against Rube. Young was roughed up for two in the first but then he settled down. Each twirler posted zeroes inning after inning. It ended 2-0 Philadelphia. Rube took on the Americans again on May 2 and threw a one-hitter this time. The lone hit was a seeing-eye roller that just barely eluded Lave Cross' glove.

A week later Rube faced Cy Young again. Rube pitched well but it didn't matter. He and his teammates were utterly powerless against the 37-year old Boston ace. He pitched a perfect game, the majors' first ever. As luck would have it, Rube was the 27th man to face Young and, after flying out harmlessly to right field, he doffed his cap to Cy. "You got us this time, old timer."

Rube managed to win his next start, but the Athletics couldn't hit to save their lives. Harry Davis was the only man generating any offense and injuries kept him out of the lineup as they often had in '03. The A's spent most of the summer mired in fifth place. Monte Cross ended up hitting just .189 and Schreck was even worse, batting an anemic .186. Rube behaved himself for a change and the boosters displayed their affection by turning out to see him.

He got a bad scare when he faced the Browns on August 2. In the third inning Harry Gleason, their diminutive second baseman, came to bat. He already had a tiny strike zone but he crouched to make it even smaller. Rube tried to throw a speedball down the middle but it sailed on him and struck Gleason behind his left ear. There was an audible crack. The boosters gasped as blood spurted out of the ear and Gleason collapsed.

Rube rushed in to him. The St. Louis trainer hurried out from behind the bench, but Rube waved him away. "I have him," Rube said. He scooped Gleason up in his arms and carried him into the Browns' clubhouse where he vomited violently. A doctor who'd been at the game came down to attend to him.

"Call an ambulance," the doctor instructed. "This man is in serious trouble."

Gleason was rushed to the Baptist Sanitarium where he was diagnosed with a severe concussion. Rube was completely unnerved and struggled through the rest of the game. As soon as it was over he rushed to check on Gleason. Although he was still groggy when Rube went into his room, Gleason was able to sit up. His head was wrapped in thick bandages.

"Harry. You gave us quite a scare. You feelin' all right?"

"Not *too* bad, but you're kinda fuzzy, Rube," Gleason said.

"But you can see?"

"I can see, but I got a helluva headache. Damn, you throw hard."

"They're usually straighter than that, Harry. I'm awful sorry. I surely was not tryin' to bean you."

"I know that. I haven't bin around long but everyone says you're one of the few twirlers that doesn't throw at hitters, not even brush backs."

"I'm always afraid I'll kill somebody, or at least knock him senseless."

"I guess I was out for a while but Doc says I'll be fine."

"That's a relief. Anything I can get ya?"

"Just the address of that pretty nurse with the big bosoms. Every time she bends over to adjust my pillow my little head starts to throb like my big one."

"Sounds as though you're gonna be all right after all."

ℓℓ   ℓℓ   ℓℓ

Luckily for Rube the close call didn't affect his pitching. He was striking batters out at a phenomenal rate, 22 in 19 innings in one stretch. Strikeouts were still a rarity with most batters choking up and trying to poke the ball into a gap. With the fences as much as 500 feet away - to allow boosters to stand in the outfield when they weren't enough seats - it seemed futile to swing for them, especially if the ball had been in play for three or four innings and had been spit on a bunch of times. He struck out eleven in front of 27,000 rooters in Chicago at the end of August and then fanned fourteen in a 13-inning shutout of Detroit. It was Rube's sixth straight win.

The A's finally went on a tear with a 10-2 road trip and, though in fourth place, were just two games behind first place New York when they headed home to take on the Cleveland Blues. The city's boosters were so enraptured with their handsome second basemen Napoleon Lajoie they had taken to calling the team the Naps. Rube pitched the opener and he was great, striking out fifteen this time. But Monte Cross threw a ball into the seats in the eleventh inning allowing Lajoie to scamper home with the winning run. Two days later before a sell-out crowd Rube whiffed ten batters and allowed Cleveland just four hits.

Because of a string of rainouts the A's were now going to face the New York Highlanders nine times in six days.

"If we can win six or seven of them we have a shot at the pennant," Connie Mack told the team before game one of a Labor Day doubleheader.

Things didn't start well. Jack Chesbro shut out the A's in the morning contest. Rube pitched the afternoon tilt and after his teammates scored twice in the first inning Rube gave up three hits and a walk in the second. Connie Mack went out to the mound.

"That's all for today, Eddie."

"What are ya talkin' about, Connie? It was only two runs."

"Just two so far. But with more to come the way you're throwing. You aren't sharp today and you know it. Now have a rest so I can use you tomorrow."

"You promise I can start tomorrow?"

"Yes, Eddie, I promise."

Connie Mack kept his promise. Rube fanned fourteen Highlanders in the first game the next day but New York reached him for four runs in the third inning and the A's got just one run. When the teams traveled to New York Rube pitched the first of the four remaining games with the Highlanders. He allowed three runs in the first inning and not even a hit the rest of the way but lost to Jack Chesbro. Rube started the last game and won it, but the A's were all but out of the race now.

On September 15 the A's took on the last-place Senators who had just lost seven out of nine to Boston to more or less hand the Americans the pennant. In the second inning a runner got caught in no man's land between first and second. Rube had been around long enough to know what to do. He ran straight at him. But when he went to apply the tag the runner deftly ducked under Rube's arm. Rube stumbled and then fell, landing hard on his right shoulder.

"I can stay in, Connie, it's not my left arm."

"I'm not taking any chances. We're probably not going to catch Boston anyway."

When Rube had his shoulder checked out he learned that it was separated. He would be out for almost two weeks. The A's went 3-8 while he was out and their season was done.

CHAPTER TWENTY NINE

SENTENCED TO A CHAIN GANG

"How many more do you think he could have had if he hadn't gotten hurt?" the reporter from *The Inquirer* asked his editor after the year's statistics were announced.

"It doesn't matter, Joe, nobody's ever going to match what he got this year," the editor said.

"People don't usually make that much of a fuss about strikeouts, but three hundred and forty-nine is just unbelievable. He could have had five more starts if he hadn't gotten injured and at the rate he was mowing them down he could have had close to four hundred. Chesbro was second. He was a hundred and ten behind Waddell and he pitched seventy-two more innings. And Rube won twenty-five, had an ERA of one sixty-four, and set a record for most consecutive scoreless innings to boot."

"Goes to show you what he can do when he lays off the bottle and gets home before sunrise," said the editor.

"Now all Connie Mack has to do is get some players who can hit."

"That's something he might want to think about."

         ℮   ℮   ℮

Rube went to St. Mary's for the winter. He worked as a woodchopper during the day and spent his evenings drinking whiskey on the veranda. One afternoon he went to see if there was anything interesting in the nearby town of Kersey. He was walking along Union Street when the clerk of a millinery shop ran out of the store yelling "Fire!" at the top of his lungs. A young boy had been shopping with his parents when he accidentally knocked over an oil can. His parents watched in horror as the oil spread along the floor to a woodstove. It immediately burst into flames.

Rube knocked the clerk out of his way and ran into the store. He saw the burning stove and realized the flames were perilously close to engulfing the little boy. He looked around and found a long piece of cloth. He wrapped it around his arms and then, with a grunt, lifted the stove right off its moorings and into the air.

"My God!" the boy's mother gasped, amazed that a man could do such a thing by himself.

Rube carried the stove out through the front doors and, to the shock of passers-by, heaved it into a snow bank.

A crowd quickly formed around Rube. The parents hugged him and told him how lucky it was that he was there to save their boy. Word of Rube's heroics spread through town almost as quickly as the oil had reached the stove. More free meals and more free drinks.

⸙ ⸙ ⸙

Connie Mack and Ben Shibe met for lunch at the owner's club on a cold day in January. The Philadelphia Club at 13th and Walnut was the oldest club for gentlemen in the country.

"Are you sure you want to take the team to New Orleans for training camp, Connie," Shibe asked when they'd ordered turtle soup and their meals.

Mack laid down his menu card and picked up his linen napkin. "It'll be a great place for exhibition games, Ben. The folks there haven't seen major league teams yet."

"You *do* know that the Mardi Gras will be on while you're there?"

"What of it?"

"Have you ever been in New Orleans during Mardi Gras?" asked the A's owner.

"No. What's it like."

"It's one big party."

"Good, the boys'll have some fun when they aren't practicing."

"What about Waddell? Aren't you worried about what he might do there?"

"He behaved himself last year, didn't he?"

"Yes, but New Orleans? You'll be letting a kid loose in a candy store."

"I realize I will need to keep an eye on him down there, Ben."

"That may not be enough. Are you planning to take Frank Newhouse with you?"

"Of course. He's the trainer. He'll need to deal with strains and pulled muscles as well as injuries."

"Let's get him to deal with Waddell too."

"What do you mean by that?"

"I mean that you should have Newhouse watch Rube, shadow him and make sure he stays out of trouble."

"If you think it's necessary."

"I don't *think* it's necessary, I know it is."

Connie called Newhouse and told him about his special assignment.

ℓℓ   ℓℓ   ℓℓ

On the train ride south the A's had a blast. Until the food ran out. The railroad officials had no idea that ballplayers, especially Rube, could eat that much. When the train made a stop at King's Mountain, Tennessee the players rushed into the station's coffee shop and devoured everything in sight. After two huge helpings of meat and potatoes the ravenous Rube polished off an entire marble cake.

When the players arrived in New Orleans, Connie Mack was delighted to see that Rube was in great shape - in spite of the way he'd feasted on the trip down. When Newhouse weighed him, the scale read 212 pounds, ten pounds less than he'd been at the end of last season.

"Never been in better shape, Frank, that wood chopping was the best thing I coulda done."

ℓℓ   ℓℓ   ℓℓ

He did nothing to embarrass Connie Mack in New Orleans and, with his broad smile and love of merriment, he was a big hit with the town fathers. They made him a member of the Eagles Club and even held a special reception in his honor. When he got up to speak he got a big laugh when he congratulated the leading citizens on their Mardi Gras. He said, "I thought I knew how to throw a baseball, but you fellas down here sure know how to throw a *party.*" He told the club members that when the season got underway he was going to mow down the Boston Americans just like Andrew Jackson mowed down the redcoats in New Orleans a hundred years ago.

One night he joined an all-male group of masked paraders who called themselves the Jefferson City Buzzards. They'd taken their name from the birds that once frequented the city's slaughterhouses. They made their way along St. Charles Avenue and Canal Street with decorated canes, dancing and mixing with the revelers who lined the route. Some wore strings of beads, others wore dresses. They sang and drank from flasks and handed out doubloons. Every couple of streets they would lie down on their backs and quiver their arms and legs in the air like dying cockroaches. Rube's favorite part was when they went into the crowds and exchanged beads and flowers for kisses.

When he took the mound against the New Orleans Pelicans 2,500 people took a break from the Mardi Gras festivities to see him pitch. Of course a lot of them brought their libations with them. The reporter from *The Picayune* wrote "Waddell is of massive build, with a genial face. His manner wins over the spectator at once. When he makes a wild pitch or gives the batter the best of the argument, he whistles and grins a grin that can be seen from the business office of the park to the locker room."

After five days in New Orleans Connie Mack decided his players were having a little *too* much fun and moved the team 300 miles north to Shreveport. Things weren't lively enough there for Rube and Ossee, so they organized a midnight football game on Stoner Avenue. The residents of its stately homes were not impressed.

The second night in Shreveport, Rube and Schreck went out to see what kind of entertainment the town had to offer. They started with the show at the Majestic Theatre, but were disappointed that its cast consisted mainly of overweight opera singers. Then they went to The Strand Theatre which was owned by two brothers, Abe and Julian Saenger. Abe produced the theatre's vaudeville shows and, to Rube's delight, Julian ran a nearby drug store that was open 24 hours. After the bars closed Schreck went to bed and Rube headed straight to its soda fountain, or as straight as he could manage.

The next night Rube talked the owner of the lounge at the Washington-Youree Hotel into staging a beauty contest among the maids and waitresses. The winner got a kiss from Rube. Schreck organized drinking contests and Rube beat all comers in arm-wrestling. Ossee was just sober enough to remind Rube to use his right arm.

        &   *&*   *&*

Disappointed with how quickly Rube had found or created mischief, Connie Mack made an arrangement with the local sheriff. Rube was snoring away in his hotel room the next morning when there was a loud knock on his door. He sat up and looked for a bathrobe to put on and then realized he was still in his clothes. His suit was soaking wet and there were ice cream stains on the lapels. He fondly remembered the tiny waitress who had won the beauty contest when he saw there was lipstick on his collar.

He rubbed his pounding temples and went to the door. Before he got it half way open the sheriff barged in. He wore a huge white cowboy hat and had flowing red handlebar moustaches. Rube noticed that a large Colt special protruded from his holster.

"I am Sheriff Dewdney and *you*, sir, are under arrest."

"Arrest? For what?" Rube demanded.

"For the things you did last evening."

Rube tried desperately to remember everything he had done. He vaguely recalled swimming in a fountain and asking the bosomy bar maid who'd finished third in the beauty contest to unbutton her blouse, but he wasn't sure that was worthy of an arrest. The sheriff took out a pair of handcuffs and clapped them on Rube's thick wrists.

"Where are you taking me?" Rube yelled. "I got a right to a lawyer, don't I?"

"You will have no lawyer. You will be tried this afternoon by Judge Mitchell and sent to work on a chain gang."

"Get Connie Mack, he'll see that I get a lawyer."

"I have already spoken with Mister Mack," said the sheriff.

"You did?"

"I spoke with Mister Mack one hour ago?"

"Then what is all this?"

"This is his idea."

"*His* idea? I don't get it."

"Your manager asked me to convince you that the town of Shreveport will not tolerate any more of your shenanigans."

"So I have to work on a chain gang?"

"No, not this time," said the sheriff, removing the handcuffs. "This was a warning. But you are not to go out on the town again during your stay here."

"Can I go fishing instead?"

"By all means, I think that would be an excellent use of your free time. In fact, I'll go with you. I know some great spots to get catfish."

"Our game'll be over around two."

"I'll meet you at the park," said Dewdney, "Mister Mack says you're quite the fisherman."

"I been known to catch my fair share."

"Bring that catcher of yours if you want, the one who was swimming in the fountain with you and the two gals from the hotel. I'll bring my brother, he can catch more fish than anybody around here."

"Maybe he can show me a thing or two."

"From what Mack says he'll have a hard time just to keep up."

Dewdney's brother caught fourteen catfish that afternoon, Rube caught twenty.

The A's headed north the next day. Their second stop was in Birmingham, Alabama and Rube went out alone. Schreck had left the team to go home for his father's funeral. This time there was no threat of a chain gang awaiting Rube, just a couple of thieves who jumped him when he left a bar to relieve himself in an alley. Rube got in a couple of licks but came out of the fight with some nasty bruises and a sore rib where one of the thugs had kicked him. Frank Newhouse could have helped, but Rube had given him the slip.

Connie Mack gave Chief Bender the ball for the A's opener against Boston. Rube's rib was still bothering him. Andy Coakley, a skinny, well-spoken 21-year old graduate of the College of the Holy Cross, got the start in the next game but in spite of his sore side Rube was sent in to try to save the day for Coakley after he allowed the Americans five runs in the first three innings. Rube allowed just four hits and got the win, but uncharacteristically registered only two strikeouts.

Ed Plank and Chief Bender started the next two games against the Highlanders and then Mack went back to Coakley. He got roughed up again and Connie told Rube to go to the corner of the park to get ready. Harry Barton, a prematurely balding 29-year-old from Chester, Pennsylvania who was trying to land a job as a catcher, went out to warm Rube up.

"You sure got your stuff today," said Barton after being almost bowled over by Rube's first few throws.

"I'm not holding back anymore, Harry, the rib's fine now."

Rube took over in the eighth and struck out the side. He struck out the first two Highlanders in the ninth as well and had a 2-2 count on Bob Unglaub, the third batter.

"It's all over but the huzzahs," Rube yelled in at Unglaub. He fired the next pitch over the outside corner and the bat never left Unglaub's shoulder. Rube threw his glove up in the air and prepared to dance his way off the mound.

"Ball three," yelled Silk O'Laughlin.

"What!" Rube bellowed. "That was right over the corner, Silk."

"Missed by six inches, Rube."

"It did no such of a thing," Rube insisted, huffing his way over to pick up his glove.

Flustered, Rube walked Unglaub but got the next batter to ground out for another win. Rube gave O'Laughlin a piece of his mind and then headed to the bench.

"You gotta put me back in the rotation now, Connie. D'ya see how quick my shoots were out there?"

"Not just yet, Eddie. No use taking any chances this early in the season. You're doing a fine job finishing games for us."

Perturbed, but with little choice, Rube went in to rescue Chief Bender two days later in Washington and gave up just one hit. When Coakley, Plank, and Bender all lost to the lowly Senators Connie finally gave Rube his first start. He rewarded Connie's faith in him by throwing a two-hit shutout. Rube didn't walk a batter and no Senator got past first base.

※ ※ ※

Harry Davis was in the middle of a very pleasant dream at 2 o'clock the next morning when he was wakened by the sound of fire bells. Sniffing for smoke and smelling none, he went to the window and opened it. Across the street from the A's hotel there were three fire wagons. Smoke was pouring out of a livery stable and some boys were hurriedly leading the horses out into the street. Davis went back to the bed and woke up his roommate Socks Seybold and they headed down the stairs. On their way they caught up to Connie Mack, Topsy Hartsell, and Danny Hoffman.

"You fellas going to see the fire?" Davis asked.

"Maybe we can lend a hand. Be careful though, it's mostly smoke now, but I saw a lot of flames when I looked out a few minutes ago," said Connie Mack.

When they got out to the street they were almost run over by panic-stricken horses. A burly old fireman came out and they asked him if there was anything they could do.

"Flames are all out now, just a whole lot of smoking straw. Thanks though."

Then another fireman came out of the livery stables. He was big too, but younger. His face was covered in soot and he wore red long johns, a yellow rubber coat, and a fireman's hat. He was dragging a hose and had a big grin on his face.

Socks Seybold was the first to realize who it was. "Son of a gun. We shoulda known Rube would beat us here."

"Hey fellas," Rube yelled. "The bells wake yuz up?"

"You all right?" Connie asked.

"Sure, Connie, why wouldn't I be?"

"No reason. When did you get here?"

"About half an hour ago. Ossee and I were playin' cards and we smelled smoke. He went to bed and I ran over here to lend a hand."

"And we sure needed the help," said the burly fireman, whose name was Big Jim Brodie. "Hard to get my men here in the middle of the night."

"Are you going to get any sleep tonight, Eddie?" asked Connie Mack.

"A bit I guess, we're almost done. Gotta get the horses somewhere else though, they're way too spooked to go back in there even if we wanted them to."

"There are some stables two blocks down," a boy who was holding the reins of a huge grey Clydesdale offered.

"Run down and see if they got room," Big Jim told him. "I'll hold the Clydesdale." The boy took off down the street and Rube's teammates headed back to their hotel.

"When we get the horses settled I'll buy you a beer," Brodie told Rube. "What's your name anyway?"

"Eddie. Folks bin callin' me Rube for the better part of ten years now though."

"You ain't the ball player, are you?"

"I am."

"I heard tell there was a ball player who was a fireman on the side? How many you been too?"

"Couldn't say for sure, Jim, I've lost count. Maybe thirty."

"Well you earned yourself a cold one tonight. The owner's gonna be grateful for what you done."

"Maybe *he'll* buy me a beer too."

℃   ℃   ℃

When he took the mound against Cleveland two days later the air was hot and so was Rube. He was firing bullets and crisp benders that had the Naps swinging at air. He struck out nine Cleveland batters and four others fouled pitches straight into Schreck's specially-designed glove. When Rube went up to bat in the eighth he was up by two runs and was working on another shutout. There were two out and Socks Seybold was on first base after blooping one over the infield.

On the second pitch Socks took off for second. The catcher threw in time to get him, but the ball sailed over the second baseman's head into centerfield. Seybold reached and rounded third and headed for home. The centerfielder picked up the ball and fired it on a line to home plate. Rube was still standing in the batter's box even though it was obvious there was about to be a play at the plate. When the centerfielder's throw came in, instead of getting out of the way, Rube swung at the ball and drove it back into play.

"What the hell are you doing!" yelled the catcher.

The bewildered umpire took a moment to get over what had just transpired and then pointed at Rube, "Interference. The runner is out!"

When Rube got back to the bench Connie Mack asked him what he thought he was doing swinging at a throw from the outfield.

"I couldn't help it, Connie. They bin feedin' me curves all afternoon. That was the first straight one I'd seen."

RUBE WADDELL
KING of the HALL of FLAKES

CHAPTER THIRTY

THE TOP GUNS STAGE A CLASSIC

Rube had now pitched thirty-seven innings without allowing a run. The scoreless streak ended in his next game when he allowed Cleveland one, but only one, while striking out ten Naps. Now he was 7-0 and his ERA was less than 1.00. Of course he led the league in strikeouts, but in Detroit things went badly from the get-go. Wild Bill Donovan tried to bunt his way on in the first and Rube threw the ball into the seats. Then two of his curves failed to bend and got lashed for base hits. Rube settled down a bit but then Germany Schaefer and Sam Crawford started bunting every time they came up. Schaefer made a big production of it, like he did with everything. He always made Rube laugh with his antics.

Batting after Crawford was a skinny 18-year old rookie called Tyrus Cobb. In the on-deck circle he swung three bats around his neck and it looked like he was showboating. He had an arrogant manner and, unlike his new teammates, Cobb wore his black uniform collar up in an aristocratic fashion.

It was clear that the other Tigers were less than fond of their new addition. They were mad that he was taking an outfield job they all thought Jimmy Barrett, Duff Cooley, or Piano Legs Hickman should have. Because of his speed, Detroit had Cobb playing center field and Sam Crawford and Matty McIntyre absolutely hated it when Cobb encroached on their territory, sometimes cutting right in front of them to take away a catch.

He was the only southerner on the team and he was a Baptist, which didn't go over too well with Charley O'Leary and Bill Coughlin and the other Irish Catholic players. If they'd known that Cobb's mother was on trial in a Georgia courtroom for the murder of his father they might have treated him a little better. Maybe not.

Cobb beat out a perfectly placed bunt in the fifth. When the next hitter singled, the rookie raced around the bases and slid into third, his feet in the air. His razor-sharp spikes slit Lave Cross open. Lave grabbed his blood-soaked leg and then got up and went after Cobb. The umpire had to pull them apart. Several A's ran out to make sure no further harm came to Cross. None of the Tigers made a move to go to Cobb's defense.

"That sorry sumbitch is a crooked as a dog's hind leg," Rube told Lave when order had been restored.

"The shit's gonna make a lot of enemies playin' like that," said Lave.

"Sam Crawford told me every man on the team hates his guts," said Rube.

"He's still sore the South lost the war."

"He ain't sore, Lave. He's still fightin' the damn thing."

His next time up Cobb stroked a single into right field. He immediately tried to steal second. The Bennett Park field was laid over an old cobblestone surface and it was a nightmare for fielders. It wasn't very conducive to sliding on either. Cobb slid head first and came up short. After a perfect throw from Schreck, Danny Murphy was waiting for the Southerner. After Murphy tagged Cobb he stuck his knee into his ear and drove his face hard into the dirt.

"How's that for a big league meal, you cocky Confederate bastard?" asked Murphy.

Cobb jumped up ready to fight but once again saw a lot of A's around but no Tigers.

"Gutless Yankee pricks," he muttered to himself. He called Murphy a bog-jumping fairy and headed off the field. Everyone noted that Cobb didn't slide head-first much after that. He preferred to go feet first and brandish his spikes anyway.

કી   કી   કી

Rain fell off and on throughout Rube's next two starts against the Senators and White Sox but he prevailed in spite of having to slop through mud whenever he had to field a bunt. In the past month he was 9-0. The rest of the staff was 14-16. The A's were in second place - mostly thanks to Rube.

One day the Philadelphia boosters presented him with an expensive safety razor in recognition of his winning streak.

"Maybe they're hopin' it'll help you win some close shaves, Rube," said Danny Murphy.

"Might have been gamblers that bought it for you, Rube," offered Socks Seybold. "You've cost some of them a heap of money. I'll bet they're hoping you slit your throat with it."

Rube beat the last place Browns and then the Naps before finally losing a couple in early June. One was a four-hitter with Sam Crawford's solo home run the only run he gave up and the other a 14-inning heartbreaker in Chicago during which he was hit in the stomach by a line drive. He beat the Browns on one day's rest but then fell apart in Washington, giving up three singles, a double, a walk, and making an error to lose 6-3.

The next afternoon in New York Ed Plank had a 7-4 lead over the Highlanders after eight. In the ninth the first two batters singled and Connie Mack brought in Rube. He got Wee Willie Keeler to ground out to preserve the victory. Connie Mack started him the next day in the first game of a July 4 doubleheader against Boston. His opponent was Cy Young.

Rube gave up a single and back-to-back doubles in the first and two runs scored. But after Young had worked out of trouble four times in his first four innings big Harry Davis tied things up with a long two-run home run in the fifth. Both teams put runners on board in the sixth but neither scored. The same thing happened in the seventh. The A's failed to score yet again in the top of the eighth.

Though there were occasional base runners, neither team scored in the ninth, tenth, eleventh, twelfth, thirteenth, fourteenth, fifteenth, sixteenth, seventeenth, eighteenth, or nineteenth innings. After three and a half hours the score was still 2-2.

Danny Murphy hit a ground ball to third in the top of the twentieth inning. Jimmy Collins gloved it but then bobbled the ball moving it to his throwing hand. Murphy was safe. Then a Cy Young speedball hit Schoolboy Knight, the rookie shortstop, in the back of the head. Knight had to leave the game. Schreck hit a pop fly to Hobe Ferris. Apparently everyone was getting a bit tired, he dropped it. Bases loaded.

It was Rube's turn to bat. He waved his bat around his head in the on-deck circle and headed to the plate. He was half way there when he stumbled over something and fell to the ground. He grabbed his left ankle and then twisted it around gently to make sure it was all right. Connie Mack hurried out to see if he was hurt.

"What happened?"

"I tripped on something."

"I don't see anything, but they've let the grass grow so long ... wait ... I see what it was."

Mack walked a few steps and bent down. He picked up the umpire's broom.

"Is that where the damn thing is," said Bert Cunningham. "I haven't seen it for three innings. They gotta cut this grass shorter. Sorry about that, Rube."

Rube stood up, brushed himself off and picked up his bat. "Never mind, Bert, it's not your fault. I'll be all right."

"The league's got to get you fellas some pocket-sized whisk brooms so you don't have to lug the big ones around," Mack told Cunningham.

"We've already told Johnson that, Connie. He hasn't gotten around to it yet. I guess we're just gonna have to buy our own."

Rube stepped into the batter's box. On the third pitch he hit a grounder to Freddy Parent at short. Parent bobbled it and Murphy scored the first run in fifteen innings. Danny Hoffman singled Schreck home and the A's had a two-run lead. Cy Young was finally worn out.

Rube got Chick Stahl to ground out to start the bottom of the twentieth, but then Bob Unglaub ripped a double to deep centerfield. There was an audible groan from the grandstand. Schreck looked in at Connie Mack, who loosened his tie a little, shrugged, and then nodded his head. This was Rube's game to win or lose. After twenty innings there was no way Mack was taking him out now.

Jimmy Collins took two close pitches for strikes and then popped out. Hobe Ferris came to the plate. He hit Rube's first offering to deep left field. Though they were exhausted too, the boosters rose to watch. Bris Lord, a handsome young rookie from nearby Uplands, Pennsylvania was in left. His entire family and half of Uplands were there to watch him.

Lord's parents didn't know whether to watch or cover their eyes. What if their son dropped it? What if he cost his team the game after twenty innings? Would any of them be able to show their faces in town? Bris, who had uncanny eyesight, ran full tilt toward the outfield fence, tracking the flight of the ball all the way. It was well hit and he didn't know if he could get to it. He was within two feet off the wall when he reached up and made the catch.

"I knew you were gonna catch it, kid, never any doubt in my mind," Rube told Lord before walking with him to the stands where his family was standing and cheering. They were thrilled that Rube would come to talk with them instead of glorying in his big win.

"That was a truly masterful performance, Mister Waddell," said Lord's father as he shook Rube's big paw.

"It's Eddie, sir. But, heck, Rube is fine. Great catch your son made there. Saved the day for me." Bris was grinning from ear to ear and his pretty young girlfriend was beaming with pride.

      ℰ   ℰ   ℰ

After the marathon, reporters went scrambling for the record books. After a lot of digging they discovered that no hurler had pitched all of a twenty-inning game since the mound had been moved back from forty-five feet. And now two men had done in the same game! For years Rube would get free drinks at bars by handing over what he claimed to be the ball he used to beat Cy Young in '05.

      ℰ   ℰ   ℰ

Given the time of year, there was still plenty of time to play the second game of the doubleheader. Andy Coakley started and gave up ten hits in the first eight innings. Luckily the Americans had scored only two runs and the A's still led heading into the ninth.

Hobe Ferris, the first batter, fouled out. Jimmy Collins was up next. He hit the first pitch into left for a single. Then Jesse Burkett hit Coakley's first pitch to him into right for another single. Connie Mack wasn't going to risk seeing this one go twenty innings.

"Where's Rube?" Connie asked Topsy Hartsell, whose place Bris Lord had taken over.

"What do you want Eddie for? The man just threw twenty innings!"

"You don't think he'll go in?"

"I didn't say that. Hell Rube'd pitch every inning if you let him."

"So where is he?"

Hartsel pointed down the right field line. Rube was lifting 200-pound weights and talking to people in the stands.

"Eddie, grab a glove. You're going in," Connie called to him.

Rube spit a long stream of tobacco juice at the ground, tipped his hat to the bugs he had been joking with, and jogged in to get his glove.

Chick Stahl was due up next. He'd been looking forward to going up against Coakley. He couldn't believe his eyes when Rube went to the mound.

"You can't be serious?" he demanded of Schreck. "How can Waddell pitch again? What the hell is Mack doing?"

"Winning the game, that's what he's doing."

Stahl didn't do any better this time than he had against Rube three hours before. He struck out, though it took five pitches this time. Bob Unglaub was up next. Rube thought of the double he had hit in the twentieth inning of the first game. He called Schreck out to the mound.

"What did he hit the last time he was up?" Rube asked.

"You mean the last time he was up against you and he doubled?"

"Ya, of course that's what I mean. I don't give a shit what he hit offa Coakley. What was it he hit for the double?"

"It was a fadeaway."

"Good, we'll tease him with that and then get him out with shoots."

Rube threw Unglaub two curves that missed the plate. Unglaub was dying for something he could hit. He never had a chance. The next two pitches were like bullets. It was getting pretty dark now but Unglaub would not have gotten a bat on them if it had been noon.

The first strike had been right down the middle, the second was so fast that Unglaub hadn't had any idea where it had ended up. He asked the umpire where it was. The umpire was relieved that Unglaub didn't know because he hadn't seen it either. He'd just heard it hit Schreck's mitt with a crack and guessed it must have been over the plate.

Not only was it getting dark, the ball had been in play for four innings and it was almost black now. Both leagues were considering a rule that would empower the umpires to decide when a new baseball should be put into play instead of the home team's manager.

Rube looked in for Ossee's sign. Instead of putting down fingers, Ossee just pounded his mitt and winked. Rube winked back.

He wound up and fired another one. It was over the plate, or so it sounded. Another loud smack in Schreck's mitt. The umpire blinked and yelled "Strike three!" as convincingly as he could. He knew Unglaub hadn't seen it. Neither had he.

Unglaub spat in disgust and trod back to the bench.

℮   ℮   ℮

"I wasn't sure we were gonna pull it off," Ossee told Rube as they downed their third beer that night. "My hand's still sore from smacking my mitt so hard."

"Would have been mighty embarrassing if the ump had looked in your mitt and found out there was no ball in it."

CHAPTER THIRTY ONE

A RECORD-BREAKING STREAK

The press right across America dubbed the 20-inning marathon between Rube and Cy Young one of the greatest games ever played. It was also the longest ever played as well, a mind-boggling three hours and thirty minutes. Both twirlers had thrown close to 300 pitches.

Rube's nation-wide notoriety reaped immediate dividends. A company paid him $500 for the right to manufacture Rube Waddell 'smooth delivery' cigars. They sold for a nickel, which was four cents more than Rube usually paid for cigars. He was delighted when twenty free boxes, one for each inning of the marathon, arrived at his door one morning.

A pharmacist from Atlanta, ironically a former alcoholic, had invented a carbonated beverage that was said to have health benefits. The drink was now being sold outside of Georgia and promoted as "The Great National Drink". It was called Coca-Cola. The marketing department convinced Napoleon Lajoie and Rube to have their names appear on billboards.

Lajoie, who had downed a lot of beers back when he played for the Phillies in the '90's but rarely drank anymore, was a natural choice for a health beverage. He was quoted on the signs as saying, "I drink Coca-Cola regularly. It is the best, most refreshing beverage an athlete can drink." Rube was the last man on earth any of his managers or teammates would associate with a soft drink, but on the billboards it said "Rube keeps Coca-Cola on the bench for an emergency and finds it REFRESHING! INVIGORATING! and SUSTAINING!"

Another company paid him two hundred dollars to lend his name to their bourbon, a beverage with which Rube was a great deal more familiar. The cigars sold well, the whiskey not so much. He was dismayed when he received only one free case of the bourbon. Maybe it was just as well.

The next week Alf Jones brought a visitor into the A's clubhouse. He was very well-dressed, sporting an ascot, a cane, and a top hat. Jones introduced him to Rube.

"This is Arthur Conan Doyle, Rube, the writer."

"Good ta know ya, Art. What paper you with?"

Connie Mack, who was nearby and overheard, struggled to suppress a guffaw.

"He's not that kind of writer Rube. He's in America promoting The Return of Sherlock Holmes," Jones explained.

"Where's this Holmes fella been?" Rube asked.

Now Mack couldn't hold it in, he laughed out loud.

"He's a fictional character. He solves murders."

"And he took off and nobody could find him?"

"Maybe he took off to fish like you do, Rube," chuckled Jasper Davis.

Ed Plank tried to help out. "Mister Doyle wrote three stories about Sherlock Holmes that a lot of people read, and now he's written another one."

"I am sorry to hear you are not an admirer, Mister Waddell, though everyone tells me you are a terrific twirler. Perhaps you could cross the pond and try retiring a few of our top batsmen," Doyle suggested.

"Didn't know you played baseball over there, Art."

"We don't, but we *do* play cricket."

"Oh, right, I've heard of cricket. A couple of catchers - Nig Clarke and Roger Bresnahan - have taken to wearing cricket pads on their shins. The other catchers are ribbin' them about it somethin' awful. Is it true your games can take days to play?"

"They can," said Doyle. "I hear that you pitched for almost an entire day last week."

"Seemed like it. Say, good luck with that writing of yours. And I hope you don't lose Holmes again," said Rube as he headed for his locker.

Ed Plank and Alf Jones tried to apologize, but Doyle told them to stop.

"The man is an absolute delight, gentlemen - like some character James Fennimore Cooper might have invented. I've heard about some of his heroics off the field, he's a real-life Paul Bunyan or Davy Crockett. You wouldn't expect a man like that to sit around reading novels would you? Your Rube is an American treasure."

In his next start Rube shut out Chicago, allowing just six hits. Then he went in for Sheldon Henley and finished off a win without surrendering a run. Then he shut out Detroit. Next he shut out Cleveland on three hits. Nobody got past first base. Then he saved a game for Andy Coakley, allowing no runs after taking over in the ninth. In the span of five days

Rube had pitched five times and pitched 47 consecutive innings of scoreless ball. Nobody had ever done that. He'd shattered Cy Young's consecutive shutout innings record. He was at the top of his game and the A's were in first place.

Andy Coakley went to talk to Connie Mack. The manager took off his hat and set it on his desk. He set down his scorecard and said, "Good game, Andy. We needed that."

"Thanks, Connie. Rube saved my bacon though. Do you mind if I ask you something?"

"Not at all, son, what is it?"

"You I know my wife and my folks are in Rhode Island."

"Yes, I know, Andy. What about it?"

"Well it's just that I haven't seen them all season and this is as close to Rhode Island as we are going to get."

"And you would like a couple of days off to go see them," Connie interrupted.

"I know it's asking a lot, but you often give Rube time off."

"We all know that Rube needs time away . . ."

"I'm not complaining, Connie, we all understand that Rube's ... special."

"Don't you worry, you can have time off to see your folks. I'll be using Plank, Bender, and Waddell the next three days anyway. You can meet us at the train station in Providence on our way to New York on Friday."

Rube started against Cy Young in the last game of the Boston series. He was wild in the first inning and gave up two walks and three hits. His scoreless streak was done. Rube was disgusted with himself and Connie Mack could tell; he took him out.

When the A's boarded the train for New York, Schreck thought Rube was acting strange - even for him.

"What's eating you?" Schreck asked on the way to the dining car.

"What are you talking about?"

"I don't know, you're just not acting like you usually do, it's like you got your knickers in a knot."

Rube gave Schreck a shove that sent him reeling. "Probably just you that's buggin' me. Come on let's eat. I'm starved."

"Course you are, we haven't eaten since breakfast two hours ago, you must be famished."

RUBE WADDELL

When the train stopped in Providence waiting there on the platform as promised was Andy Coakley. He was always a snappy dresser and today he looked quite the dandy in a freshly-pressed suit and starched white collar. He was wearing a straw hat with a small bright red ribbon in it. Rube and Schreck were looking out the window.

"How long's Coakley been in the big leagues?" asked Rube.

"Three years I think. Why?"

"Plenty long enough to know the rule then."

"What rule are you talking about?"

"The one that says nobody wears straw hats after Labor Day," Rube explained.

"Oh, right. We're supposed to put a fist through them and throw them out."

"And what happens if you don't smash your hat by Labor Day?"

"Somebody smashes it *for* you."

"That's the rule and everybody knows it."

"And if they don't know it, you go out of your way to smash their hat for them."

"I have been known to bust a few hats here and there."

"Here and there? Are you kidding me? You must have set some kind of straw hat smashing record by now."

"Looks as though I'm going to have to help Andy and take care of the hat smashing for him."

"I suppose nothing would stop you."

Rube put a hand over his heart. "It's my sworn duty as a veteran ball player."

He tore off the train and down the platform to where Coakley was gathering up his bags. He ran right at him and reached to snatch the hat off his head. Coakley looked up just in time to see someone coming straight for him. He figured it must be some maniac or robber. He deftly stepped to the side and swung a suitcase at the onrushing demon.

The bag caught Rube squarely in the face. He figured that Coakley had done it on purpose. He roared like a crazed grizzly bear and went after him.

By now several other players had seen the altercation and rushed in. They knew Coakley hadn't hit Rube on purpose and they tried to pull him away. But Rube was in no mood to back down. He threw one teammate after another over his shoulder as if they were bags of potatoes.

More teammates arrived and they finally managed to knock Rube off his feet. He landed hard on the pavement. On his shoulder. His *left* shoulder.

"Are you all right?" Ossee asked when they got back on the train. "You landed pretty hard back there."

"It hurt, but not all that much. Move over. I want to sit by the window."

Given Rube's mood and what had just transpired, Ossee obliged and gave Rube the window seat. Rube reached into his pocket and took out a silver flask. Then he took off his suit jacket, raised his window several inches, and sat back. His left side was up against the open window.

"That's pretty cold air coming in there, Eddie."

"So?"

"Are you sure that's wise, with you having just hurt your shoulder back there?"

"I don't imagine it'll make it any worse," said Rube, taking a long pull on his flask.

"Suit yourself. But I would close that window if I were you."

"Well you're not me. Now give me some peace and quiet."

Rube went to see Connie Mack two days later. He was close to tears. Connie looked up. He couldn't remember when he'd seen Rube so concerned about anything. "What is it, Eddie? You look as though you've seen a ghost."

"It's my arm, Connie. I was shaving this morning and I heard a click in my shoulder. After that I could barely lift my arm."

"Hold on a minute," said Connie. He went to a closet and rummaged around. He came out with an old catcher's mitt back from his playing days. Rube gave him a funny look.

"Have you forgotten I used to be a catcher? Grab a ball and try tossing me a few."

Rube got a baseball out of a bag that was hanging on the doorknob and got his glove. His first throw just barely reached Connie. Rube grimaced in pain. His next throw bounced twenty feet in front of the plate. He grabbed his shoulder and yelped in agony.

It was evident that he would not be pitching again for quite some time. Would the A's be able to win the pennant without him?

RUBE WADDELL
KING *of the* HALL *of* FLAKES

CHAPTER THIRTY TWO

DID THE GAMBLERS
GET TO WADDELL?

The White Sox were really the only team with a chance to catch the A's. In the first week after Rube's injury they gained a little ground, but not much. Ed Plank, Chief Bender, and Andy Coakley picked up the slack and the Athletics hit better than they had all year.

Connie Mack tried sending Rube in to pitch just once. The A's were down by seven runs and the game was all but out of reach. The first batter Rube faced drilled a pitch into deep right for a double. The next hitter laced one almost all the way to the distant center field fence. Connie didn't need to see any more.

"It was evident to the most superficial observer," wrote Alf Jones, "that Waddell was not right."

Rube kept bugging Mack to let him pitch again but Connie kept turning him down. On September 28 Ed Plank struck out a dozen batters in a huge win over Chicago and the next day Chief Bender held the White Sox to one run while the A's lashed six extra base hits. Without any invitation from Connie Mack, Rube went out and warmed up in hopes of starting the next game.

As usual, he started his warm up by swinging his arms around his shoulders. He heard a loud snap. "Oh, no," he said to himself.

He gingerly moved his left arm back and forth. Miraculously, or so it seemed to him, there was no pain. "Hot damn," he yelled to Schreck. "Ossee, my arm's all better!" Rube hurried to tell Connie Mack the good news.

"Let's wait and see, Eddie. You've told me several times that your arm was healed and it wasn't." He got his glove and had Rube throw him a few. He got them to the plate this time and they had a little bit of speed, but no movement.

"Can I start, Connie?"

"Not today, Eddie. I don't want to risk making it worse. Plank will start."

"He just pitched two days ago, Connie. Nothing against him, Ed's a swell fellow, but you know he's not like I am ... or like I *was*. He can't pitch without a few days' rest."

"He'll have to. I am not taking a chance on you right now."

              ℓ   *ℓ*   *ℓ*

Plank gave up twelve hits and four runs. The whole time Connie Mack kept thinking that if Rube were healthy he'd be making monkeys of the Hitless Wonders. The White Sox left town just a game back of the A's, but when they got back to Chicago they turned into their own worst enemies. First they lost two games to the lowly Senators, then they lost to the St. Louis Browns, who were even worse. The A's clinched the pennant.

The baseball bugs in Philadelphia went wild. There had been no World Series the year before due to the animosity between the National and American Leagues but now the war was finally over. The two pennant-winning teams would meet; the A's would play the New York Giants for the championship. It was time to see if Rube would be able to pitch in the Series. Ed Plank matched up fairly well with the Giants' number two starter Iron Joe McGinnity, but the A's would certainly need Rube to take on Christy Mathewson.

              ℓ   *ℓ*   *ℓ*

Andy Coakley struggled and lasted just two innings against the Senators in a game that now meant nothing. Connie called for Rube.

"How much you have to drink last night?" Schreck asked him.

"I don't know. You were with me. If you don't remember I sure as hell don't. I didn't figure to pitch today."

"Well, hung, sober, or pissed to the gills, this is your chance to show Connie you can pitch in the Series so don't fuck it up."

With the pennant clinched there were a lot of empty seats, but the small crowd sent up a roar when they saw that Rube was going in to pitch. He started badly, walking three batters in his first inning before getting the third out on a hard groundball to Harry Davis.

"He sure isn't throwing very hard but I thought his arm was ruined," Alf Jones said to Lou Brisken from *The Philadelphia Record*.

"That's what they want us to believe," said Brisken.

"What's that supposed to mean?"

"You haven't heard the rumors?"

"What rumors are you talking about, Lou?"

"It's all been worked out. The gamblers have things figured out before they even happen and they're usually spot on."

"Meaning what?" Jones asked.

"Meaning that they figured the A's were going to win the pennant and they got to Waddell."

"All right, Lou, I guess you're going to have to spell it out for me. I've only been covering baseball a couple of seasons and apparently I don't know how these things work."

"Most folks figure it's all above board, Alf. It's not. The gamblers wait until the odds are in and then they decide which team they can make the most money from. In this particular scenario the best thing is to have the odds close on account of Waddell matching up so well against Mathewson."

"But?" said Jones.

"But Waddell ain't gonna pitch. So they make a pile bettin' on the Giants."

"What if Waddell does pitch? The man's always had a rubber arm. So what if he's got a sore shoulder? Hell, he can pitch twenty innings and come back and throw the next day."

"Are you thick in the head? You must be if you still haven't figured it out."

"Figured out what for Christ's sakes? You mean those stories out of New York that Rube's afraid to take on Mathewson? That's bullshit and you know it. Rube would be in seventh heaven going up against Mathewson in the Series."

"He's not yellow, the gamblers got to him, Alf. Pure and simple. They gave Rube a thousand bucks and a few cases of good old Kentucky bourbon and promised him hot, easy women every night and Rube agreed to stay hurt."

"He's never laid down for gamblers before, at least as far as anyone I've ever talked to knows."

"Maybe not, but it seems pretty gol darned shady that the best pitcher in the American League, a man who can pitch pretty nearly every day and has never had a serious injury, happens to get hurt just before the World Series."

"You may be right, Lou. It does seem a might fishy. But that's three innings now without giving up a run. Let's see how he does the rest of the way."

"Suit yourself, Alf. But I tell you, they got to Waddell and he ain't gonna pitch in the Series."

RUBE WADDELL

For the next several minutes the most recurring sounds in the stadium were the echoes resounding off the empty seats. They were echoes from the cracks of bats as the feeble Senators smacked Rube's deliveries all over the park. His shoots had nowhere near their usual velocity, his curves had no bite, and he struggled to find the strike zone. Being badly hung over didn't help. In the sixth inning he fell down trying to field a routine comebacker to the mound. In the eighth he gave up four straight hits, something he'd never done before. He uncorked a wild pitch and when he tried to pick a runner off first he missed Harry Davis by ten feet. In all, he walked five and gave up six runs. There was no chance he was going to be able to pitch in the World Series.

Thousands of New Yorkers descended on Philadelphia with bundles of cash to put down on the Series. Rube was in a foul mood as the A's assembled for their team photo before the first game. When Alf Jones spotted him in the stands talking to some cranks a few minutes later he came down from the press box to talk to him.

"Hey, Rube, how's that shoulder of yours?"

"Just great, Alf, just fuckin' great."

"You hearing what they're saying about you?"

"What? About me bein' afraid to go up against Mathewson?"

"Ya."

"Well it's nothin' but a foul lie, and people oughta know that."

"What about the gamblers plying you with money, booze, and prostitutes to keep you from pitching?"

"That's hogwash. I wouldn't take money to throw a ballgame. Never have, never will. And I like women, but I don't go for hookers."

Rube nipped from his silver flask throughout the game. His presence did nothing to dispel the rumors. No shady characters approached him, just some arrogant cranks from New York.

"Too gutless to take on Mathewson?" one yelled.

"Havin' a good time with those whores?" another called out.

Rube wanted to punch the loudmouth bastards but his arm hurt too much.

All such talk was ridiculous. Rube badly wanted to be out there, especially when he saw his teammates struggle mightily against Mathewson. He shut them out in Game One.

"Sure would have been great to see the two go head to head," Alf

Jones said to Lou Brisken. "Remember how Rube pitched April through August. This could have been a real classic with the two of them locking horns."

          ℓℓ   *ℓℓ*   *ℓℓ*

With the A's down three games to one, a desperate Connie Mack had Rube warm up before Game Five. He had nothing. His fastest throws had absolutely no zip and he couldn't curve the ball in the least. His control was no better and he would have been hammered mercilessly. He threw one pitch right into the grandstand. Luckily it lacked Rube's usual velocity. It hit a booster square in the head.

It would be Mathewson, not the injured Waddell, who would get all the glory in the 1905 Series with three consecutive shutouts. No one could ever top that performance. The only consolation for Rube was that, with the A's bats as ice cold as they were, he probably couldn't have won anyway.

Lou Brisken wrote about Waddell's absence in *The Record.*

> *"With Waddell at the height of his powers it is sad indeed that he was robbed of the opportunity to perform on baseball's largest stage, the World Series competition. Waddell's 287 strikeouts this year would have been a record except for the fact that he himself has surpassed that total in each of the past two seasons. He led all twirlers with 46 appearances, won 26 games in spite of injuries and feeble run support from his team on several occasions, and compiled a miserly Earned Run Average of 1.48. Baseball enthusiasts will always ponder how marvelous three duels between Waddell and Mathewson could have been."*

Poor Andy Coakley would be hounded by cranks for years about "the straw hat that kept Rube Waddell out of the '05 Series." He was booed so badly and so often Connie Mack finally had to send him to the National League.

RUBE WADDELL
KING *of the* HALL *of* FLAKES

CHAPTER THIRTY THREE

A HERO AGAIN

Rube spent the winter with his parents in St. Mary's. They'd opened a grocery store and Rube helped out there a bit. He spent most of his time hunting and fishing, but wherever he went he was a celebrity. He was so popular with the folks in Elk County that some actually thought about getting him to run for governor.

"I don't think he'd garner many votes from the Prohibitionists," mused one such supporter.

Rube went to Philadelphia a few times to be treated by Dr. McFarland, who was the closest thing to a team doctor the A's had. He x-rayed Rube's arm and put him on an exercise routine that soon put the elasticity back in his arm and restored almost all of the velocity he'd possessed in his younger days. His waistline was not what it had been though. He'd polished off too many groceries and several glasses of beer every day had added to his girth as well.

On March 1 he was at the train station with his teammates for their journey to Montgomery, Alabama. Connie Mack hadn't even considered a return to New Orleans with all of its diversions. Once again their train was derailed and once again Rube took the lead in the rescue operation. The engine was damaged beyond repair and he helped the railway men hitch the cars to a mail train on its way from Atlanta.

Once they were back underway again Mack called Rube to his car. He had bad news for him. "Eddie, I am afraid we are going to be cutting your salary this season," he told Rube.

"But Connie, I had my best year last season. Sure, not quite as many strikeouts, but I led the league in a whole bunch of things."

"Yes, but you have obviously not exercised this winter, except perhaps your drinking arm. You're overweight and may not been in proper condition to start the season. Furthermore, your tomfoolery last August over that infernal straw hat may have cost us the World Series."

"How much are you cutting me?"

"Instead of twenty-four hundred dollars you'll receive twelve hundred."

"So you're not gonna give me five dollars every week like before?"

"No, Eddie, I will now be giving you two dollars and fifty cents each week."

"Can I have that now?"

"As soon as we get to Montgomery. You won't be needing it until then."

Mack gave him his $2.50 in an envelope when they were getting off the train, as well as an extra dollar out of his own pocket.

*   &   &*

The roster would be nearly the same one that had won in the pennant in '05. Rookie Jack Coombs was going to take over Weldon Henley's place in the starting rotation and John Knight would move to third base so Monte Cross could return to short. Rube was happy to see that Bris Lord was taking Danny Hoffman's spot in the outfield. Lord's parents had sent Rube a beautiful tie pin in appreciation for the kindness he'd shown their son.

Rube and Ossee had a few of the players up to their room on the second floor of The Montgomery Manor. They generally preferred the lower floors. If the hotel had no elevator it was a lot easier to stagger up one or two flights of stairs than five or six after a night of carousing.

The next morning Rube woke up in a hospital bed. He hurt all over, though it didn't seem as if anything was broken. He yelled for a nurse. A sour-faced woman who had a small moustache and her hair wrenched into a bun eventually came to see what he was hollering about.

Rube was taken aback by her appearance. "That face'd make a freight train take a dirt road," he thought to himself.

"What happened to me?" he asked.

"You had a very bad fall, Mister Waddell."

"A fall? From *where*?"

"Perhaps you should ask your friend. He just arrived. I will bring him in."

A couple of minutes later Schreck came in.

"Eddie, you're alive! Anything broken?"

Rube looked at the nurse.

She said, "Mister Waddell has no broken bones, only some very bad bruises. He was very fortunate. It could have been much worse."

"She hasn't told me what happened."

"You don't remember?"

"No. For God's sake, what was it? Did a streetcar hit me? A delivery wagon?"

"We didn't go out last night, Eddie."

"That's right. We stayed in and had a couple of drinks in the room with some of the boys."

"The boys had a couple of drinks. You and I may have had more."

"What makes you say that?"

"Because around midnight you got the idea you could fly."

"I what?"

"You bet everybody that you could fly."

"I *did*? What I do then?"

"You stood on a chair and jumped out the window."

"For the love of Pete. Why didn't you stop me?"

"I'd bet a hundred dollars you could do it."

℮ ℮ ℮

Rube missed just two days of practice. He had been lucky indeed. Connie decided it was best to have him throw batting practice rather than start him in an exhibition game. His teammates smashed his pitches all over the Montgomery field.

"I don't think Rube's got it anymore," Harry Davis told Danny Murphy.

"I got a feeling you're right, Jasper. His pitches are just floating over the plate."

Though they'd been keeping their voices down, Schreck overheard them.

"Hey, Eddie."

"What?"

"I just heard Davis and Murphy talking about you."

"What did they say?"

"They say you haven't got any speed anymore. Cuz of the way you've been lobbing them up there like tomatoes in batting practice."

"What d'ya think I should do?"

"Davis has another turn. Lob some more to Topsy and when Davis comes up show him what you got."

Hartsel was the next batter. Rube threw him five pitches, all right down the middle, and all very slow. Topsy belted each of them to the wall.

Harry Davis and Danny Murphy looked at each other and sighed.

"Poor Rube," said Murphy. "What do you figure Connie's gonna do with him?"

"Well he sure as hell can't use him when he's throwing like that."

"I suppose not. He must have hurt it real bad last year. Rube's gonna be heartbroken when Connie cuts him loose."

Davis grabbed a bat. It was his turn.

"You gonna take it easy on him, Harry?" Murphy asked.

"What good would that do? It'd only prolong the agony."

"I suppose. Might as well make it obvious so Rube'll see he's finished and Connie won't feel so bad."

"I'm gonna see if I can put one over the fence."

Davis strode to the plate. Rube looked in at him and pretended to be worried. He made a show of rubbing his left shoulder and shook his head at Schreck.

"Take it easy," Ossee yelled out, "you don't have to prove anything?"

Rube threw a pitch that was outside and painfully slow. He pretended to grimace. The next pitch was so slow it didn't even reach home.

"Try and get it to the plate at least," yelled Schreck.

"I'm tryin', I'm tryin'." Rube took off his cap and wiped his brow. Slowly he put his cap back on and kicked the rubber.

"It's all right, Eddie," called Schreck. "You can do it."

The next pitch went by Harry Davis in a flash. It started waist high and was up around his neck when it flew across the plate before smacking into Schreck's mitt. Scheck fell backwards, partly because of the speed and partly because he was laughing so hard at the look on Davis' face.

"What the fuck?" Davis grunted.

The next two pitches were even faster, though that seemed impossible. Davis returned to the bench with his head down.

"I think I *missed* it, Harry," Danny Murphy said to him, cupping his hand over his eyes to block the sun and looking around the outfield. "Which fence did you hit it over?"

"Very funny, smart ass."

"Looks like Rube isn't all washed up after all."

"Apparently not."

        *   *   *

Rube and Ossee were walking back to the hotel after the practice and noticed that a crowd had gathered on a corner.

"What's going on there?" Rube asked a kid who was trying to push his way to the front so he could see better.

"Some delivery fella got his wagon stuck in the trolley tracks. Now the whole line's gettin' backed up."

"How long they been tryin' to get it out?" Rube asked, gesturing at the men who were straining to dislodge the wagon.

"About ten minutes I guess," said the kid.

Rube stepped forward. "How's about you let me have a try at it?"

The crew was happy for a break, though they were certain there was no way that one man could budge, much less move the wagon by himself. They took handkerchiefs out of their pockets to wipe the sweat from their brows and stepped back out of Rube's way.

"That fellow is Rube Waddell," one worker told another.

The other man just looked at him.

"From the A's," the worker explained.

The other man, who had just arrived from Italy, said, "I gotta no idea whata you is a talkin' about."

Rube went to the back of the wagon. He bent over and put his back up against it. Then he reached under and put his hands under the bottom. At first the wagon didn't budge. The men smiled at one another. Rube grunted and applied a little more force. Slowly the wagon began moving, just inches at first, then up and right out of the tracks.

"Fuck, that son of a bitch is strong!" the driver of the wagon exclaimed, looking around to be sure none of the women present could hear him.

"Is he ever!" another crewman agreed. "Lucky he came by. We mighta been here all day."

         * * *

The next day Rube was a hero on the field. The A's were playing an exhibition game against a team from the nearby college. In the fourth inning Rube walked one of the college kids. As he jogged to first base the lone umpire came out from behind the plate to position himself behind the mound where he could see home plate but also be close to second in case the runner tried to steal.

Rube was taking it easy on the collegians, throwing only a little harder than he had in the batting practice before Harry Davis needed to be straightened out. The next hitter was the biggest kid on the college team. A girl wearing a pink bonnet called out to him from the stands. "Hit one for me, Ralph. You can do it."

Rube smiled. Then he threw a floater right over the plate. Ossee chuckled. The kid hit a line shot up the middle. It was headed right for the umpire. Rube had no time to get his glove up to catch it and the umpire had no time to duck. Rube stuck out his left hand and caught the ball. If it had traveled another few inches it would have struck the umpire in the head. The crowd gasped.

Rube's hand hurt like hell but he felt better when the umpire thanked him. "You just saved my life, Rube. That shot was so fast it would surely have killed me."

The *Montgomery Advertiser* mentioned the remarkable catch in an article about a fire that had broken out a few hours after the game.

> *"Rube Waddell, who is in our city with the Philadelphia Athletics base ball club, attended a fire on Decatur Street last evening and helped colored men fight the flames. They were able to spare a part of the residence from destruction. The property damage is insignificant as the home was the property of a Negro family. On his way to his hotel afterwards Waddell was set upon while walking along Bell Street. Negro highwaymen apparently hit the player over the head. The blow left Waddell with a nasty gash. The attackers took $40 from the twirler."*

Rube tried to get Connie Mack to give him the $40 that had been stolen. Connie was quite sure that Rube had helped put out the fire and he wasn't surprised that he'd been foolish enough to walk around streets in a bad part of town in the middle of the night, but he had a very hard time swallowing that Rube would have be carrying $40. He reluctantly gave Rube $20, which he figured was probably about $19.50 more than he'd actually had in his pockets.

CHAPTER THIRTY FOUR

TOO SORE TO THROW

As the '06 season got underway it became more and more obvious that Rube's performance was being affected by his carousing. Clear-headed, he shut out the Senators and the Americans. Then he went out and celebrated. Hung over and bleary-eyed against Boston, he walked seven batters, let a ground ball go through his legs, and threw a wild pitch that allowed a run to score. He lasted only six innings. Connie had a long talk with him after the game. He told him he was letting the team down, that a lot of people depended on him and the A's needed him at his best or they had no chance to win another pennant. Rube listened.

Rube bore down and tried his best. He shut out Cleveland and then he blanked Chicago. In only one inning did he allow two runners to reach base. In his next start, against the Tigers, he pitched a masterful one-hitter. The only safety was a bunt by Tyrus Cobb. It was a third straight shutout. Rube didn't care that much that he'd just missed a no-hitter again, but he hated that it was Cobb that spoiled it.

Thanks to Rube's latest streak the A's were now in first place. Schreck suggested they go celebrate.

"Nah, I got to behave myself, Ossee. Connie says I can't let the team down, I'm going for a ride instead."

"Suit yourself. I'm going for a drink."

⌁ ⌁ ⌁

Rube went home and got his Labrador retriever, whom he had named Connie Mack. The canine Connie Mack was always excited to go anywhere with Rube and his tail wagged a mile a minute. Rube rented a carriage and the two headed along Ridge Street. It was a beautiful afternoon. Several people recognized Rube and waved. He stopped to get ice cream and gave Connie Mack a few licks of it.

They journeyed on, Rube whistling his favorite tunes and tipping his derby when they passed pretty girls. Some kids ran along beside them for a while. Rube stopped the carriage a couple of times so the kids could pet Connie Mack.

"Rube, look out!" a young boy yelled as the carriage reached the corner of 23rd and Ridge.

A delivery wagon loaded with beer barrels was headed straight for them. The teamster had obviously lost control. Rube pulled on the reins as hard as he could and narrowly avoided a head-on collision, but the carriage flipped over. Rube jumped to safety, as did Connie Mack, but Rube caught his thumb in the carriage's whip socket. It was his left thumb and it was throbbing as Rube got to his feet and assured onlookers he wasn't hurt.

Connie Mack had run off. He was nowhere to be found. The teamster insisted on taking Rube to the hospital to have his thumb looked at. The x-rays revealed a fracture. When he showed Doc McFarlane he was told he would be out for at least two weeks.

The newspapers reported on the accident and asked the public to be on the lookout for a Labrador retriever that answered to the name Connie Mack. Rube got a huge ovation when he went to the A's game the next day. He wore his best suit and sat in the press section smoking cigars and showing off his cast.

"Hey Rube," said a crank sitting just behind him. "You hear 'bout that women's team in Kansas?"

"What about 'em?" Rube asked.

"They're called the Kansas Bloomer Girls but some of their players are really men. They got a hard-throwing pitcher named Joe Wood but he goes by the name of Lucy Totton. Another feller goes by Dolly Madison."

"Ya don't say," said Rube, a little bored by this news, though he was picturing girls playing in bloomers.

"And another feller, a lefty twirler calls himself Lady Waddell."

"I'll warrant ya he's a fine pitcher," said Rube, "and the best lookin' one of the bunch."

        ℓc   *ℓc*   *ℓc*

Rube removed the cast before he was supposed to and then begged Connie Mack to let him pitch. Mack reluctantly agreed. The Hitless Wonders were in town. The damaged thumb didn't affect Rube's speed but it did affect his control, he walked seven batters in the first three innings. In the fourth he eased up on the speed to gain more control and the White Sox ripped his pitchers to every corner of the park, scoring five runs before anyone was out.

Clearly Rube was not yet ready. Chicago swept the series and the

A's fell to third place. Rube went on a bender. He drank and slept in a saloon in a seedy part of St. Louis for three straight days and nights. When the team moved on to Detroit, Rube went to see Connie Mack and told him his hip was hurting. He asked Connie to let him go up to Mount Clemens for a little bit of fishing.

"Be careful with the thumb and be ready to pitch when you get back, Eddie. Do you hear me?"

"Loud and clear, boss. See you in two days."

&c   &c   &c

Rube laid off the bottle and caught some of the biggest fish the folks in Mount Clemens had seen. When he got back Connie Mack sent him out against Addie Joss and the Naps. The A's managed just five hits. Rube gave up seven hits, walked three, uncorked a wild pitch, and struck out only five Naps. But he drew a walk off Joss and then scored on a bad hop single and that was all he needed. It was another shutout and the A's were back in first place.

It was good to get the win, but when Rube and Ossee went out for a few beers after the game Rube was holding his left thumb. He asked the bartender for a glass of ice water and then submerged the thumb in it.

"I don't think I shoulda gone fishing, Ossee. All that casting put a strain on it. "

"You're going to have to be careful with it or it's never going to heal," Schreck told him.

&c   &c   &c

Rube's next start was against Washington. The Senators didn't hit much better than the White Sox had, but Rube's control was awful. After walking five in the first three innings he held back on the speed and the Senators teed off on him. They stranded eight runners but four others scored and the A's managed just two runs. Rube begged Connie for another chance against Washington. Connie said yes, and it didn't take long for him to regret it. They did better by one, scoring five runs this time, though two were unearned.

Ben Shibe went to Connie Mack's office after the loss.

"You know it isn't just the thumb, don't you Connie?"

"I know, Ben. It's the drinking again. He just cannot leave the stuff alone."

"Should we get rid of Schreck?"

"No, that wouldn't be fair. Schreck's having a good year with the bat and it's not as if he is pouring the drinks down Rube's throat. He'd be drinking just as much without Schreck, he'd just be doing it alone."

Mack gave Rube the ball on July the 4th against the Highlanders. After a morning shower the field was muddy. Clark Griffith had his players bunt in hopes that Rube would slip. He managed to keep his footing and, though New York had a runner on every inning, Rube neatly worked out of jams the whole afternoon, stranded eleven, and won 3-1.

In his next start he struck out eleven in an extra-inning win over the Naps. But once again he was erratic, issuing five walks and hitting a batter. When Schreck won the game for him with a two-run double in the tenth the crowd of 22,000 Philadelphia rooters went berserk.

When Detroit came into town Chief Bender took sick as he quite often did. He was known to enjoy a beverage or two once in a while himself. Connie Mack asked Rube to pitch on short rest. Before the game he and Schreck were playing pepper with Topsy Hartsel and Bris Lord. Schreck playfully whipped the ball at Rube. His reflexes had always been amazing, but not this time. The hard throw hit him squarely on his bad thumb. It immediately began to swell.

"It's not that bad, Connie," I can still throw.

"You know what happens when the thumb is swollen, Eddie. You have trouble getting the ball over the plate with any speed so you ease up and get hit hard."

Rube shut out the Tigers in the first two innings and was delighted when he struck out Ty Cobb. The paranoid and foul-tempered Georgian, who apparently was now sleeping with a loaded revolver under his pillow, glared at him. He spat a stream of tobacco juice as he picked up his glove from where he'd left it behind third base and ran out to his position.

The third inning proved Rube's undoing. He walked a batter and surrendered two singles and a double. The Tigers scored four runs and Rube was lifted for a pinch hitter when it was his turn up. Swinging a bat bothered the thumb too.

After the game Connie Mack sent Rube for X-rays. They revealed a split along the bone. He wouldn't be pitching for a while. When the A's left on a road trip Rube, whose record stood at 12-4, stayed home. He decided to go fishing, but this time though he wore a brace so the casting wouldn't hurt his thumb.

The Inquirer had a laugh over Rube's favourite pastime.

> *In fishing it is Rube's delight*
> *To take a bottle on the trip.*

And though he doesn't always get a bite
He always thinks to take a nip.

On July 25 Rube tested the thumb against Detroit. He lasted two innings. He struggled with his control again and berated the umpire so badly that he was thrown out of the game. He didn't mind, his thumb was killing him.

The A's maintained a slim lead, but four teams were now breathing down their necks. Luckily, Cleveland and Detroit had key players out with injuries. Chicago was healthy but they still weren't hitting enough to mount a charge. The Highlanders were doing better than anyone expected. Willie Keeler, Hal Chase, who made great plays at first unless he had money down on the game, and Kid Elberfeld were all batting over .300. When Rube finally rejoined the A's in Chicago on August 5 they were just two games in front of New York.

He started against the White Sox after they'd won the first two games of the five-game series. Ed Walsh pitched for Chicago and the A's could do nothing with his spitballs. They didn't get a single runner past first base. Rube shut out the White Sox for five innings but then faded fast and was taken out. He wasn't the only A's pitcher who struggled against Chicago. The White Sox won a doubleheader the next day and took over first place with the sweep.

The Athletics traveled to St. Louis for another five-game series, hoping to regain the lead with a sweep of Jimmy McAleer's light-hitting Browns. The A's lost the Friday and Saturday games though, each by one run, and then Chief Bender got roughed up for seven runs in a third straight loss on Sunday. It could have been more. After three innings of drizzle the baseball was sopping wet and the Chief was having a tough time gripping it. George Stone hit a line drive foul along the left field fence where Rube was warming up in case Connie wanted to have him bail out Bender. Rube noticed the umpire wasn't watching. He chuckled and threw the dry ball he'd been using in and kept the wet one. Bender did a lot better after the switcheroo. That night, Rube and Ossee went out on the town, even though the teams would play a doubleheader the next day and Rube was going to start the first game. They made their way from bar to bar in hopes that people would recognize them and buy them drinks.

At the Cattleman's Bar and Grill they hooked up with a group of baseball enthusiasts who said they wished the Browns had some stars like the A's.

"If you pitched for us we'd have a decent chance of winning a pennant," said a big fellow in a cowboy hat with a handlebar moustache. "You want a whiskey or a beer?"

"Make it a shot of the redeye," said Rube. "And how about one for my pal Ossee here?"

The man patted Rube hard on the back. "Not a problem." He signaled to the bartender for a round of whiskeys. "Would you consider playing for the Browns if you ever left Philly, Rube?"

"I most certainly would. This is a helluva town. Kind of hot this time of year though."

"It was so hot last night we slept on the roof of our hotel again," said Ossee.

"It's deadly out there on the field in the afternoon," said Rube. "Hotter than nickel night at the whore house."

"I can just imagine. It's hot enough to fry an egg in the grandstand. Why don't you do what the Browns do?"

"What's that?" asked Schreck.

"They put a head of lettuce in an ice box and then tear off leaves during the game."

"What for?" asked Rube.

"They stick the leaves under their caps to keep cool."

"What a great idea!" Rube yelled, almost knocking over his whiskey. "I'm gonna do just that. That way I might not sweat off ten pounds every damn time I pitch here."

"How's the th, th, th, thumb, Rube?" asked the man's friend, who wore expensive clothes and a derby and talked with a stutter.

"Don't tell the Browns, but it's actually not a hundred per cent yet."

"You gonna be able to pitch tomorrow?" asked the man with the big moustache.

"I surely will."

"Can you win though? What have the A's lost now, eight in a row? You fellas are going to be out of the pennant race if you lose many more."

"I tell you what, my good man," said Rube, pausing to empty his glass, "not only can I win, I am *going* to win. And if I do not . . . if I do not . . . I will quit baseball."

"You'll what?" asked Schreck incredulously, choking on his drink.

"Now don't go making st, st, st, statements like that, Rube," stuttered the man in the expensive suit.

"At least not in front of witnesses," said his friend.

Rube stood up - with more than a little difficulty. "I tell you, one and all, that I will win tomorrow or I am done with the game of baseball," Rube repeated.

Schreck just shook his head. "Well that had better be your last one of those then," he said as the bartender set a new drink in front of Rube. "I notice you promised to quit baseball, not drinking."

Rube put an arm around Schreck's shoulders. "I'm drunk my friend, not hysterical."

His eyes were more than a little bloodshot when he took the mound the next morning. He carefully adjusted his cap to make sure the cold leaf of lettuce wouldn't fall out. The Browns' boosters had heard about Rube's vow to quit playing if he lost and taunted him throughout the game.

"Nice knowin' ya, Rube," yelled one. "You gonna be a full-time actor now?"

"Hey Rube, how much does fishing pay?" Rube" hollered another.

His curves did not have their former snap but his shoots were nearly as fast as they had been before the injury. He struck out only three batters but allowed just six hits and kept posting zeroes. He was glad the Browns weren't bunting. Maybe they were too hot to try beating them out. When it was over the A's had their first win in a week, an 8-0 shutout. Rube would not have to quit the game.

Chief Bender had just pitched the day before, Ed Plank was injured, and Jack Coombs was sick. So Connie Mack asked Rube if he could go again.

"I'd be delighted," said Rube, heading to the ice box. "I am cool as a cucumber, Connie. Or at least a head of lettuce."

Rube struck out two and shut out the Browns in the first inning of the second game. He gave up a single to the first batter in the second and the next hitter hit a slow roller to John Knight at third. He scooped it up and threw the ball five feet over Harry Davis at first. The next batter lined a single. The next one hit a grounder to Monte Cross at short. He picked it up and threw it into the grandstand.

"My hand's sweaty as hell," he told Rube.

Flustered, Rube gave up another hit, this time to the outfield. Topsy Hartsel fielded it and then threw wide of third base. Five runs scored and Connie mercifully took Rube out.

It wasn't as warm in Cleveland when the A's got there. They managed two wins, two losses, and a tie. Rube pitched and lost the third game. He and Schreck were both badly hung over. The A's didn't give Rube much of a chance, getting just two hits. The A's were 3-11 over the past two weeks and now Socks Seybold, Danny Murphy, and Bris Lord were out with injuries. The White Sox had won twelve straight and were pulling away from the pack.

When the A's got back to Philadelphia their supporters were in a foul mood. They weren't interested in hearing about injuries and illnesses and there were a lot of murmurs about how Rube's drinking was affecting his performance.

On August 22 Jack Coombs was coasting along with a 5-1 lead. Then he gave up a pair of runs and the boo birds started up. Fearing the worst, Connie Mack sent Rube in to restore order. He got as many boos as cheers. It rattled him but he fired the first pitch right down the middle. A chorus of mock huzzahs emanated from the grandstand. Luckily Rube was able to retire the side without further damage and the A's won, but the next time he pitched in relief he gave up a long double to Sam Crawford to lose the game in the tenth. The cranks let him have it. "Go get another drink," one shouted.

Rube didn't need to go anywhere for a drink. He'd been sipping from a flask the whole afternoon. So much for the billboards pronouncing that Rube Waddell drank Coca-Cola on the bench.

In his next start he shut out the Tigers for six innings but tired in the seventh and ended up being pulled for a pinch hitter. His performance still inspired *The Inquirer* to say that he "had given a suggestion of his old-time form."

In his next start in St. Louis he held onto the ball and let a runner steal third. He'd forgotten that there was a man on. Then he fumbled a bunt and the runner raced across the plate. On another play, Topsy Hartsel threw the ball to Schreck who caught it and just stood there as the runner slid home safely. Rube allowed fourteen hits - and this was the lowly Browns.

The A's were done. Rube and Ossee sat out the second game in St. Louis. But rather than sit on the bench they went to the bar under the Sportsman's Park grandstand. They had just ordered their third drink when a tall, thin man in a suit approached them.

"Holy shit!" said Schreck. It was Connie Mack.

Schreck was sent home to Philadelphia. The newspapers conjectured that he was finished with the A's.

℔ ℔ ℔

Ed Plank and Chief Bender had been left behind to pitch in some exhibition games or else Mack would have sent Rube home too. Mack had left other players behind to play in exhibitions as well, so he called up some rookies. One was a promising infielder from Columbia University named Eddie Collins. Rube was being punished by having to arrive early and pitch batting practice.

"Grab a bat," Mack told Collins, "You have ten minutes to show us what you've got."

Rube thought it was fun to throw his hardest against the rookies. He blazed one pitch after another over the plate. After nearly thirty pitches Collins had yet to make contact.

When his time was up Collins trudged back to the bench dejectedly. "I'm going back to Columbia, Mister Mack. I hit great in the college league and I thought I was ready for big league pitching. Obviously I'm not."

"Don't be so hard on yourself, or so hasty, Mister Collins. You have a great future in this game."

"Half of those pitches I never even saw."

"Listen son, when Rube is throwing like that there is not a man alive that can get a hit off him."

That made Collins feel a little better, and when he watched the other rookies, they did no better than he had. When the regulars took their turns Rube eased off and let them hit.

After the practice was over Rube went to Collins and gave him some advice.

"You have a good name, Eddie."

"Pardon?"

"Eddie. It's a good name."

"What makes you say that, Rube?"

"Cuz it's my name too."

"Oh, right, I should have thought of that. Obviously Rube is just a name people have given you."

"You mean saddled me with."

"You don't like it?"

"Why would anybody like to be called Rube?"

RUBE WADDELL

"It still bothers you after all this time?"

"Not that much anymore. It did for a long time, but I finally got used to it."

"Do you always throw that hard in a game, Rube? I mean, Eddie."

"No I do not, I save the hard stuff for when I really need an out. That way I can throw a lot more innings."

"That makes sense."

"Anybody who wants to win twenty or more games year after year had better not try to throw bullets every inning. All the top pitchers pace themselves, Cy, Matty, all of 'em."

"Well then, maybe I'll get a few hits after all."

"Mind a piece of advice?"

"Of course not, I clearly need some."

"You obviously got good eyesight and reflexes, and you've got quick wrists, otherwise you would never have hit as well as you did in college. Try standing back in the box a bit. Gives you a little more chance to see what the pitch is gonna do. And don't hold your bat so high, takes too long to get around on a fast one."

"All right, I'll try that."

"And crouch down a little, you're standing up too straight."

"Why? So I have a smaller strike zone?"

"No. So your eyes are closer to the strike zone."

"Thanks, Rube. Sorry, it just feels funny calling you Eddie."

"No need to, Rube'll be fine."

§   §   §

Rube mostly mopped up lost causes the rest of the year. After a game in New York, Rube was walking back to the hotel by himself when a motor car sideswiped him. The vehicle was a roadster, a large, expensive automobile. It was driven by a chauffeur and there was a well-dressed man was in the back seat. The car didn't stop after clipping Rube. He hadn't been hurt, but he'd been knocked down. He got up and looked at his suit. It was dirty and torn. Rube was mad.

"What do you think you're doing? Come back here!" he yelled.

The car didn't stop. It didn't slow down either. It was traveling at about twelve or fifteen miles per hour. Rube tore after it. Pedestrians were startled to see a big man in a torn suit sprinting through the streets. They jumped out of his way as he ran, dodging telephone poles and knocking over garbage cans. All of a sudden a woman appeared out of a shop. She was pushing a baby carriage. She gasped as she saw Rube barreling toward her and her baby. He hurtled the stroller, tipped his hat, and kept on running.

Rube caught up to the motor car when it slowed to turn a corner. He jumped onto the sideboard. The shocked driver and passenger stared at the giant, who was clearly out of his mind.

"What the devil do you think you are doing?" demanded the passenger. He was wearing a pin-striped wool suit and had a huge diamond pin in his pink silk tie.

"That was a nice trick back there," panted Rube.

"To what *trick* are you referring?" asked the passenger.

"The one where your horseless carriage ran into me."

"It did no such thing, I assure you," said the passenger.

"It sure as hell did. Do you think I *threw* myself to the ground?"

"That is impossible, we would never…"

"Actually, sir, I believe this man may be right. I thought I felt a bump along the side about a block and a half back. I *thought* we may have brushed against something."

"Some *one*, you mean," Rube corrected him.

"James! Why did you not stop?"

"I wasn't sure. I didn't hear anyone yell out."

"That's because this contraption of yours is so gol dang noisy."

"Are you injured?" asked the passenger, his tone less pompous now.

"I don't believe that I am."

"Well, my apologies, on behalf of my chauffeur. He has been a most excellent driver … until today that is."

"I am going to need more than an apology, mister."

"What else is it that you require, my good man?"

"A new suit is what I require. Can you not see this one is now dirty and torn?"

"I suppose a little. How much will it cost to replace it?"

"It was my very best suit. Set me back close to fifteen dollars."

"That is quite a lot for a suit."

"Like I said. It was my best."

"Fine. Anything to be on our way." He took out his embroidered wallet and removed a five dollar bill and a ten and handed them to Rube.

"Drive on, James, I must be at the Ritz-Carlton in ten minutes."

The motor car pulled away. Rube jumped off the sideboard and chuckled to himself. The suit had cost only seven dollars but he figured he deserved *something* for his trouble.

RUBE WADDELL

When the season was over Rube pitched in three exhibition games. One was against the Philadelphia Giants, one of the top clubs in the Negro League. Rube struck out eleven. He pitched in two other exhibitions in Scranton and Wilkes-Barre and struck out seventeen in each of them.

CHAPTER THIRTY FIVE

I'LL BET SHE'S GOT SOME
SNAP IN HER GARTERS.

Rube had won twelve out of sixteen before the thumb injury. He'd had six shutouts and his E.R.A. had been 1.40. But after getting hurt because of Schreck's clowning around in that game of pepper Rube had lost twelve of his last sixteen starts. Perhaps worse, he'd been booed at home for the first time. He was not used to it and he didn't like it. The rooters had thought his hard-drinking lifestyle humorous when Rube was winning all the time, but as soon as things went bad for the A's they stopped finding it so funny. Connie Mack believed that alcohol was not only contributing to Rube's injuries, but seriously affecting his recovery from them as well.

Would Rube be able to bounce back or was he worn out and washed up at twenty-nine? A lot of other pitchers had been. The year Rube broke into the majors, Kid Nichols was twenty-nine and had gone 92-37 over his last three seasons, throwing an average of 375 innings a year - far fewer than the 425 he'd averaged his first six years. After sliding to 53-51 in his next three seasons he retired.

"This is easy, once you get the hang of it," Rube told the lovely young girl who was holding his hand to keep him from falling. Her name was Emily and she had beautiful green eyes. She felt tiny roller skating alongside Rube.

They had met at a soda fountain the day before. He was spending the off season in St. Mary's again and when they had struck up a conversation she had told him how much she loved to roller skate.

"You're looking a lot steadier now, Rube," called the owner of the rink a few minutes. "Those skates better?"

"Ya, Burt. Those other ones were way too tight."

Rube and Emily picked up a bit of speed as they hit the straight stretch along the side boards. The ribbons from her bonnet flowed out behind them in a stream of yellow.

"Do you take to everything this quickly?" she asked.

"Pretty near everything. Motorcycle riding and alligator wrestling took a few minutes I guess."

"Alligator wrestling! What would possess anyone to try that?"

"Just somethin' different, I like to try new things."

"But isn't that awfully dangerous?"

"Not if you stay on top and behind the gator. Course you got to watch out for his tail."

"Are you free to come here again tomorrow, Rube?"

"Sure. Once I help out my ma and pa at the store a while. I got to unload a couple of wagons and stock some shelves for them. Then I'll go to your place and get you."

"Maybe we should just meet here."

"What's the matter, Emily, you got a beau?"

"No, it isn't that."

"What is it then?"

"My parents grew up in England, during Queen's Victoria's reign," she explained.

"So?"

"So they have very strict rules when it comes to girls going out."

"Like what?" Rube asked.

"Like a girl should never be alone with a man. There must always be an escort."

"So I can't walk you home after we're done skating?"

"No. I will have to go home with one of the other girls," she said, pointing to her friends. They were talking and giggling on the benches behind the side boards.

As Rube and Emily skated by them he heard one of them say, "He's so big. Emily looks like a little girl skating beside him. He'd have to get down on his knees to kiss her."

"I would think so," said another girl. She had pony tails and scores of freckles. Rube heard more giggles as they skated away.

Emily and Rube skated together almost every afternoon. He would like to have done a lot more than hold her hand, but she said her parents would disown her if she was courted by a ball player ten years her senior. A lot of the time she just watched while Rube skated on his own, tearing around the rink at breakneck speed. He became an excellent skater, almost as fast as the local champion.

ℰℓ   ℰℓ   ℰℓ

The combination of skating and working at the grocery store got Rube into terrific condition. When he got back to Philadelphia he played a few games with an amateur roller polo team. He was a trim 210 pounds when he met the other A's at the train station. Alf Jones reported that he looked "as hard as nails."

"Looking pretty fit, Eddie," said Schreck, smacking Rube in the stomach.

"You too, Ossee, you chase a lot of fast girls around this winter?"

"Nope. I ran *away* from a lot though. Mack told me I had better be in shape this year or I'm through."

"You quit drinkin'?"

"I got in shape, I didn't become a teetotaler."

This time Connie Mack was taking the A's to Marlin, Texas. The train ride south went smoothly this time.

"Where the fuck is Marlin, Texas?" Socks Seybold asked the teammates he was playing cards with.

"I hear it's about a hundred miles from Dallas," said Topsy Hartsel.

"What's there?"

"Cowboys and coyotes," said Harry Davis.

The town was tiny and surrounded by forests. There didn't seem to be anything to do but hunt. Rube and several of his teammates decided to try their luck as soon as the first workout was over. Sam Erwin, the corpulent new club secretary, had come south with the team. He made a reputation for himself on the train ride.

"Land sakes alive, that fellow eats almost as much as Rube," Danny Murphy declared after Erwin had tucked away three steaks and a half a dozen roasted potatoes.

"He ate a whole pie after lunch," Socks Seybold added.

As Rube and the other hunters were getting ready, Erwin went up to them and gave them a challenge.

"Gentleman. I would like to make you a wager," he said.

"On what?" asked Harry Davis.

"I bet that I can eat everything that you bring back."

"Really? Everything, Sam?" asked Topsy Hartsel. "That may be quite a lot. Rube here is quite the hunter."

"Everything," Erwin repeated.

"What if you can't?" Davis asked.

"If I can't, I will take you all for dinner at the most expensive restaurant in Philadelphia as soon as we get home."

"And if you can?"

"You can buy me a box of cigars."

"You're on," said Hartsel, shaking Erwin's hand.

"Ya, Sam, you got yourself a bet," said Rube, grabbing his gun and heading out the door.

        *   *   *

The players came back two hours later. All they had were three rabbits. Rube wasn't with them.

"Well, the rabbits will make a nice little stew at least. Looks as though I won the bet, gentlemen."

"Not so fast, Sam. *We* may have struck out, but Rube's not back yet?" said Harry Davis. "He went off on his own a while ago. He should be back soon."

Topsy Hartsel peered out the dust-covered window. "Here he comes now."

"What's that he's dragging?" asked Sam Erwin.

"It looks pretty big. Might be a moose," offered Topsy Hartsel.

"Too small. Maybe it's a deer."

"You're gonna get venison," Harry Davis said to Erwin. "Lucky you."

"That doesn't look like a deer to me," said Danny Murphy, squinting through the window.

Rube stopped outside and let go of the animal he'd been dragging. He wiped his brow, a big grin on his face. Now the beast was close enough for everyone to recognize. It was not a deer or a moose. Its ears were much too big. It was a mule.

"The bet is off," Sam announced.

That night Rube was forcibly seized from the lobby of the Worth Hotel. He was taken to a nearby hall and initiated into the Marlin Mystic Knights of the Bovine, an order of wealthy cattlemen. The next day Rube proudly rode in their parade on a bucking bronco.

        *   *   *

Connie Mack had chosen Texas because the New York Giants were training there. He and the Giants' manager John McGraw had calculated that there would be a lot of people who would pay money to see the 1905 World Series opponents play each other. The A's traveled to Dallas three times to play exhibitions against the Giants. When Rube was scheduled to pitch 6,000 people showed up, the biggest crowd ever to attend a baseball game in Texas. He pitched and then disappeared. Unknown to Connie Mack and Sam Erwin, Rube was spending his time drilling with the rookies who were trying to get on with the Dallas Fire Department and he was intent on qualifying.

Three days after his disappearance John McGraw and some of his players were sitting out in front of their hotel, the St. Charles, smoking and talking about the exhibition games they still had left before heading north.

"Why hasn't Waddell pitched against us the last couple of days?" Roger Bresnahan asked McGraw. "He drew a big crowd the last time."

"He's taken off again," said McGraw. "Does it all the time. Probably out trying to drink the state of Texas dry."

Everyone looked up as a hook and ladder whizzed by. They were shocked when they recognized the driver. He was in full uniform and wore a very serious expression.

"Isn't that Waddell driving that truck?" asked Iron Joe McGinnity.

"It surely is, there's no mistaking him," said Christy Mathewson.

"Rube!" they called. "Rube!" they all yelled at him again. He never looked their way. He was completely focused on his driving.

"I've never seen Rube look so serious," said McGraw.

    *   *   *

"I'm sorry, Chief," Connie Mack said to the head of the Dallas Fire Department, "but Mister Waddell is employed by the Philadelphia Athletics baseball club and he is in Texas to train for the upcoming season."

"But he finished at the top of the class. He handles the equipment and fights fires better than most of my ten-year veterans."

"He has a great deal of experience fighting fires and very much enjoys doing so. He's a hero in several of the towns he's played in for saving a number of buildings and several lives, perhaps as many as thirteen in fact. But the fact remains that he is a professional ball player."

"You mean he can't stay and join our force?" the Chief asked.

"I'm afraid not, Chief. But if there is a fire while we're here, I'm quite sure he'll be there."

    *   *   *

Rube rejoined the club for the rest of the exhibition games. After one of them he and Ossee asked the Giants what the food was like at the St. Charles.

"It's great," Bresnahan told them.

"You have to try the steak," said McGinnity. They didn't notice that McGinnity was grinning when he made the recommendation.

        ℮   *℮*   *℮*

"A couple of your finest steaks," Ossee told their waiter, a young fellow with a huge cow-lick. "We want them rare, with garlic, onions, and mushrooms, and roast potatoes on the side."

When the waiter got inside the kitchen he shouted the order. The owner walked over to the cook and winked. "Make those steaks the *ballplayer* ones, Grady."

"Oh, right," said the cook with a nod. He went and got two of the cheapest steaks out of the fridge.

While Rube and Ossee waited for their dinners they had a drink. Then they had another. And then another. They started ogling the female diners. A stunning redhead went by, her hips swaying from side to side.

"Look at that one," said Rube, "I would rather watch her walk than eat fried chicken."

"She has quite a rustle in her bustle," sighed Schreck.

"I'll bet she's got some snap in her garters too," added Rube.

        ℮   *℮*   *℮*

"About time," Ossee told the waiter when he finally brought their meals.

"This is the toughest god-damned steak I've ever been served," Rube told Ossee a minute later.

"I can hardly even chew this fucking thing," said Schreck.

Their voices were getting louder and louder.

Rube tried another bite of his steak. "I wouldn't serve this to my dog," he said.

"Maybe it's the mule you shot in Marlin," Schreck suggested.

"He'da tasted better than this," said Rube.

"What are we gonna do about them?" asked Schreck.

Rube got a mischievous look in his eye. "Wait here," he said, getting up and heading out of the dining room.

        ℮   *℮*   *℮*

He came back in ten minutes. Somewhere he had found two hammers and some nails. To the shock of the other patrons Rube and Ossee proceeded to loudly nail their steaks to the dining room wall. The hotel manager ordered them to leave and never return.

CHAPTER THIRTY SIX

CONNIE HIRES A MUMMY

Rube didn't start the season opener. He didn't start the next day either. He was clearly not Connie Mack's favorite twirler anymore. Mack had Ed Plank and Chief Bender and, after a mediocre '06 season, Sunny Jim Dygert looked ready to join the rotation. Rube finally got into a game in relief and he shut out the Boston Americans for seven innings. But, when he gave up two hits in the ninth, Mack pulled him, a move that wouldn't have even crossed his mind two years ago.

Rube had a 4-2 lead after eight in New York but he'd struck out only one batter. When he walked the leadoff man in the ninth and the second batter drove a single through the infield, Mack once again took him out. Plank went in and promptly gave up the lead. Rube sat on the bench muttering to himself. Mack ignored him.

Rube was mad. He took off and no one saw him for ten days. On April 27 Mack called in the press and told them he was suspending Rube for thirty days.

"Contrary to the orders he was given, Waddell continues to drink alcohol to excess and keep late hours and bad company," Mack told the reporters. "He continues to arrive at the park in no condition to perform effectively and he has become a liability to the team."

❧   ❧   ❧

Rube read the newspapers the next morning and went to see Connie Mack.

"I wasn't out drinking, Connie. Honest. I was in a Turkish bath," Rube explained. "I heard it was the best way to purge alcohol from your body."

"We used to be able to trust what you told us, but this time you'll have to provide an affidavit to prove you were there," Mack told him.

"I will, Connie. I will."

Rube returned the next day with the required affidavit and Mack, flabbergasted that Rube had been able to come up with it, reluctantly reinstated him.

He still didn't trust Rube enough to put him into the rotation and used him only in relief. Sometimes he did all right, sometimes he got shelled. After the first month of the 1907 season Rube had just one win.

&c &c &c

Harry Davis went to his locker. He pulled up a stool so he could talk to Rube about his recent struggles.

"I know you don't want to throw spitters, Rube, but what about trying the emery ball?"

"The what?"

"The emery ball. A lot of twirlers are throwing it now."

"They are?"

"You know how players often leave their gloves on the field when their team goes in to bat?"

"Like that time in Detroit you knocked home Topsy with the winning run cuz you hit one to right and it ricocheted off his glove before Cobb could make a play on it. Cobb was mad as a hornet when it skipped by him. What about it?"

"Well sometimes on my way in I'll pick up a glove to toss it to a fella who's running out to his position."

"And?"

"Well, sometimes I find something sewn inside."

"What?"

"A piece of emery paper."

"What's it for?"

"For rubbing the ball with, to scratch it, so the pitcher has something to use besides the laces to make it break sharper."

"My curves break plenty."

"Not as much as they used to."

"Sounds a lot like cheatin' to me," Rube grunted.

"A course it's cheating. But only if you get caught. And it'd be me or one of the other infielders doing it, not you. You wouldn't have to have the emery paper in your glove."

"I don't think so, Jasper. Wouldn't be as much fun striking people out if I wasn't playin' square. I don't like cheatin'."

&c &c &c

On May 13 Rube finally got to start a game at home against Chicago, but only because Chief Bender showed up coughing and sneezing. Mack didn't want the whole team to come down with the flu so he sent Bender home. Rube was thrilled that he was finally getting to start. A smattering of hoots and boos greeted him as he took the mound. His first pitch, a shoot, sailed high over Schreck's head. His second, a curve, bounced five feet in front of home plate.

"Settle down, Eddie," Schreck yelled out.

Rube tried another shoot. It was almost as high as the first. He tried a wobbler, which wobbled way inside. Another shoot, another ball. A puzzler, another ball. A fadeaway, another ball, now six straight. He couldn't get *anything* over the plate.

The next pitch was outside but the batter swung at it and dribbled it to Harry Davis, who stepped on first for the out. The next batter swung at a high one and popped it up. Rube started to feel better. He struck out the next hitter for out number three.

He proceeded to shut out the White Sox for eight innings, giving up just one hit. In the ninth he let up a bit and Chicago scored a run on two hits but Rube finally had a win.

Connie Mack shook his hand when he came off the mound. "Careful how much you celebrate, Eddie."

"It'll be water for me tonight, Connie, don't you worry."

Rube did drink water that night as he'd promised, but he mixed it with generous quantities of bourbon.

        ℓℓ   ℓℓ   ℓℓ

Three days later Rube got another start, in St. Louis. It was clear from the outset that he had been celebrating his success against the White Sox in several establishments. Rube had a lot of friends in St. Louis. One night, he couldn't remember which, he and Schreck had met up with the fellows they'd been drinking with the year before, the ones Rube had told he would quit baseball if he didn't win the next day.

The next morning Rube's eyes were blurry and so were Schreck's. They looked as though they should be sleeping it off instead of trying to play a major league ball game. The Browns murdered Rube, patiently drawing walks when he couldn't find the strike zone and belting his pitches when he did. Uncharacteristically, Rube hit two batters. He would have yelled to them that he was sorry, as he usually did, but his head was pounding too badly. After he'd given up six runs to the last-place Browns, Mack took him out and Schreck out.

        ℓℓ   ℓℓ   ℓℓ

That night some of the A's were sitting on the porch of their hotel. It was too hot to sleep. At eleven o'clock a taxi pulled up in front of the hotel. Rube jumped out.

"A bit early for you to be calling it a night, isn't it?" yelled Harry Davis.

Rube went around to the other side of the cab. He hauled out a big man and threw him over his shoulder.

"Just droppin' this lug off," Rube explained.

"Who is he?" Davis asked.

"He's a detective. Connie's had him keepin' tabs on me. The man just cannot hold his liquor."

Rube deposited the man on the front lawn and then got back into the taxi. "Back to the bar," the others heard Rube tell the driver.

Rube and Schreck behaved themselves in Detroit. They didn't go out and they didn't destroy their hotel room. The team was no longer welcome in the hotel where Rube and Schreck had played football. Now, wherever they stayed, Connie Mack made sure that their room was right next door to his. Getting some sleep helped. Rube shut out the Tigers on six hits. After losing a close one to Addie Joss, Rube took the mound for the second game of a Decoration Day doubleheader in Boston. It went twelve innings and Rube went the whole way, chalking up strikeouts like the Rube Waddell of old, fourteen of them by the time it was over.

When the A's finally returned home from their western swing they hosted the White Sox. Ed Plank got shelled in the first game, then Rube got a chance against the defending champions. His speedballs had lots of zip, his curves were sharp and in on the wrists of the right-handed batters, and his fadeaways were right over the outside corner every time. After all Rube's years in the majors it was still hard for batters to adjust to the fact that he could curve pitches either way.

He retired the first nine straight, striking out seven of them. In the eighth inning he knocked in the winning run with a single. The A's badly needed the victory, which put them above .500 for the first time in weeks and moved them into fourth place.

One of the things affected most by his hard drinking and late night carousing was Rube's fielding. When they saw he was "under the weather" teams bunted on him relentlessly. But he made three terrific plays when he faced the Browns at home and shut them out on three hits, a far cry from how they had smacked him around in St. Louis.

Rube played pool and had a couple of beers after the St. Louis games and was talked into going to Camden, New Jersey to referee a boxing match that night. Rube put on a show, as he always did. After the match ended he did some boxing of his own.

He went to a tavern called The Red Onion in a seedy part of Camden.

The floor was decorated in peanut shells and tobacco juice stains. Rube was about to have something to eat when one of the regulars at the bar warned him that people had found maggots in the meat a few days ago. Rube decided to stick to alcohol. Things were going fine until a loud-mouth Irishman began harassing him.

"My, oh my, if it isn't the great Rube Waddell, come to grace us with his presence?" the man taunted from the other end of the bar. He was big and he had an ugly scar on his left cheek. It was hard to see since he hadn't shaved in a while. Rube was generally a good-natured drinker and he did his best to ignore the hooligan, whose name was apparently Brady. His friends were finding him hilarious.

"How many balls did you throw into the stands this week, Rube?" Brady asked loud enough for everyone in the place to hear. Rube was still smiling, but under the table he was clenching his fists.

"Those Browns sure pounded the shit outta Rube's pitches last week, didn't they boys?" Brady said to his friends. They roared.

Rube got out of his seat. He had in mind simply to tell Brady to leave him alone. But when he got close to the loudmouth, Brady stood up and took a swing at Rube. Rube wasn't ready for it and the blow knocked him backwards. He fell against a wall and when he regained his balance he went at Brady with both fists.

Rube managed to inflict some damage, landing a few punches and being on the wrong end of some as well. He finally knocked Brady out. His friends dragged him outside in hopes that the fresh air would wake him up. Rube had more drinks. They were on the house because the manager felt bad that the man had bothered him. The bartender gave him a steak to put over his right eye, which was already swelling and turning an ugly shade of purple.

He woke up with a terrible headache the next morning. He had a terrible taste in his mouth. It took him a while to realize where he was. He was lying in a jail cell. The smell coming from a pail in the corner was putrid. A rat scurried across the floor. Rube's tie and suit jacket were gone. Eventually a guard came and led him into a courtroom. There was a bailiff and a magistrate. Rube was led to the docket and told to be seated.

A man in a dark grey suit motioned to a policeman standing at the back and he went out a door. When he returned a minute later he was leading what appeared to be an Egyptian mummy by the arm. It was tall and obviously a man, but it was hard to tell since he was wrapped in bandages.

The man in the grey suit started talking. He said this badly injured man was a citizen of Camden and he had been assaulted by the defendant, George Edward Waddell, the night before.

"Get that man to a hospital immediately," the magistrate instructed the policeman. "It looks as though he may die."

The mummy was taken away. Rube was white as a ghost. The magistrate declared that Rube would be released only with a $300 bond on condition that he display good behavior.

"I swear I will behave," Rube told Connie Mack when he arrived to bail Rube out. What Rube didn't know was that Mack had arranged the whole charade. The magistrate was actually a police lieutenant and the mummy was not the man Rube had fought with. He was the court's janitor. Connie had made a $200 donation to the Police Widows Fund and the whole thing had been staged to scare Rube. It worked. Rube actually behaved himself. For a while.

CHAPTER THIRTY SEVEN

HAS CONNIE MACK HAD ENOUGH?

June started well for Rube. He beat Washington on the fourth. After some early hits, the Senators didn't get a runner past first base in the last five innings. The White Sox came into town and they hammered Ed Plank for twelve hits and six runs in the first game of the series. Connie Mack decided to send Rube out against them on a day's rest, against Ed Walsh, Chicago's ace. Walsh pitched well, as always loading up the ball with generous applications of tobacco juice, and held the A's to two runs. It wasn't good enough, Rube struck out eleven and shut out the White Sox.

He was even better three days later against St. Louis. He shut out the Browns on six hits and when the game ended he'd rung up thirty strikeouts in his last three starts and had pitched twenty-three straight scoreless innings. He got the streak up to thirty innings before allowing three hits and a walk in losing to Cleveland in the ninth.

Rube struggled in his next start against Detroit. He and Schreck had been drinking the night before, but not together. Schreck was starting to resent the way Connie Mack punished him whenever he showed up drunk or hung over but usually let Rube off the hook for one reason or another.

When the Tigers got some early hits Schreck started getting on Rube. "Those shoots aren't quite so fast these days, are they?" he chided. Then he remarked that Rube's curves weren't as sharp either.

Rube threw one in the dirt the next inning and then stood on the mound when the ball scooted past Schreck and the runner on third scored.

"Ever cross your mind to cover the plate?" Schreck yelled.

Two innings later, with a runner on third and two out, Schreck called for a curve and Rube threw an inside shoot instead. Schreck rolled the ball back to the mound. It bounced off a stone and out of Rube's reach. The runner dashed home. When the inning ended Connie Mack took them both out of the game.

He gave them a chance to redeem themselves against the Tigers two days later but to Mack's disgust they were both hung over again. The result was the same. Mack replaced the two reprobates early and the A's lost.

On the train ride to Boston Connie Mack had a long talk with Rube. "You can't keep this up. You're thirty years old and you look forty. The drink is taking a dreadful toll on you. When you're sober you're still a terrific pitcher but you must start taking care of yourself."

Rube stared down at the floor. "I know, Connie, I know. I just can't recover like I used to. It's just that I have a hard time saying no when friends are buying me rounds."

"Are they really friends if they're causing you to lose your skills and your edge?"

"I suppose not. Are you going to let me pitch in Boston?"

"I haven't decided." He paused for a moment. "Are you going to be ready to pitch? You certainly were not the last two times I used you."

"What if I stay in the lobby tonight and drink nothing but soda?"

"Fine, Edward. I'll check the lobby and you had better be there."

"I will, you'll see."

Mack was amazed to see Rube sitting in the lobby every time he checked it. Rube even went to bed early. When he started against the Americans the next morning he struck out twelve and threw his fourth shutout of the season. "Though he is now thirty years old there is no doubt that when Waddell is in form he is still nearly unhittable," *The Boston Post* remarked the next day.

But as quickly as Rube recovered, he just as quickly fell off the wagon. In New York he lost after taking a 6-0 lead into the fifth. Two days later the Highlanders reached him for seven runs and when he went into the next game in the fourth he was pounded for seven hits and six runs in three innings.

When they returned to Philadelphia the A's were mired in fourth place. Connie Mack called a practice. Rube didn't show up. When Chief Bender gave up three runs in the fifth inning the next day against Detroit, Mack sent Billy Jones, the batboy, to find Rube. Billy looked all through the grandstands and finally found Rube sleeping in the clubhouse. Mack was livid but he decided the best punishment would be to send Rube in immediately. He gave up six runs. The rumors began. Connie Mack was going to trade or sell Rube Waddell.

"How much longer are you going to put up with him, Connie?" asked Sam Irwin after the game.

"I don't know, Sam."

"Have you had any offers?"

"I have, and one of them is so serious that I am going to Chicago tomorrow to discuss it."

"We play in St. Louis tomorrow," Irwin pointed out.

"I'm perfectly well aware of that fact, Sam, but I must go and find out what the White Sox have to offer us in the event we do decide to trade Rube."

"Are you going to tell people why you're missing the game?"

"No, I'm not. I'm saying that I'm going on family business."

"You don't have any family in Chicago, do you?"

"Maybe I do, maybe I don't."

The players were surprised to learn that Mack was missing a game. He had told Schreck to manage during his absence. Like a lot of catchers, including Mack himself in his early days, Schreck was a student of the game and he knew the pitchers better than anyone else.

Schreck sent Chief Bender to the hill even though Rube hadn't started in a week. Bender did fine, until the eighth. Enjoying a 2-0 lead he gave up four runs. Schreck told Rube to get in there and put out the flames before the game was out of reach.

"Glad to, skipper," said Rube. He could never hold a grudge.

Rube struck out the first two batters he faced to end the eighth and then shut out the Browns again in the ninth while his teammates rallied to tie the game. He shut out St. Louis again in the tenth, and the eleventh, and in the twelfth, striking out the Browns' best three hitters one after the other. The A's finally pushed a run across and Rube had a much-needed win.

The next morning the reporters hounded Mack to see if he was trading Waddell.

"Is that why you went to Chicago, Connie?" one asked.

"Listen, gentlemen, the Athletics have no intention of releasing Waddell. He is a little out of condition but he is working hard and the reports of his shortcomings are made from whole cloth."

"You've shown remarkable patience with Waddell, Connie, but you can't be too thrilled with the way he keeps showing up unprepared to pitch?" said another one of the scribes.

"It is true that I was sore at Waddell when I left for Chicago. He is wonderfully talented and should remain one of the game's greatest twirlers. They tell me he pitched a whale of a game yesterday and I suppose he is going to behave himself now and pitch effectively for us."

He'd delivered the lines convincingly. The reporters looked at one another. Could they really swallow what the canny manager was feeding them? They had their doubts.

The next day Rube shut out the Browns on five hits. Three days later he beat the Naps in Cleveland. From the fifth to the eighth he set down fifteen straight batters, striking out nine of them. He was as sharp as he'd ever been. Surprisingly, he didn't go out to celebrate the way he had before whenever he was in Cleveland. He was pleased with himself, he had three straight wins.

Rube's eyes were the clearest Mack had seen them in quite some time when he faced the Tigers two days later. He struck out twelve, including a seething Ty Cobb twice, but his teammates made four errors that did him in.

"Another good one, Eddie. I'm proud of you," Connie Mack told him after the game.

"I just love to strike out Cobb. Did you see him after the second one?"

"I did. I have heard some terrible cursing in my day but that Cobb takes the prize. His eyes were on fire and it looked as though steam was going to come out his ears."

When the A's returned to Philadelphia they had an important series with the White Sox. Connie Mack started Rube in the first game. He was not quite as sharp as he had been of late and allowed base runners in almost every inning. But five different times, with runners in scoring position he calmly struck out a batter to retire the side. When Rube behaved himself and arrived ready to pitch he could still strike out anybody when he needed to.

In the eighth the White Sox put together a walk, a steal, a sacrifice bunt, and a sacrifice fly to take a 1-0 lead and the A's still hadn't scored. In Detroit his teammates had let him down in the field. Now they were letting him down at the plate. When Socks Seybold started the bottom of the ninth with a single it was the A's first hit in four innings. Schreck came to the plate.

"Get me a run, Ossee," Rube called out from the on-deck circle.

Schreck smiled, spit out some tobacco juice, and stepped into the box. He tapped his bat on the plate and hitched up his pants. Then he lined the first pitch for a double into right. Seybold scored easily.

"There's your run," he yelled as Rube strode to the plate. Rube really wanted to knock in Schreck and get the win.

"Shit," he muttered to himself when he saw that Connie Mack was signaling for a bunt. "Makes sense though. None out, pitcher up, get the winning run over to third." Still, he didn't feel like bunting.

Rube fouled off the first two pitches. Mack wasn't sure he'd tried very hard. Reluctantly, he took off the bunt sign. Rube hid a smile. The next pitch was high but the one after it was right down the middle. Rube hit it, but not quite squarely. It fell just out of Patsy Dougherty's reach and Schreck took off for third. Dougherty fielded the ball as Connie Mack signaled for Schreck to hold up at third. Schreck ignored him. Dougherty fired the ball to Billy Sullivan at home.

Sullivan caught the throw on a hop and moved to block the plate. Schreck hit him head-on like a runaway train and sent him flying through the air. The cranks grimaced as Sullivan landed on his back six feet from the plate.

Sullivan couldn't breathe. Rube ran in from second base and pulled him up. "Billy, are you still with us?" he asked.

No response.

"Billy, can you . . . "

"Let go uv me, Rube," Billy gasped. "Yer fixin' to break me bones with dat bear hug uv yers and squeeze the life outta me into the bargain." He looked at Schreck. "Nice one, I'll get ya fer dat one day though, you can be sure uv dat."

"He's fine," Schreck told Rube. "But next time you want to knock in the winning run make sure there's no play at the plate, at least not if *I'm* the one trying to score."

As Rube and Ossee were leaving the park a half hour later a man who looked to be in his fifties approached them. He had bushy side whiskers and wore a tailor-made wool suit in spite of the heat. He had his bowler in one hand and was using his other hand to wipe his brow with a silk handkerchief.

"Another masterful display of pitching and a timely hit as well, Rube," said the man. "My name is Hampton, Henry James Hampton and I'm a great admirer of your abilities . . . and of yours Schreck. I'm afraid I am unable to pronounce your full name."

"Never mind, Mister Hampton, nobody can."

"As for me, Henry will do just fine. What's say I buy you fellows a drink in recognition of a job well done?"

"Sad to say I cannot accept your generous offer," Schreck told him. "I have a previous engagement."

"Who is she?" Rube asked.

"A gentleman never tells," Schreck said with a wink at Hampton.

"And you, Rube? Do you have other plans for the evening?"

"Well I was sorta planning to quench my thirst somewhere. It was pretty dusty out there today."

"Then a drink it is. I know just the place."

They got into Hampton's cherry red motor car. Rube thanked the elderly chauffeur when he held the door open for him. Hampton told Rube the automobile was a Pierce Racine Touring Model and that he'd had it shipped to Philadelphia by train from Chicago. The place Hampton had chosen to go to for a drink turned out to be his private club. Rube thought the chandelier in the foyer must have weighed a ton. He was close. A waiter in a tuxedo brought them a bucket of ice. It held a bottle of champagne that was older than Rube. "It's a Seventy-Six, Mister Hampton," said the waiter.

"A centennial vintage, how patriotic," said Hampton, allowing the waiter to fill their crystal goblets.

"That is mighty tasty wine, Mister Hampton," said Rube after draining his glass.

"It's Henry, Rube. I get enough of Mr. Hampton at the bank."

"You work at a bank?" Rube asked.

"Actually, my father owns it."

&c.   &c.   &c.

They finished the bottle in short order and the waiter brought them bowls of oysters and mushrooms in a mouth-watering sauce. Then he brought them another bottle of champagne. They had duck à l'orange and roasted quail for dinner. When their dishes had been cleared the waiter brought two snifters filled with brandy.

"It's French. Like the champagne," Hampton told Rube, as he handed him a cigar that Rube guessed cost more than Connie Mack paid him for a week.

Rube took a sip. He knew it was not polite to gulp expensive liquor. "It burns on the way down, but it sure tastes special."

Hampton laughed. "Say, it occurs to me that tomorrow is Sunday."

"I believe it is," Rube agreed, wondering why that mattered.

"Thanks to our Quaker forefathers the good people of Philadelphia are not exposed to such pursuits as baseball playing on Sundays."

Rube was confused. "You mean the Quakers *ball team* doesn't play on Sundays?" he asked. "Henry, I don't think the Quakers are playing on *any* days of the week now. Didn't they fold up?"

Henry roared with delight. "No, no, I didn't mean the defunct baseball club of that name. I was referring to the religious zealots who founded this pious city."

Rube had never heard of three of the words Hampton had just used, but he decided to have another sip of brandy rather than ask what they meant.

"It's just that due to the ban on Sunday baseball you'll not have a game tomorrow."

"No. I mean, yes, that's right. We don't play tomorrow. Why?"

"I was thinking that it will likely be dreadfully hot again tomorrow and it might be an idea to take a run up to my cottage in Atlantic City."

"What would we do there?"

"Well, we could take a roller carriage ride along the boardwalk, have a few drinks at the hotel, take in a sideshow or two, and then have mint juleps on the veranda and watch the ladies in their bathing costumes."

"Will your wife be there?"

"No, she will not, America is much too *colonial* for her. My wife chooses to spend her summers on the Riviera. What about yours?"

"I don't have a wife anymore, Henry."

"Well then, there's nothing tying you down. How would you like to see Atlantic City? It's growing like a house afire these days."

"That sounds delightful, a capital suggestion," said Rube, mimicking a remark he'd overheard from someone sitting at a nearby table. "How are we gonna get there?"

"We shall take my boat. It will take a few hours, but the breeze will be wonderful."

ℓ   ℓ   ℓ

Hampton had a crew of five on his boat, which was a 42-foot yacht. During the cruise he asked Rube a lot of questions about where he'd grown up and how he'd learned to throw baseballs the way he did. Hampton said he had seen his first game just a few years ago and had become fascinated by its symmetry and pastoral origins. Rube had no idea what he was talking about.

They moored at a huge dock half a mile north of Atlantic City. An enormous manicured lawn led up to a Gothic mansion. Rube guessed it must have a hundred rooms. There was a row of stables and outbuildings beside it, Hampton called it a mews.

"What's this?" Rube asked.

"The family cottage," Hampton told him.

After some difficulty Hampton's valet found some casual clothes that belonged to one of the servants that were large enough for Rube to wear and he and Hampton headed into town in an expensive carriage pulled by the finest looking horse Rube had ever seen. Hampton rented a roller carriage and they traveled along the new boardwalk. Rube could hardly believe the number of people on the beach. It was after eight o'clock but there were still thousands of men, women, and children wading in the Atlantic to cool down. Though the rest of their bodies were modestly covered by their bathing costumes it was odd to see women's exposed shins and ankles.

"There are some real beauties down there on the beach, Henry," Rube exclaimed.

"Yes, indeed, I never tire of coming down here to gaze at them. Sometimes I even invite a couple of them up to the cottage for cool drinks."

"That's mighty gracious of you," chuckled Rube.

After taking in a couple of shows the two men had a midnight dinner on the veranda of the United States Hotel. Torches lit up the shoreline below and several bonfires burned on the beach. Rube and Hampton didn't get back to his cottage until three in the morning.

The next day they drank and swam, mostly they drank. Rube missed the nine p.m. train. He was so drunk he might have fallen off it anyway. He did not appear for the Athletics' game on Monday.

CHAPTER THIRTY EIGHT

ON AND OFF THE WAGON

"Where the hell was he this time?" Harry Davis asked Danny Murphy.

"Gallivanting around Atlantic City with some banker's son apparently. Livin' the life of the idle rich."

"And forgetting we're in a pennant race," snorted Davis.

A lot of the A's had just about had enough of Rube's antics. His act was wearing thin. Nobody found him very amusing anymore. Harry Davis, Topsy Hartsel, and Danny Murphy went to see Connie Mack after the game, which the A's had lost. He stood up when they entered his room.

"What did you want to see me about boys?" Connie asked. "Would you like some coffee?"

Davis had been chosen to do the talking. "We're not here on a social call, Connie, we got something serious we need to say."

"I see," said Mack, sitting back down.

"I'll come straight to the point," said Davis. He was fidgeting a little with his hat. The other players looked a bit sheepish.

"Please do," said Mack.

"We think it's time you got rid of Rube."

Connie Mack said nothing.

"We all know he's a great pitcher."

"He is," Mack agreed.

"It isn't his pitching that's the problem," Davis continued. "It's all his clowning and carousing."

"He's always done that, Harry."

"Yes, Connie, he's always been a drinker, but now the drinking is getting worse, a lot worse, and you know it."

"I have tried . . ."

"Connie, we *know* you've tried. You've tried *everything*. Hell, you've been like a father to Waddell. And look how he repays you."

"Rube lacks the maturity to take care of himself."

"Why don't you let somebody else babysit him for a while? You've done enough," said Hartsell. "He's hurting the team."

"He still draws big crowds. A lot bigger than Plank or Bender. No one knows what will happen when Rube pitches."

"So?"

"So if I get rid of Rube the team's revenue will drop."

"And?"

"And we wouldn't be able to pay you fellas as much."

The players looked at one another. That hadn't occurred to them. "Are you just sayin' dat cuz you want ta keep him?" asked Murphy.

"No I'm not, Danny. It's simple arithmetic. The less money we take in, the less we can pay out."

Connie's logic sank in and it took the wind out of the group's sails. They left, muttering to one another as they did.

      *   *   *

Connie Mack started Rube in the last game of the series and the light-hitting White Sox clawed their way to a win with bunts, walks, sacrifices, bad hop grounders, and a couple of scratch hits. Rube's shoots lacked their usual zip. The drinking was sapping his strength. Connie Mack decided to give him a few days off. Instead of resting, Rube went on a bender.

      *   *   *

When Mack started him against Cleveland, Rube's eyes looked terrible. He was shaky in the first, giving up a hit and two walks to load the bases with one out. Then he fooled Rabbit Nill with a bender and fired an inside shoot past Nig Clarke to get the third out. The cranks went wild. They hadn't had that many chances to cheer Rube of late.

"You still got it Rube," one yelled.

They kept right on cheering through the next six innings as the Naps kept swinging and missing or hitting harmless dribblers.

"These Naps oughta change their name to Napkins," Rube told Schreck as they headed to the bench after Rube had rung up another strikeout.

"Why's that?" Schreck asked.

"Cuz they *fold up* so easy."

Glenn Liebhart, the Naps' pitcher, led off the seventh with a seeing-eye single to left. Bunk Congalton was next up. He bunted. Rube fielded it, but his throw to second to get the lead runner pulled Monte Cross off the bag. Runners on first and second, no one out. Everybody knew another bunt was coming.

Elmer Flick was the next batter. He squared to bunt but popped the ball meekly in front of the plate instead. Rube charged in and dove for it. The ball squirted out of his glove as Rube hit the ground with a thud. He landed in a heap on top of his left arm. The bugs groaned.

Rube's arm hurt, but his head hurt worse. He hadn't slept much last night. He was gagging too, which struck everybody as odd until Rube was able to get his breath and explain that in the fall he had swallowed his wad of chewing tobacco. Connie Mack checked his arm, looked into his bloodshot eyes, and took him out.

The A's had a doubleheader with Cleveland the next day. Ed Plank beat Addie Joss in the first game and Connie Mack started Billy Bartley in the second. He'd been in the majors for two years and had started just four games. He had yet to win one.

The first batter walked. Elmer Flick followed with a double and Nap Lajoie singled. Mack told Billy to take a seat. He sent in a rookie whose name was Sam Hope. The papers had been quipping that if Rube could not stay off the bottle there was still "Sam Hope for the A's." Perhaps not. Hope gave up three straight hits.

The Naps had batted through the order and now the score was 6-0. With two of the most powerful hitters in the league due up, it seemed a good time for Mack to see how bad Rube's arm was. Reporters were claiming that the Philadelphia rooters were giving up on Rube, but when he took the mound a lot of them hooted and hollered in delight.

Muscular Elmer Flick strode to the plate. He'd led the league in triples for three straight years and was en route to another .300 season. Rube knew Flick was a free swinger. He struck him out with a hard shoot that followed a nasty wobbler. Then he got Lajoie, who was struggling a little and might not bat .300 for a change, to pop up to Schreck against the screen and the inning was finally over. The A's bat came alive and they scored eleven runs. Rube struck out eight the rest of the way and allowed just five hits. He threw his glove in the air after fanning the last batter, but he wasn't tempted to do handsprings or cartwheels this time.

When Mack sent him out to throw on the sidelines during the game the next day there was a loud roar from the grandstand. "So much for Philadelphia's baseball enthusiasts losing faith in Waddell," Alf Jones wrote the next day.

The Athletics traveled to Detroit and Rube started the first game on one day's rest. He held his old teammate Sam Crawford hitless, but *he* was no longer the Tigers' toughest out. Ty Cobb was their most feared hitter now. He led the team with four homers and had already knocked in ninety runs.

Cobb ripped a single through the infield his first time up on one of Rube's inside shoots. When he tried to steal second Schreck fired the ball to Danny Murphy in time to get Cobb. But when Murphy bent to apply the tag Cobb kicked his leg viciously. His spikes, which he always made sure were razor sharp, tore into Murphy's left shin and blood poured out of three deep gashes. Murphy had to leave the game.

Cobb came up again in the third with two on and two out. He usually held his hands a few inches apart on the bat so that he could punch the ball wherever he saw a hole in the defense. Rube noticed that this time Cobb had them together down at the knob.

"He's looking to drive one deep this time," Rube muttered to himself.

"See if you can get another one of those lame ass shoots by me, sousepaw," Cobb yelled out.

Rube was sorely tempted to throw an inside shoot right into Cobb's ear. Instead he threw one right over the heart of the plate. Cobb's eyes lit up like a kid on Christmas morning and he took a vicious cut at the ball.

There was a sound, but it wasn't the sharp crack of the bat Cobb had expected. He'd popped the ball up. Harry Davis camped out under it on the base line in front of first. Cobb threw his bat in disgust and then set out to run Davis over.

With his eyes skyward, Davis didn't see Cobb coming and he was bowled over. He flew four feet and then lay on the ground gasping for breath. Rube picked up the ball Davis had dropped and bent over him to see if he was all right. Schreck grabbed Cobb from behind and threw him down.

The umpire ran in to prevent a bench-clearing brawl. When Cobb got up and headed to first base the umpire yelled, "The batter-runner is out for interference." Cobb snarled and headed to the bench.

"Too bad you didn't hit the ball as hard as you cold-cocked Davis, you cheatin' son-of-a-bitch," yelled Rube.

Cobb started for the mound but the umpire stepped in front of him. He put his face up to Cobb's. "After the stunt you just pulled if you take one step toward the mound I'll throw you right out of the game." Cobb started to say something but thought better of it. He stormed off the field.

Rube struck out seven and went on to win the game 7-3 and move the A's into first place.

That night Rube went out to celebrate. He was still celebrating the next night and was delighted to run into the police constable who had helped him trick Connie Mack into giving him ten dollars to pay an imaginary fine two years before.

He was in rough shape when he took the mound the next day. He threw eight straight balls to the first two batters and when the next three hitters reached base a disgusted Connie Mack took him out.

After the game the A's took trolley cars down to the docks where they boarded a steamer for the trip across Lake Erie to play in Cleveland. Rube sipped from a flask most of the way and cursed the seagulls who landed on the deck looking for scraps of food. He was in no condition to start a game against the Naps but Mack sent him in to pitch the last two innings of the second game of the series. The A's led by a run. Rube gave up two hits, walked two batters, and surrendered the lead.

Luckily for Rube, who was persona non grata with his teammates for drinking so heavily in the midst of the pennant race, the A's tied the game in the bottom of the eighth when Danny Murphy hit the ball through a knothole in the left field fence.

"Talk about the luck of the Irish," Schreck said when Murphy, who was still laughing, got back to the bench.

"Keep it tied for us," Connie Mack told Rube as he went out for the ninth.

Rube walked the first two batters and then Nig Clarke ripped a double to right that cleared the bases. Mack pulled Rube out, but the damage was done. The A's lost a game they'd badly needed to win in order to stay in first. Rube was digging his own grave.

&c &c &c

Mack tried Rube again the last game in Cleveland even though once more he was hung over. He walked three of the first five batters. Nap Lajoie hit a wicked liner right at Topsy Hartsel then Bill Hinchman hit one that landed in front of Hartsel. As he raced in for it the ball bounded over his glove and all of the runners scored. Mack sent Rube to the showers.

Ed Plank started the first game when the A's reached Chicago and lost it 4-1. Chief Bender did better the next day, holding the White Sox to four hits. The A's still lost 1-0 and things were getting desperate. Connie Mack had no choice but to start Rube for the last game of the series.

He'd be facing Ed Walsh.

On the walk from South Side Park to their hotel Connie Mack pleaded with Rube. "You'll have to stay in tonight and be at your absolute best tomorrow against Walsh. We didn't score a run today against Doc White and Walsh is twice the hurler he is."

"I know we have to win tomorrow, Connie. You can count on me to be ready this time."

"If you're not, there may not be a next time."

A couple of boys were tagging along. They were trying to get Rube to go and play with them as he had the last time he was in Chicago. Uncharacteristically, Rube ignored them so he could give Connie his full attention.

"What do you mean, there may not be a next time?"

"I have been very patient with you these past couple of years as your drinking has become more and more of a problem. Ben Shibe is on me to let you go and now some of the other players are too."

"No one has been better to me than you have. You've always..."

"Not anymore. I cannot tolerate any more irresponsible behavior. We need wins and we need them badly. Plank and Bender are pitching pretty well, and so are Coombs and Dygert. But you're still our best pitcher when you're not on the drink. You just cannot keep letting us down."

One of the boys tugged on Rube's sleeve. "Come on, Rube, come play with us."

Rube shooed the lad away. "Not now," he told him.

"I will stay in tonight. I promise. You can even put a guard on my door if you like."

"Edward, you and I both know that if you want to go out on the town you will find a way, no matter what I do."

Rube hesitated. "Well, I suppose that's true . . . but there'll be no shenanigans tonight, I'll be good. And *tomorrow* I'll be great. You'll see." He turned to the boys. "All right, one quick game, but I'm throwing underhand, I gotta save my shoots for the White Sox."

"What's this?" said a heavy-set man in a derby as he went through the brand new turnstiles at South Side Park and was handed a card with printing on one side.

"It's a poem?" explained the young ticket-taker.

"What do I want with a poem at a ball game?" the man asked.

"We want people to chant the lines. It's about Waddell. He's pitching today."

"I know. That's why I came. Win or lose, Rube generally puts on a show."

The White Sox had printed 15,000 copies of the poem, which someone had written about Rube. The man read it when he got to his seat. He thought it simple, but humorous.

You've been drinking and cannot see the plate.

Rummy Rube, a trouncing'll be your fate.

He chuckled and then took up the chant along with the rest of the crowd as Rube took the mound.

In the past Rube been easily distracted by Hugh Jennings and John McGraw waving toys and puppies and had sometimes been put off his game by noises and yells from the stands, but this time he was all business. He looked at Connie Mack, who was pacing back and forth in front of the bench tapping his lineup card against his hip. Rube smiled and spit a stream of tobacco juice toward the plate. "Let's get 'em, Ossee," he called to his friend.

"Saints preserve us, old Reuben has got his stuff today," said Patsy Dougherty when he got back to the bench after striking out on three pitches to start the bottom of the first.

"He sure is fast," said Jiggs Donahue after he'd struck out. "I could hardly even see the fucking ball."

"Do you hear them hitting Schreck's mitt?" said Billy Sullivan.

"I imagine they can hear them across the street," said Donahue.

Rube mixed in some fadeaways and curves and a couple of puzzlers, but he stuck mostly to shoots. He struck out the side in the fifth and the sixth and the cranks gave up their mindless chanting and actually started to applaud him. The A's had reached Ed Walsh for two runs in the first and that was all they'd need. Rube shut out the White Sox on three hits, two of them feeble grounders that infielders should easily have reached.

"Nobody ever lived who can hit those pitches," said George Davis, the Chicago shortstop, after flailing helplessly at three pitches to end the game. It was Rube's thirteenth strikeout. He'd shut out the White Sox and put the A's back in first place. Connie Mack couldn't help but shake his head and think how easy winning pennants would be if only Rube were sober all the time.

RUBE WADDELL
KING of the HALL of FLAKES

CHAPTER THIRTY NINE

BLOWING HIS LAST CHANCES

Rube's next start was against St. Louis and he held the Browns to two hits while striking out eleven. Though he'd blown a couple of leads after coming on in relief, he had now won five of his last six starts and his record stood at 18-10. In spite of the hard fall, his shoulder was fine.

The A's headed home to play back-to-back doubleheaders against Washington. Rube and Ossee watched as the Senators' highly publicized new prospect warmed up to face Rube in the second game on Monday. The A's had lost the morning game 3-1 to fall one game behind first-place Detroit.

"That new kid's fast," said Rube. "What's his name?"

"Willard Johnson," answered Schreck. "No, wait, *Walter* Johnson. He's from somewhere out west."

"He surely does throw hard shoots," said Rube.

The tall and lanky rookie, who was said to be painfully shy, had extraordinarily long arms. He eased through eight innings using a sidearm slingshot style that contrasted sharply with Rube's straight overhand delivery. But in the ninth inning he got the jitters, lost his control, and walked three men. The next batter hit a grounder to Johnson. He picked it up and threw the ball well over the first baseman's head. Rube bested the rookie 3-2.

The next day Jimmy Dygert won the opener 15-6 even though his spitters weren't really fooling anybody. Rube pitched the second game, which was called after five innings, and won it 9-1. The A's held onto first place by a half game.

The Boston Americans came to town and a huge crowd turned out to see Rube take on Cy Young. Having just celebrated his fortieth birthday, Young was coming off his worst year, one in which he'd won only thirteen games against twenty-one losses. He was gamely struggling to return to the 20-win mark this year. He pitched well, keeping the A's to just six hits, but there could easily have been more. His outfielders made several great catches for him.

Rube didn't get the same kind of support. Danny Murphy booted a ball in the second, Jasper Davis dropped one in the fourth, Monte Cross let one go through his legs in the sixth, Murphy threw wide to first in the seventh, and Harry Davis dropped another in the eighth and then seemed to take a short nap before picking it up. Rube knew full well what was going on. His teammates were still mad at him over the trip to Atlantic City. They were making the errors on purpose.

At least *some* of the A's tried to help Rube. Fred Parent hit a ball into the deepest spot in left field in the fourth, but Topsy Hartsel ran at full speed and caught the ball over his shoulder to rob him of a sure triple or inside-the-park home run.

"Thank you, Topsy," Rube said to himself, "at least *you're* still with me."

When Heinie Wagner hit a little pop fly behind second base Danny Murphy pretended not to be able to reach it. Socks Seybold raced all the way in from right field and dove to catch it just before it hit the grass. He shot Murphy a dirty look. "Nice try," he told him sardonically.

"There's another still with me," thought Rube.

With a runner on in the seventh thanks to a wide throw to first by Danny Murphy, Cy Young lined a pitch that hooked sharply into the right field corner. Seybold got to that one too, just barely.

The hits came to a halt after eight innings. Rube and Cy bore down and retired batter after batter on three pitches, sometimes four. It was as if there was no point in anyone even going up to the plate. A minute after they stepped into the box they'd trudge back to the bench after being made to look as though they'd never had a bat in their hands.

It was still 0-0 after nine, after ten, after eleven, and after twelve. It was still not four o'clock - the first twelve innings had taken only an hour and fifty-five minutes to play. But it was a humid afternoon and a mist had blended with smoke from the nearby railway yard and blanketed the field. The umpire had no choice but to call the game, he didn't want anybody killed by one of Young or Waddell's shoots that they never saw.

Rube failed to cover first twice in a 6-6 tie in his next start on Friday the 13th of September and - after being given a week off - lost 4-1 to the sixth-place Browns on the 20th. He was spending a lot of nights at the Grog Barrel in Camden and it showed. He hadn't won a game in the last sixteen days of the tight pennant race. The A's were lucky to be tied with Detroit for first.

Connie Mack sent Rube out for the opener of a three-game set with the White Sox. Rube wasn't sharp, but his fielders made one mental error after another. Mack left Rube in the whole game, an 8-3 loss. Ed Plank pitched a 5-0 shutout the next day, his eighth whitewash and twenty-fourth win, and Jimmy Dygert beat the Pale Hose 3-1 the next day, allowing the Hitless Wonders only two safeties.

Nineteen thousand bugs showed up for a Friday afternoon game with Detroit. Since Dygert had pitched the day before and Chief Bender had a sore shoulder, Rube was the obvious choice to start the game. But not this year, certainly not after the way he'd behaved the past few weeks. Mack went with Plank on one day's rest. He battled but lost a close one 5-4 and the A's fell a game and a half back of the Tigers.

After rain had prevented play on Saturday and Sunday twenty-four thousand cranks showed up for a Monday doubleheader, the biggest weekday crowd ever. Thousands more were turned away. People with strategically-located windows in surrounding apartment buildings sold admittance to their rooms for a ridiculous five dollars a head. A man across the street from the park rented out pieces of his roof for $3.25. The rooters brought cowbells, bicycle horns, bugles, and anything else they could get think of to rattle the Tigers. Downtown, thousands more bugs massed in front of *The Inquirer* office to listen to announcers with megaphones relay the game's proceedings phoned in from the press box.

Jimmy Dygert started against Wild Bill Donovan. He shut out Detroit in the first and the A's scored four in their half of the inning to give him a healthy lead. The boosters were giddy. It was a great start to the day.

The first batter in the second singled off Dygert. The next one grounded the ball right to him. He threw to second to start an easy double play, but his throw was wide and pulled Danny Murphy off the bag. The runners were sacrificed to second and third and the next man up hit a comebacker to Dygert. He grabbed it and threw to third to get the runner, who'd broken for the plate. This throw was wild too and a run scored. The next batter drew a walk and now the bases were loaded.

Mack was surprised to find Rube on the bench for once. "I need you to put a stop to this," he told him, "we absolutely have to win this game." Mack would have preferred to use Plank, but he needed him for the second game.

"No rest for the wicked," said Rube. It took him a while to find his glove. Then he stuck a fresh wad of tobacco into his cheek and headed to the mound. There was a murmur in the stands as the cranks realized who was taking over.

"With Rube goin' in this would have been a lead-pipe cinch in the old days," a man in the front row told his son.

"Not anymore," said the boy.

"Tough luck, Jimmy," Rube said as he took the ball. He toyed with the rosin bag for a minute. Since Dygert had not been hurt, no warm-up throws were allowed. "Don't fuck this up," he told himself.

Rube struck out Davy Jones on four pitches. Now there were two out. He threw two wide ones to Germany Schaefer and the cranks started to look at one another and shake their heads. Rube fired the next three straight over the plate and strode off the mound with a big grin on his face. The crowd went berserk. Was it possible the old Rube was back yet again?

He struck out four more Tigers over the next two innings and the boosters were loving it. He had now fanned six of the eight men he'd faced, including the adorable Ty Cobb. The A's scored two runs off Wild Bill in the second and another two in the fifth. Rube had a 7-1 lead. Things were looking good.

Wild Bill led off the seventh and hit a high lazy fly to center. Rube could hardly believe his eyes when Oldring dropped it. It was a can of corn. Flabbergasted, Rube walked Davy Jones, the only batter he walked today. The next hitter grounded right to Monte Cross. The ball caromed off his glove. It should have been a routine double play. Up came the always dangerous Sam Crawford, Rube's buddy on the Grand Rapids club back in '99. He ripped the first pitch for a double. Both runners scored.

Up came Ty Cobb. To the disgust of almost everyone he was leading the league in hitting. The A's bench jockeys began razzing him. They were taking a big chance doing so. When a team had heckled him during a spring training exhibition game Cobb had lined fourteen vicious line drives right at their bench.

Rube managed to get him to ground one to Danny Murphy who had an easy play to get Crawford at home. With a four-run lead, Murphy elected to go to first and keep Cobb off the bases. A run scored, but Rube wasn't upset. Who could blame him? Murphy had terrible scars from the last time Cobb had gone into second hard against the A's.

Rube struck out the next batter. Though he had given up just one hit, four runs had scored and the lead was down to 7-5. Schreck singled in a run in the bottom of the seventh and made it 8-5. Germany Schaefer got the Tigers' only hit of the eighth, a double. He stole third when Jimmy Collins was late covering the bag on Schreck's perfect throw and then scored on a grounder to second. The lead was back to two with an inning to play.

Sam Crawford led off the ninth with a single to left. Up came Cobb.

"Why don't you put in Bender to finish it off?" Jimmy Dygert asked Connie Mack.

"Rube's only allowed three hits and *everybody* has trouble with Crawford," answered Mack.

"Ya, but now it's *Cobb.*"

"We know Rube will bear down against him. He despises the man."

Rube was careful. He threw three straight benders to Cobb. Each one just missed the plate. Cobb smiled as the umpire called ball three. Rube threw another curve. This one caught the corner. Rube decided to try one more. It caught the corner too. The count was full.

By now you could cut the air with a knife. Some cranks covered their eyes, hoping that when they uncovered them Rube would have registered another big strikeout. Cobb usually leaned forward to improve his chances of making contact. He rarely swung for the fences, though he often bragged that he could reach them easily if he wanted to. This time he pulled back a bit. He was sure Rube would throw a shoot this time. He did. There was a loud crack as bat met ball. It sailed over the right field fence and bounced in the middle of 29th Street. There was nothing but silence. The park was like a tomb.

Cobb leered at Rube as he circled the bases. It was the first and last home run he would hit off Rube and it had come at a perfect time. The score was tied.

As the ball exited the park Connie Mack fell backwards right off the bench. He landed on the bat rack. When he was helped to his feet he rubbed the back of his head, retrieved his hat, and told Ed Plank to take over.

After fourteen innings, by which time Rube had emptied two flasks of bourbon under the grandstand, the game was called. Even though all the runs in the disastrous seventh had been unearned and the hits had come off the bats of two of the league's best hitters, almost everyone blamed Rube. At this point the A's couldn't afford to lose any games, especially to Detroit.

The Tigers moved on to Washington where they took three straight from the Senators. The Naps came to Philadelphia for the last home stand. Jimmy Dygert beat them in the first game but Ed Plank lost the second when his teammates made errors on crucial plays. Dygert beat Cleveland again in the last game of their series and the A's went to Washington for a do-or-die doubleheader.

℮ ℮ ℮

Plank lost the first game to Walter Johnson 1-0 in ten innings and Connie Mack sent Dygert, who'd pitched the day before to face the Senators in the second game.

"Why aren't you starting Coombs or Bender or Waddell?" asked Alf Jones. "Dygert's pitched three times in the last five days."

"Coombs and Bender are hurt," answered Mack.

"I didn't know. What about *Waddell*?"

"Waddell is drunk."

Dygert won the game and the A's now had just two left, in Washington. They had to win both or the Tigers had the pennant.

℮ ℮ ℮

Connie Mack was desperate. In the first game he started Charlie Fritz, a 19-year old he'd seen pitch in New Orleans. Fritz shut out the Senators for three innings, then his nerves got the better of him and he walked two and hit a batter in the fourth.

Mack sent in Harry Vickers, who had just joined the team after winning twenty-five games for the Williamsport Millionaires of the Tri-State League. Because he threw hard and was a left hander, the Williamsport folks had nicknamed him Rube. While the new Rube was putting on his new uniform Connie Mack sent in the old Rube, hoping he could hold the fort, at least for a couple of batters. Rube faced just one. He ripped a double and Mack took Rube out. Now he'd completely lost confidence in him.

Vickers came in and won the game, 4-2 in fifteen innings. Then he started the second game and went five innings without allowing a hit. The game was called because of darkness. It was just what the *old* Rube would have done before alcohol got the better of him. Detroit beat St. Louis that day and took the pennant in spite of Dygert and Vickers' heroics. Vickers had won himself a place on the A's staff for 1908 and every baseball crank in Philadelphia knew whose place he'd likely be taking.

CHAPTER FORTY

BLACKTIPS AND OYSTERS

Because of his behavior in the final weeks of the '07 season the A's had missed winning the pennant and Rube had failed to win twenty games. He'd ended up at 19 and 13, which was better than his 15-17 mark in '06 but not much. And, for the sixth straight time, he'd led the league in strikeouts with 232. Ed Walsh wasn't too far back, fanning 206 with his soggy ones, but he'd pitched a whopping 422 innings to Rube's 285. His E.R.A. had been a fairly impressive 2.15 which was better than Ed Plank's, but Plank had won twenty-four games. Dygert had done a lot better than Rube, going 21-8 and Bender was nearly as effective in spite of his injuries and ailments at 16-8.

🚲 🚲 🚲

After a quick barnstorming tour the players put together to make up for the fact that they wouldn't be getting World Series shares, Rube headed to Mobile, Alabama where his parents were spending the winter. He often went to Sneaky Pete's Oyster Bar. Its doors were usually open and a warm breeze blew through. One afternoon he sat at the bar drinking beer with two men named Henry and Gunther who were ardent fishermen. They munched on peanuts and watched Rube wolf down one raw oyster after another.

"Do you always eat that many oysters, Rube?" Henry asked.

"Usually," Rube told him. He called to the owner, "Pete, how many oysters do I generally eat when I come in?"

Pete was busy adding up receipts. He was a young man but his hairline was already receding. He set down the receipts, thought for a second, and then answered, "You usually eat a whole box, Rube."

"How many oysters are there in a box?' Gunther asked.

"Six dozen," Pete told him.

"You eat seventy-two oysters in one sitting!" Henry exclaimed.

"I've always had a good appetite," said Rube.

"I should *think* so," said Gunther.

"Zack Mitchell is the only man who can eat more oysters than Rube," Pete told them.

"What!" Rube blurted. "Some fella eats more oysters than I do?"

"Well, yes, Zack comes in and sometimes eats a box and a *quarter*," Pete explained.

"You get him in here and we'll see who can eat more," Rube demanded.

Pete thought for a moment. "I guess I could arrange a contest. It might be a big draw. How about Friday night?"

"Fine with me," said Rube.

               ℓ   ℓ   ℓ

Henry and Gunther spent most of the afternoon bragging about sharks they'd caught. They invited Rube to go shark fishing with them that night. They didn't have to ask twice.

Gunther had a boat and they had extra gear that Rube could use. He would need a very strong rod and a lot of line, five hundred yards or more. They headed out at 7 o'clock. It was a beautiful evening and Rube enjoyed the smell of the Gulf air as they sailed toward Dauphin Island. There was a gentle breeze and hundreds of seagulls soared above them.

The trip took only a few minutes. They anchored up current from a spot where sharks regularly scavenged around a pair of old shipwrecks. The tide was coming in and the flow was strong. Henry said that made sharks more likely to grab bait. Henry and Gunther put harnesses on and handed one to Rube.

"I won't be needin' that," said Rube.

"Are you sure, Rube? Sharks put up quite a fight, they've nearly pulled me right out of the boat a few times," said Gunther.

"I imagine, I'll be fine," Rube answered. "I can put up a pretty fair fight myself."

They got their bait ready. The other men used squid, Rube used shrimp and jackfish that he deftly sliced into pieces.

All of a sudden Rube hopped over the side. Henry and Gunther looked at one another.

"What in the hell is he doing?" Henry asked Gunther.

"I'm not entirely sure," Gunther answered, scratching his head.

They watched as Rube spread the shrimp and jackfish bits through the shallow water. He attached them to cork rigs to keep them from falling to the bottom.

"He seems to know what he's doing," Gunther told Henry. "Rube, are you really going to stand in the water?"

"Why not?"

"Oh, no reason, I was just wondering."

They caught plenty of saltwater catfish, but they were after sharks. Rube started hopping the jig bait up and down when he saw a shark lurking on the horizon. When it got a bit closer Gunther recognized it as a blacktip. It was bluish gray and it had a distinctive white stripe on its flank. Rube knew blacktip were aggressive but more cautious than other sharks and that they kept their distance at first. He also knew they were among the best-tasting sharks. The blacktip burst out of the water and then spun around before dropping back into the ocean.

"Look out!" yelled Henry.

Rube looked behind him. He didn't see anything.

"By your *feet!*" Gunther explained.

Rube looked down and saw a stingray. It was inches from his left foot.

"Those things are very dangerous. Watch out. If you just move away slowly and leave them alone they'll just swim away."

"What if you pick them up?" Rube asked.

Once again Henry and Gunther looked at each another.

"What in tarnation are you talking about?" Henry asked.

"How are you going to pick it up?" asked Gunther.

"By the tail," Rube answered.

With that he reached down and grabbed the stingray by the tail. Gunther and Henry gasped. With a huge grin on his face Rube twirled the helpless stingray around over his head and then pretended he was going to throw it into the boat.

"Rube! Don't!" Henry screamed.

But Rube had turned his back to them. He drew the stingray back and then flung it. It sailed through the air and landed with a loud slap on the surface the better part of two hundred feet away. Rube laughed and, after a second or two, so did Henry and Gunther. They weren't sure they had just seen what they had just seen.

Their attention returned to the blacktip. It was moving toward the bait. Slowly and cautiously it approached, turning its head from left to right and back again in order to pick up the scent of the fresh bait. It went for Rube's jackfish and he pulled hard. The shark had the bait and the hook. Rube was surprised by the shark's weight. Blacktips were much smaller than bull sharks but this one had to be over a hundred pounds.

It immediately sped away, swimming faster than anything Rube had ever seen. He let the line out and let the shark make a run for it. The shark was two hundred yards away within seconds. Rube let out more line and then he started to pull the blacktip in. Henry and Gunther were amazed by his strength and by the way he was able to keep his footing, especially without a harness. It put up a struggle and Rube was relieved that it didn't break his line with its teeth or its tail. After forty-five minutes he finally reeled it in.

"Throw me the gaff," he yelled.

Gunther set it on the water and then pushed it to Rube, who picked it up and expertly gaffed the huge blackfish through the shoulders. Even though the shark was all but helpless now, Rube was careful to keep his hands out of the way of its mouth and tail.

"That was *some* fight," said Gunther.

"That is *some* blacktip," said Henry. "All the ones we've caught were forty or fifty pounds. That fellow has to be over a hundred."

"I wager he's gonna taste pretty good," said Rube.

That night he and his new friends had a feast. He chopped the shark into bits, added lemon, pepper, garlic, and parsley and then cooked it slowly on Henry's backyard grill. Henry invited some of their neighbors to share Rube's prize catch.

When he woke up the next morning Henry realized that he'd passed out in a chair in the middle of the yard. The last thing he remembered was Rube telling stories and challenging people to arm wrestle. He was already gone, even though the sun had just come up. He'd left a note that read, "Thanks for a great night of fishing and fun. Sorry I could not stay to help with the mess."

Henry looked around. The yard was littered with empty beer bottles and there was a bucket brimming with fish bones. There were about a hundred flies buzzing around it. Henry heard a noise behind him that sounded like a groan. It was Gunther. He'd passed out sitting up against the fence.

"Damn but Rube can put away the drinks," he said, trying to block the sun from his eyes.

"He can fish pretty well too," said Gunther.

"Not much at cleaning up, but he did me a big favor last night," said Henry.

"What kind of favor?" asked Gunther.

"Haven't you noticed what's gone?" Henry asked.

Gunther looked around. He thought for a moment. "Oh, now I see. That enormous branch, the one that got struck by lightning and fell in your yard last month." He looked at the spot where it had been.

"The two of us couldn't even budge it," said Henry, "and Rube picked it up like it was a bag of groceries and heaved it into the creek."

"I seem to recall him throwing a couple of your *guests* into the creek too," said Gunther.

"I guess they had it coming, telling Rube Cy Young deserved to beat him in that game Rube kept bragging about."

"They'll know better next time. Rube's friendly, but he's a bit off his rocker."

"More than a bit I'd say."

On Friday night, Rube went to Sneaky Pete's. There were hand-painted signs out front advertising the oyster-eating contest. There were so many people inside he had a hard time getting through the crowd.

"What do I win if I out eat the man?" Rube asked Pete.

"The winner doesn't have to pay for the oysters he eats and he gets five dollars," said the bartender.

"Where is this Zack fellow?" Rube asked.

"Over there," said Pete, pointing to a huge man in overalls. He was bald and had a patch over his right eye. Rube went over to introduce himself, Zack just grunted.

Pete pointed them to a table where the contest would be staged. A buxom waitress with dancing blue eyes brought them huge pots of steaming oysters.

"What's your name?" Rube asked her. He was sure he hadn't seen her at Sneaky's Pete's before. Or anywhere else for that matter. He knew he would have remembered if he had.

She gave Rube a big smile, happy to be asked. "My name is Esmeralda," she answered. She was very pretty, though she had a tiny space between her front teeth. She had a saucy way about her. Rube guessed she was about the same age he was.

"Pleasure to make your acquaintance," Rube told her. She smiled again and then took a deep breath, knowing full well that it would make her large breasts swell even larger.

"Can we just get started?" Zack Mitchell grunted.

"Fine with me," said Rube. "I haven't eaten a thing since lunch."

They dug into the pots and started tossing oysters into their mouths. The spectators gathered around. Even though he was new in town, almost all of them were cheering for Rube. Zack Mitchell wasn't the type to make friends. Neither man showed any sign of slowing down after they had finished a box of oysters. They matched one another until they had each finished off a second.

"That is a hundred and forty-four for each contestant," Pete announced, with more formality than the occasion probably warranted. He was enjoying himself and thinking about all the beers the spectators were ordering.

"Bring out more oysters, Esmeralda," he instructed.

Zack Mitchell began to sweat profusely when he neared a hundred and seventy-five oysters. Then he started holding his stomach and belching. Rube looked at him, shrugged and kept eating.

Mitchell pushed his plate away after choking down his hundred and ninetieth oyster. It looked as though he was going to be violently ill. As he ran out the back door to the outhouse, the crowd watched him. They struggled not to laugh, no doubt thinking they could not have eaten anywhere near that many oysters themselves. They looked back at Rube. He was still going, but he paused for a moment.

"Pete," Rube called out.

"Yes, Rube," he answered.

"I am going to require another beer to wash these down," he said.

"I'll get you one," said Esmeralda. Rube popped another oyster in his mouth as she headed for the bar.

When she brought his beer she bent over Rube so he had a full view down her blouse at her breasts. She winked and whispered, "Whatever you want, Rube."

Rube ate a few more oysters, wiped his mouth with a napkin, pushed his chair back from the table, and stood up. Pete rushed over and held up his right arm. "We have a winner. Rube Waddell by a score of two hundred and ten to one hundred and ninety."

The spectators crowded around Rube as Pete handed him a five-dollar bill.

After things quieted down, Rube went to the end of the bar, where Esmeralda was putting clean mugs on a shelf. He looked straight at her chest and said, "That is one amazing pair of ... earrings you have, Esmeralda."

She smiled and tugged at one of her long, dangling earrings. "I'm glad you noticed them."

"They're pretty hard to miss," grinned Rube, still staring at her breasts.

She came around the bar and sidled up close to Rube. "Speaking of *hard*, is it true that oysters have an effect on a man's desire to . . . to . . . spend time with a girl?"

"They do, and with all the oysters I ate tonight I'm gonna have to let out my trousers in more than just the waist."

"Perhaps I can help you with that problem," said Esmeralda. She looked around to see if anyone was watching and then ran her hand slowly down the front of Rube's trousers. She looked in his eyes and gulped. "Why, Rube, it seems as though it's not just your *appetite* that's enormous."

She looked over at the clock above the bar. "I'm done in twenty minutes," she said, "then we can go to my place. I'm not a nurse, but I may be able to help you with that extraordinary swelling of yours."

Esmeralda helped relieve Rube's 'swelling' five times that night.

                        ɛ   ɛ   ɛ

RUBE WADDELL
KING *of the* HALL *of* FLAKES

CHAPTER FORTY ONE

SOLD IN THE BEST INTERESTS
OF THE BALL CLUB

Before leaving for Spring Training Harry Davis and Topsy Hartsel went to see Connie Mack.

"What's the matter, boys, didn't you get your train tickets?" he asked. "Or did your wives tell you they'd miss you too much and beg you to stay home?"

Davis and Hartsel weren't in the mood for jokes. "No, Connie, we came to see you about Rube," said Davis.

"I see," said Mack. "Are you here to ask me to make him the team captain?" Mack asked.

"That is definitely not why we're here," said Davis.

"What is it then?" Mack asked.

"When we came to see you before about getting rid of Rube you talked us out of it," Davis reminded him.

"Yes, I did. I told you it would mean I'd have to cut salaries due to the loss of revenue," said Mack.

"Well, with the way Rube is drinking and carousing and letting himself go, we just don't see where Rube is going to be able to pitch many more times anyway," said Davis.

"You may be right about that," said Mack, rubbing his chin. "It's an awful shame the way he's wasting his talent, he could have five or six more great years in him."

Hartsel chimed in, "It's not just Harry and me, there's seven of us, Connie. I won't name the others, but none of us will go to camp if Waddell is still on the club."

"You feel that strongly about it?" asked Mack.

"We do," said Davis. "We won't play another game with the man. We all know how much talent he has, but he's let the team down too many times."

"I guess you might as well know, I looked in to sending him to Chicago last year."

"So *that's* where you went when you missed the St. Louis game," said Hartsel. "But you told the reporters ..."

"Never mind what I told the reporters. As for your request, let me handle it, I've been asking around to see if another club is interested in Rube and I think you'll be hearing something soon."

"All right then. It sure is too bad, Rube used to be a lot of fun. Now even the boosters are against him."

"I know we need left-handed pitching, Colonel, but are you sure you want to take a chance on Waddell?" Jimmy McAleer asked Robert Hedges, the owner of the St. Louis Browns.

Hedges was 56, handsome and clean-shaven, with straight white teeth and a warm smile. A lot of people called him Colonel, but because of his good nature many of the rooters had taken to calling him Uncle Bob. He regularly greeted spectators at the gate and often admitted entire families for free. His office was large, with handsome furnishing.

"I know what you're going to say, Jimmy," said Hedges. "The man is a drinker."

"That's a bit like saying a salmon is a swimmer," said McAleer. "His drinking was always bad, but last year I heard it got down right terrible."

"He would be a big draw, Jimmy. I don't know if two major league teams can survive here much longer. This isn't New York or Philadelphia. It may well come down to us or the Cardinals."

"How much is Connie Mack asking for Waddell?" McAleer asked.

"Five thousand dollars," Hedges told him.

"I see. And how much are you planning to pay Waddell?"

"Twelve hundred dollars. Connie Mack told me he cut him back from twenty-four hundred to twelve hundred a couple of years ago."

"And how much do you figure he would make for you?"

"If he pitches twenty times and the gate goes up by two or three thousand each time he'll bring in an additional twenty thousand dollars."

"I guess I can see why you'd want him."

"You cured Hack Spence of his drinking ways, Jimmy. Maybe you can do the same for Waddell."

"Well, one thing is sure. If he stays sober he'll win us a lot of games. He could even give us a chance to challenge for the pennant."

"See what you can get out of the big lug," said Hedges, slapping McAleer on the back. "Win the pennant and I'll use some of the money

Waddell makes us to give you a nice bonus."

lc   lc   lc

Rube was still in Mobile when he heard. He was sitting in a chair in Bernie McCay's poolroom with his feet up on the woodstove, tossing a cue ball up in the air and gazing out the window. "There surely are a lot of horseless carriages on the streets nowadays," he said to no one in particular.

A young man wearing horn-rimmed spectacles and a cheap cotton suit came in. He looked around the poolroom. When he spotted Rube he headed over to him purposefully.

"Mister Waddell?" he asked, though there was no mistaking the famous visitor.

"At your service," said Rube.

"I'm from The Mobile Dispatch. We have just received news by wire."

"I'm guessing that the news has something to do with me," said Rube.

"Yes. There's a report from Philadelphia that, in the best interests of the ball club, the Athletics have sold your rights to the St. Louis Browns."

"In the best interests of the club. Well isn't that a fine how do you do? It would appear that I wore out my welcome in Philly. Did it say how much they got for me?"

"No it didn't. There were no players involved, just cash."

"I see," said Rube, tossing the ball in the air again.

"How do you feel about it?" the reporter asked.

"Well I feel just fine. To be honest, I was kinda looking for a change. I liked the people in Philadelphia and all and Connie Mack was always good to me, but I've been in one place quite a long time and believe I can do better work on another team. There's no place I'd like to play in more than St. Louey. I am going to show the A's that they've made a big mistake, that I got a whole lot of good baseball left in me."

"I'm sure you will, Rube, I mean Mister Waddell," said the young reporter.

"Say, who's my new boss?"

"I beg your pardon."

"What is the name of the owner of the St. Louis club?"

"Oh, right, sorry. His name is Robert Hedges."

Rube said goodbye to his new friends at the pool hall and hurried to the telegraph office. He counted the change in his pocket and decided the message would have to be a brief one. It read . . .

To Robert Hedges, Sportsman's Park, St. Louis, Missouri.
Glad of deal. Send $100 at once so I can come. G.E. Waddell

Robert Hedges didn't send his new star a hundred dollars. He sent a train ticket instead.

ℓℓ   ℓℓ   ℓℓ

That Friday night Rube boarded a train for St. Louis. He got there on Valentine's Day and spent his first night in town at the Standard Theater watching wrestling matches. The sports pages had been full of talk about "the Great and Eccentric Southpaw."

"Hey, everybody," shouted a spectator. "It's Rube Waddell!"

There was a murmur and then a buzz in the audience as all heads turned to see the big man.

"Speech, speech!" people began to chant.

Never shy, Rube got up on stage and told the excited crowd how thrilled he was to be playing for the Browns and how he still had a lot of speedy shoots and tricky deliveries up his sleeve.

He got a room in the Southern Hotel. The next morning he put on his best suit and went to see Robert Hedges at Sportsman's Park.

"Glad to meet you, Rube," said Hedges as they shook hands. "Good Lord, you have huge hands. Cigar?"

"Don't mind if I do, Mister Hedges," answered Rube as he reached into the humidor. "I will help myself to another for later if that's all right."

"By all means. Take three or four," said Hedges. "You can call me Colonel if you like."

"Much obliged. And would you mind not callin' me Rube, Colonel? I know it's what nearly everybody calls me, but I never did like it."

"What did Connie Mack call you?"

"He's called me Eddie ever since he managed me in the Western League."

"Eddie's kind of a young-sounding name for a man of thirty. How about we call you George? That is your first name, is it not?"

"Yes it is." Rube scratched his chin and thought for a moment. "Say, I think I would like that, Colonel. No one's ever called me George. It sounds kinda distinguished and . . . educated."

"We already have a George, George Stone, but I don't think anyone will confuse the two of you. He's a westerner and four inches shorter and forty pounds lighter than you. Besides, all the players call him Stones."

"Then George will answer just fine."

"You look to be in pretty fine shape, George?" Hedges remarked. "What have you been doing to stay in condition?"

"Well, I was training a boxer for a while and I ran five or more miles with him each day, and I played in some exhibition games in Alabama."

Hedges hesitated then said, "Jimmy McAleer says you did a great deal of drinking last season."

"I won't try to deny that, Colonel. But I have not had a drink in a month. From now on baseball is going to be serious business for me."

"I'm happy to hear you say so."

"What are you planning to pay me, Colonel?"

"Twelve hundred dollars."

"I was hoping for a lot..."

"I'm afraid the amount is not negotiable, George. I run this ball club as a business and I'm in the process of rebuilding the stadium. I can't spare any more funds for salaries."

Rube frowned. "Cobb and Wagner are making seven or eight grand and they don't put fannies in the seats the way I do. Besides I expect to win twenty-eight games for you this year."

"That would be terrific, George. I tell what I'll do for you. In addition to your salary I'll pay your room and board for the entire season."

Rube's frown faded a little. "Well I suppose..."

"And, instead of the usual three dollars a day for meal money players receive, in light of your famously gargantuan appetite, you'll get four dollars a day."

"That'd be mighty swell of ya, Colonel."

"Do you need a little walking around money?" asked Hedges, taking out his billfold.

"Well, a hundred would sure . . . "

"Here's fifty dollars. Try not to spend it all at once."

Rube's face lit up as he pocketed the money. "Thanks Colonel." He grabbed two more cigars before heading out the door.

℃   ℃   ℃

Rube spent the next three afternoons at *The St. Louis Post-Dispatch* sports department. He worked with a cub reporter named Harvey Stiles on a series of five articles for kids. The first one advised them not to try pitching until their bodies had matured. Rube walked around Stiles' tiny office with his thumbs in his suspenders and pontificated. Stiles scratched madly on a pad with a tiny pencil.

"Throwing curves and fadeaways can ruin a young man's arm if it is not yet ready for the strain," Rube dictated as though he was delivering the Ten Commandments to Moses. In the second installment Rube talked about how pitchers need to ignore things going on around them, such as spectators heckling them and teammates making bad plays.

"Do not let yourself get rattled," he advised. "Leave your nerves at home."

His third pearl of wisdom advised youngsters to work on their speed rather than their curves. "Fast, late-breaking curves are a lot harder to hit than slow ones. Do all the stretching you can to get snap into your arm. A half an hour a day at least."

Rube's fourth pronouncement advised young pitchers to get to know their catchers so they can work together, especially with runners on base.

"There is not a catcher on Earth that can throw a runner out if the pitcher ignores him. Keep your runners close and your catcher will thank you. Treat him right and he will pull your close pitches into the strike zone, treat him badly and you will notice that there are a lot of passed balls."

The final chapter told kids who wanted to pitch to learn the hitters' strengths and weaknesses. "There is no point in wearing your arm out throwing a bunch of fast pitches to a man who can't hit a curve to save his soul."

"Anything else, Rube?" Stiles asked.

Rube thought for a minute.

"Yes," he said earnestly. Stiles put his pencil tip to his tongue and prepared to begin scribbling again.

"Tell the boys not to play with their peckers the morning before a game."

Stiles stopped writing and looked at Rube in disbelief. "Do you really think we should . . ."

"I was just joshin' with ya, Harry. Now, where do I pick up my twenty-five dollars?"

A GREAT FIRST IMPRESSION

Robert Hedges had also signed Bill Dinneen, who had been Boston's best pitcher five years ago, and Hobe Ferris, who'd been one of the Americans' infielders. The Browns would now be the oldest team in the league. To get his veterans in condition, Jimmy McAleer took them to French Lick Springs, Indiana two weeks before training camp.

"Where did you get all this fancy equipment, Jimmy?" asked Bill Dinneen.

"A gym uptown," McAleer answered.

"You going to show us how to use it?"

"I can do that, Jimmy," said Rube.

With that, Rube took the other veterans from one piece of equipment to the next, showing them not just how to use them, but how to get the most benefit out of them. He pulled so hard on the arms of the rowing machine McAleer was afraid he was going to row it right through the wall and off down the street. Bill Dinneen thought he'd done pretty well on the bench press, lifting two hundred and twenty pounds.

"Nice job, Bill," said Rube. "My turn."

Rube added two fifty pound weights and lifted the bar fifteen times without breaking a sweat. When the two men played catch with a medicine ball Rube knocked Dinneen flat on his back. Rube also led the group in the daily calisthenics that McAleer had ordered. He was first out the door and the first back in when the group did a grueling ten-mile run each morning. The rest straggled in as much as twenty minutes after Rube, who wore a big grin through all the training.

After packing away enormous suppers Rube would play soccer with any of the other veterans who had any energy left. One night he wasn't able to convince anyone to play, so he headed into town. As always he made friends quickly and ended up spending the evening refereeing badger fights.

RUBE WADDELL

"I have to admit I was worried about how serious Waddell would be, but he's actually in terrific condition, by far the best of any of the veterans," McAleer told a reporter who'd come from St. Louis to watch the unusual pre-training camp proceedings. "I couldn't be happier with the shape he was in when he reported and with the work he's been doing here."

"How do you think he'll perform for you?" the reporter asked.

"Waddell looks better than I've ever seen him," declared McAleer. "He is one of the most likable and easiest men in the world to handle and I think he's going to pitch good ball for me this year."

"Off the record, Jimmy," the reporter whispered. "Is the big fellow drinking?" asked the reporter.

"Not a drop so far. But Lord love a duck, the man can put away a heap of food."

After two weeks of extra conditioning the veterans traveled to Shreveport to join the rest of the team for Spring Training. Since he was already in good shape, Rube was selected as one of the Browns to play in a series of exhibition games to make money to defray the training expenses. In his first start in Monroe, Louisiana he struggled to find the plate and gave up four early runs but still had a four-run lead in the ninth. After giving up a leadoff single he decided to do a little showboating. He purposely walked the next two batters to load the bases.

He threw fastballs to the next hitter, who just barely managed to get his bat on the ball and popped it up just out of the reach of the infielders. Thanks to an errant throw from Dode Criss, the rookie right fielder, all three runners scored. Rube's lead was down to a single run. He shrugged his big shoulders, grinned and then struck out the next two batters on six pitches.

He was feeling good after the win and got into a mock wrestling match under the stands with Criss over his bad throw. Unfortunately, his spikes caught on a nail and he fell against a hot steam pipe. Rube yelped in pain. The rookie was mortified that he'd contributed to the team's new star getting hurt.

"I am so sorry," Dode sputtered, "I didn't mean to ..."

Rube consoled him. "Listen to me, Dode, I been burned a lot worse than this fightin' fires. Never you mind. It's not my pitchin' arm and it'll be just fine after I soak it in cold milk."

Rube was okay. He hoped Jimmy McAleer back in Shreveport wouldn't hear about what happened. The rookie outfielder wasn't the only one who wanted to make a good impression on the manager.

        ℮   ℮   ℮

The weather took a turn for the worse and no exhibitions could be played for a few days. A local farmer who introduced himself as Jed Wickens found Rube sitting under an overhang smoking a "Rube Waddell smooth delivery" cigar. The farmer said he had always been an admirer and showed him a new rod and reel he'd just bought. He asked Rube if he would like to go fishing with him on the Red River. Rube was delighted. He invited a couple of his new friends on the team and the four of them headed out in the pouring rain. Rube never cared about getting a little wet if he was fishing.

When they reached the spot the farmer said was the best for catching walleye he offered Rube a pull on his canteen. "Best shine in the county," he stated proudly.

Rube took the canteen and was about to take a swig. Then he stopped and handed it back to Wickens. "No thank you, Jed. Believe me, I would love to, but I got to be good. McAleer will skin me alive if he learns I had a drink."

The other three together caught eight fish. Rube left the others and found a spot of his own where he caught fifteen.

        ℮   ℮   ℮

As was the case in Philadelphia, the crosstown rivals in St. Louis played a yearly exhibition series before the start of the season. Rube was picked to start the second game against the Cardinals and 25,000 bugs turned up to see the city's new attraction. It was the biggest crowd Sportsman's Park had ever held and it was just an exhibition game. Rube did not disappoint, striking out nine even though he lost by one run.

The reporter for *The St. Louis Post-Dispatch* did some arithmetic and wrote that the Browns' owner had raked in $17,000 that afternoon, maybe more depending upon how many of the new and popular cooked wieners on a bun had been sold. Not even counting the spectators he'd drawn to the exhibition games in Louisiana, Rube had earned Hedges more than three times what he paid for him and the season hadn't even started. Rube drew close to 20,000 when he pitched in his second exhibition against the Cardinals and then 22,000 to the sixth and last. He was making Hedges money hand over fist.

Rube found a rooming house not far from the stadium and one night while he was sitting on the veranda one of the female boarders came out to catch some of the evening breeze. It was only May but St. Louis was already heating up. Rube thought she was well dressed for a woman staying in a boarding house and he wondered why she was alone. As he was screwing up the courage to talk to her, the landlady's husband came out and sat in the rocker between them. He began reading a newspaper, *The St. Louis Globe Democrat*.

After a few minutes had passed the man spoke. "Say Rube," I just found an editorial about you, "listen to what this fellow says."

Rube was more interested in what the young woman thought of him, but figured he should be polite. "What does he have to say about me?" Rube asked, hoping the woman would be impressed by it.

The man cleared his throat, set down his pipe so he could hold the paper with both hands, and then read, "Rube Waddell has lent excitement and high hopes to what otherwise promised to be another drab season of discontent for St. Louis baseball enthusiasts. Waddell as he appears today is what he seems always to have been, inscrutable, unfathomable, and as simple as a child. No one has plumbed the depths of his moods; yet everyone knows him as a sociable, overgrown boy. It is hard to see Rube today and believe all the indiscretions credited to him. Lean of face and trim at one hundred and ninety-six pounds of muscle, he seems a carefully-cared for athlete rather than one accustomed to heaping vagaries on the altar of pleasure."

"I'd like to show that gal a certain part of me that's overgrown and plumb her depths," Rube thought to himself as the female guest got up and walked into the house. She smiled at him as she passed but he wasn't sure how friendly or inviting she meant to be.

⚓ ⚓ ⚓

His much anticipated first regular season start came on April 17 in Chicago. As he laced up his shoes in the clubhouse he looked around the room. He'd taken a few minutes to read about his new teammates in *The Sporting News*. If he was going to win the twenty-eight games he'd promised Hedges he was going to need some talent around him.

Three other pitchers would be competing with him for starts. Spitballer Harry Howell, the ace of the staff, had given up fewer than two runs a game in '07, yet he was just 16-15. "Not a good sign," Rube had thought. Their next best pitcher had been Jack Powell. At 34, he had to be getting toward the end of his career. Barney Pelty, whom the newspapers called "the Yiddish Curver", had been 12-21 in '07 after an excellent season the year before. His curves had not had much snap. Rube recalled hitting a couple of them a long way.

Now he saw why the Browns had needed pitching so badly and he wished he'd stuck to his guns and turned down the paltry salary Hedges was paying him. He thought about how many people had turned up to see him pitch against the Cardinals in the exhibition games and shook his head. He decided he should at least have grabbed more of Hedges' cigars.

Rube recalled facing the Browns over the past couple of seasons and remembered that he hadn't had much trouble with their hitters. No wonder Howell had lost so many games. Rube knew that Tubby Spencer, the Browns' young catcher, came from Oil City, Pennsylvania just a few miles from where he was born. He recalled hitting him in the stomach with a pitch. His real name was Edward and he'd been saddled with an even less flattering nickname than Rube. Last year he'd rebounded from a horrible '06 season during which he hit just .176. He'd been awfully lucky to hang on with the Browns.

Handsome and dapper Tom Jones, a veteran at first base, was also from Pennsylvania. He was very good with the bat, having hit close to .300 four times. But everyone knew he had an iron glove at first. Jimmy Williams was at second. He was a mediocre fielder at best and not very good with a bat either. He was the same age as Rube but the Browns were his fourth team, which said a lot. Rube knew Hobe Ferris, the third baseman, well. Mostly he knew that Hobe let a lot of balls go through his legs.

Bobby Wallace, the shortstop, was 34 now. This would be his tenth year in St. Louis. He'd hit .324 back in '01 when Rube had broken into the majors but hadn't come close to that since. At least he was still good with the glove. It was lucky Rube didn't know that Wallace was making $6,500 a year, more than five times what he was being paid. Leftfielder George Stone was the Browns' best hitter. He'd hit .358 in '06 and .324 in '07. Rube wished the Browns had a couple of more hitters like 'Stones'.

Rube didn't know much about Charlie Jones, the Browns' right fielder, but he'd played with Danny Hoffman, the centerfielder. They'd been teammates in Philadelphia before Hoffman was sent to New York. Dode Criss was trying to take Hoffman's job and Rube thought he might just get it. Hoffman had stolen thirty bases in '07 but he'd struck out 103 times, which was unheard of. There were only three other players in the league who'd struck out more than seventy times.

Rube took the mound feeling a bit nervous in front of his new teammates. As a result, he walked four batters in the first three innings. But after the Browns finally scored a run in the seventh Rube finished with a great assortment of speedballs, curves, wobblers, and puzzlers. He retired the White Sox in order in the seventh, eighth, and ninth and gave up just one hit the whole game, a single to Jake Atz. It was the only ball hit out of the infield.

"Whale of a game, George," McAleer told Rube as he was stripping down to his red underwear. "See what behaving yourself does for you."

"Seems as though I've got a few good years left in this wing after all," said Rube.

"Seems like." said McAleer. "Oh, I almost forgot. The Colonel told me to give you this." He handed Rube a twenty dollar bill. Rube was thrilled. For a moment he forget how rotten his salary was.

CHAPTER FORTY THREE

TALKIN' WITH TEDDY

When the Browns returned to St. Louis, Robert Hedges called Rube into his office. Rube helped himself to some of the owner's cigars and sat down in a large leather chair.

"That's a very nice suit, George," said Hedges. "I am glad to see you are spending your money wisely."

"I'm still on the straight and narrow, Colonel."

"Well your clean living may be paying off for you, George," said Hedges. "I just heard from a company that makes soap. They want you to say you use nothing but their product when you shower after a game."

"Ain't that a hoot? I've put my name on cigars, whiskey, and Coca-Cola but never soap. What kinda soap is it?"

"I'm not sure, but they are going to pay you five hundred dollars."

"Hell, for that kinda money I'd shower in molasses."

Since Rube didn't have a bank account, he got Robert Hedges to cash the soap company's check for him after he'd signed *Edward Waddell* on the back in his distinct and flowing style. He ended up giving $200 of the endorsement money to a boys' club so they could buy baseball equipment and take the kids on excursions. He never used the soap. Privately he told anyone who asked that he thought it smelled like cow dung.

        ⚾   ⚾   ⚾

The Browns wore their new home uniforms for their first game in St. Louis. The players now wore brown stockings and their new white shirts had brown trim. The team logo - a fleur de lis - was on the chest now instead of the sleeve.

Rube pitched the home opener on April 24 before a Friday crowd of 9,000, which was a lot more than expected on a weekday. He threw a four-hitter and the Browns moved into very unfamiliar territory - first place. The crosstown Cardinals were last in the National League. Then Rube disappeared. He told people he had gone fishing but several of the

Browns suspected he had gone on a bender.

When he finally turned up on May 4 the Browns were playing the Tigers. Jimmy McAleer said nothing but, "You're pitching today, George."

"How do you like that?" Bobby Wallace muttered. "The scoundrel's gone ten days and McAleer says nothing."

"Get used to it, Bob," said Hobe Ferris. "There are different rules for Rube than everybody else."

"Why's that?' Wallace demanded.

"It's just the way it has to be," Ferris answered. "He's not like anyone else, he's just a big kid."

Rube set down the first two Detroit hitters. Then Sam Crawford hit a dribbler to Jimmy Williams. He'd been playing back with the powerful Crawford at the plate and didn't get to it in time to throw him out. Next up was Ty Cobb, batting in the Tigers' cleanup slot for good now. Rube tried to throw one outside to him but it caught enough of the strike zone for Cobb to turn on and slam into right field. Crawford scored easily. A murmur went through the crowd.

Bill Dinneen turned to Harry Howell, who was beside him on the bench. "If Rube's been on a binge this whole time the Tigers are gonna tear him apart."

"Maybe, Bill, but it *was* Cobb after all," said Howell. "He eats everybody alive. He never saw a fast one he didn't jump all over."

"We'll see," said Dinneen.

That run was the only one Detroit scored. Unfortunately the Browns didn't score at all. It was still 1-0 when the sky darkened in the seventh and rain poured down. After a twenty-minute downpour the umpire called the game. It was a tough loss.

"Did you hear what your old manager Fred Clarke's invented, George?" Hobe Ferris asked Rube after the game had been called.

"What's that, Hobe?"

"It's a huge piece of canvas on a roller."

"What's it for?" asked Rube.

"It's to spread over the diamond when it starts to rain. He calls it a tarpaulin. When the rain lets up you roll it back up and the field is dry enough to keep playing on."

"Fred was always a clever fella," said Rube. "He worked a deal and had his sense of humor pulled out with his teeth."

"I heard he's working on shades to put on the outfielders' caps so they don't lose the ball in the sun. Lots of new things comin' into the game," said Ferris. "Like old Roger Bresnahan in Brooklyn wearing cricket pads on his legs - shin guards he calls 'em - so he can move right up in behind the batter instead of staying back outta the way a foul tips. Says it makes it easier to throw out base stealers."

"Ya, I was tellin' that writer about them, the English fella who's found this friend of his called Holmes."

      ℃ ℃ ℃

Five days later McAleer started Rube again, this time against Chicago. The White Sox scored four runs on a walk, three bunts, and a double, all in the first inning. Rube had an early shower. Since he'd pitched for only ten minutes, McAleer sent him out again the very next day. In the second inning he dropped a ball that had been hit softly back up the middle. He could probably have caught it with his cap ten years ago. Twice he had to cover first base. The first time Tom Jones dove to his right and somehow came up with the ball. He tossed it to Rube, who dropped it. An inning later Jones made another nice play. This time Rube didn't drop the ball. He tripped over the bag before the throw reached him.

At the plate he struck out four times. The season was still young but Rube still didn't have a hit. The St. Louis papers were not kind after the loss. One said, "Rube did everything but run the bases for Chicago."

      ℃ ℃ ℃

When the Browns headed east they were out of first place, but not by a lot. Their first stop was in Washington against the sad-sack Senators and the Browns were invited to the White House to meet President Roosevelt. All of the players were in awe of the imposing hero of San Juan Hill. All except Rube.

When the other Browns were introduced to Roosevelt they almost bowed and curtsied. Some were actually trembling and everyone was far too nervous to say anything but "Nice to meet you, Mister President."

When Rube's turn came he grabbed Roosevelt's hand and shook it vigorously. "Pleasure to make your acquaintance, Teddy. Any of the Roughriders around?"

Roosevelt stared at Rube and then his huge belly began to shake.

Jimmy McAleer almost fainted. "George, you can't talk to the ..."

But Roosevelt held up a hand to stop him. He had a huge smile under his big moustaches.

"That's quite a handshake you have there, Rube. And those are the biggest paws I've seen apart from a grizzly bear. As to your question, no, I'm sorry but there are no Roughriders here today, just you ball players and a bunch of stuffy members of my cabinet who are about as lively as turtles."

"Doesn't sound like a whole lotta fun around here, Teddy. Why don't you and me go huntin' some time?"

"That a *great* idea. I'll see if can escape this place some day. Have some champagne."

"Do you not have any good whiskey here in your house, Teddy?"

"I have a bottle of Kentucky bourbon a supporter sent me as a gift. I think he'd much rather I shared it with ballplayers than politicians or lobbyists."

A puzzled expression came over Rube. "I didn't see anybody in the lobby when we came in."

Roosevelt let go another enormous belly laugh. Rube reached into his breast pocket and pulled out a cigar. "Here, Teddy, have a *Rube Waddell* cigar."

Roosevelt read the label and laughed again. "I'd be delighted, thank you, Rube." He put his arm around Rube's big shoulders and the two walked to the bar cabinet together discussing where to hunt.

McAleer shook his head and muttered, "That joker even makes friends at the fuckin' White House."

    *   *   *

Harry Howell won the first game in Washington and Bill Dinneen won the second. Rube pitched the third game and lost 4-0. He was sweating profusely and didn't look like he was having much fun. His record stood at 2-5.

"We need something to perk George up, get him motivated," Tom Jones told Jimmy McAleer.

"That shouldn't be a problem considering where we're headed next," said McAleer.

"What do you mean? Oh, that's right, we're going to Philly."

"If that doesn't light a fire under Rube, nothin' will."

    *   *   *

"Why aren't you starting Rube?" George Stone asked McAleer when he saw the lineup card for the first game in Philadelphia.

"I want him really riled up when he pitches," McAleer told him.

Stone pointed to the stands where a huge crowd was chanting, "Rube, Rube, we want Rube!"

"They'll just have to come back tomorrow," said McAleer.

    *   *   *

A delegation came out on the field and presented Rube with a fishing pole and a medal that read "To a great hurler and hero of Philadelphia base ball enthusiasts." They declared Rube 'King for the Day'. A huge moan went through the crowd when Harry Howell took the mound. He pitched well, but the Browns lost.

McAleer didn't start Rube in the second game either. Another big crowd who had come to see Rube went away disappointed even though the A's beat the Browns again.

By now Rube was fairly chomping at the bit. He wanted to have a go at his old team and show them he still had it. He'd learned that Davis and a bunch of other A's had all but forced Connie Mack to get rid of him.

Jimmy McAleer made a simple announcement to reporters after the game was over. "Rube will pitch tomorrow." An average weekday crowd numbered 4,000. More than 20,000 showed up for game three. Several offices and two factories closed early to allow their workers to see their former ace.

A thunderous roar erupted from the crowd when they saw that Rube would indeed be the starter for St. Louis. He made a theatrical bow and waved his cap over his head. Another roar. The game was held up when another delegation made a presentation to Rube. This time it was a shotgun and an expensive gun case. There was no way Rube could ever have afforded them.

He tried to contain his excitement but still walked the first batter. Then Topsy Hartsel laid down a bunt. Rube fielded it cleanly but Tom Jones had raced in for it and Jimmy Williams neglected to cover first. Two batters, two base runners. Rube struck out the next two hitters, each on four pitches, and then got Socks Seybold to pop up. He waved off the infielders and caught the ball himself bare-handed.

The A's scored two runs in the second by virtue of walks, bunts, and sloppy fielding by the Browns. Hartsel led off the third and reached on another bunt. He moved to second on yet another bunt. The A's were well aware of Rube's biggest weakness.

Rube watched Hartsel as he danced off second. He knew he was looking to steal third. Rube waited. Hartsel danced and shuffled some more, inching farther and farther off the bag. Without so much as a twitch to give away what he was doing, Rube fired a bullet to Bobby Wallace, who had silently snuck in behind Hartsel. He was caught completely flat-footed and Wallace nonchalantly applied the tag.

Then Rube put an end to the Athletics' shenanigans. His former team didn't get a single hit the rest of the afternoon. Rube chuckled when he struck out Harry Davis for the third time.

"Still glad you talked Connie into dumping me, Jasper?" he yelled at him.

"I dunno what you're talkin' about," Davis called back.

"Never mind, it's water under the bridge now. What's it like havin' me on the other side?"

"For what it's worth, I never said you weren't a great pitcher, Rube."

The Browns' bats finally came alive against Chief Bender and the crowd cheered even though the home side was losing its lead. Danny Hoffman hit a double against his former mates and George Stone knocked Chief Bender out of the game with a two-run home run. After Rube struck out the side in the ninth the Browns walked off with a 5-2 win.

Robert Hedges, who had made the trip to Philadelphia, ran into Connie Mack under the grandstand. "The man can still pitch," said Mack. "He may not be able to hit a lick anymore and he's having more and more trouble with the bunts, but he still has an arm like a catapult."

"That he does, Connie, and McAleer knows he's the best we have."

"I imagine he's making you some money."

"Our gate receipts are up sixty per cent, Connie. How about yours?"

"Ours are *down* thirty per cent. But my hair's stopped turning white and I'm sleeping like a baby."

     *   *   *

McAleer gave Rube a few days of rest and then started him in the Browns' last game against the Naps. He threw seven strong innings and had a lead when he came to bat in the top of the eighth. He hit a looper just over Nap Lajoie's head for his first hit of the year. The leadoff hitter, Bobby Wallace, was up next and he sacrificed Rube over to second. Heinie Berger, the Cleveland pitcher, tried to pick Rube off. He dove back to the bag in time but there was an awful crunch when his head made contact with Lajoie's knee.

"You all right, Eddie?" Lajoie asked Rube, who was rocking back and forth in apparent agony.

"I believe my neck is broken," Rube told him.

McAleer wasn't sure the injury was as bad as Rube was saying. It was a hot afternoon and he suspected Rube was badly in need of a cold beer, but he took him out anyway. Bill Dinneen took over and managed to hold onto the lead.

When he seemed fine minutes after the game ended his teammates teased him about his close shave with death. Rube was about to let them have it when a big grin spread across his face. "Let's go upstairs and have a drink, fellas. Just beer, and three is my limit."

"Hardly enough to wet your whistle, George," said Hobe Ferris.

"Just enough to hold me 'til I get uptown. Got to leave room for dinner."

"You liking the steaks here in Saint Louis, George?"

"I sure am, had a delicious 32-ounzer last night."

"What's that, half a cow?"

"Pretty near, I guess. Might have the other half tonight. If they don't want me to drink I got to keep up my strength up somehow."

RUBE WADDELL
KING *of the* **HALL** *of* **FLAKES**

CHAPTER FORTY FOUR

STAYING ON THE WATER WAGON

The Browns were playing well and were still in first place when the Athletics visited St. Louis in early June. Rube whitewashed them 10-0. He struck out only two batters, but almost all of the eight hits he gave up were scratch singles. Particularly satisfying was the fact that his opponent was Rube Vickers, the rookie who had shown him up before the A's gave up on him.

When asked if he'd had to throw hard to beat his former mates Rube was unusually philosophical. "What's the use of a fellow throwing his arm away to win a game of baseball? Especially when he has a big lead like I had today? From now on I am going to use my head and save my arm for when I really need to get an out."

James Crusinberry wrote a tongue-in-cheek column in The Post-Dispatch about the suddenly thoughtful twirler. "Instead of going fishing on his days off, Rube will now spend his time in the public library reading Darwin and Shakespeare."

"I heard of that Shakespeare fellow but who's Darwin?' he asked Hobe Ferris.

"I think he plays left field for Cincinnati," Ferris told him, hiding a grin.

"Can't be too good a player if I never heard of him, musta hurt his eyes reading books."

&c &c &c

Rube's next win came at the expense of young Walter Johnson. After coming in to start the fifth inning he struck out six and gave up just one hit. After 41 innings of work for the Browns, Rube's E.R.A. stood at 1.30 and he'd evened up his record at 6-6. He was still laying off the whiskey and showing everyone just how good he still was.

Four days later he faced the Boston Americans and rookie Ed Cicotte, whose nickname was Froggy because of his French-Canadian heritage. Rube outpitched Cicotte, but the Browns booted the ball around the diamond for five errors. Then Rube started grooving pitches down the middle in frustration.

Tubby Spencer finally came out to the mound after Boston got their fourth straight hit. "What are you doing out here, George? You're just lobbing 'em in."

Rube gestured toward the infielders, shrugged his shoulders and said, "Shit, Tubby, I might as well let those guys get their cuts the way our boys are kicking the ball around."

The Americans took three in a row and the Browns fell into second place.

Jimmy McAleer could see that his team needed some kind of a distraction. He called Rube into his office. Rube looked for a cigar box but there wasn't one. Seeing what he was after, McAleer offered him a cigarette instead.

Rube took one and lit it up. "What can I do for you, Jim? I haven't done anything you'd wanna fine me for, least not that I can think of."

"No, George, it's nothing like that, I have a job for you," said McAleer, taking a drag of his own cigarette.

Puzzled, Rube asked, "A baseball job?"

"No, a fishing job."

"A fishing job? I didn't know there was one available, I'da put in for it."

"We have a couple of days before we play again and I want you to take the boys fishing. Get them away from the park, let them relax, get their minds off baseball for a bit."

"That'd be swell. You got any particular spot in mind?"

"I was thinking of Creve Coeur Lake."

"Up in Maryland Heights? Yeah, that's a good spot. I've bin there a few times already."

"Get as many of the players as you can. Some'll want to spend time at home instead but I imagine most of them will go."

"Can you gimme fifteen dollars for supplies? I'll have to rent boats and get some gear."

"Here's twenty," said McAleer, handing Rube two ten dollar bills. Have some fun and bring me back a couple of beauties."

"Be glad to. See you on Thursday."

       ℓ   ℓ   ℓ

All but four of the Browns joined Rube and they had a great time. Rube got them grubs, plugs, night-crawlers, and minnows and showed them the best spots on the lake. He knew a river channel where the fish hid in the rocks. He left some of the men there and then led an expedition out into deeper waters. The water was just warm enough for what Rube was after - largemouth bass.

Schools of crappies swam by and the players in his boat caught some nice-sized blue catfish, but Rube waited patiently for largemouth. He would gladly settle for a walleye, but he hadn't heard of anyone catching one on Creve Coeur since he'd come to St. Louis. They'd been out for just over two hours when Rube, who had appeared to be asleep, straightened up in his seat and looked out over the water. He had a big grin on his face. Twenty minutes later Rube hauled a huge walleye in over the side of the boat.

"That bugger has to go thirty-five pounds," said Lou Criger.

Rube lifted the fish higher and then handed it to Criger. His arm dropped as he took the weight that had seemed like nothing to Rube.

"Hell, that's more like *forty*-five, George, nice catch."

Rube expertly pulled his hook out of the walleye's mouth and threw the fish into his bucket. By the time they headed back it was joined by two largemouth bass that looked to be close to twenty pounds each.

They had a huge bonfire on the shore that night. Rube cut up his catch like an experienced chef and then got the coals just the way he wanted them. They roasted potatoes and soaked the fish in lemon. Having thought of everything, Rube had bought some chickens to fry up for the players who hadn't caught anything and really didn't like fish anyway.

His teammates knew Rube was trying hard to stay on the water wagon but they'd brought along a couple of boxes of beer. While they ate, Rube told stories about some of the fish he'd caught and game that he'd shot. Then, after producing a box of Rube Waddell cigars, he taught his teammates some of the raunchy songs he'd learned during his travels.

The next day he caught five largemouth and another walleye, though this one was a bit smaller. He took those back to his manager. McAleer accepted only a couple of the bass, saying they'd last his family for a week.

When they got back to work the relaxed Browns won all of their next five games. The team was fielding a lot better for their other starters than they had for Rube and had a chance to move back into first place with a win over Detroit on June 24th. McAleer gave the ball to Rube.

The Tigers started ragging him from the get-go and they never let up. They all knew that Rube loved animals, especially dogs, so their manager Hugh Jennings, who had learned lots of tricks in his glory days with the Orioles, had his players hold up puppies on the bench and in the coaching boxes to distract him. "Look, Rube," they yelled, "ain't he a cutie? I'll bet you'd love to take him home right now."

"You like that one, hayseed?" Ty Cobb yelled. "Well, I'm going to drown it."

"That so, Cobb?" Rube called back. "Well make sure you go down with him. You'd make a lot of folks real happy." Cobb's teammates hid their smiles behind their gloves.

In spite of the puppies and in spite of the Tigers calling Rube every name they could think of, he kept his cool and kept mowing down the Detroit batters. The Browns' bats came alive and Rube won easily 7-1.

He got a start on July 2 against Chicago and was pounded for three runs on four hits in the one inning he lasted. It didn't help that his fielders committed five errors. He wondered if that was a major league record for one inning.

Rube usually responded well to big crowds, but in front of 15,000 on July the 4th he seemed to show that he was no longer the Rube of old. He got roughed up and once again lasted just an inning. McAleer told him he wouldn't pitch in the next series against Cleveland and sent him on ahead alone to Philadelphia. Rube drank a quart of whiskey on the train.

When the rest of the team arrived in Philadelphia they couldn't find Rube anywhere. Since his bed at the hotel hadn't been slept in, everyone was shocked when Rube appeared bright-eyed and bushy-tailed for the game the next day.

"Let me start, Jimmy," he begged McAleer.

"All right, George, you can start. You've been terrific against the A's all year. But you had better throw better than you have been lately," said McAleer.

"I know I've been horseshit the last two times out, but today's gonna be different."

Rube knew he had been letting his teammates down, but to his relief he didn't disappoint them this time out.

"His fast ones are not quite as quick as they used to be," Tubby Spencer told Jimmy McAleer after Rube struck out the last two batters in the fifth, "but his overhand curves are droppin' like rocks in a well."

In the seventh Ossee Schreckonghost came up as a pinch hitter. Schreck was a backup catcher these days so Rube hadn't faced him yet.

He knew Rube's pitches and patterns better than anyone and he went up to the plate with a plan. But having a plan and executing it were two different things. Ossee struck out on four pitches.

"I guess you still got a few tricks up those long sleeves of yours," Ossee called out to him.

Rube winked at his old friend. "One or two," he yelled back. He ended up with a nine strikeout, 6-0 shutout.

Over the last two weeks of July and the first week of August Rube was unbeatable, chalking up six straight wins to boost his once woeful record to 14-9. In the last of the wins he beat the Americans, who'd been clobbering the Browns all year. He even got two hits, doubling his total for the season. He sealed his victory with a home run that sailed over the Bull Durham sign into the bleachers.

"Fucking Waddell," Lindy Stokes grunted to the other gamblers he was sitting with. "He's cost me a god damned fortune these last three weeks."

"You weren't bellyaching when you were making a pile a dough bettin' against him in May and June," said Suitcase O'Shea, "takin' advantage of all the saps who thought he could still pitch like when he was twenty."

"Turns out the bastard still *can* pitch like he's twenty," said Stokes.

"You know what you gotta do," said O'Shea.

"What's that?" asked Stokes.

"Get him drunk before every game."

"Hell, he used to do that on his own. He's only done it once this year from what I heard - on the way to Philly. And he won the next day anyway. This water wagon he's on is killin' me."

"I imagine it's pretty hard on Rube too."

RUBE WADDELL
KING *of the* HALL *of* FLAKES

CHAPTER FORTY FIVE

KEEPING HIS TEAM ALIVE

Rube finally lost to the Athletics on August 14, though he pitched well. He struck out eleven in beating the Senators 4-2 five days later and on the 19th he faced the Highlanders in New York and won again.

"Wallace has a sore hand, Schweitzer has a dislocated hip, and I'm releasing Charlie Jones," Jimmy McAleer told Robert Hedges. "The man just cannot hit big league pitching."

They were sitting in Hedges' office. Sunlight streamed through the window, revealing a million tiny dust particles. The sweet smell of coffee filled Jimmy McAleer's nostrils as he watched curls of steam rise from the Colonel's China cup.

"Who will you get to replace Jones?" Hedges asked.

"I've signed Emmett Heidrick."

"Heidrick? He hasn't played in three years!"

"There's no one else available this time of the year, Colonel. Believe me, I've looked all over."

"Is Powell's ankle still bothering him?"

"It is, and his arm's still not right."

"Where would we be without Waddell?" Hedges asked his manager.

"I don't know, Colonel. Do you realize he has every single one of our wins in the last four weeks?"

"It's lucky for us the Tigers have finally started losing some games," said Hedges as he took out a cigar and cut the end off. "Otherwise, we'd be out of the race."

"We're not going to stay ahead of Chicago and Cleveland unless we start winning more," said McAleer. "We just played nine games against the three worst teams in the league and we only won three. Well, *Rube* won three."

Hedges got out of his chair and walked to the window. He squinted into the sunlight and then put his face up close to the glass.

"Who's the big fellow painting the fence, Jimmy?"

McAleer joined him at the window. "What do you mean, Colonel? As I recall all four of the painters are short fellas."

"Look at the man on the end," said Hedges.

"He is tall," McAleer agreed. "Must have just joined the crew. He's not wearing the same . . . wait a minute, Colonel. That isn't a painter."

"Who is it, then?"

"It's Rube."

"Well, I'll be damned. So it is."

"You sure are getting your money's worth out of him. He was taking tickets and selling programs before the game yesterday."

"He is making me a bundle, Jimmy. Our attendance is up sixty per cent."

"How are the Athletics drawing since Rube came over here?"

"Their gate is down more than thirty percent. Rube was their biggest draw."

"And you know what, Colonel" said McAleer, looking back out the window.

"What's that, Jimmy?"

"He's a heck of a painter too."

&c &c &c

The White Sox came to town for four games. It was no surprise who would pitch game one, their ace Ed Walsh. He was starting every second game for Chicago as they tried to overtake the second-place Browns. Rube struck out eight and beat Walsh 4-0. The Tigers lost to Cleveland and St. Louis was just a game and a half game back in spite of their recent slump. But the Browns dropped the second game to Chicago and the third as well. St. Louis had to win the fourth game and Jimmy McAleer went with Rube.

The Browns scored one run in the third and three more in the sixth and Rube had given up just one run on two hits heading into the ninth, but he looked tired. His control was a bit off and he was having to throw a lot of pitches. He felt as though he'd pitched fifteen innings, not eight. But he struck out two in the ninth and got the other batter to ground out. He won again and his record now stood at 18-10, not bad for a castoff.

Harry Powell, Bill Dinneen, and Barney Pelty were nowhere near as effective against the Naps in the next three games and Cleveland struck what might just prove to be a death blow to the Browns with a four-game sweep.

They returned home for what would be their biggest series yet against

Detroit. "How ya feeling, George?" Jimmy McAleer as they got off the train.

"Not so bad, Jimmy, my arm's a little tired but nothing serious. Why?"

"I need you to start tomorrow. We can't drop any farther back than we are."

Rube smiled. It felt like the good old days in Philadelphia when Connie Mack would tell him, "Eddie, I really need you tomorrow."

"You can count on me, Jimmy," he said, "I'd love to get back at those bastards after the shit they pulled on me the last time."

After falling a run behind, Rube drove in the tying run in the third inning and then shut out the Tigers for the next eight. In the St. Louis half of the eleventh Tom Jones led off with a single to right and then stole second. Bobby Wallace lined one into right between Crawford and Cobb to score Jones and the Browns had a crucial 2-1 victory. They were still in the race.

℘   ℘   ℘

Every game was life or death now and McAleer knew he had to keep Rube on the water wagon. He decided to send him fishing for the two days before his next start. He came back rested and refreshed and pitched well against Detroit, who had beaten his teammates in both games while he was away. But all afternoon weakly-hit balls kept innocently bounding just out of the reach of outstretched gloves and the Tigers reeled off a third straight win to all but eliminate the Browns from the race.

Desperate, Jimmy McAleer went with Rube two days later against the Americans. Tom Jones dropped a pop fly, Bobby Wallace booted a groundball, and Tubby Spencer dropped a throw from the outfield all in the same inning. Boston scored two unearned runs. It was all Boston could manage off Rube, but the Browns didn't score at all. They were running out of time.

The Senators came to town and Rube Waddell and Walter Johnson, the two fastest twirlers in baseball, were going to face each other in 90 degree heat at 1 p.m. The Browns' morning practice ended at 10:30 with no sign of Rube. Jimmy McAleer was nervous. He dashed up the stairs to the club's offices. Panting, he burst into the Colonel's office without knocking.

"What the devil is it?" asked Hedges.

"Waddell's gone," McAleer sputtered.

"Gone?"

"He missed the whole practice and nobody knows where he is."

"We're going to have a sellout crowd here expecting him to take on Johnson in less than two hours."

"I know, I know."

"John! Get in here right now," Hedges shouted.

John Poston, his private secretary, ran into the office. "What is it, sir?"

"You've got to find Rube. Nobody's seen him."

"Where shall I look?"

"He must have fallen off the wagon. Connie Mack told me this happens when he's under a lot of pressure."

"But he's behaved so well all year."

"Try every bar in the neighborhood," said McAleer, "I don't know where else to look."

Poston ran to his office, grabbed his hat and hurried down to the street two steps at a time. He dashed in and out of seven bars. Rube had been in five of them. Oddly though, he hadn't had a drink in any. He'd merely joked with the patrons and talked about what he would do to the Senators and that Johnson kid. Finally Poston found someone who thought he knew where Rube had gone.

"Try the Cardinals' park," said a grizzled old-timer with a day's growth of white whiskers. "I heard him say somethin' about goin' there," said the man between puffs on his corn pipe.

Poston hopped a trolley car and got to League Park in just under fifteen minutes. It was now just forty-five minutes until Rube was supposed to pitch. Poston spotted him right away. He was at the entrance to the fairgrounds across the street from the Cardinals' stadium. He was selling the wieners in a bun people had nicknamed hot dogs.

"Ten cents!" yelled Rube.

"What in God's name are you doing?" asked Poston.

Rube gestured toward a hairy man who was even bigger than Rube. "That fella and I are selling these wieners in buns," Rube explained innocently.

Poston thought about telling Rube how inappropriate and downright bizarre it was for a major league star to be selling hot dogs outside another team's park, but simply said, "We have to go, you're scheduled to pitch in a few minutes. There will be a huge crowd there to see you."

"Can't leave yet, John."

"What do you mean you can't leave?"

"I can't leave 'til I'm sold out."

Poston was flabbergasted but he tried to maintain his composure. As calmly and patiently as he could he asked, "How many do you have left?"

Rube looked inside his basket and counted. "Seventeen."

Poston took out his billfold. "Here's two dollars. I'll take them all."

Rube pulled out the hot dogs and handed them to Poston, who quickly handed them out to delighted fair-goers. Rube went and handed the big fellow the money he'd made and the man handed him back two dollars. As Rube smiled and said thanks Poston grabbed his arm and hurried him onto a trolley car.

Rube whistled as he put on his uniform in the Browns' locker room. He strode out to the sidelines to the deafening cheers of the crowd, threw five warm-up pitches on the sidelines, and went to the mound.

He and Johnson were both in top form. Each gave up just one run in nine innings. Five times the Senators got a runner as far as third base only to watch in frustration as Rube calmly struck out the next hitter. His strikeouts kept piling up. Cranks all over the league were talking about how many batters Johnson was striking out. Rube wanted to prove that *he* was still the master.

In the tenth, Rube struck out the side. In the home half of the frame Tom Jones singled and stole second and Danny Hoffman ripped one of Johnson's rare curves into right to win the game. In spite of the important, much-watched, and gratifying win, for Rube it was yet another near miss. Several times he had come close to no-hitters and perfect games without getting one. For his part, poor Walter Johnson, who was a top-notch hitter, not only suffered a tough loss, he struck out four times.

Rube's next outing was a three-hit shutout of the Americans, his nineteenth win. But his colleagues weren't racking up victories the way he was. Cleveland had won seven straight to pass the Tigers. The Browns stood third now. Once again, McAleer sent Rube out against the Americans on one day's rest. He fanned two in the first and retired the first two hitters in the second but then three straight base hits and an error produced a pair of runs. The Browns did their best but couldn't get *any*. Twice George Stone hit rockets to deep center field more than 400 feet but speedy Tris Speaker hauled them down even though he played much shallower than any other centerfielder dared.

Rube didn't falter, allowing only two more batters to reach base after the three hits in the second, but it was all for naught. The Browns were now four games back of Detroit who'd regained the lead in the tight race.

ℓℓ   ℓℓ   ℓℓ

The Browns faced the Tigers in a win at all costs series and Rube was sent out to save the season. With so much riding on the game Rube, who could not even remember the last time he'd had a drink, was nervous. He was also exhausted. Pitching repeatedly on a day's rest had been a piece of candy for Rube in '02, '03, and '04, but not anymore. He gave up three runs in the first inning. Crawford and Cobb were the culprits as usual.

When he went to the bench, Jimmy McAleer told him he was putting in Harry Howell. "You gave it all you could, George. Have a rest, I might need you again tomorrow if we can pull this thing out."

This time his teammates got the runs back. St. Louis had a one-run lead after eight. Matty McIntyre led off the ninth with a single. Crawford doubled him home to tie the game. Cobb hit a liner that hit the ground right in front of Harry Howell. He deftly fielded it and threw out Crawford at third.

On the next pitch, before Cobb had a chance to steal second, Claude Rosseau hit the ball into right centerfield. Cobb took off. The ball rolled into an exit runway that would normally have been empty. But when Al Schweitzer went to retrieve it he had to run in among the spectators who had been allowed on the field after all of Bennett Park's seats had been filled.

"Ground rule double!" yelled Jimmy McAleer, trying to help umpire Jack Sheridan.

Normally a ball that went in among spectators was ruled a double. That would mean that Cobb would have to stop at third. Cobb, of course, kept right on running. He scored easily and for some reason Sheridan allowed the run to stand. The Browns were done. They could no longer catch the Tigers.

They had four games left, but they would be meaningless. In spite of his lousy start Rube had turned out to be the ace of the staff, winning nineteen games. But for the first time since 1901 he hadn't led the league in strikeouts. Ed Walsh put 269 moist third strikes past hitters while Rube registered 232 dry ones. Rube did it in 285 innings. Walsh pitched a record 464.

In August a young left-hander named Richard Marquard had pitched a no-hitter against Columbus. He was so impressive that the New York Giants signed him immediately. His blazing speed was enough to earn him a nickname. For the rest of his career he would be known known as Rube Marquard.

The St. Louis sports reporters couldn't say enough about what Rube had meant to the team and the city in his first year as a Brown. His teammates showered him with praise too.

"Rube really won me over," Hobe Ferris was quoted as saying. "He stood the gaff in fine style and, though he was of no good to us in April and May, he was our mainstay from then on and gave us a chance to win it all."

George Stone said, "Rube didn't have a friend on the team last spring, but he won us all over with his big heart and determination to stay dry and give us his best. We didn't expect him to last a week but he kept on the straight and narrow path and was temperate the entire season. I give him a lot of credit for throwing off his bad ways and swinging into line. If he keeps up like that next year he's bound to pitch us to a pennant."

ℓ   *ℓ*   *ℓ*

In Philadelphia Connie Mack called the 'Get rid of Waddell' cabal into his office. He set his hat on the side of his desk, pulled a piece of paper toward him, and put on his spectacles.

"Well boys, I guess you must be pretty happy about how things turned out," he said, looking at the figures on the page. "You had me send Rube off to St. Louis and their attendance went from four hundred and fifty thousand to six hundred and twenty thousand. That's half a million more in revenue all things considered."

He looked around from man to man, allowing time for his words to sink in before continuing. "Last year we finished twenty-three games ahead of the Browns and drew six hundred and twenty-five thousand. This year, we ended up sixteen games behind them and drew only four hundred and fifty thousand. That's a drop of ..." he paused again and licked the end of his pencil, pretending to do the subtraction, though of course he already had. "One hundred and seventy-five thousand." Worked out pretty well, didn't it? You don't need to bother asking for raises after making me pull that move." The players just stared sullenly at their shoe tops.

ℓ   *ℓ*   *ℓ*

RUBE WADDELL

Rube was a big hit again when the Browns tried to make up for missing out on World Series checks by going on an exhibition circuit. George Jones could hardly believe the way locals appeared out of nowhere when they heard Rube was in town to pitch.

"We chalk the sidewalks with 'Rube Waddell is going to pitch tomorrow at 2 o'clock'. When we get to the ballpark it's always full of people chanting his name. And after the game's over, Rube always fools with the kids, tells jokes to their dads, and then takes off. And no matter if the county's been dry for twenty years, somehow he comes back driving a wagon full of beer."

CHAPTER **FORTY SIX**

"I AIN'T BUGHOUSE"

Robert Hedges continued to pay Rube's room and board throughout the winter and, to provide him with spending money, gave him two dollars each week. To keep him out of trouble, he offered him the position of 'gamesman' for as long as the hunting season lasted.

At the end of the season Rube had excitedly told him that he was thinking of opening a saloon with Bugs Raymond who pitched for the Giants. Hedges tried to recall what he'd read about the man. Then it came to him. Raymond, it was said, drank so heavily that he had a great curve because when he breathed on the baseball it got woozy too.

Hedges was relieved when Rube gave up on the idea and accepted the gamesman job. Hedges, his family, and his staff enjoyed a steady and delicious diet of fish, venison, quail, rabbit, duck, and pheasant. When he was teased by someone on his way through the streets of St. Louis with his latest catch, Rube yelled at him, "I ain't bughouse! It's my job! And don't call me Rube, it's Mister Waddell."

He went duck hunting near a small lake just east of St. Louis on a crisp but sunny day toward the end of November with the gun the Philadelphia boosters had given him. When the noise of a blast from his rifle subsided he heard cries for help coming from the lake and quickly spotted a boat that had capsized. He set down the gun and ran right into the lake.

There had been two men in the boat. One man could swim and was making for shore. The other couldn't. Rube quickly righted the boat and hauled him into it. Back on shore he built a fire and the three enjoyed a big meal of trout, duck, and rabbit stew, along with a couple of jars of moonshine.

*   &   &*

Though Rube put on a couple of pounds in the off season, he was still in good shape. Which was more than could be said for Bill Dinneen. He had Rube's affinity for spirits, but not his considerable tolerance. Harry

Howell had a torn ligament in his throwing arm. Things were not looking good for the Browns.

When the team reported for their checkups and weigh-ins at the start of spring training at French Lick and Rube took off his shirt McAleer exclaimed, "Look at that back, I see a pennant in those big shoulders."

McAleer sent the team out for hikes in the woods to help with their conditioning. One route was a seven-mile trek to Outlaw's Cave and back. On the way back Rube told his group he knew the woods and claimed there was a shortcut. They figured he'd spent a lot more time in the wild than they had, so they decided to follow him. The group ended up getting back for lunch nearly two hours later than the rest of the team.

"Heckuva shortcut, George," said Tom Jones. Rube didn't hear him. He was already desperately shovelling food into his mouth.

*   &   &*

Robert Hedges had bought 36-year old Lou Criger, Cy Young's 'personal catcher' for many years, from the Americans to replace the heavyweight but light-hitting Tubby Spencer. Rube looked forward to pitching to Criger. The Browns were a *really* old team now. With the profits from Rube's appearances the year before, Robert Hedges had added a double deck grandstand to Sportsman's Park. He raised ticket prices to seventy-five cents for unreserved seats, a dollar for second row seats, $1.25 for front row seats, and a whopping $1.50 for box seats in the new upper deck. Few could afford them.

The week before the '09 season got underway Rube made a tidy $500 during intermissions at the American Theatre delivering a monologue of stories about his childhood in Butler and the high points of his career that was only loosely based on the truth. Every night he was called out for encores. The night before Opening Day, he served as the 'official cake carver' at the wedding of a boxer and his showgirl fiancée.

*   &   &*

Rube got the year off to a fine start, hurling nine innings of shutout ball at the Cleveland Naps. The Browns also scored no runs. In the tenth Lajoie hit a ball to center that Danny Hoffman came in on. He realized his mistake too late and the ball soared over his head and rolled to the fence for a triple. Miffed at Murphy's mistake, Rube gave up two doubles and when the Browns were retired three straight in their half of the inning he and the team had their first loss.

His next outing, against Chicago, was a disaster. In the first five innings he struck out seven but surrendered nine hits and five runs. Three were unearned, as the Browns made four errors. Given another shot at the Palehose two days later, he took a shutout into the ninth. A walk, a sacrifice bunt, and a scratch single later the Hitless Wonders had a 1-0 victory. The Browns managed just three hits on the day.

Rube faced Cleveland again four days later and the result was predictable given the Browns' lack of offense, another 1-0 loss for Rube. When April ended Rube had an 0-4 record - in spite of an 0.45 ERA. St. Louis sat in last place.

In his fifth start Rube took on the first-place Tigers and gave up just five hits, none to Ty Cobb. Cobb did reach base on a walk in the sixth. He stole second and was sacrificed over to third. With Rube so effective Cobb doubted anyone would knock him in so he decided to steal home.

Rube watched him from the corner of his eye. When Cobb began inching toward home Rube pretended to go into his windup and then abruptly stopped and stepped off the rubber. Cobb had no choice but to continue toward home and Rube easily threw him out.

"That was a balk, you hayseed pig fucker!" screamed Cobb. He headed toward Rube bent on revenge but Lou Criger grabbed him from behind.

Cobb managed to stay in the game but he got his manager Hugh Jennings tossed when he tried to defend his foul-tempered star. Cobb's face was beet red when Rube struck him out in the ninth. He smashed his bat so hard on the plate that he broke it in two.

The Browns won it 4-2 but then lost their next two and remained mired in the basement. "The Browns are not hitting, and Rube Waddell is the only man who is pitching well," *The Globe Democrat* reported.

In Washington he allowed a run in the first and that was all. In the third he took matters into his own hands and doubled in a runner from first. The Browns won again the next day, handing Walter Johnson his fifth loss in six starts. He was getting about as much support from his teammates as Rube was and after his great rookie season the newspapers were unfairly calling him a flash in the pan.

After beating the Highlanders, whom some rooters were beginning to call the Yankees, Rube shut out Boston. Four days later Rube shut out the Americans again. They got four hits and three were infield singles. "Waddell is doing his level best to carry the Browns on his broad shoulders," said *The Globe Democrat*.

A cub reporter by the name of Grantland Rice attended Rube's next start against Cleveland. He wrote . . .

The Rube had a 1-0 lead as the final frame commenced. The first man up got only a portion of the sphere but muscled a Texas Leaguer just over the head of the shortstop. The next man hit one to the third baseman, who booted it. Perhaps a tad dismayed, the Rube walked the next man and now had the misfortune of facing Larry Lajoie, Bill Bradley, and Elmer Flick, the Cleveland Nine's premier batsmen, with the sacks drunk. The Rube called for time and sauntered over to the box seats where sat a pair of finely dressed young women whose acquaintance Waddell had apparently previously made. Rube told them, "Ladies, I will be with you in two minutes."

He then returned to the pitching box without a care in the world and proceeded to blaze nine straight strikes past Lajoie, Bradley, and Flick, and the game was over and the Rube could boast to his female friends of his third straight whitewash."

CHAPTER FORTY SEVEN

FALLING OFF THE WAGON
AND THE MOUND

From May 13 to the end of the month Rube was 5-0. He had single-handedly hauled the Browns up to fifth place. After beating the Senators, he had seven wins in his last eight decisions. He'd pitched out of turn against Washington so he could go on ahead of the team to Chicago to take part in the Grand American Trap-Shooting Tournament. He finished third and won fifteen dollars. After celebrating away his winnings he lasted just six innings against the White Sox, but Jack Powell rescued it for him. The Browns moved on to Cleveland and Rube lasted eight this time, losing 3-1.

Rube was hit in the wrist by a line drive in his next start. Reporters marveled that his arm hadn't been broken. He was out of the lineup for ten days. When he game back he won his tenth game, but the opposition was Joe Cantillon's lowly Senators, who were playing .280 baseball. His teammates assumed he was still on the water wagon. They were wrong.

$\text{\it lc} \qquad \text{\it lc} \qquad \text{\it lc}$

Rube was scheduled to pitch the first game when the Browns hosted Detroit for a series. Sportsman's Park had no clubhouses so the Tigers changed into their uniforms at their hotel and then climbed onto a tally-ho pulled by four horses. A group of kids ran alongside, jeering at them and throwing things. Germany Schaefer barely ducked out of the way of a tomato.

"That was close," Wild Bill Donovan chuckled.

The kids had been hoping to bombard Ty Cobb with fruit and vegetables but he had chosen to walk and had left early. He told people he wanted to sharpen his spikes before the game but no one knew if he really did that or just said so to intimidate enemy basemen. It was just as well, he would probably have chased after any kid brave enough to throw something at him and there was no telling what he would have done had he caught him. The year before Cobb had gone into the stands and beaten a heckler senseless even though the man was crippled.

RUBE WADDELL

A couple of blocks from the stadium the tally-ho passed a saloon. Its front doors swung open and a large man in a linen suit came out with a huge beer mug in his hand.

"Isn't that Rube?" Schaefer asked Sam Crawford.

"It sure is," said Crawford.

Rube saw them. He waved and yelled, "Hey Tigers, you're going to leave the park with your tails between your legs today."

"What a fool," said Schaefer.

"Yes, but a fool who can still throw mighty hard."

"He seems to be taking his preparations pretty seriously," chuckled Schaefer.

Rube hoisted his beer and broke into song. "The barmaid's a sweet lass, with long golden hair. She works hard and she never quits. The barflies all eye her, but you must beware. She'll deck you if you grab her . . . tips."

"Nice tune, Rube," Crawford called out, "romantic stuff."

er   er   er

The Tigers were surprised when Rube was on the mound to start the game. He seemed a bit wobbly, but he threw strikes. Though his curves weren't as sharp as they usually were, he still retired the side in order in each of the first three innings.

In the fourth the first batter reached on an error and Rube walked the next man on four straight pitches. When Jimmy Austin came up Rube was determined to throw strikes. His first pitch was right down the middle. Austin hit it over the left field fence. As he trotted around the bases Rube turned around and followed him with his eyes. They were half closed and Rube was having trouble focusing. The turning made him dizzy. He put his hand to his forehead and then fell over backwards, landing in a heap.

The crowd roared, they'd never seen anything that funny at a ball game. The Tigers laughed - all except Ty Cobb - and even Rube's teammates had a good chuckle. Jimmy McAleer shook his head and plodded out to the mound.

"Get out of here, you don't want to pitch anyway," he said to Rube.

Rube swatted at the dirt on the seat of his pants. He took off his cap and waved to the crowd. He walked to the bench to a chorus of huzzahs. The cranks would have a story to tell about the day they saw Rube Waddell fall off the mound.

Rube pitched the 4th of July home game against Detroit and the

Tigers knocked the ball all over the field. Luckily it was usually right at someone. He held a 1-0 lead going into the eighth but then tired. A double, triple, single, and walk later he was out of the game. His next start was against the Yankees and he didn't finish it either after stopping a line drive with his wrist. His next appearance was in relief of Powell against Philadelphia. He went into the game in the fourth and held the Athletics scoreless until the eleventh. Connie Mack put Chief Bender in to pitch the twelfth and Dode Criss deposited his second pitch into the bleachers. Rube, who had given up just three hits in eight innings, got the win.

℞ ℞ ℞

Back in the rotation, Rube beat the last-place Senators. He seemed to toy with them. "They made nine hits in all," wrote James Crusinberry, "but Rube seemed to give them five of those as presents. When men were on base, Rube was able to strike out the batter if he so desired."

Rube lost his next start in New York, where he complained to reporters that he could never get any sleep. They chuckled at that one, knowing that he hardly ever *tried*. The Browns then traveled to Philadelphia to play in the Athletics' new park, which Ben Shibe had immodestly named after himself. In the eighth, Rube forgot there was a runner on first. Realizing it, the crowd yelled "Rube, Rube!" even though he no longer pitched for their side. But he just stood there and held onto the ball while the runner jogged to second base. He allowed four hits and one run in ten innings.

In the eleventh, Eddie Collins, who still couldn't get around on Rube's shoots, dragged a bunt down the first base line. Jones gobbled it up, but Rube neglected to cover first and Collins was safe. Danny Murphy sacrificed him to second and, after fouling off seven pitches, Harry Davis ripped a single to right to drive Collins in with the winning run. Rube's boozing and late nights seemed harmless when he won in spite of them, but they were not so funny when he lost track of runners and fielded miserably. The 5-0 streak suddenly seemed a distant memory. Rube was losing right along with the rest of the St. Louis pitchers. If it wasn't a lack of hitting it was lousy fielding.

℞ ℞ ℞

Rube threw well in his next start against New York until he hit Hal Chase with a pitch. That rattled him and Jimmy McAleer had to take him out. He made the rounds the night before his next start in Washington and this time the Senators turned the tables and toyed with him. Rube gave up eleven hits, walked three, and lost 6-1.

After the game he went over to Tom Jones, who was just about to get in the shower. "Tom," he asked, "have I ever given up eleven hits before?"

"Not since you joined the Browns you haven't. I don't know about before that but I know we sure never got that many hits off you when you were with the A's."

"I'm scared, Tom."

"What d'ya mean? Scared about what?'

"I'm scared about my arm. I've had off games or bad innings - like at the start of last year. But now I can't just rear back and blaze the ball by people like I used to be able to whenever I needed to."

"You're getting older, just like the rest of us. We're not exactly a team of youngsters, more like grey beards."

"I don't know what to do?"

"Maybe you could take a little better care of yourself, George. Just a thought."

    ℓ   ℓ   ℓ

His aging arm didn't fare any better in Philadelphia. The back-to-back starts and extra-inning complete games of his younger days were finally taking their toll. Rube was definitely not the unhittable twirler he once was. About that there could be no doubt. He allowed eight runs this time, all of them earned. After the game he just sat on his stool and stared at the floor.

"I've never seen Rube looking so glum," said Jimmy Collins.

"You know what it is, don't you?" Hobe Ferris asked him.

"What?" asked Collins.

"Nobody made a fuss when he got to town. Nobody showed up at the train station to see him the way they always have when we've come into Philly. Not even the kids that always used to be waiting to crowd around him."

"You're right, Hobe, I never thought about it."

    ℓ   ℓ   ℓ

The next day an article appeared in *The Inquirer.* It was entitled "Heroes in Baseball Do Not Last Forever".

> *"The man whose name and fame were broadcast by local scribes and whose every appearance on the field was the signal for wild yells and whoops from the boosters has come in for*

practically no notices on this visit. There was not a single cheer today for Waddell, the man who almost single-handedly pitched the Athletics to the championship in other years. The incident is a lesson to all young stars that the boosters will not remember their deeds for long."

The next day another sports columnist remarked that Rube had been able to stay on top of his game in spite of "a multitude of meanderings into forbidden paths such as have wrecked the careers of many box artists." But now, he claimed, Rube was no longer a dominant pitcher.

Waddell has yet to post a game with ten strikeouts this season, despite having a physique unlike any other in the game. He is losing the prestige which made him a box-office attraction beyond compare. Hedges paid him a few thousand dollars and he paid for himself in his first three starts in St. Louis. He has added many thousands to the Browns' exchequer since then with paid admissions that would never have arrived at the park but for the fact that Rube was scheduled to work. But with the fading of his sensational strikeout work the glamor that surrounded him is dissipating."

Rube made headlines when the Browns went to Cleveland, but not for anything he did at the ballpark. A warehouse at Wirick's Storage exploded and exhausted firemen struggled with a rope that was lashed to a wall they were trying to pull down. Rube had heard the fire bells and raced to find out what was going on. He immediately saw that the rope wasn't firmly attached and he ran into the flames which had already burned four men who had attempted to fasten it properly.

"It's not gonna hold," yelled Rube.

"What?" said a man who seemed to be in charge.

"We gotta tie a knot in it, fast!" Rube shouted. He ran up a ladder and showed the fireman how to hook the rope around the wall and use a sailor's knot to secure it. Once tied, Rube grabbed the rope and, with his enormous strength added, the wall came down.

When he climbed back down a policeman went over to him. "Do you have a permit to be on this crew?" he inquired.

"No, I haven't," answered Rube.

"Well who are you then?" asked the constable.

Rube shrugged his shoulders, said, "I'm nobody, only Rube Waddell is all," and walked alone back to the hotel.

      ℰ   ℰ   ℰ

Back in St. Louis Rube got knocked out of the box in just four innings by the Americans, who were now usually being called the Red Sox. When the Athletics came to town they beat him up for five runs in five innings. Frank Baker hit two terrific long drives. Hedges knew the cause and called Rube into his office.

He got right to the point. Rube was going to reach for a cigar as he always did, but thought better of it when he saw the stern look on the Colonel's face. He just took off his hat and sat down.

"Did you see what *The Post-Dispatch* is calling you this morning?" asked Hedges. He didn't wait for an answer. "A monument to waste, that's what they are calling you. And they're speculating that you will be sent to the American Association."

"Are you going to . . . "

Hedges cut him off. "No, I am not sending you to the minor leagues, not now anyway. But because of the condition in which you took the mound again this afternoon you are suspended for one week. Following that week you will report to me two hours before each game or one hour before practice on non-game days for a sobriety test. If you fail a single test you will be released. Do you understand me?"

"I do," said Rube, staring at his hat. "I'm sorry, Colonel, real sorry. I know I've let you down."

The Colonel could see that he was on the verge of tears. "No, George. It's not me who you've let down. It's yourself."

      ℰ   ℰ   ℰ

When the Browns went to Detroit James Crusinberry, the reporter from Chicago, recognized Rube walking through the lobby of the hotel the team was staying in. He was carrying two buckets. Chips of ice were falling out onto the carpet.

"What have you got there, Rube, beer?" Durst asked.

"Come on up and see," said Rube as he headed toward the elevator. "I'm in three nineteen."

Deciding that Rube was the kind of fellow who always shared anything he had and that he wouldn't mind a glass or two of beer, Durst headed up to 319. The door was open when he got there. He looked around, expecting to find beer glasses. All he saw was Rube sitting beside the tub with a stick in his hand. He was stirring the water. When Crusinberry went to see what Rube had in the tub he saw three large fish.

"Howdy, Jim. Glad you could make it."

Crusinberry stared at the fish.

Seeing the confused look on his face, Rube explained, "I never liked this hotel's food. You wanna join me for dinner?"

℔   ℔   ℔

Crusinberry followed the Browns to St. Louis, where he watched Rube take on the White Sox. He could hardly believe his ears when Rube took the mound.

"Can you believe that?" he asked a reporter sitting next to him. The small crowd was jeering and booing Rube.

"Waddell's been a bum lately. People are getting tired of it," the reporter explained.

Rube drilled the leadoff batter in the ribs. The hoots and catcalls got louder. The count on the next hitter went to 3-1 before he grounded to Jimmy Collins, who fielded it cleanly starting a double play. Rube struck out the next man on three pitches.

With two out in the second the next hitter bunted one towards the mound.

"Watch this, Crusinberry," said the reporter. "He's been kicking these all year."

But Rube deftly scooped up the ball and fired a strike to Jones at first and was out of the inning. There was a light smattering of applause.

Rube began throwing harder, with most of the speed of his youth. He struck out at least one batter every inning, sometimes two. The jeers turned to huzzahs and Rube ended up with a tidy three-hit shutout.

℔   ℔   ℔

Two days later the Browns played a double header against the Tigers, who were coasting to their third straight pennant. Jack Powell started the first game and the Browns had a 3-0 lead after four innings. They ended up losing 12-5.

"Who wants to pitch?" Jimmy McAleer asked before the second game. The pitchers all looked at one another. Remembering what carnage the Detroit lineup had wrought during the past hour and a half, everyone declined.

Finally someone yelled, "Let George do it."

All eyes turned to Rube.

He hesitated for just a second. "I'll go, Jimmy."

Though he'd done it all the time when he was younger, Rube hadn't pitched on one day's rest in quite a while.

"Are you sure, George?" McAleer asked.

"Gimme the ball, Jimmy. I can stop them."

Wild Bill Donovan started for Detroit. He'd acquired a bright pink gin blossom as a result of his hard drinking. Rube and Donovan kept walking batters and giving up hits, but neither broke down. After eight innings the score was 3-3. The umpire declared it too dark to continue and called the game. Though there were almost three weeks left to play Rube didn't pitch again. His arm was dead.

℮   ℮   ℮

As the season came to an end, with the Browns firmly entrenched in seventh place, Tom Jones was sold to Detroit.

"I wish I was going with him," said Jimmy Collins, who was sitting in the locker room when he heard the news. Jimmy McAleer came into the room.

"Hedges keepin' you on?" Collins asked.

"I'm not waiting around to find out," McAleer told him.

"Where you going?"

"Washington. I'm taking over as skipper of the Senators."

"What about Joe Cantillon? What's happening to him?"

"I understand he's takin' over the Minneapolis Millers, in the American Association."

"The *Senators*, Jimmy?" asked Tom Jones. "Finishing second last wasn't good enough for you? You have to take over the team that finished *dead* last?"

"What can I say, Tom, I'm a bear for punishment."

When asked if he wanted Waddell back for the 1910 season Robert Hedges said nothing. Even if he had, Rube wouldn't have heard about it. The day after the season ended he was off hunting in the wilds.

CHAPTER FORTY EIGHT

STRIKE ONE AGAINST RUBE

Once again Rube spent the off season as the Browns' official game and fish supplier at ten dollars a month. Hedges wisely had him pick up his money on Monday mornings rather than Friday afternoon. Rube did some of his hunting in New Mexico, where he also rode horses and played some baseball. When he wanted to return to St. Louis he wired Hedges for money to settle his bills and pay for his train ticket. Hedges sent him $75 which got Rube only as far as Kansas City due to stops for refreshment along the way and the fact that he had given twenty dollars to a hobo he'd befriended at the train station.

Robert Hedges had hired a new manager, Jack O'Connor. He was apparently less than thrilled that Hedges had decided to keep Rube. Before the start of the 1910 season Hedges called Rube into his office. Knowing Rube had probably smoked all of his enormous supply of Rube Waddell cigars he gave him ten of his. Rube stuffed nine in his pockets and lit up the other one.

"I've established an incentive system for you this year, George," said Hedges.

"What's an incentive, Colonel?"

"It is a reward for good performance or behavior."

"How's it gonna work?"

"The first time you misbehave you'll be fined twenty-five dollars. The second time you misbehave you will be fined fifty and the third time you will be suspended, without pay."

"Those sure don't sound like rewards to me, Colonel. Those sound a lot like punishments."

"The reward, the incentive, is that if you go the full season without consuming intoxicants, that is liquor, you will receive a bonus of a thousand dollars."

"Oh," was all Rube said. He was deep in thought.

"And I should add that the new manager, whom I believe you know from your time in Pittsburgh several years ago . . . "

"When he refused to catch if I was pitching," Rube pointed out.

"I was not aware of that. Regardless, the new manager has decreed . . . announced, that no player is to imbibe intoxicating spirits. So you will not be alone on the water wagon."

"He's gonna have some unhappy players," Rube muttered.

"Perhaps, but at least they'll arrive at the ball park ready to perform."

"How many of the fellas are comin' back, Colonel?"

"Al Schweitzer, Bobby Wallace, George Stone, and Danny Hoffman?"

"What about pitchers?"

"Jack Powell, Barney Pelty, and yourself."

"That's it! Just eight of us?"

"That's right, George, we had to make changes, the team was getting too old to compete."

"Who's comin' in?"

Hedges picked up a piece of paper from his desk, scanned it, and then told Rube about the new players. "Jim Stephens is going to catch, Pat Newnan will play first base, Frank Truesdale will play second, and Al Schweitzer will be full-time in the outfield. And Joe Lake and Farmer Ray will join our pitching staff."

"That's quite a collection of stars you're countin' on, Colonel. Little Nemo, I mean Stephens, hasn't hit better than two hundred the last few years, Cheese Schweitzer hit around two twenty last season, and I recall Joe Lake losin' twenty-two games for New York a couple a years ago. And I never heard of Truesdale, Farmer Ray, or Pat Newfellow at all."

"Do I need to remind you that we finished seventh last year, George?" said Hedges.

"You're gonna be thinking seventh looks pretty fine after a few weeks with those players."

"That will do, I have business I must attend to. Remember the incentive system."

"The what? Oh, right, the punishment plan," mocked Rube, getting up to leave.

"Call it what you will, but abide by it, or *else*," Hedges concluded.

"Fine," muttered Rube on his way out the door.

      ℔   *℔*   *℔*

The previous spring, just before his string of shutouts, Rube had gone to a party that his landlords, Mr. and Mrs. Rupenthal, had thrown for a girl who was in town for a visit. She reminded Rube of Florence but she was even prettier, and when she spoke she sounded like a genuine Southern belle. She had wavy ash-blonde hair and blue bedroom eyes, and she wore a silk lavender dress.

"This is George Waddell, Madge," said Mrs. Rupenthal. "He is boarding with us. He's a baseballist for the Browns. George, this is Miss Madge Maguire, she is from New Orleans and this little get-together is a celebration of her eighteenth birthday."

"My, but aren't *you* a tall drink of water," said Madge.

Rube turned a bit red and then extended his hand. Madge's hand disappeared inside his. "My goodness, what huge hands you have, Mister Waddell," she purred.

Mrs. Rupenthal smiled and slipped away to leave the two alone.

"It is Mister *Waddell* is it not? That is what our hostess called you?"

"Yes, George Edward Waddell. When I was young people called me Eddie, but my teammates call me George because they know I don't much care for my nickname."

"Do you mean you do not care to be called Eddie?"

"No, I never minded being called Eddie?"

"Then what was it that people had been calling you?"

"Rube."

"I declare. Rube? I can certainly see why you might not care for such a name as that. Say, could you be Rube Waddell, the famous baseball twirler?"

"I could be and I am."

"I've often seen your name in the newspapers and I have heard my father and his friends tell stories about you."

"Well I hope you didn't believe all of them, Miss Maguire," said Rube. He hoped he was making a good impression.

"Is it true that you do cartwheels after you strike batters out?"

"I've been known to on occasion. Not as often as I used to though. The cranks eat it up when I do it."

"The cranks?"

"It's what us ball players call the boosters that come to the game. People are startin' to call them fans."

"Is that because they wave fans when it's hot?' Madge asked.

Rube was pleased to be able to explain things to this beautiful girl. He was thinking about what might be under those bustles and ruffles. "No, 'fan' is short for fanatic, cuz some of the boosters seem like their whole life is riding on whether their team wins or loses. As if a dang ball game could mean that much to anybody."

"Do you pitch with your right hand or your left hand?"

"Well, I can throw pretty good with my right hand, but I pitch with my left."

"So you are what they call a southpaw then?"

"That's right."

"And where does that term come from?"

Rube was really enjoying educating the sweet young thing. He wondered if there would ever be things he could teach her under the covers. "Well, they position the diamonds in ballparks so that the afternoon sun won't be shining into the batters' eyes and when the pitcher is standing on the mound his left arm is to the south."

"That makes sense. Is it true that you pull people out of fires, George?"

He was delighted she was calling him George. "I have been known to do that from time to time."

& & &

The two began a whirlwind romance. When women saw them together, they muttered their disapproval over the obvious difference in their ages. Men just grinned and tipped their hats. Reporters conjectured that Rube had somehow hypnotized the young girl, though their readers doubted that was a skill he possessed.

Rube told Madge he was thirty-one and that was what he wrote on the wedding license. He was a really thirty-three. In spite of lying about his age Rube made a solemn pledge. "My marriage to Miss Maguire will make a better man out of me. I have stopped drinking and Madge will keep me on the water wagon. I'm in better condition than I've been in for years. I believe that the happy part of my life has just begun."

A reporter went up to Madge before a game. He made a comment about the difference in their ages and then asked if she had heard the rumors that Rube had another lady friend in St. Louis. Madge chose to ignore the comment and the question and said, "I have admired Mister Waddell since the first time I saw him and I am giving my life to him because I love him, not because I was hypnotized by him."

& & &

Rube had a hard time concentrating during the training camp in Hot Springs. He wrote a series of romantic letters to Madge that, in addition to pet names and professions of affection, included promises to kill any man he ever caught walking with her.

After a few days in Hot Springs Rube developed terrible stomach pains which the doctor diagnosed as ptomaine poisoning. He was in such agony when he slept that he repeatedly banged his head against the headboard and the bedroom wall and bent the bed's brass rods with his clenched hands.

He got into trouble only once. He decided to visit the music halls in Houston one night and when Jack O'Connor made his rounds at eleven Rube's bed was empty. He finally came in just after 2 a.m. He'd hoped to sneak in without being noticed but O'Connor was waiting for him, along with the entire team. They were dying to find out what O'Connor would do.

"Do you know what time it is?" O'Connor raged.

"I can't say as I do, Jack. I guess it must be pretty late."

"It is two o'clock in the morning."

"That late? Are you certain?"

"*Absolutely* certain. I am sending you home for breaking curfew," O'Connor snapped.

"But Jack, it's the ptomaine - the aches and pains - I just can't sleep. I didn't think it would hurt to go and listen to some music for a while."

"Come over here and let me smell you for whiskey," O'Connor commanded.

Rube complied. The players leaned forward, as if they might be able to smell liquor or, even better, cheap perfume. All O'Connor could smell was tobacco. He looked into Rube's eyes. They seemed clear.

"All right, Rube, but no more midnight trips to town. Understand?"

"I do, Jack, I do."

"And Rube."

"Yes Jack."

"That was strike one!"

The players trudged back to bed, disappointed there were no fireworks. Of course O'Connor put Rube through a brutal workout the next morning. He survived it and was ready to pitch the next day. Robert Hedges, who had heard about Rube's late night trip to Houston, was there to watch. The Browns took on the Galveston Sand Crabs. Rube pitched three innings and gave up two hits, walked two, and allowed one run. Hedges was not overly impressed and let into Rube after the game. He sobbed while Hedges told him that he was out of patience and would tolerate no more misconduct. Rube was a lot more contrite than he had been when the two had last spoken in the owner's office.

After Hedges stormed out, Bobby Wallace went over and sat down beside Rube. "He was pretty rough on you, George. You didn't pitch that bad."

"It was dumb of me to go to Houston."

"It wasn't one of your *smarter* moves."

"You know I had a dream last night, Bobby."

"What about?"

"It was strange. A train of day coaches came down the hall of the hotel and stopped in front of my door. A conductor dressed like an umpire was punching tickets with a catcher's mitt. He got off the train and yelled, 'All aboard for the minor leagues!' Then a man who looked like Hedges came up and folded the train up and put it in his pocket. He had a bunch of waivers in his hand and a baseball bat wrapped in barbed wire. Then the telephone rang and woke me up."

Rube redeemed himself somewhat with strong performances in his next two spring outings, including one in which he gave up just two hits over six innings. At least one St. Louis paper was impressed with Rube as the team arrived for the 1910 season. Billy Murphy, the sports editor of the *St. Louis Star*, wrote,

> "Rube Waddell looks the same as he did ten years ago. He has not lost an ounce of speed or a dot of confidence. The bridegroom should be in for another good season."

Jack O'Connor put Rube into the first game of the season in the ninth inning. The Browns held a one-run lead. The first batter he faced grounded out to first. The second man grounded out to short. Rube smiled and threw three darts past the next batter to end the game.

The boosters stood and applauded and then roared with delight as Rube did cartwheels off the mound. Pat Newnam and Frank Truesdale, the rookies, stood and stared at each other. "I really didn't think those stories I'd read about him could be true," said Truesdale.

"Apparently they are," said Newnam.

CHAPTER FORTY NINE

BATTLING MADGE AND THE HUSTLERS

O'Connor figured it would keep Rube on his toes if he thought he might be sent into games every day or two. He used Rube in relief against Chicago and he pitched four shutout innings. The Browns rallied from behind and Rube stole a win from Ed Walsh. The next day he relieved Barney Peltry against the Tigers and won it in the twelfth. The Browns won three out of five and Rube had either won or saved each of them.

He came down with a sore stomach toward the end of April and couldn't pitch. Then the weather turned lousy and O'Connor decided to go with his younger pitchers, figuring that they would handle the cold, rainy conditions better. Rube would start no more.

Madge kept nagging him that he wasn't giving her enough money, so he got a job tending bar. He didn't mind that they paid him in whiskey and beer instead of cash. Madge *did.*

One night he came home around 8:30. "Your dinner's on the table," Madge told him icily.

Rube shrugged and sat down. Before he had even picked up his fork and knife Madge marched over to him, took hold of the tablecloth, and gave it a severe jerk. It flew off the table and everything on it went crashing to the floor. Then she dashed up the stairs as Rube dabbed away at the carrots, mashed potatoes, and gravy that had splattered all over his clothes. Madge came back down with Rube's two best suits.

"What are you fixing to do with those?" Rube demanded.

Madge went to the kitchen woodstove, yanked open the door, and tossed in the suits. Rube grabbed her arm, reached back to hit her and then stormed out. "You are a crazy woman. I'll sleep with the fellows at the fire hall," he yelled.

Madge screamed, "Or with floozies, like you do most nights!"

President Taft decided to take in a ballgame when he visited St. Louis at the beginning of May. Before it started Robert Hedges had the Browns line up to be introduced to him. Rube was supposed to pitch that day but he hadn't arrived.

Suddenly Rube broke through the ranks, sidled up to the portly commander-in-chief, and stuck out his hand. "Hey, Prez, good to make yer acquaintance."

"As am I, Rube," said Taft. Robert Hedges was mortified, but the president seemed fine with Rube's impertinence. Then Rube pulled Taft around by the arm until he could find a photographer to take a picture of the two of them together.

"Rube should be caged up whenever there is a special occasion at Sportsman's Park," commented one reporter acidly.

Madge was at the game and was thoroughly embarrassed by her husband's behavior. "Now I see why they call him a rube," she muttered to herself.

*   *   *

At home that night she let him know exactly how she felt about his behavior. "You're not pitching, you aren't bringing home pay checks, and you're drinking again!"

When Rube got up the next morning her bags were packed and she announced that she was going back to live with her mother in New Orleans.

*   *   *

When the Browns traveled to Boston, Jack O'Connor decided to start Rube in the first game. There was a large crowd and they gave Rube a tremendous ovation. He pitched well. After three innings he had three strikeouts and he hadn't given up a run. When he went up to hit against Ed Cicotte, Rube batted from the right side. He figured it would give him a better chance against the young speedballer. The move backfired badly. Cicotte's first pitch was fast and it rose and veered sharply inside on Rube. He instinctively raised his arms to protect himself and the ball struck him on his left elbow.

Rube went down in a heap, writhing in pain. O'Connor sent a runner in for him. Rube wouldn't be pitching again any time soon. That night he got bad news, the elbow was fractured. It would have to be in a splint for weeks and the doctor said there was only a remote possibility that Rube would ever pitch again.

He would no longer draw a salary from the Browns. He had no savings

- he'd still never had a bank account. Whatever he made or borrowed he spent or gave away. In July he took a job driving a delivery truck for three meals a day. It didn't sound as though Madge would be coming back to him any time soon. She told a reporter who went to see her that Rube had been awful to her.

"No eighteen year old girl has ever been treated so horribly. He promised me he would not drink and he did, every day. I was forced to try to pay the bills and run the household on less than five dollars a week. He is crazy and I intend to have him examined mentally by the court and put away. I would have gone crazy myself if I'd stayed with him. He said he liked excitement but I got tired of being the excitement every night. When I finally gave up arguing with him he'd bring home pictures of other women to try to make me jealous."

When the reporter wrote his story he noted that the poor girl had been reduced to posing in a variety of undergarments for the "Made in St. Louis" show at the Coliseum and had modeled for the Ferguson-McKinley Dry Goods Company for a dollar for each pound she weighed - 120. He claimed Madge was becoming known as "the pajama girl". In truth, though she did need the money, Madge loved having men ogle her.

Rube's arm eventually healed enough that Hedges reinstated him on August 1 and O'Connor started him. He was ahead 5-4 in the ninth when he gave up a single, hit a batter, and threw two wild pitches. O'Connor took him out. Tellingly, Rube had not struck out a single batter. Hedges released him the next day.

         ℔   ℔   ℔

Iron Man Joe McGinnity, whom Rube might have faced in the 1905 World Series but for the straw hat fiasco, had retired from the New York Giants in '08 and was now part owner of the Newark Bengals of the Eastern League. He was also their primary pitcher in spite of his age. By the end of July he had thrown 279 innings and, because he lacked faith in his young starters, he was pitching both ends of double headers as he had with the Giants. He knew he couldn't keep it up. The Bengals were in a fight for the pennant with the Rochester Hustlers and McGinnity needed an addition to his pitching staff to head them off. He decided to see if Rube had anything left. He sent him a train ticket and sent him in to pitch against the Montreal Royals as soon as he reached the ballpark. Rube struck out five, walked only two, and won 7-1, the Royals' only run coming in the ninth when the affair was already settled.

The Newark Star was impressed. "Rube had everything he possessed in his palmiest days. His curves had baffling breaks and his speed was marvellous."

A few days later he threw five shutout innings before twisting his ankle and leaving the game. The very next day McGinnity started him again against Rube Vickers. Connie Mack had released him and now he was pitching for Jack Dunn's Baltimore Orioles. Rube Vickers struggled in front of the biggest crowd ever to see a ball game in Newark, giving up eleven hits and four runs. Rube the original gave up seven hits and no runs.

He knew he had something to prove and pulled no shenanigans on or off the field. By the middle of September he had eight wins and just two losses, one in which the Bengals had been shut out and the other a one-run loss in extra innings.

The Bengals stayed in the race thanks to Rube, who drew huge crowds to the park, but they fell just short of the championship. Meanwhile, the St. Louis Browns had not come close to challenging for the American League flag like they had in '08. They finished seventh, 36 games out of first.

The highlight of his time in Newark - where he made a lot of friends as usual - was a Labour Day shooting contest he was invited to enter. He beat all shooters except the club champion, hitting 172 of 200 targets. His eyes hadn't failed him yet.

CHAPTER FIFTY

RUBE MEETS THE MILLERS

Rube hoped that Robert Hedges would want him back for the 1911 season. But Hedges had decided that he'd had more than enough of Rube's antics and even the big crowds he drew weren't enough to sway him. Joe Cantillon, the former umpire who'd persuaded Rube to join the all-stars' barnstorming tour of the west coast, had accepted the job of managing the Washington Senators. He'd come to regret it. He had discovered Walter Johnson, but he had passed on Joe Jackson, declaring that the line drive smasher was a bush leaguer and wouldn't cut it in the big leagues. Cantillon's three years in Washington were positively dreadful. But the Minneapolis Millers team he had taken over as owner and manager after being replaced by Jimmy McAleer were perennial front-runners and had won the 1910 American Association championship.

Cantillon knew Rube and what he could do. He'd heard how well he had pitched for Newark and he wasn't bothered that Rube's behaviour was often eccentric. Cantillon was a good 'ol boy from Kentucky and there were plenty of characters in those hills. Most of all, he knew that - win or lose - Rube would put rear ends in the seats.

Rube was glad that someone wanted him, even though he could remember reading in *The Baseball Magazine,* that the American Association was "the Graveyard of the Major Leagues". He hoped that if he did well in Minneapolis a big league team would send for him.

Against her mother's wishes and her own better judgement, Madge had forgiven Rube and she sent his signed contract to Cantillon along with a letter that said she was looking forward to coming to Minneapolis and would help her husband make good there. She added that the Browns had never given him a square deal and that much of what had been written about him was absolutely false.

Of course Madge herself had been the source for many of the bad things written about Rube. Among other things she had publically accused Rube of throwing water bottles at her after coming home drunk. *The St. Louis Dispatch* kidded that Rube had "used her as home plate and that his control was excellent - unless the water was mixed with liquor."

A reporter from *The Minneapolis Journal* visited Joe Cantillon to get his views on his latest addition.

"I know that Waddell has created some problems for his managers over the years," said Cantillon, "but I am not worrying one bit. He is a great twirler with many victories left in his amazing left arm. I plan to use him a lot and, when he is not pitching, I hope we can spend some time on Lake Minnetonka taking a crack at the bass together."

&   &   &

The Millers held their spring training camp in Hickman, Kentucky on the Mississippi. Ironically, though it was in a 'dry' county, it regularly suffered flood damage. It was Cantillon's home town and he'd had steam and shower bath rooms built above the Hickman Drug Company offices. The players stayed at the Laclede Hotel, where the patrons talked about their gross neglect of table manners.

For Rube and Madge it was like the honeymoon they'd missed out on. They were given their own room and Rube got Madge to put on the underwear she'd worn in the advertisements before pulling it off and carrying her to bed. The bed squeaked and squeaked and the other players ribbed Rube about his impressive stamina.

"Sure be great if you could keep on goin' like that on the mound," one told him. "You're gonna wear that pretty little thing out."

"Or die tryin'," said Rube.

&   &   &

He and Madge spent a lot of time in the hotel lobby too. He told people about his duels with Cy Young and Christy Mathewson and she talked about the society life in New Orleans and about how those awful men positively drooled when she'd modeled in silk nightclothes. A local scribe noted that Rube was acting like a perfect gentleman and that the lovebirds were almost inseparable. Madge sat in the bleachers during exhibition games and she even attended the workouts.

Rube felt right at home with the Hickman townsfolk. Of course he joined the fire department and led the local minstrel band on their parades. He also prevented an irate mule that had reduced a carriage to splinters from inflicting serious damage to nearby storefronts by grabbing its bridle and wrestling it into submission. His feat drew a large crowd and earned him a big round of applause and a free lunch from a relieved store owner.

Rube knew a few of his new teammates. He'd played with Jimmy Williams and Hobe Ferris and against Claude Rossman and zany Nick Altrock, who'd pitched for the Hitless Wonders when Rube was in his prime. Altrock had settled in with the Millers at the age of thirty-six and was almost as entertaining as Rube. Before games he performed sleight-of-hand tricks and did strongman stunts. Sometimes a bird flew out of his cap.

The Tribune positively gushed with accounts of Rube.

> *"Waddell is in the pink of condition at an even 200 pounds with not an ounce of fat on his frame. He is taking care of himself and is confident he still has the goods up his sleeve. His catcher's glove booms like a Salvation Army drum when he throws a speedball and the bewildered batters swing two and three times at his knuckle pitches before the ball dances over the plate. His curves make the hitters put both feet in the bucket."*

Claude Rossman told a reporter that when he'd batted behind Crawford and Cobb during his stint with the Tigers he had never seen anybody better than Waddell and that it was positively amazing to see how the man drew a crowd everywhere he went.

One day it poured rain all morning and afternoon and the next day Joe Cantillon cancelled practice because of the soggy grounds. Rube told the other Millers that he was putting together a hunting expedition upriver to Wolf Island where the geese were plentiful and easy to bag. Cantillon took care of an old flatboat owned by Charlie Comiskey that he had named *The Whitesox*. It was perfect for hunting and fishing trips, but it was in an awful state of repair. Rube found one of its propeller tubes was packed with driftwood, rail pieces, tin cans, empty bottles, and even dead swine, but after a quick clean out the party tooted off up the river with Rube at the wheel.

The Whitesox was chugging through the mudflats when the hunters heard a loud crack. The tiller cord had snapped off the pilot's wheel. The boat took a nose dive toward the Missouri side of the river. That it would crash was not in doubt, it was only a matter of where. Rube took command, grabbing the loose cable and diligently pulling and twisting it until *The Whitesox* was headed toward a soft landing. Once aground, a broomstick, several button hooks, and some twine effected the necessary repairs and the party headed back upriver. When they reached Wolf Island they found an old-timer and Rube asked him about the wolves.

"Don't you worry 'bout them mister, they all up and swam over to Missouri in the middle of a gunboat battle durin' the War with the North."

Reassured, Rube instructed the cook they had brought from their hotel to get lunch ready. He used the boat's stove to heat water and served a fine spread of boiled cabbage, ham, and onions. Hobe Ferris, a city boy who had been having a dreadful time up until now, brightened a little.

After lunch Rube steered *The Whitesox* up a chute alongside the island and the engine noise frightened thousands of geese out of nearby fields. He reassured the others that the birds would come back and then dug several pits around which he placed decoys he'd made. He called them tin boosters. The others didn't think they looked much like geese.

"That's a lot of decoys, Rube," said Jimmy Williams. "It looks like a suffragette convention."

"Can't be," said Hobe Ferris, "the decoys aren't squawking."

After a long and uncomfortable wait in the holes Williams yelled, "There they are!"

Before the words were out of his mouth Rube had fired. He hit a bird and it fell to the ground. It was crippled but not dead and the others laughed their heads off as Hobe Ferris chased it all around the island. The others managed to bag a few geese. Rube's total was eight, all huge 12-pounders. Darkness began to fall so, without any lights to guide him, Rube piloted *the Whitesox* back down the river, striking several stumps and narrowly missing two other boats.

ℓ   ℓ   ℓ

"Much damage?" Cantillon asked when they got back.

"Nothin' to speak of Joe," said Rube nonchalantly. "It's time that cheapskate Comiskey got a new boat anyway. Man's as tight as a wet boot. "

"He is a little on the stingy side," said Cantillon. "I understand he doesn't pay his players much."

"Comiskey has ball players and he has money," said Rube. "He just doesn't like the two of them to get together."

ℓ   ℓ   ℓ

When the Millers traveled to Toledo to begin the season Cantillon delighted the crowd of 9,000 by starting Rube in the opener against the Mud Hens. He worked slowly. His control wasn't pinpoint, but he held Toledo scoreless for seven innings. Having heard that Rube had trouble fielding bunts the Mud Hens laid down one after another. Rube fielded all but one of them cleanly and recorded eight assists. Two days later Rube faced the Mud Hens again. He gave up a few hits, including a long triple when he eased up and grooved one to the Toledo starter Cy Slapnicky, but he beat Slap 4-2.

Rube and Madge moved into a cabin on a small lake a couple of miles from Minneapolis. Rube fished every morning from dawn until whatever time Madge came out of the cabin. She would yawn, blink at the sunlight, stretch her arms, and look out at Rube. Then she would pull the ribbon out of her hair and let it fall to her shoulders. "Would you like to give me a bath again this morning?" she'd call out, as she let her robe fall to the ground to reveal her gorgeous naked body. Rube would row to shore so fast there was a wake behind his boat.

Everywhere the team went Rube was a big hit. Fathers in Louisville and Columbus and Milwaukee told their sons how Rube had pitched there when he was just starting out. In early June the Millers were in first place and Rube's record stood at 6-0. Then his speed abruptly deserted him and his curves suddenly had no snap. He lost his next six straight. Cantillon was desperate. He tried two rookie pitchers, Pug Cavet and Vinegar Bill Essick. Neither one worked out. If they had, Cantillon might have given Rube his walking papers.

Rube, who was always clean-shaven, told everyone who would listen that he wouldn't shave until he won.

"I wonder how long his beard's gonna be by Labour Day," Nick Altrock joked to Hobe Ferris.

But Rube won the very next day, striking out nine Brewers. Madge was in the stands and a reporter asked if she was relieved that her husband won.

"I am extremely happy that Edward won, I can't abide side *whiskers* much less beards."

In his next start Rube had a 5-4 lead in the sixth. In the seventh he surrendered three straight hits. When the next batter bunted, Rube fielded it and then just stood still holding on to the ball. He never did throw to a base. He walked off the field before Cantillon could scramble to the mound to replace him.

In his next start Rube gave up four straight hits in the first and, when the next batter bunted and the first baseman fielded it, Rube neglected to cover first. Everyone knew the problem. He was drinking again.

CHAPTER FIFTY ONE

TAKING OUT YINGLING
AND THE WADDELL RENAISSANCE

Rube pitched a lot in the first two weeks of May and hardly ever in the last two weeks. Cantillon knew he was in no condition to. When he was scheduled to pitch Cantillon would go with someone else. He never gave an explanation but people could guess what was wrong. The few times Rube *did* pitch he couldn't field bunts and could hardly run the bases. Twice, after drawing walks, he was thrown out easily at second when the next batter hit singles that ended up as fielders' choices because of Rube's lack of effort.

He got a couple of wins in early June, though neither was very impressive. Then he had a two-run lead against Toledo until his teammates committed four errors in the ninth to blow it. The Millers sank to fourth place. They badly needed Rube to start winning. He came through with one of his best performances of the season when he struck out nine and beat the Milwaukee Brewers 2-1. The win may have saved his job, Cantillon had already released Nick Altrock.

On June 19 the umpire announced, "Pitching for Toledo, Yingling, Pitching for Minneapolis, Waddell" to a cascade of groans and boos. The Minneapolis rooters, who had been so thrilled when he had arrived and then started so well, had completely soured on him. They'd read stories about how he kept a whiskey bottle in the dugout. But Rube surprised everyone, especially Joe Cantillon, when he gave up just four hits and struck out eight to beat Earl Yingling and Toledo 3-1.

The joy was short-lived. Warming up for his next start he threw a warmup pitch twenty feet over the catcher's head and hit a boy in the stands. Luckily he wasn't hurt. Rube lasted three shaky innings. Reporters speculated that Rube would soon be let go. Cantillon didn't use him for two straight weeks. But when he took the mound again he pitched five perfect innings before allowing a home run. He struck out two in the eighth and another two in the ninth for the victory and a reprieve.

Joe Cantillon took Rube aside. "Listen, we have a really important series with second place Toledo starting tomorrow. I want you to pitch the first game and the third game. You have got to take good care of yourself so you're ready. Do you understand?"

"Of course, Joe. I'll win both games for you."

"We'll be facing Yingling and he's always tough on us."

"Got ya, Joe, see you tomorrow."

ℓℓ ℓℓ ℓℓ

But Joe did not see Rube the next day, or the one after, or the one after that. Strangely, Yingling missed the games as well. Rube finally showed up on Friday morning, the day after the end of the Toledo series.

As soon as Rube came into the clubhouse Cantillon let him have it with both barrels. "I told you to take care of yourself and be ready to pitch!" he bellowed.

"I did take care of myself, Joe."

"Did you now?"

"Yes I did. And I took care of Yingling for you too. I took him fishing with me."

Rube reached into a basket he was carrying and hauled out a string of walleyes and northern pike.

"I know how you eat fish on Friday, Joe. Look what I brought you."

Joe smiled and forgave Rube. Two days later Cantillon got a bill. Rube had purchased the string of fish and charged them to Joe. Cantillon had no idea where Rube had actually taken Yingling. He suspected that he'd talked him into going on a bender.

A week later Rube disappeared for two days and returned with another string of fish. This time they were trout. When he handed them to Cantillon he took one off the string and slapped Rube in the face with it.

ℓℓ ℓℓ ℓℓ

Madge was through. She left. "His craziness is too much for me," she told a reporter who caught up to her as she was boarding a train for St. Louis.

Rube's teammates thought he would be despondent. He was just the opposite. The day after Madge left he struck out nine and got a key hit that gave the Millers a win. He won again three days later. The next day the team was up 3-0 when Red Killefer gave up three runs in the fifth.

Cantillon sent Rube in to save the day and he threw hitless ball the rest of the way. In the top of the ninth he singled and then huffed and puffed his way around to score the go-ahead run when Otis Clymer rapped a double to right. In the bottom of the inning Rube struck out the side.

He decided to file for a divorce and was delighted when Madge didn't contest it. She knew she wouldn't get any money out of Rube. He was a free man again and he felt great. As suddenly as his prowess on the mound had disappeared, it had reappeared just as suddenly. He won seven straight. The newspapers called it "the Waddell Renaissance". When the Millers went to Milwaukee for a five-game series Rube pitched in four of them. He won three of the games, including a two-hitter, and saved another.

On his one off day he was wondering around the stadium looking for entertainment when he ran into an old friend, the Brewers' club secretary Walter Dickinson.

"Eddie! What's new with you?" asked Dickinson.

"Well, Walt, the bride left me."

"How do you feel about that?"

"I wouldn't exactly say I'm torn up about it."

"I saw you wondering around. What were you looking for?"

"Oh, I'm just a might bored is all. Joe says I can't pitch today. Anything I can do to pass the time?"

Dickinson took off his hat and scratched his head. "Well, you could help me out by counting the gate receipts. The lad that usually does it didn't show up."

Dickenson led Rube to the office and showed him what to do. Rube started right in. He'd been counting the ticket stubs and the cash for only a few minutes when three policemen stormed into the ticket office. Someone had told them that some big fellow was about to make off with the money from the game. One of the constables grabbed Rube from behind. Having no idea who it was, he swung around and hurled the big policeman against a wall. The other two froze in their tracks. Luckily Dickenson ran in and hurriedly explained that Rube had been *asked* to count the money before the policemen either took him away or found themselves stuffed into trash cans.

He won his next three and Cantillon sent him out in the first game of a series in Louisville. Rube was warming up when he heard loud popping noises. He knew what they were. He told Cantillon the stitching in his glove had come loose and ran into the clubhouse. He never came out.

There was a gun club next door to the park and they were staging a trap-shooting contest. Cantillon was livid. But when Rube arrived at the hotel as the Millers were going into the dining room for supper Cantillon could tell that he hadn't been drinking. Rube had a big smile on his face and something under his arm. It was a beautiful mahogany gun case. Rube opened it and inside was a very expensive rifle.

"I won," Rube announced.

"What?" asked Cantillon.

"The trap shootin' competition."

"And they gave you this rifle and case?"

"That's right. And I am givin' it to you." Rube handed it to Cantillon.

"You're giving it to . . . me?" Cantillon stammered.

"That's right, Joe. For all that you've put up with from me."

Cantillon was touched, it was hard to stay mad at a man like Rube.

&c &c &c

Rube got a shutout in the Millers' last game. They finished first with a 99-66 record. Rube had won 22 and lost 12, the best record in the league. Some of the Millers were signed by major league teams. Not Rube. In spite of his record and his second half success, major league owners and managers had heard far too many reports of his incessant drinking.

&c &c &c

Joe Cantillon invited Rube to stay on his 30-acre farm on a lake near Hickman and the two spent a lot of happy days hunting and fishing. Until the rains came. Rube packed a valise and announced that he was going away.

"Where are you headed, Rube?" Joe asked, wondering how he would pay his way.

"I am joining a traveling theater group that's gonna perform in some towns along the Mississippi."

"What will you be doing?" asked Joe.

"Acting a bit and tellin' baseball stories I imagine. They know I'm not a hoofer or a crooner."

Rube got big rounds of applause for his stories and did reasonably well in the one-act plays he starred in. He made it to every show except one. A fire had broken out a few blocks from where the group was performing and he'd dashed off to help put it out.

&c &c &c

"Waddell looks hard as iron," a reporter wrote at the start of the Millers' 1912 training camp. "He is as big as a coalhouse and as clear of eye as a kid." Cantillon had been smart. The hunting and fishing had kept Rube off the bottle. His 1912 contract would pay him $10 per week - for "basic expenses". If he finished the season without drinking he'd get another $1,000.

The team had just returned to the LaClede Hotel after a workout when alarm bells rang. This time it wasn't a fire. There had been so much rain that the levees were in danger of giving way. Rube immediately ran out the door. The other players went to help put sandbags where they'd be needed to hold back the water. Rube was already hard at work. He kept at it all day and throughout the night stopping only to pull a group of children out of the rushing water.

The rains refused to let up and on April 1 the levees burst. Hickman was under eight feet of water and 2,000 people were left homeless. The governor sent tents, but there was nowhere to put them up.

No one would be playing baseball in Hickman any time soon, so Joe Cantillon arranged for boats to take the players to Owensboro. Rube didn't want to leave but there wasn't much else he could do. Owensboro was home to fourteen bourbon distilleries. The townsfolk were delighted to host the team and the distillery owners happily invited the players to tour their facilities. They were encouraged to sample the product - in glasses, flasks, quart jars, and even full jugs.

After visiting a couple of the players at their hotel a reporter noted that "there was enough bourbon in their rooms to float The Titanic". He rued his clever words the next week when the telegraph service reported the shocking news that the great ship had sunk on its maiden voyage.

At first Rube refused the complimentary drinks. He eventually gave way, not wanting to hurt the distillers' feelings. Then he started going back for second and third tours. Sometimes he wore a false beard so people wouldn't know he was back again.

The Millers opened their season with trips to Louisville, Columbus, and Toledo. Rube didn't pitch at all. He was too drunk. When he finally sobered up enough to start he was lit up for five hits and three runs in the first four innings. In the fifth he tried to field a bunt and fell flat on his face. He got up and threw the ball into the stands behind first base. Cantillon took him out.

     ℓ   ℓ   ℓ

It was ten days before he got another chance and he was terrific. He gave up just four hits and two runs, both unearned. But the Millers were held scoreless for the first time in the season.

Four days later he had a shutout going in the sixth when he mishandled a bunt and then walked the next two batters.

"The bases are loaded. Just like Rube usually is," Hobe Ferris chuckled to himself.

Rube struck out the next hitter on three pitches. He fired two strikes past the next batter and stopped to wave to the crowd.

"What the hell is he doing?" Joe Cantillon asked no one in particular.

"It's all over," Rube yelled.

Five years before the major league batters he faced would have waved helplessly at his next speedball. Now a minor leaguer hit it into the seats for a grand slam home run.

     ℓ   ℓ   ℓ

It was May 26 and Rube had not won a single game. As fond of him as Joe Cantillon was, Rube had pretty well run out of chances. It was sad to see him try and fail so miserably. Rube said he had a sore elbow, but age and drink were the real contributors to his downfall. He started that day and, to everyone's amazement, he was sober. He struck out nine and pitched a no-hitter for seven innings. With a big lead he relaxed and gave up a couple of hits but won easily. He even singled and scored a run.

Rube had a two-run lead when he took the mound in the first inning of the Millers' next home game. Cantillon had elected to have his team bat first so they could get a crack at the baseball before it had been batted around and softened up with spit. He walked the first batter on four pitches and hit the next two. Cantillon lifted him. Rube was drunk, again.

In July Rube missed two weeks with an attack of gallstones. The Millers didn't miss him. For the first time in his career he was not drawing crowds when he pitched.

     ℓ   ℓ   ℓ

By the middle of August, after a loss to the Indianapolis Indians, Rube's record stood at 6-7. Two weeks later he shut them out in the first game of a double header.

"Lemme pitch the second one too," Rube begged Cantillon, who knew that Rube had actually stayed in for a change the night before. Cantillon agreed and Rube put the Indians out three straight in the first. The crowd roared its approval. Rube was back. Or was he? Over the next two innings he gave up six hits and four runs and Cantillon took him out.

"Didn't he used to be a great pitcher?" a small boy asked his father.

"One of the best," his dad said. "Back in the day he would pitch both games of a double header like he was taking a stroll in the park."

"Was he as good as Walter Johnson is?"

"He was better. Johnson is fast but he can't throw all the pitches Rube could throw. I saw him pitch in Chicago once and he was a marvel. Batters couldn't hit a lick off him. They just watched his pitches go by, shrugged, and traipsed back to the bench like beaten puppies."

⚜   ⚜   ⚜

The Millers took the championship ring with Rube winning four games in August to finish at 11-8. The Millers played a series against the Western League champion Denver Bulls, losing four games to one. Rube didn't pitch a single inning. The newspapers were generous, simply reporting that "Waddell was deemed unable to play."

RUBE WADDELL
KING of the HALL of FLAKES

CHAPTER FIFTY TWO

SINKING TO C LEVEL
AND THE FINAL OUT

The Millers returned to Hickman for Spring Training and on March 22 there was more flooding. A group of Negroes was brought in to help lay down more sandbags. No whites would do the dangerous work. Mounted state policemen with rifles made sure the Negroes stayed on the job. Most carried one bag, bigger men struggled to carry two. They were naked to the waist and sang "I Stood on the River Jordan" as they toiled in the rushing waters. Evidence of the devastation upriver swept past them, a wagon wheel, a clothes-drying rack, then a rocking chair.

There was *one* white man among the Negroes. It was Rube. He staggered forward against the heavy current, carrying three sandbags and singing - off key - right along with his fellow crew members. After working throughout the day and night and helping two teenagers to safety after their rowboat capsized, Rube suffered a relapse and was rushed to see a doctor.

"Have you seen anyone about your breathing?" the doctor asked him.

"The last time I had a real bad cough someone told me to go south, so I went to St. Louis. I didn't have any money so I got picked up for vagrancy. The police were gonna throw me in jail, but when they heard how bad I was coughing they took me to a hospital instead."

"Well this is a lung ailment," the doctor told Rube. "On top of pneumonia, you're suffering from pleurisy and it's fairly severe. I am going to prescribe creosote, but I must warn you, it is extremely caustic."

"What's caustic mean?" asked Rube.

"Corrosive."

"What's corrosive mean?"

"It means that this will burn right through your stomach if you're not careful. You need to take two teaspoons, not tablespoons, teaspoons -

and no more than that - once a day."

Rube slid the bottle into his back pocket and got up off the examination table.

"How much do I owe ya, doc?"

"Don't worry about that, just take care of yourself. Stay warm and stay in bed. Do not go out in this weather, whatever you do. And no more than two spoonfuls of that creosote a day, do you hear me?"

"Sure do. Thanks, doc."

ℓℓ   ℓℓ   ℓℓ

On the morning of April 12, the day of the Millers' home opener, Rube got up and got dressed. As he pulled on his trousers he had another terrible coughing fit. This time it was so bad he could hardly breathe.

When he finally recovered, he remembered the creosote. He got it off the top of the dresser and gulped down the entire bottle in one swallow. He gasped, choked, and doubled over in agony. The burning sensation in the pit of his stomach was worse than any pain he'd ever felt, even having his wrists and arms singed in fires.

After several agonizing minutes he was able to stand and then to walk, gingerly at first, holding onto furniture. Slowly his strength returned. He thought of going back to bed but he could see through the sheer curtains that the sun was shining outside. Obviously the rain had stopped when the temperature had dropped the day before.

He went to the window and looked out. He was thrilled to see that the ground was covered in snow and that his neighbors' children were out building snowmen and throwing snowballs. He ran downstairs, threw on a light coat, and headed outside to join them.

ℓℓ   ℓℓ   ℓℓ

Wid Conroy passed by later on his way to the park. "Rube, what the hell are you doing?" he demanded. "You're supposed to be in bed."

"Hey, Wid. I saw these kids out here and thought I'd give 'em a hand with their snowman."

"How long have you been out here?"

"'Bout two hours, I guess."

"Two hours!"

"Say, what time is it anyway?"

Conroy got out his pocket watch. "Goin' for ten-thirty. Why?"

"Promised a crew down on the docks I'd help 'em clear ice outta the harbor. Gotta go."

Conroy stared in disbelief as Rube ran off.

Around two o'clock Rube told the crew he had to go and headed to the park to help get the field ready for the game. He suffered another relapse, his lungs were hemorrhaging. This time he was taken to the hospital.

A week later he reported to Joe Cantillon. "I figure I can play again Joe, my breathin's a lot better."

Cantillon agreed to let him pitch, but Rube was obviously in a severely weakened condition. In his first exhibition game he gave up sixteen hits in just four innings.

Cantillon sat down next to Rube on the bench. He could tell how disappointed he was.

"Listen Rube, we all know what you can do when you're healthy, but you're nowhere near healthy right now and you just cannot pitch at this level."

"What are ya sayin', Joe?"

"They've started a new league up north with teams in Grand Forks, Winnipeg, Superior, Wisconsin, Duluth, and Virginia, Minnesota. They have a team in Minneapolis too. My brother is one of the owners, they're called the Broncos. We want you to pitch for them."

"What level of ball is that?"

Cantillon hesitated before answering. "It's C level, Rube."

"C Ball. Are you joshin' me?"

"No, Rube. I'm serious. It would just be until you get your health back."

"You promise, Joe? I'd just have to show them I can still pitch and then I can come back to the Millers?"

"Absolutely. You have my word."

"All right, I won't be gone long. I'll be back here in less than a month, you'll see."

"I'll be glad to have you back, everybody will. Now you take care of yourself. Take it easy. Get your rest and don't do anything crazy up there."

That was advice Rube simply never took.

When he pitched his first game for the Broncos it was clear that he was still very weak. He gave up ten hits in four innings. In the fifth he yielded six runs. Even worse, while running to cover first base on a weak grounder he got spiked in the leg. The deep cut got so badly infected the doctors considered amputation.

But Rube made another one of his miracle recoveries and was pitching again at the beginning of May. It seemed as though the old Rube Waddell was back. He knew he was pitching against weak competition, but he made mincemeat out of the Grand Forks Flickertails. They hit just three balls out of the infield and Rube struck out ten in a complete game shutout.

After the game Rube sent a telegram to Joe Cantillon to tell him that he was back in shape and ready to rejoin the Millers. He got a reply the next morning. "Good to hear from you. Too early to tell if you are ready. Keep working hard, Cantillon."

Bob Unglaub, the Broncos' manager, greeted Rube when he arrived at the park the next day. When Rube saw him, he thought back to the 20-inning game against Cy Young on July the 4th, 1905. He could still remember striking out Bob Unglaub on three pitches to end the sixteenth inning. Now Unglaub was his boss.

"Hey Rube. You looked good out there yesterday."

"If you say so, Bob."

"I guess I'll send you back out there against Grand Forks again today."

"No you won't," Rube snapped. "I quit."

His next and last team would be the Duluth Ore Diggers. They played in the same league as the Broncos. Rube would still be at C level. They were in last place so they were more than happy to have Rube. He met the Ore Diggers at their hotel. He liked his new teammates. They tried to get him to talk about his big games against Mathewson, Johnson, and Cy Young. But Rube just said that was a long time ago and asked them about the hunting and fishing in Duluth. His new manager, Spike Shannon, who'd once played for the New York Giants, asked him how he felt.

"Good as the day Connie Mack found me, Spike," Rube told him.

"Sure you are, Rube, no doubt about it," said Shannon. "See you tomorrow. We play at two."

Spike Shannon didn't see Rube the next day or the one after. He wondered what had happened to his newest player. The next week the Ore Diggers were playing the Superior Red Sox. The Diggers had a 5-2 lead after eight innings but the Red Sox scored twice and had two runners on with nobody out. Things looked gloomy. It was going to be just another entry in the loss column.

Rube walked nonchalantly out of the clubhouse and strolled to the mound. Spike Shannon had no idea what was happening. "Well I'll be a monkey's uncle, where did he come from?"

Rube walked up to the pitcher and put out his glove. The pitcher, who looked sixteen but may have been eighteen or nineteen, assumed that Shannon had sent Rube in. He gave him the ball.

"Rube Waddell," Rube called in to the umpire.

Delighted to be able to announce the appearance of a once great and famous major leaguer, the umpire turned to the stands and bellowed, "Now pitching for the Ore Diggers . . . Rube Waddell." There was an enthusiastic cheer from the stands.

"Is that really Rube Waddell?" hundreds of cranks whispered to the people around them.

It took Rube just eleven pitches to strike out the next three batters. In his next start Rube struck out twelve and went the distance. The team drew big crowds when there was a chance Rube might pitch. Sometimes he coached first or third and entertained the boosters. Sometimes he played first base. Shannon put him in the outfield one time but he dropped three fly balls.

Then the coughing started. He never complained about it, but it was a terrible thing to watch.

"It's an absolute shame," Spike Shannon told his wife one night. "After a pitch, Rube doubles over and he coughs so violently it seems his big frame is gonna shatter. Then he pulls himself together, heaves and puts all his concentration into gearing up for the next pitch. When he throws it the bum at the plate, who couldn't have managed a clean *bunt* off him back in the day, smacks it to the farthest reaches of the park."

&c   &c   &c

On July 9 he collapsed and had to be carried off the field. Ten days later he lost to the Winona Highbrows 9-0. As sick and weak and ineffective as he was, as always, Rube made friends. The mayor invited him to join the Elks Club and he was allowed to stay at their clubhouse. He spent a lot of time at the mayor's lodge on Lake Vermillion as well. They caught whitefish and rainbow trout and shot quail, grey squirrels, and loads of wild turkeys.

He loved to visit the zoo at Olcott Park and play with the kids that went there. The zoo had four old black bears. Rube would climb into their cage and jostle with them. He gave them names. Two of them were good-natured. The male he named Connie Mack and the female Tilly Schaefer, after fun-loving Germany Schaefer. Another bear was a bit ornery and Rube called him John McGraw. The fourth bear was downright mean and Rube had to be wary of him. Rube named *him* Ty Cobb.

When the season ended Rube headed back to Hickman and stayed with Joe Cantillon. Before long he developed an infection in his throat and he could barely speak above a whisper. He still had gut-wrenching stomach pains from the creosote. When a doctor diagnosed him with tuberculosis Cantillon arranged for Rube to be sent to stay with his sister Maude in San Antonia. Maybe the hot, dry Texas climate would save him. When Maude saw Rube she was shocked that the brother she had once teased for growing so big and so fast was nothing but a shell.

The Ore Diggers sent him a contract for the 1914 season. He sent it back unsigned with a note that said, "I would like to play, but I could never get into shape. I am writing this from bed. I have lost fifty-four pounds and am as weak as a kitten. I can't walk twenty feet."

Maude checked him into a sanatorium. Joe Cantillon paid most of his expenses and Connie Mack sent a check for the rest. Unknown to Rube, three of the bears at Olcott Park had died, all but the cantankerous Ty Cobb.

Wild Bill Donovan was spending the winter in Texas and he went to visit Rube. He could hardly believe his eyes when he saw him. He weighed just over a hundred pounds. Beside his bed there was a picture of Rube and Schreck in their A's uniforms. Tears welled up in Donovan's eyes. "We used to call them the Batty Brothers," he muttered to himself." He got in touch with Connie Mack, who contacted Rube's parents. Mack told them they must get to San Antonio as soon as possible.

Mack and Rube's parents arrived on March 31 and drove out to the sanatorium the next day. They got there at noon and hurried to his room. A nurse met them in the hall. A sobbing Maude was with her. She told them, "I'm so very sorry, Mister and Missus Waddell. Your son died an hour ago."

It was April Fool's Day, 1914. A few hours later the zookeeper at Olcott Park announced that the last of the four black bears had died.

Alf Jones went to Connie Mack's house the week after Rube's funeral to get his reflections on Rube's passing.

"The game of baseball will never see such a combination of wackiness and greatness," Mack told him. "We owe two pennants to his skill and if it were not for the accident that kept him out of the Nineteen Hundred and Five World Series we would surely have cleaned up the Giants. He was the greatest pitcher in the game and, although he was widely known for his many eccentricities, he was more sinned against than sinning. Rube had the biggest heart of any man I ever managed. When a comrade was sick he was the first one to his side and the last to leave him. If he had any money it went for some gift for the man. I am very sorry for the passing of the wonderful southpaw."

Jones read Connie what Billy Murphy had written about Rube in the *St. Louis Star.* "A boy he lived and a boy he died. He knew naught of the great problems of sociology or philosophy, but lived in the realm of love, adventure, romance, gallantry, and grace."

Murphy had written a story that Joe Cantillon had related to him. Jones read it to Connie. "Cantillon told of how Rube had invited everyone who passed a store in Hickman at Christmas to come in and get fitted for a new pair of shoes. The merchant thought Rube had gone daffy and wanted to know if he should stop him. Joe told him 'no, let Rube have his fun, and if he can't pay for it I will.' He gave away forty pair. Rube was lonesome and the Christmas spirit was upon him and he couldn't do anything else that would have brought him more pleasure."

Connie smiled. "That certainly sounds like Rube."

The telephone rang. Connie's daughter answered it.

"Yes, this is Connie Mack's residence. I am his daughter, Alicia. To whom am I speaking?"

She paused, listened and said, "Yes, yes, of course, we . . . " Another pause. "Oh no! That's terrible news. I am very sorry for you all, I shall tell my father. Thank you so much for calling. Please let us know when the arrangements have been made."

"Who was that, Alicia?" asked her father.

"It was Ossee Schreckengost's sister."

"What's happened?"

"He told the family that life wouldn't be any fun anymore now that Rube is gone. She said he stopped eating and just gave up. He passed away this morning."

"That's terrible," said Connie. "I can still picture the two of them laughing and fooling together. I gave them the dickens more times than I can count, but I swear they were a lovable pair of cutups."

RUBE WADDELL

When Jones was leaving Alicia Mack went with him to the door. She handed him his hat and put a hand over his forearm. "You know, Mister Jones, I never did get to meet Rube. But whenever my father talked about him there was a gleam in his eye. I think it broke his heart a little when he had to let him go."

It occurred to Jones to find out what Walter Johnson, baseball's *new* king of the mound, thought of Rube. He learned from another reporter that Johnson had just had a telephone line stretched to his farm in Kansas and he called Johnson that night.

"Rube Waddell was the greatest pitcher I ever looked at," Johnson told him. "He was eccentric and all that, but in sheer ability he never had an equal. Waddell stuck out like a beacon light."

The papers ran the news of Rube's death on the front page. There were several tributes and stories about his eccentric behavior and his kind-heartedness. There was also an acknowledgement that Rube was baseball's first big drawing card and that he'd been responsible for the first big wave of ballpark improvement and expansion since the stands wouldn't hold all the boosters that wanted to see him pitch and carry on. Some writers went so far as to claim he had saved the infant American League from bankruptcy.

Among the tributes was one from an unexpected source. A young reporter asked crusty John McGraw to name the best players of all time at each position. To no one's surprise his starting right-handed pitcher was his former ace Christy Mathewson.

"How about the best leftie of all time, Mister McGraw," the reporter asked.

"No doubt about that, son," answered McGraw. "That would be Rube Waddell."

RUBE WADDELL
KING *of the* HALL *of* FLAKES

RUBE WADDELL
KING *of the* HALL *of* FLAKES

ABOUT THE AUTHOR

As a boy, Will Braund's life revolved around playing baseball. He played every day and on weekends, with only short breaks for meals. He hung up his glove at 39 as the third baseman and manager of a men's league team but later worked as an instructor for the Toronto Blue Jays at their summer camp for teenagers.

After earning an Honors degree in History he taught for several years, during which he was nominated for the Governor General's Award for Excellence in Teaching. After being promoted to principal he was elected Chair of the 1,100 member Toronto School Administrators' Association and later named to the Executive of the Ontario Principals' Council.

Will lives north of Toronto with his beautiful wife Trudy and their son Tyler and close to their older son Matthew.

Will reads voraciously about the history of baseball. Along with two former teammates he started a blog called lateinningsblogspot.com to which he is the main contributor on the subject of baseball history. While interested by the biographies of a lot of players, Will has never not found anyone who had a more fascinating and even bizarre life and career than Rube Waddell.

His second historical novel, released in December 2016, is "Babe Ruth & the 1927 Yankees Have the Best Summer Ever," a fun-filled ride with the greatest and most colorful team ever.